Sex, Strategy and the Stratosphere

Also by Albert J. Mills

ORGANIZATIONAL RULES (1991)
GENDERING ORGANIZATIONAL ANALYSIS (1992)
READING ORGANIZATIONAL THEORY (1995)
MANAGING THE ORGANIZATIONAL MELTING POT (1997)
GENDER, IDENTITY AND THE CULTURE OF ORGANIZATIONS (2002)
IDENTITY POLITICS AT WORK (2004)

Sex, Strategy and the Stratosphere

Airlines and the Gendering of Organizational Culture

By Albert J. Mills

First published in 2006 by
PALGRAVE MACMILLAN
Houndmills, Basingstoke, Hampshire RG21 6XS and
175 Fifth Avenue, New York, N.Y. 10010
Companies and representatives throughout the world.

PALGRAVE MACMILLAN is the global academic imprint of the Palgrave
Macmillan division of St. Martin's Press, LLC and of Palgrave Macmillan Ltd.
Macmillan® is a registered trademark in the United States, United Kingdom
and other countries. Palgrave is a registered trademark in the European
Union and other countries.

ISBN-13: 978–1–4039–9857–6 hardback
ISBN-10: 1–4039–9857–4 hardback

This book is printed on paper suitable for recycling and made from fully
managed and sustained forest sources.

A catalogue record for this book is available from the British Library.

Library of Congress Cataloging-in-Publication Data

Mills, Albert J., 1945–
    Sex, strategy, and stratosphere : airlines and the gendering of organizational
culture / by Albert J. Mills.
        p. cm.
    Includes bibliographical references and index.
    ISBN 1–4039–9857–4 (cloth)
        1. Sex role in the work environment – Case studies. 2. Sexual division
of labor – Case studies. 3. Corporate culture – Case studies. 4. British Airways.
5. Pan American World Airways, Inc. 6. Air Canada. 7. Feminist theory. I. Title:
Airlines and the gendering of organizational culture. II. Title.

HD6060.6.M55 2006
331.4′813877—dc22   2005057922

10 9 8 7 6 5 4 3 2 1
15 14 13 12 11 10 09 08 07 06

Printed and bound in Great Britain by
Antony Rowe Ltd, Chippenham and Eastbourne

For Sue and Phil Helms, who made the airline business a decent place to work – thanks for being there

Contents

List of Tables

List of Figures

List of Exhibits

List of Abbreviations

AAJC	Associated Airways Joint
ACA	Aviation Corporation of America
ACOAS	Aviation Corporation of the Americas
AGCAL	Atlantic, Gulf and Caribbean Air Lines
Airco	Aircraft Manufacturing Company
ALSSA	Air Line Stewards and Stewardesses Association
American	American Airways (and then American Airlines after 1934)
ATA	Air Transport Auxiliary
ATC	Air Training Corps
ATS	Auxiliary Territorial Service
ATT	Aircraft Transport and Travel
AVCO	Aviation Corporation
BA	British Airways
BAL	British Airways Ltd.
BALPA	British Air Line Pilots' Association
BAT	Boeing Air Transport (forerunner of United Air Lines)
BBC	British Broadcasting Corporation
BEA	British European Airways
BMAN	British Marine Air Navigation Company
BOAC	British Overseas Airways Corporation
BSA	British Small Arms Company
BSAA	British South American Airways
BWIA	British West Indian Airways
BWPA	British Women Pilots' Association
CAB	Civil Aviation Board (US)
CAG	Civil Air Guard
CALSA	Canadian Air Line Stewardesses Association
CAWU	Clerical and Administrative Workers Union
CGEA	Cie. des Grands Express Aériens
CMA	Compagnie Messageries Aériennes
CMAM	Compania Mexicana de Aviacion
CNAC	China National Aviation Corp
CNR	Canadian National Railways
CPR	Canadian Pacific Railway
CSCA	Civil Service Clerical Association
Eastern	Eastern Air Transport (and then Eastern Airlines after 1934)
EEOC	Equal Employment Opportunity Commission
ESG	Equality Steering Group (Internal Committee in British Airways, 1991)

FANY	First Aid Nursing Yeomanry
FLQ	Liberation Front of Quebec
GPO	General Post Office
GWR	Great Western Railway
HPT	Handley Page Transport Ltd.
IAL	Imperial Airways Ltd.
IATA	International Air Transport Association
ICAN	International Commission for Air Navigation
ICAO	International Civil Aviation Organization
Instone	Instone Airlines Ltd.
KLM	Koninklijke Luchtvaart Maatschappij (Royal Dutch Airlines)
NOW	National Organization of Women
NUSEC	National Union of Societies for Equal Citizenship
NYA	New York Airways Inc.
NYRBA	New York, Rio, Buenos Aires Lines
OCA	Old Comrades' Association of the Women's Royal Air Force
Pan Am	Pan American Airways
Panagra	Pan American-Grace Airways
PPF	Putting People First (BA culture change slogan)
RAF	Royal Air Force
RAS	Railway Air Service
RFC	Royal Flying Corps
RNAS	Royal Naval Air Service
SAS	Scandinavian Airlines System
SBAC	Society of British Aircraft Constructors
SCADTA	Columbo-German Aerial Transport Company
SFWR	Stewardesses for Women's Rights
SSHRC	Social Sciences and Humanities Research Council of Canada
TCA	Trans-Canada Air Lines
TGWU	Transport and General Workers Union
TMO	Traffic Managers' Office
TUC	Trades Union Congress
TWA	Transcontinental and Western Airline (and then Trans World Airways)
TWU	Transport Workers Union
UAL	United Air Lines
WAAC	Women's Army Auxiliary Corps
WAAF	Women's Auxiliary Air Force
WASPS	Women's Airforce Service Pilots
WBA	Wide Bodied Aircraft
WCA	Western Canada Airways
WI	Women's Institute

WIAE	West Indian Aerial Express
WJAC	Women's Junior Air Corp
WRAF	Women's Royal Air Force
WRNS	Women's Royal Naval Service
WSPU	Women's Social and Political Union

Acknowledgements

Writing a book relies on so many people. My profound thanks go to the late Barbara Roberts, feminist historian and friend, for pointing me in the right direction. It was Barbara who encouraged my abiding interest in archival research. I am deeply sorry that she will not be able to see this work in print or to share her insights with me.

My sincere thanks go to the Social Science and Humanities Research Council for providing the necessary funding to make this research possible. In particular I'm grateful to Marta Calás and two anonymous reviewers for their confidence in the project and my ability to carry it out.

Once on my journey, I would not have gotten very far without the help of several people. I am particularly grateful to Fred Huntley, the archivist in charge of the British Airways (BA) archive collection and London's Heathrow Airport. Fred's assistance was invaluable. His knowledge, and love of the company that he served so well, helped to guide me through a wealth of material. Fred was more than just a guide; his warmth and friendship saw me through many a day at the archive. Although we had our disagreements on the gendered character of the organization, I hope there will be much in the book that will engage his interest. And I'm sure that he will realize that I came to share his affection for the airline. I would also like to thank Jack Ligertwood, who is in charge of BA's collection of uniforms, for his generosity and humour during my time at the archives.

During the course of my study I spoke with many current and former employees of BA who are too numerous to mention but I would like to thank them for their time and interest. I do, however, want to single out a few former BA staff who generously gave of their time in helping me gain a sense of the airline at different points in time: my appreciation goes to Jakey Adams, Francine Carville, Betty Chappel (Linsay-Wood), Jeannie Lardner (Sutherland), Betty Paige (Hill), Geoffrey Pett and Major Michael Vaughan – I can only hope that I have done justice to what they had to say.

My deepest appreciation also goes to Mark Ducharme and Fiona Smith Hale at the National Aviation Museum in Ottawa, and Craig Likness and Marcia Evanson at the Otto G. Richter Library at the University of Miami. Mark was extremely kind not only in helping me (and my co-researcher, Jean Helms Mills) find our way around the Air Canada files but in providing us with office space on the numerous days we found our way to the Museum. Fiona provided wonderful advice and assistance on the library collection and facilities. In Miami, Craig and Marcia were welcoming from the beginning and offered not only tremendous clues to existing works on Pan American Airways (Pan Am) but also detailed advice on the Pan Am collection. Both combined a willingness to help us navigate our way around Florida as well as being ever willing to engage in discussions of masculinities at work.

I'd also like to thank Stephen, Sue and Phil Helms, as well as Errol ('Mitch') Mitchell, Ross Brown, Rudy Cormier, Marina and Bob Young, and an untold number of Air Canada employees and retirees for sharing their experiences and insights into the airline.

Finally, in the actual writing and publishing of the book I've come to rely on many people for support and encouragement, including a number of friends, colleagues and students. They are all special and played an important role, but I'd like to thank Kelly Dye and Gabie Durepos for their friendship and the direct help they have given to the project. Jacky Kippenberger, the Commissioning Editor for Business and Management at Palgrave, is a complete gem – she had the creative ability to see the book's potential where more short-sighted others could not get past a single idea. Jacky had the foresight and willingness to ask questions and encouraged me to see the book in a different way. Thanks Jacky, your support has meant a lot. Finally, my deepest thanks goes to my co-researcher, wife, best friend and companion – Jean Helms Mills. She has helped me immensely through our common interest in feminism and other scholarly pursuits, and by being there.

1
Gender, Culture and Commercial Airways

Genealogies attempt to demonstrate how objectifying forms of reason (and their regimes of truth and knowledge) have been made, as
historically contingent rather than eternally necessary forces.
Consequently, 'they can be unmade, as long as we know how it was
they were made'.

Foucault (1988), quoted in Best and Kellner (1991: 57)

Introduction

Feminist in intent,[1] the premise of this book is that we are better placed to
redress workplace discrimination the more we know how it develops, is
maintained and changes over time. In the narrowest sense of the word, the
reference to *sex* in the book's title is about how people are discriminated
against because of their physiological characteristics. But it is more than
that. The book explores how workplace practices shape our understandings
of masculinity, femininity and sexual attraction. Thus, the book is about
how basic physiological differences between men and women ('sex') are
translated into culturally specific patterns of behaviour ('gender') which
become attached to the sexes in given work settings (Oakley, 1972).

The distinction between sex and gender is far from problematic. It is difficult to talk in terms of women and men without appearing to reference some
degree of essentialism (Rakow, 1986), yet it is hard to avoid such terms when
discussing the realities of embodied people who are discriminated against
because of their biological features (Calás and Smirich, 1992). In this book
attention is drawn to that tension through a focus on the impact of discrimination both *on* women and men and on the social construction *of* women
and men. The processes whereby notions of men and women develop and
the discriminatory outcomes associated with those notions are referred to as
gendering (Mills and Tancred, 1992).

Studies of gender suggest that notions of womanhood and manhood are outcomes of a multitude of factors that constitute the cultural milieu of society (Ginsburg and Lowenhaupt Tsing, 1990; Ryan, 1979). Depending on perspective, these factors may include language, attitudes, behaviour patterns, symbolism, dress, beliefs, values, stories, rites, rituals, ceremonies and physical artefacts in some combination. Arguably, these cultural influences are not simply reproduced, maintained and changed at a societal level but develop from specific social groupings, including organizations[2] (Gherardi, 1995; Maddock, 1999) that operate at a local (e.g., individual organization), meso (e.g., industry specific companies), macro (e.g., the economy) and theoretical (e.g., the idea of the organization) level.[3] This book examines the interface between societal understandings of gender and the role of organizational culture in the reproduction and generation of gendered notions of men and women, tracing the development of gendered notions and practices through the development of British Airways (BA) and two contrasting airlines – Air Canada and Pan American Airways (Pan Am).

This brings us to the second aspect of the book's title – *strategy*. Unlike with families, we tend to attribute rational ends to the functioning of organizations (e.g., profits, service provision, charity). This process is reinforced when an organization develops sets of specific and stated aims and develops strategies for achieving them. However, not all strategies are consciously developed and may arise out of a combination of spoken and unspoken assumptions that can be detected as a pattern in a stream of action, whether the pattern is an intended outcome or 'realized despite, or in the absence of, intentions' (Mintzberg, Brunet and Waters, 1986: 4).[4] Arguably, the strategic pursuit of assumed ends shape the cultures and relationships within the organization (Deal and Kennedy, 1982; Pettigrew, 1979). The gendered nature of such patterns is the focus of this book and is explored through employment practices and sales strategies. Specifically, the book examines how organizational strategies give rise to a complex of organizational rules which come to form the basis of gendered organizational cultures (Mills, 1988a).

Like gender, the notion of organizational culture is contested (Hatch, 1997; Martin, 2002) and few studies of organizational culture discuss gender (Wilson, 2001). Here organizational culture is viewed as a root metaphor that provides a useful framework for making sense of gender at work.[5] Its value lies in its potential for capturing the configuration of factors that influence lived experiences, in particular the ways in which people experience gendered realities at work, including sex discrimination, prohibitions against homosexuality, sexual harassment and the privileging of particular forms of masculinity. Thus, some gendered realities are experienced through employment practices that privilege some people and exclude and/or marginalize others. Organizational culture is viewed as dynamic, developing and changing over time. By definition, the culture of an organization refers to an *established* set of practices, beliefs and artefacts that have taken time to develop and as such should be studied over time and in social context (Dellheim, 1986; Kieser, 1989).

The third element of the book's title is the *stratosphere* and speaks to the fact that the gendering of organizational culture is explored through the development of selected airline companies. The choice of commercial aviation as an area of study was arrived at not only because of its influence on popular culture, including enduring images of idealized masculinity[6] and femininity[7] (Corn, 1983; Lovegrove, 2000; Nielsen, 1982), but also because of the importance of airlines within national economies, foreign policy and the growth of international trade (Allen, 1978; Hudson, 1972; Sampson, 1984; Smith, 1944; Stevenson, 1987). Airlines have also been the subject of a number of feminist analyses (Cadogan, 1992; Due Billing and Alvesson, 1994; Hochschild, 1983; Kane, 1974). Within this framework, BA was an especially interesting starting point. It is the world's oldest surviving commercial airline (Penrose, 1980b)[8] and served for many years as 'the chosen instrument' of British foreign policy (Sampson, 1984). It is one of the world's largest airlines[9] and an important part of the British economy (Corke, 1986). In addition, research was facilitated by the fact that BA has an established and accessible archive and has been the subject of a number of published histories.[10]

A focus on the organizational culture of a single organization (BA) over time allows an in-depth and far-reaching study that explores the relationship between internal (organization) and external (social) factors at different periods. Studies of other airlines – particularly Air Canada and Pan American Airways (Pan Am) but also several other airlines – are drawn on for points of comparison to allow examination of the extent to which gendered practices are characteristic of a particular organizational culture or provide more general clues about organizational culture across similar organizations. This reflects the overall research project, which set out to study a single organization over time and then draw on studies of comparable airlines in other English-speaking countries.[11] The choice of comparative airlines was dictated by similar concerns of socio-economic significance and access. Pan Am was the first, and for decades the only, international airline in the United States and has had an important influence on that country's economy, foreign policy and popular culture (Hudson and Pettifer, 1979; Josephson, 1944; Sampson, 1984).Its extensive archive is housed at the University of Miami. Air Canada, as the country's first truly transnational and international airline, played a similar role in the life of Canada. It too has an extensive archive – housed at the Canada Aviation Museum in Ottawa. Additionally, both Pan Am and Air Canada had close connections with BA over many decades.[12]

Studying the gendering of organizational culture: A rules approach

The gendering of airlines is explored through a rules approach (Helms Mills and Mills, 2000; Mills, 1988a, 1988b; Mills and Murgatroyd, 1991). Rules are defined as 'phenomena whose basic characteristic is that of generally controlling, constraining, guiding and defining social action' (Mills and Murgatroyd, 1991: 3–4). They exist in written and unwritten, formal and informal, legalistic, normative, and moralistic forms. Rules do not 'wholly rely for their efficacy on being known or understood by each and every member of a given situation into which they are applied' (Mills and Murgatroyd, 1991: 4) but they do arise out of the enactment of organizational actors who differ in their rule-making powers. The notion of rules, thus, attempts to synthesize 'both the enabling and constraining aspects of rule-governed conduct' by taking into account 'the inescapable fact that rules are created by actors but that they simultaneously constrain the action alternatives to them over a series of decision-making situations' (Reed, 1992: 183).

Rules as organizational culture

Patterns of behaviour, symbolism, dress and other factors characterize the culture of an organization, but are manifestations of something deeper, the cultural dynamic that generates ways of being in an organization. Some theories root the cultural dynamic in underlying beliefs and values (Schein, 1992), responses to uncertainties and chaos (Trice and Beyer, 1993), or strategic choices (Eldridge and Crombie, 1974). All of these approaches underplay the role of ownership and the exercise of power and control that determine many of the underlying values, and precede the ability to make choices and deal with uncertainty.

In seeking to understand what lies *behind* cultural processes the rules approach is grounded in Clegg's (1981: 545) notion of organizational control as achieved through rules that 'formulate the structure underlying the apparent surface of organizational life'. It is argued that control is the dynamic through which organizational rules are developed. In many ways rules define organizations and how they are experienced. Organizations arise out of the desire of some individuals or groups (e.g., entrepreneurs, share-holders, policy-makers, philanthropists, social activists, etc.) to achieve certain ends. In the process they recruit others to help them to achieve their ends and this creates pressure for the co-ordination and control of the various activities that people engage in. This, in turn, leads to the development of a series of rules or 'outline steps for the conduct of action [that], depending upon combinations of circumstances and actors, [will] be experienced as controlling, guiding and/or defining' (Mills and Murgatroyd, 1991: 30).

It is the configuration of informal and formal rules that shape the culture of an organization as it deals with various legal requirements, adopts or adapts to extant management practices, utilizes technology, absorbs, reflects or attempts to change the social attitudes that members bring to the organization, develops human resources practices, and attempts to control aspects of its external operating environment (Clegg, 1981; Mills and Murgatroyd, 1991). Specific configurations of rules provide the basis for patterns of behaviour that appear as 'the way things are done around here'. In other words, rules form the experiential framework of organizational culture. But rules develop and change through the actions of numerous actors as they establish, enact, enforce, misunderstand, resist and/or break the rules. It is the configuration of rules and the actors involved that constitute a specific culture. Thus, organizational culture is defined as 'composed of a particular configuration of 'rules', enactment and resistance' (Mills, 1988a: 366).

As important elements of the cultural arrangements of modern society (Denhardt, 1981), organizations can be said to influence and be influenced by gender. Thus, it can be argued that organizations are important cultural sites where notions of masculinity and femininity are mediated, developed and resisted (Burrell, 1984).[13] Important clues to the processing of gender and discriminatory practices are explored through the dynamic and configuration of organizational rules. Throughout the book I have tried to identify how rules – particularly configurations of rules – contribute to the gendering of organizations, where they support and where they arrest the process of discrimination, and how rules change and become more or less gendered in the process.

Formal rules

The context for the establishment of an organizational culture is the establishment of a series of formal rules that come to dominate organizational activities, in particular the 'manner in which groups and individuals combine to get things done' (Eldridge and Crombie, 1974: 89), who gets to do them and how people are rewarded in the process.

Formal rules are expectations and requirements, written or unwritten, routinely associated with the pursuit of organizational purposes, activities or goals, which are perceived as legitimate or 'normal'. It is hard to avoid a rationalized view of organizations and hence of organizational culture because organizations are formally established, constituted by a series of formal, written rules, and they often present themselves in a coherent light through such things as marketing and corporate image. This overly rational image of the organization is not the whole reality but it is an important element of the experience of organizations. Formal rules constitute an important aspect of the experience of organizational life through such things as recruitment and hiring practices, job descriptions, and a variety of human resource practices governing absences, leaves, health benefits, wage and salary rates, promotion steps and processes, disciplinary action, and even dress codes, all of which can have an impact on gender.

Formal rules are established in response to a number of factors that start with the perceived purposes (e.g., profitability, political power, charitable work) of the founding members and the desire of those in charge to lay down guidelines and limitations to those that they recruit. This process continues and is modified by those who subsequently take over positions of power and authority within the organization. Beyond the specific needs for co-ordination and control, rules enter the life of an organization in various ways that have implications for gender, including legal requirements,[14] the introduction of technology,[15] the employment of specific management practices,[16] the reproduction of dominant social values about the relative worth of men and women,[17] the development of social practices designed to integrate employees,[18] and the establishment of job specializations and practices to deal with perceived environmental demands.[19]

Informal rules

Informal rules are also an important focal point of the study of organizational culture because 'doing gender' is a constant aspect of organizational life and is influenced through a number of face-to-face interactions (Hearn and Parkin, 1987).

In the process of formal organizational development a series of informal rules develop alongside formal rules. Informal rules are those norms of behaviour that arise within the context of workplace associations but which do not develop to meet the defined goals or activities of the organization. People develop various forms of association at work (e.g., social groups, friendships, unofficial pressure groups) beyond those that are officially defined (e.g., a specific unit, division or department). In the process of developing informal groups or relationships people typically develop norms that govern aspects of their behaviour. Sometimes informal rules may complement the formal rules such as friendships that contribute to a sense of corporate belonging and identity (Wicks, 1998), or they may come into contradiction with formal rules where employees' peer pressure is used to restrict output (Rose, 1978).

Rules and organizational actors

Through examination of the development of gendered rules in airlines we need to understand the players who brought them into being, sustained them, challenged them and changed them. People develop rules in several ways. Principally, rules develop and are changed by powerful actors such as founders and senior managers (Pettigrew, 1985; Trice and Beyer, 1984)[20] so attention is paid to the role of leading managers in the history of BA, Air Canada and Pan Am. Once rules are established managers and supervisors are charged with enacting and enforcing them and, in the process, rules are negotiated, unintentionally misapplied, or resisted (Mills and Murgatroyd, 1991). Thus, where possible, attempts have been made to reflect the viewpoints of other employees within the airlines. Actors also develop rules as responses to unique situations and rules are influenced by meta-rules as actors reproduce social values (e.g., discriminatory notions of women) that are translated into organizational practices (e.g., pay inequities).

That rules are the creation of actors is often lost on people as they confront rules as concrete and standing above human action. That is part of the power of rules and helps to explain how certain discriminatory practices are viewed as 'normal' and beyond the action of selected individuals.[21] By ignoring the role of individuals, however, it is possible to lose sight of how certain rules come into being. To that end, the study connects 'forms of action to structural features by focusing on the diverse social practices through which actors construct rule matrices that shape their interaction and the institutionalized forms which it reproduces' (Reed, 1992: 183).

Organizational rules in context

Analysis of rules and key actors involved in the culture of organizations is used to identify those mundane practices that sustain or challenge discriminatory practices and to identify how practices change over time. But this needs to be done in context. It is theoretically possible but untenable to study an organization as fully separate from the broader society in which it is located (Dellheim, 1986; Kieser, 1994). We cannot, for example, understand the sharp increase in female employees in the early 1940s without reference to the Second World War.

The rules approach views the organization as 'an interrelated network of social practices through which a wide multiplicity of activities are assembled to form institutionalized frameworks or patterns of collective action sustained over time and place by a matrix of rules' (Reed, 1992: 183). The focus on the relationship between control and rules should be seen as a systematic attempt to understand and explain 'the political and ideological practices through which 'organizations' are assembled and sustained as viable social collectives' (Reed, 1992: 133). Here the book draws on the work of Foucault and Unger.

Foucault and discourse

While the notion of organizational rules is useful for capturing the various expectations that guide and constrain behaviour, it does not explain how some of those expectations *cohere* into a way of thinking or behaving, nor how coherence is contested and rule-bound behaviour changed. Foucault provides a useful way of understanding not only how organizational actors generate and act in accordance with consistent behaviour expectations, but also how they come to resist dominant notions.

Focusing on 'histories of experience', Foucault contends that human subjectivity is constructed within and as a result of given 'discursive practices' constituted as discourse (Gutting, 1996). In other words, discursive practices give rise to a multitude of experiences, some of which are translated into expectations or rules of action through the development of various discourses. Thus, for example, in order for gendered experiences to take on the power of rules some of those experiences need to cohere in a way that makes sense to a significant number of people. As Sawicki (1996: 300) expresses it, 'discursive practices that construct gender are rule-governed structures of intelligibility that both constrain and enable identity formations'. The notion of discourse, the empowering of certain ideas through their appearance as 'knowledge', helps to explain how certain rules come to be accepted by those involved. For example, femininity and masculinity can be seen as 'fictions linked to fantasies deeply embedded in the social world which can take on the status of fact when inscribed with the powerful practices [...] through which we are regulated' (Walker, 1990, quoted in Ussher, 1991: 13). By analyzing key discourses in the selected airline companies the book tracks dominant sets of rules and explains their power and weaknesses over time.

Unger and formative contexts

The culture of organizations can be thought of as existing within a broader socio-political context (Eldridge and Crombie, 1974; Ouchi, 1981; Pascale and Athos, 1981). The rules approach contends that 'the social values and institutions of a given country influence the rule formation within organizations in that country' (Mills and Murgatroyd, 1991: 26) Roberto Unger provides a way of understanding these meta rules that is helpful in understanding gendered processes and change. He argues, 'the origins of social arrangement lie in past social conflicts and the institutional and imaginative arrangement which followed their resolution. [These] 'formative contexts' are deep seated and pragmatic in their effects on everyday life [and] provide an implicit model of how social life should be led' (Unger, 1987, quoted in Blackler, 1992: 283). Unger's notion of formative contexts links activity at the local level with dominant social assumptions about the character of social life and helps to explain how people come to reproduce existing practices. Following the First World War, for example, it is not unreasonable to speculate that, in Britain, the dominant view that 'woman's place was in the home' (Pugh, 1992) influenced the hiring practices of British airlines, with this 'imaginative' worldview leading to gendered rules and institutional practices.

Feminist study of organizational culture over time: A question of history

Broadly speaking, feminist studies of organizational culture follow two main research strategies in regard to time, focussed on either long-term or short-term study (e.g., a 'snap shot' or moment in time). The former approach is exemplified by Morgan's (1988) study of the culture of the Canadian Public Service over much of the twentieth century. The latter approach is exampled by Wilson's (1997; 2002) study of 'Finco', which examined aspects of culture over a relatively short period of time. Neither approach is more valid than the other. Short-term studies provide an understanding of existing organizational cultures and their established practices and help us to gauge the type, range and localization of discriminatory practices at a given point. Long-term studies, on the other hand, allow us to assess how discriminatory practices come into being, are maintained and changed/or can be changed over time. Both strategies involve unique problems.

Feminism and historiography

The study of an organizational culture over time involves the construction of a history of sorts and there are different feminist approaches to the study of history, including history by women, history about women and history written from a feminist point of view (Humphreys, 1994). The first approach is closely linked to the consciousness-raising polemics of the women's movement and focuses on bringing 'a woman's point of view' to the analysis of history. In Humphreys's (1994: 87) view, 'there are now signs of increasing awareness that history written exclusively about, by and for women can never achieve more than ghetto significance'. Nonetheless, this approach retains strong adherents among 'women-in-management' scholars who argue that female researchers need to study the impact of organizations, including organizational culture, on women. This has generated a number of studies that not only identify specific areas of workplace discrimination but also the 'special' or 'unique' qualities that women bring to the workplace (Marshall, 1984). The second approach focuses on 'including women in the historical record' (Davis, 1994: 85). Again this has its critics. Humphreys (1994: 87) argues that women's history 'faces the challenge of showing that it can transform and enrich the mainstream historical tradition which it accuses of bias, rather than merely filling in some intestinal gaps in the picture' (see also Scott, 1987). Nonetheless, there have been a number of interesting and valuable studies of organizational culture from this perspective. In particular Susan Porter Benson (1978; 1981; 1986) has explored the contribution of women to the development of work cultures in the US sales industry. The third approach sees the subject matter of women's history as 'the history of conceptions of gender (i.e., of 'men' and 'women' as social, not natural beings) and of the social relationships and experiences to which gender ideologies are tied, rather than as the history of 'women' in isolation' (Humphreys, 1994: 87). This ranges from social constructionist to postfeminist approaches. For example, Gherardi's (1995: 19) 'cultural approach to organizational culture investigates how the symbolic construction of gender comes about, how it varies from one culture to another, and how the preferences system sustains social thought on gender', while Czarniawska and

Calás (1997: 327) contend that gendering is likely 'an important outcome of modernization processes' and that 'contemporary notions of gender identity might be associated with westernization, internationalization, and transnational activities worldwide'. This book attempts to steer a course between the second and third of the three approaches. It is primarily focused on the history of conceptions of gender while keeping in view the voices of women as politically embodied actors.

The choice of feminist historiography was an important starting point for the study of organizational culture over time but a starting point nonetheless. Several other issues were confronted, not least of which were questions about the nature of history, progress, subjectivities, context and cultural traces.

History as discourse

In studying BA, Air Canada and Pan Am I have had to rely to some extent on a number of written histories of each company. Corporate histories are useful in providing clues to key personnel, events and incidents in a company over time but they are also problematic. Clearly, the intent of the corporate historian differs significantly from that of the feminist work undertaken for this book. Here the starting point was to understand how organizational cultures become gendered. This was the organizing principle behind the choice to study selected airlines. This approach differs from corporate and business histories not only in its focus but also the raison d'etre for studying a particular organization.

The company historian is drawn to the object of study through a particular fascination with the company and/or as a result of a commission to undertake a history. Robert Daley's (1980) study of Pan Am, for example, was embarked upon from a deep-rooted interest in commercial aviation and the role of Pan Am in the process, while John Pudney's (1959) history of the British Overseas Airways Corporation (BOAC) was written at the invitation of company 'chairman' Sir Gerard d'Erlanger. The company historian focuses on the selected company in terms of its stated purposes (e.g., the provision of an airline service), setting out to document how well it met its objectives over time. Indeed, the 'systematic study of individual firms on the basis of their business records' (Tosh, 1991 quoted in Rowlinson and Procter, 1999: 380) serves to highlight some factors to the exclusion of others. This often means that not only is gender ignored but that the problem of gender is compounded where associations between masculinity and business are naturalized. For example, accounts of the founding of BA focus mainly on warfare and the role of the First World War in encouraging technological developments; histories of Air Canada focus on such things as geography, rugged terrain and the role of bush piloting in forging a national airline; while studies of Pan Am tend to focus on the role of finance capitalists and cut-throat competition in the building of commercial aviation in the United States. Masculinity is embedded in each layer. The reader is left with the unassailable impression that commercial aviation is quite naturally a male business. Indeed some commentators argue that it is hardly unexpected that women were not involved in aviation at this time. Yet this ignores the role of men and masculinity in the absence of women. Arguably, through the problematization of masculinity (Collinson and Hearn, 1994) we can begin to make sense of how and why women were excluded from commercial aviation. As these examples suggest, history is 'one of a series of discourses about the world', (Jenkins, 1994: 5) and historiography is a 'manifestation of the historian's perspective as a 'narrator' (Jenkins, 1994: 12). This approach to history allows the feminist researcher to see the limitations of existing histories by identifying their underlying purposes, to resist any tendency to objectify events by reminding her that any particular study is a selective marshalling of events and ideas to illuminate current practices and concerns, and to increase sensitivity to different discourses over time and their influence on the viewpoint as well as the subjectivities of those involved.

Change versus progress

A key problem to be addressed in reading the cultural history of an organization is the question of time, change and progress. An inherent problem within histories is the modernist tendency to present history as a progressive unfolding of events (Jenkins, 1994). St. John Turner (1976), for example, through selected chronologies of events, paints a picture of Pan Am as a modern and progressive company. The problem is confounded where he links this to a gendered discourse of progress built around the heroics of men and masculinity, including the 'personal determination' of the company leader (p.9), the 'distinguished men' and the First World War heroes who graced the airline's board (p.11), and the 'technical excellence' of the chief engineer which 'was a vital contribution to the progress made' (p.13).

The issue of progress is a difficult one that depends as much on the researcher's political agenda as it does on her notion of time, gender and the construction of historical accounts. Here we should distinguish between a standard for judging whether things can be said to have improved and the notion of a universal unfolding of human development and enlightenment. Clearly it is possible to say that things have improved for women without implying that the change is part of the progressive unfolding of history. Indeed, it is hard to challenge discriminatory practices without reference to alternative (i.e., better) practices. Nonetheless, there is no shortage of accounts that suggest a progressive advancement of women over time (Calás and Smircich, 1996). Yet, even if a standard of female advancement could be agreed, there is evidence that the history of female employment has not followed a path of linear development (Ehrenreich and English, 1974). Higonnet, Jensen, Michel and Weitz (1987: 4) argue that, 'gender systems are not fixed, but respond and contribute to change'. From the perspective, gender can be characterized as undergoing a paradoxical process of progress and regress, or a 'double helix' (Higonnet and Higonnet, 1987). The validity of this observation can be judged at several points throughout the book through a focus on, for example, the fluctuation in the percentage of female employees, the range of jobs open to women, the number of women on airline boards, and the imaging of male and female airline employees at different points in time.

In confronting the problem of progress time itself is an issue that needs to be unpacked. The idea of progress is closely associated with the notion of time as a continuous process. Reed's (1990) account of BA, for example, presents an unbroken chains of events that links the first international commercial flight in 1919 by Aircraft Transport and Travel (ATT) to BA's operations in the late 1980s. Yet, it may be crises rather than the progression that tell us more about an organization. Weick (1995) argues that such 'organizational shocks' are in fact challenges to ongoing sensemaking and the precursor of new ways of making sense. This notion of organizational shocks and changed sensemaking offers the feminist researcher the possibility of identifying how gendered understanding change and can be changed again.

Thus, it might be suggested that a potentially fruitful way of studying time is not as a continuous process but as a series of 'junctures'. In other words, the history of a given organization should not be seen as a series of progressively changing events but as a series of key time frames, which shape how things were viewed at a given period of time. To understand a particular time frame we need to piece together the various factors – rules, actors, discourses and formative contexts – which shaped the worldview of organizational members at the time (Helms Mills and Mills, 2000). In brief, while a particular set of factors may come together to create particular ways of viewing the world a change in those factors can lead to a change in the subjectivity of those involved, creating different ways of viewing the world over time. To understand a particular juncture we need to understand not only the main features involved but also the particular subjectivity of the time.

Gender in context

A focus on 'gender systems' (Higonnet *et al.*, 1987) moves beyond study of the impact of events *on* women to analysis of the role of gender representations in the creation *of* gendered identities. It moves beyond the politically important question of discrimination *against* women to consider the impact of discriminatory practices on the social construction *of* women (Humphreys, 1994); beyond consideration of women and femininities to include analysis of men and masculinities (Collinson, 1988; Maier, 1997); and beyond a narrow focus on heterosexuality to include homosexuality (Weeks, 1990).

Hufton (1994: 82) contends that we need to focus not simply on how men have come to understand women but also themselves, that the history of women should become 'the history of mentalities'. Davis (1994: 86) suggests that, 'women's history must always be comparative, women's experience compared to men'. Kimmel (1987: 14) makes a similar argument from a social constructive perspective that 'definitions of masculinity are historically reactive to changing definitions of femininity'.

Collinson and Hearn (1994:18) argue 'men and masculinity are frequently central to organizational analyses, yet they remain taken for granted, hidden and unexamined'. They go on to argue for the study of 'multiple masculinities' in the development and maintenance of different gendered outcomes, concluding that 'more research studies are needed that critically examine the conditions, processes and consequences through which the power and status of men and masculinities are reproduced within organizational and managerial practices'.

In terms of sexual preference, Weeks (1990: 1) argues that the centrality given to the concept of sexuality as a definable and universal experience 'constitutes a problem for historians, for it ignores the great variety of cultural patterns that history reveals, and the very different meanings given to what we blithely label as "sexual activity".' In other words, a key part of the process of the construction of gendered identities includes the assignment of specific forms of sexual preference that say something profound about the man or woman so labelled.

Through a focus on masculinities, femininities and sexual preference the organizational construction of gender can be explored in all its complexities (Hearn and Parkin, 1987). This means interrogating historical materials and accounts to identify the influence of gender on the events described and on the construction of the narrative itself (Hufton, 1974).

An understanding of gender 'requires sensitivity to contextualization' (John, 1994: 90). Hufton (1994: 82), for example, contends that we need 'to locate [women] in the social, economic, religious, political and psychological *monde immobile* of traditional society'. This means that any reading of historical accounts and archival material must be understood in context; that to understand the gendered subjectivities of the actors involved we need to understand the discourses in which they were located and the relationships in which they were involved. To do otherwise is not only to judge a particular period by our standards alone (Thompson, 1977) but also to misjudge the nature of some of the processes under study. In the mid-1940s, for example, the senior management of BOAC and British European Airways (BEA) developed an equity policy for dealing with the hiring of flight attendants (see Chapter 5). Yet two decades later both airlines used eroticized imagery of female flight attendants to sell tickets (Chapter 6). To understand the apparent dramatic shift in policy we need to understand something of the thinking in Britain in the austere period of the late-1940s compared with that in the so-called swinging sixties. Thus, an understanding of the significance and meanings of practices and artefacts needs to take into account the social and organizational discourses in which they were located. Contexts are themselves problematic and take us to the issue of cultural traces and the construction of a sense of history as a continuous process.

Cultural traces

Understanding specific contexts in time is far from easy. In the construction of corporate histories accounts inevitably draw upon 'memories' or 'traces' from a variety of sources, including corporate documents,[22] films, artefacts[23] and informants.[24] These accounts are usually framed within the context of organizational memories in which some memories are privileged over others. That is, they are selected representations of events that have been given prominence by more powerful members of the organization, including managers, editors, corporate accountants, marketing personnel and film producers.

Reviewing these historical traces, it is clear that corporate memories are highly selective. They are framed by the context and needs of the corporate managers. Sometimes, as in the case of annual reports, they are constructed for specific reasons (e.g., legal requirements) and audiences (e.g., shareholders), thereby excluding a range of people and activities not deemed central to the focus. Other times they may arise, as in the case of in-house newsletters, out of the broad pursuit of building a sense of organization and commitment.

For the feminist scholar these memories are problematic in several ways. Primarily they focus on men and male-associated activities that are framed by concerns with the development of the company (e.g., efficiency, growth, profitability, etc.). In part this is useful in providing insights into the role of masculinity and organizational development (Collinson and Hearn, 1994, 1996), and the character of the dominant corporate discourse of the time (Benschop and Meihuizen, 2002; Tinker and Neimark, 1987). But it is also problematic in that excluded from corporate memories are a number of mundane events, processes and informal rules that contribute to the gendering of organizational culture. As Douglas (1986: 69–70) contends,

> When we look closely at the construction of past time, we find the process has very little to do with the past at all and everything to do with the present. Institutions create shadowed places in which nothing can be seen and no questions asked. They make other areas show finely discriminated detail, which is closely scrutinized and ordered. History emerges in an unintended shape as a result of practices directed to immediate, practical ends.

Douglas (1986: 70) goes on to suggest that, 'to watch these practices establish selective principles that highlight some kind of events and obscure others is to inspect the social order operating on individual minds'. That is true to a certain extent. Corporate images are often powerful in their impact and may not only reflect but create an organization's discourse. To that end, the study of corporate culture can draw on corporate materials to reveal a powerful element of the imaging process to which people were exposed over time. However, a note of caution is required because

> we cannot simply accept at face value the written records or people's memories; we cannot assume that women's experience lies outside officially constructed contexts, as a definably separate, 'purer' commentary on politics. Instead we must read the evidence we accumulate for what it reveals about how people appropriate and use political discourse, how they are shaped by it and in turn redefine its meaning.
>
> Scott (1987: 29)[25]

Constructing a sense of organization over time

The cues that corporate historians rely on to construct the history of a selected organization are linked to ongoing debates within capitalism concerning property rights, efficiency and the political economy of organizational success. As such they have varying links to ongoing discourse on the nature of masculinity and femininity. This influences the sense of continuity that gives an organization a history and it decides which voices are heard and which are not.

The image of a single company operating uninterrupted for a period of 50 years or more is only achieved by a focus on a combination of extracted cues that, in turn, depend on the purpose of the researcher. The particular interests and purpose of the historian shape the way that s/he constructs a history, in particular providing the framework for the 'extracted cues' that lead to a certain 'discovery' (Weick, 1995). Airline histories, as with other company histories, rely on a combination of extracted cues that include legal status, acquisitions and mergers, organizational size, socio-political status, organizational memory and a coherence of key personnel across time. These cues are all highly problematic when attempting to examine gendered relations over time through an organizational culture lens.

Corporate law, by delineating the legal realm of a particular company, provides the business historian with a ready made set of boundaries within which to focus attention. Nonetheless, legal status can be problematic, particularly in regard to the study of organizational culture over time. British Airways, for example, came into being in 1974 through an amalgamation of BEA and BOAC. In order to trace the organizational culture prior to 1974 we have to follow developments in BEA and/or BOAC back to their origins and then trace those origins back through their predecessors (see Figure 1.1). Nor is it easy to trace the organizational culture forward from 1974 as BA acquired a number of large airlines over that timeframe. As we can see from Figure 1.1, BA's official viewpoint is that the airline was created out of fifty-six different airlines.

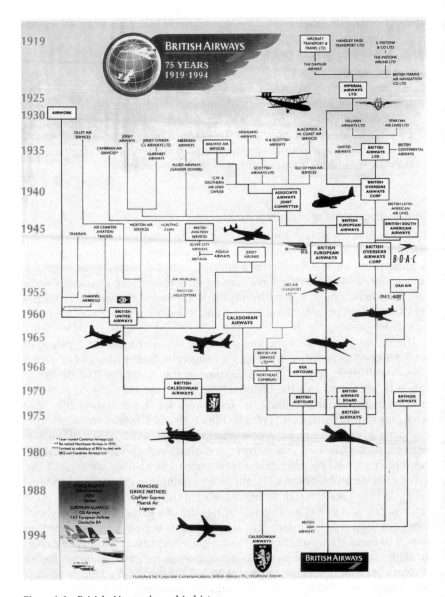

Figure 1.1   British Airways' graphic history

Source: *British Airways News*, Special Anniversary Issue, August 1994.

Nor are the legal roots of Pan Am straightforward. The original Pan American Airways Inc. was founded in March 1927 but was bought out by Atlantic, Gulf and Caribbean Air Lines (AGCAL) and then merged another holding company – the Aviation Corporation of America (ACA). A new holding company – the Aviation Corporation of the Americas (ACOAS) – was established, and its operating subsidiary was called Pan American Airways Inc. Over the next three decades the company acquired substantial ownership (ranging from 30.1% to 100%) in twenty-four airlines, in 18 countries. In the post-Second World War era Pan Am owned a chain of hotels, established an aerospace division and, in 1980, merged with National Airlines (see Table 1.1).

Until recently it is somewhat easier to trace the roots of Air Canada but the process was not entirely without its problems. The airline was originally

Table 1.1   The founding of Pan American Airways and its acquisitions, 1927–91

The formation of Pan American Airways, Inc. and the Aviation Corps of the Americas

1927   Pan American Airways Inc. (Pan Am) (established by the Bevier group)
       Atlantic, Gulf and Caribbean Air Lines (AGCAL) (holding company – established by the Hoyt group; buys out Pan Am)
       Aviation Corp of America (ACA) (holding company – established by the Trippe group; acquires 52% of Pan Am)
       West Indian Aerial Express (WIAE) (airline – established by Basil Rowe)
       Juan Trippe named president and general manager of Pan Am.
1928   Aviation Corps of the Americas (ACOAS) (holding company formed from merged assets of the ACA and AGCAL. Acquires WIAE).

Companies developed or acquired by Pan Am

1929   Compania Mexicana de Aviacion (CMAM) (interest relinquished in 1968)
       Huff-Darland Dusters – renamed Peruvian Airways
       Chilean Airways
       Pan American–Grace Airways (Panagra) (established 50/50 by Pan Am and Grace Co., partnership dissolved in 1966)
1930   Columbo–German Aerial Transport Company (SCADTA) (secretly acquired by Pan Am)
       New York, Rio, Buenos Aires Lines [NYRBA]
       New York Airways Inc. (NYA) (formed by Pan Am as part of the Bermuda agreement with IAL)
       Panair do Brasil (interest relinquished in 1961)
1932   Aerovias Centrales (Mexico) (absorbed by CMAM in 1935)
       Pacific Alaska Airways
       Uraba, Medellin and Central Airways (54% holding; company dissolved in 1961)
       Compania Cubana de Aviacion (interest relinquished in 1954)
1933   China National Aviation Corp (CNAC) (45% holding; nationalized by the Chinese in 1949)
1940   Aeronaves de Mexico (40% holding; nationalized in 1959)
       Aerovias de Guatemala (40% holding; interest dissolved in 1945)
1943   Aerovias Venezolanas (30.1% holding)
       Bahamas Airways (45% holding; interest dissolved in 1948)

continued

Table 1.1 Continued

1944	Compania Panamena de Aviacion (40% holding; interest dissolved in 1971)
	Compania Dominicana de Aviacion (40% holding; interest dissolved in 1957)
	Lineas Aereas de Nigaragua (40% holding)
	Servicio Aereo de Honduras (40% holding; interest dissolved in 1970)
1945	Lineas Areas Costarricenses (40% holding; interest dissolved in 1970)
1949	Middle East Airlines (36% holding; interest dissolved in 1955)
1953	Guided Missile Range Division formed
1957	Philippine Air Lines (20% holding; interest dissolved in 1968)
1973	Intercontinental Hotels Group established.
1980	National Airlines (merged with Pan Am).
1981	Pan Am sells of Inter-Continental Hotels Group.
1985	Pan Am sells Pacific Division to UAL.
1991	Pan Am folds.

Source: Table compiled from Pan Am Annual Reports, Bender and Altschul (1982), Daley (1980) and St. John Turner (1976).

called Trans-Canada Air Lines (TCA) when it was established by an act of parliament in 1937 as the aviation arm of the Canadian National Railways (CNR). With a few notable exceptions the company retained it core legal operating status until 1977 when it was fully recognized as a separate entity from CNR and again in 1988, when it was privatized. Concerned with francophone sensibilities, the airline underwent a legal name change in 1965, adopting the more bilingually friendly Air Canada name. Its main foray into acquisition came in the 1970s when it purchased an interest in an aviation consulting company, a hotel chain, a cargo operation, small aircraft trading and a regional airline (Nordair). It also established an airline charter operation (Touram). At the end of the 1990s Air Canada merged with Canadian Airlines (see Table 1.2). The merger presents a problem for someone beginning a study today because she would face the complexity of unravelling the current Air Canada from its predecessors, which, through Canadian Airlines alone, involves dozens of airlines merged and acquired over time, and whose personnel play a substantial role in the airline today.

Company mergers also create problems for the scholar who is interested in tracing the impact of organizational dynamics in a single company over time. What, for example, can be said to link developments in one company with developments in another? To what extent is it possible to speak of events in one company, in one period of time, as if they are relevant to another company at a different point in time? We are still left with the central question of how did the practices in any one company come to influence the practices in BA, Pan Am and Air Canada, and which companies were more influential in the process?

Table 1.2 A schematic history of Air Canada

1937	Canadian Government establishes Trans-Canadian Air Lines (TCA) – under the control of the Canadian National Railways (CNR)
1965	TCA changes name to Air Canada
1973	Air Canada purchases Econair Canada Holidays Ltd (later called Touram Inc.)
1977	Air Canada Act, makes the airline a stand-alone Crown corporation, separate from Canadian National Railway
1979	Air Canada takes over Nordair
1981	Air Canada becomes legally separate from CNR Purchases 30% interest in Innotech Aviation Ltd
1984	Air Canada sells Nordair; buys 20% share of Global Travel
1988	Air Canada privatized
1999	Air Canada merges with Canadian Airlines; retains the name Air Canada

Organizational construction and gendered accounts

Although it is difficult to construct a coherent sense of organization over time there are a number of feminist strategies for dealing with the problems involved. To begin with, it is less important for feminist research than it is for corporate history to focus on a particular company over time: an organization's legal boundaries and its culture are often two different things. While the corporate historian is concerned to document how particular legal boundaries were established and maintained, the feminist approach to the study of organizational culture in this book is concerned to understand how particular social arrangements impact people's understandings of gender. This suggests that it is more important to focus on a particular set of regularized social interactions and follow them through several periods of development and change. This means that a particular aspect of an organization should be studied and traced over time. In the case of BA the book traces particular sets of relationships that constituted core aspects of an organization over time. This means focusing on such things as piloting, stewarding and selected administrative relationships in BA's predecessor Imperial Airways Ltd (IAL) and studying the impact on those relationships on merger with British Airways Ltd (BAL) in 1939. Similarly, those same sets of relationships – identified through specific but changing personnel – were followed through BOAC and the new BA. Less important were relationships within the various merged or acquired companies, except in their impact on the culture under study. Thus, company names – such as IAL, BOAC and BA – were less important for the boundaries that they delineated as for the meanings they bestowed on selected sets of relationships. In a similar vein, and for purposes of comparison, the book traces employment practices through Pan Am's US-based head office and divisional headquarters but leaves out of account the various foreign airlines in which the company had a large holding. In regards to Air Canada the book focuses on employment practices prior to its merger with Canadian Airlines.

Finally, any study has to have a cut-off point and for various reasons I have chosen to end this study in 1991. That was the year that Pan Am went out of business and it is also eight years before Air Canada merged with Canadian Airlines. Thus, for relative ease of comparative analysis, and the tracing of cultural processes, 1991 serves as a useful stopping place although, where it is crucial to the story, I have included more recent events.

Outline of the book

The gendering of airline culture over time is explored through a focus on selected employment practices related to the hiring and promotion of women. This serves three purposes. First, it documents significant changes in the employment of women over time. Second, it serves as a focus for identifying attitudes to (and the social construction of) women and men in a given period. Third, it identifies points of change, which act as a guide to cultural factors that may serve to maintain and change social constructions of gender, and associated practices.

Using this method, eight distinct periods are identified over the life of BA. Each period is viewed as a juncture or 'a concurrence of events which create a moment in time – a series of images, impressions and experiences which act to give the appearance of a coherent whole and which influence how [an] organization is understood' (Mills and Ryan, 2001: 64).[26]

Focusing primarily on BA, Chapter 2 deals with the first of the junctures, namely the absence of female employees in the period 1919–24. Chapter 3 examines the introduction and growth of female clerical work in the 1930s. Chapter 4 looks at the rapid expansion of female employment during the war years. Chapter 5 examines the consolidation and 'normalization' of female employment in the immediate post-war era, 1945–60. Chapter 6 discusses the eroticization of female labour in the 1960s and 1970s. Chapter 7 traces the making of an employment equity discourse through three distinct junctures, (1) equity struggles in the mid-1975s to 1980s, (2) the development and consolidation of professionalized female labour, 1980–90, and (3) the rise of the woman manager in the 1990s. The final chapter provides a summary of what we can learn from analysis of the gendering of organizational culture over time. Throughout each chapter comparative developments are explored through analysis of selected changes in Air Canada and Pan Am.

2
The Gendering of Civil Aviation, 1919–24

In other respects, [Hounslow] this old R.A.F. aerodrome, approached by a narrow tarmac road, was unattractive. It was irregular in shape, grass covered, with a crude, lightly tarmaced apron. It boasted one international touch. One gable of its twin sheds bore the legend 'CUSTOMS': the other, triumphantly the word 'DOUANE'. In a converted wartime shed, a neat waitress in cap and apron served teas, cut sandwiches and was sometime able to do a packed lunch of sorts for adventurous travellers to enjoy during the two and a half hour trip to the other side.

Pudney (1959: 49)

Introduction

Following the First World War a number of British airlines began commercial operations. ATT was the first to offer a regularly scheduled passenger service, flying passengers from London to Paris on 25 August, followed by Handley Page Transport Ltd (HPT) one week later. In October Instone Airlines Ltd (Instone) began flying the same routes but by the end of the year three airlines faced competition from Royal Dutch Airlines (KLM)[1] and two French airlines, Compagnie Messageries Aériennes and Cie. des Grands Express Aériens (CMA and CGEA).[2] By 1923 only HPT and Instone had survived. ATT was closed down in 1920 when its parent company, the Aircraft Manufacturing Company (Airco), was taken over by the British Small Arms Company (BSA) and replaced by the Daimler Airway, jointly owned by BSA and the Daimler car group. In 1923 a fourth British airline called British Marine Air Navigation Company (BMAN) began international operations.[3] In 1924, the British government stepped in to support civil aviation by recommending the merger of Daimler, HPT, Instone and BMAN into a single company, to be called Imperial Airways and subsidized for a period of ten years.

In the United States the post-First World War government undertook air-mail service and left the transportation of passengers to private entrepreneurs. Many of the early commercial ventures were run by veterans operating air-taxis with war-surplus aircraft but few survived the competition (Bender and Altschul, 1982). Early ventures included Aero Ltd, which flew passengers between New York and Atlantic City as early as 1919, Aeromarine and West Indies Airways, both of whom flew services from Key West to Havana the same year, and Long Island Airways, which was established in 1922 by a young financier by the name of Juan Trippe. However, it wasn't until the passage of the first Air Mail Act in 1925, which provided mail subsidies to private contractors, that commercial aviation began to take off (Smith, 1944).

In Canada commercial aviation in the post-First World War era took a different turn. Government airmail subsidies did not come into effect until mid-1927, and it was ten years later that the first (government-owned) transnational airline – Trans-Canada Air Lines (TCA) – was established (Milberry, 1979). In the meantime passengers along the heavily populated East–West routes were serviced by two national railway systems run by the Canadian Pacific Railway (CPR) and the government-owned CNR. Instead, many of the hundreds of returning wartime combat flyers turned to bush piloting;[4] servicing mining, timber and oil interests in Northern and remote areas of the country.

One thing that stands out in these early years of commercial aviation is the almost total absence of women at any level. In North America this may be accounted for by the fact that airline services were small operations, built around the activities of military veterans, and few women played a role in the military.[5] As airline ventures grew the masculine character of the industry was enhanced in the United States as they came under the control of financiers and venture capitalists and in Canada by the male dominant nature of bush piloting (Foster, 1990; Time-Life, 1983). In the United Kingdom, despite the overwhelming military character of the airlines, the near-exclusion of women from the industry has to be explained in the face of the availability of some 32,000 air force-trained female personnel and important post-war social and legislative changes.

At this juncture: A look inside British Airlines, 1919–24

In numerous ways, the early British airlines had the look and feel of masculine preserves.[6] Power and authority were concentrated in male hands; all tasks, with almost no exception, were classified as male jobs; symbols and artefacts referenced wartime military activity; company advertising focussed on images of the heroic pilot; and there was an overwhelming feel of military camaraderie. A description of the early days of ATT at Croydon airport, for example, refers to pioneer airway men, working in a former military aerodrome, in an environment that 'reminded one forcibly of a Wild West township' (Robert Brenard, AT&T employee, quoted in Pudney, 1959: 54).

Power and authority

In 1919 Major-General Sykes, former First World War Chief of Air Staff, characterized commercial aviation as 'a child of war and a military development pure and simple' (quoted in Penrose, 1980b: 9). This was an accurate description of the emerging airlines. With one exception, men who had made their fortune building warplanes founded the airline companies; the exception was Instone, whose founders made their fortune through wartime shipping. Founding owners included George Holt Thomas (ATT), Frederick Handley Page (HPT), Colonel Frank Searle, Major George Woods Humphrey, Hubert Scott-Paine (BMAN), Sir Samuel Instone and Alfred Instone. All the airlines were managed and staffed by former air force officers. ATT was run by Major-General Sir Sefton Brancker (Managing Director) and Colonel Frank Searle (Master-General of Personnel).[7] Brancker and Holt Thomas (Chair) were key members of the ATT Board of Directors (King, 1989; Pudney, 1959).[8] Woods Humphery managed HPT,[9] and, with the collapse of ATT in 1920, Searle and Woods Humphery combined with BSA to establish the Daimler Airway. Searle took on the post of managing director and Woods Humphery that of general manager.[10] At Instone Sir Samuel Instone controlled the airline but his younger brother Alfred was in charge of the day-to-day running of the company.[11]

The gendered patterning of work[12]

In the immediate post-First World War era men filled all levels of commercial aviation – from the Department of Civil Aviation[13] to the airlines and airports. Many were recruited from the armed forces, particularly the air forces. Airline recruitment replicated air force practices, with senior air force officers in the ranks of senior and middle management, pilots drawn from the ranks of wartime bomber and fighter pilots, and engineers and mechanics recruited from wartime ground crews. In the airlines the only work open to women was secretarial and clerical jobs, but even the latter was considered primarily men's work (see Figure 2.1), and, with the exception of waitressing, female employment did not exist in airport work. There were less than a handful of women employed in British airlines at this time, including 'Miss Wyton,' who worked for the ATT Flight Manager (Bamford, 1986: 29) and Dorothy Young, an ATT clerical employee (Young, 1987).[14] When ATT collapsed Young went to work for KLM at Croydon airport until October 1921 and Wyton joined the French airline CMA on 1 May 1922.[15] At the new Daimler Airway Doris Moore was employed as the secretary to the Managing Director, a post she held between 1922 and 1924 (British Overseas Airways Corporation, 1946g).[16]

100% male-associated job (task and role descriptions)	<--------------- ---------------- --------------->			100% female-associated job (task and role descriptions)
Airport				**Airport**
Chief control officer				
Air traffic controller				
Customs officer				
Security				
Van driver				Waitress
Porter				
Airlines				**Airlines**
Owner				
Chairman				
Director general				
Director				
Commercial director				
Senior manager				
General manager				
Managing director				
London manager				
Paris manager				
Manager				
Station manager				
Office manager				
Master-general of Personnel				
Business manager				
Publicity manager				
Public relations manager				
Chief financial accountant				
Chief accountant	Accounting+			
Chief pilot				
Pilot				
Radio operator				
Flight engineer				
Steward				
Cabin boy				
Maintenance foreman				
Mechanic foreman				
Section leader				
Air mechanic				
Section engineer				
Engineer				
Mechanic				
Mechanical engineer				
Ground mechanic				
Freight handler				
Loader				
Flight and wireless monitoring				
Meteorologist				
Commercial man		Clerical work		Secretary
Outside representative				
Canvasser		Ticket sales+		
Commissionaire				
Office boy				

+ Only in the London offices of the French airline CMA were women employed in these tasks.

Figure 2.1 The division of labour in civil aviation in Britain, 1919–24

As airlines expanded their passenger services the new positions went to male employees. In 1922 Instone hired men as 'commissionaires' to 'shepherd passengers to their seats' (Penrose, 1973: 99) and as 'stewards' on its inaugural London-Brussels-Cologne flight (Instone, 1938). That same year Daimler hired fourteen-year-old 'cabin boys' as the world's first flight attendants, serving coffee from a vacuum flask during flight (Learmonth, Nash and Cluett, 1983: 61).[17] For various different reasons, all three innovations were discontinued due, respectively, to drunkenness, economic viability and a fatal plane crash that killed all on board.[18]

Symbols and artefacts

Male-associated symbolism dominated the new airlines and was derived from two sources, wartime air force associations and the luxury travel business. From the very beginning, wartime military symbols and artefacts permeated almost every aspect of commercial aviation but as the industry grew airlines began to mimic other luxury travel organizations, taking on some of the trappings of rail and ocean-going businesses[19] and contributing to a new 'service' masculinity.

In the first two years of operation British airlines operated with military bombers that had been converted to passenger service. The Handley Page 0/400 bomber, for example, carried up to twelve passengers seated on lightweight wicker chairs, with space for two more in the former gunner's cockpit. Entry to the open cockpit was reminiscent of wartime rather than commercial aviation, with the passengers having 'to crawl through a small trap-door in the bulkhead between the two cockpits' (McIntosh, 1963: 41). The planes were flown from former wartime Royal Air Force (RAF) aerodromes by air force pilots,[20] in their military uniforms and flying suits, using their wartime ranks. Even the passengers sometimes ended up in the First World War flying kit (Pudney, 1959: 38). Eventually, custom-built passenger planes and airline uniforms were developed.

In 1922 airlines began to take on new types of masculine associations with the introduction of uniforms, terms and roles (i.e., stewarding) that mirrored those in other luxury travel organizations. Instone was the first to introduce uniforms. Copying the outfits worn on ocean liners, the airline dress their pilots and operational staff in navy cut uniforms, consisting of blue serge and brass buttons (Instone, 1938: 94–95).[21] The company renamed the general manager 'the Commodore', signifying his rank by the use of 'gold braid on his navy blue suit with reefer coat and brass buttons' (ibid.). Even the commissionaire was dressed in a uniform 'adorned with silver braid and the company's initials' (Penrose, 1973: 99).

Imaging the employee: Male identity in airline advertising and narratives

From the early days, airline managers utilized advertising and other forms of publicity to sell airline tickets.[22] The major problem confronting airlines at the time was not simply competition but the widespread perception of flying as dangerous. To overcome this airlines focussed their advertising on safety, using particular images of the pilot to make the point. Instone, for example, advertised itself as 'the safety line', informing passengers that 'No Other Company Has Such A Unique Record For Safety' and assuring them of 'Safety, Comfort and Speed' through the use of 'British Machines' and 'British Pilots' (Instone, 1938: plate xx).[23] The company also produced signed photographs of their pilots, which were handed out to passengers along with accompanying details of the pilot's achievements.

In airline advertising the pervasive image is of the rugged flyer, schooled in wartime flying, facing the new and dangerous hazards of commercial aviation with courage, fortitude and loyalty.[24] It was argued that, 'The real criterion of success was not the aeroplane but the skill, enthusiasm, devotion, and determination of the pilots – and theirs was the spirit which had taken the RAF to victory' (Penrose, 1980b: 16).[25] This image was not only the stuff of advertisements but informed the airline narratives of the time and successive histories of commercial aviation. Passengers were sold the idea that, in the unlikely event of danger, they would be in the safe hands of an experienced and brave flyer. It is little wonder that commercial pilots came to be looked up to as gods and heroes (Corn, 1983; Learmonth *et al.*, 1983). The image of the heroic pilot was kept alive through countless retelling over the years in official accounts, including company histories and pilot biographies.[26]

Certainly commercial flying *was* dangerous in its early days and pilots did need a certain amount of bravery and skill to fly the planes. Nonetheless, as stories they are selective accounts that highlight some aspects of flying to the exclusion of others, particularly the more mundane, routine aspects of flying. Given the complete absence of female flyers in commercial aviation it was inevitable that the object of the stories (i.e., danger and heroism) came to be associated with the subjects involved (i.e., male flyers).

Gendered interactions

At the heart of an organizational culture are the multifarious interactions between people. Those in leadership positions often have a powerful influence on the culture (Bryman, 1986; Deal and Kennedy, 1982; Schein, 1992) but the role of employees and their influence on the informal rules also need to be taken into account (Mills and Murgatroyd, 1991; Schultz, 1995), particularly in the development of gendered 'sub-structures' (Acker, 1992). The biggest single factor influencing relations between men in the early airlines was air force experience. This informed leadership style and camaraderie throughout the airlines.

Leadership

The airline entrepreneurs influenced the fledgling industry more by their hiring practices than force of personality. During the First World War both Holt Thomas and Handley Page hired women to work in their engineering concerns (King, 1989) but this seems due to wartime practice and expediency rather than any particular commitment. Instone hired few women to work in its mining and shipping businesses.[27] At the war's end, with the ending of government contracts, these three companies fired all their female and most of their male employees (King, 1989; Learmonth *et al.*, 1983).

Frederick Handley Page had a direct influence on the running of his airline. Strong willed, and masterful, he discouraged independent thinking and ran the airline as a 'benevolent autocrat' (King, 1989; Penrose, 1980b;

Pudney, 1959). He was immensely popular with employees 'because he was an approachable man's man who remembered one's name and made uproariously funny speeches at staff parties' (Bamford, 1986: 2). In contrast George Holt Thomas, Hubert Scott-Paine and Sir Samuel Instone were matter-of-fact and businesslike, leaving much of the running of their companies to the former airmen that they hired as senior managers.

One of the most influential RAF officers in the airline business was former Air Vice Marshall Sir Sefton Brancker – 'a typical Army officer, debonair and dashing, at times quixotic, on the surface a trifle orthodox but at bottom sound and rugged, [but] a shade too conservative' (Collier, 1959: 131). His leadership style was that of the paternalistic military officer, prepared to look out for those who followed orders but intolerant of those who challenged or were a threat to order. He was, for example, anti-union, seeing them as 'an evil element'.[28] His manner was flippant and occasionally aggressive, yet he was well respected by the men under his command (King, 1989: 209). His dealings with women were another matter.

In many ways his attitude to women was typical of men brought up in Victorian Britain, 'courteous, even gallant, to women of all ages though he liked them young and pretty'(Collier, 1959: 122). In other ways he was ahead of his time in his advocacy of female recruitment to the armed forces in time of war.[29] He was also 'the first comparatively senior officer in the War Office to employ a woman driver and one of the first to have a Lady Secretary' (Brancker, quoted in Beauman, 1971: 19). Brancker's view was fuelled by a combination of patronization, wartime exigencies and a genuine belief in women's capabilities. All three factors remained a part of his approach to women in subsequent years.

Framed by a belief in the importance of men to warfare, Brancker viewed the employment of women as 'a proper arrangement whereby large numbers of men could be released to the trenches and to the front' (ibid.). Towards the end of the First World War, as the newly appointed RAF Master-General of Personnel (MGP), Brancker made the organization of the Women's Royal Air Force (WRAF) his first priority, yet his dealings with the WRAF Commandant, Lady Violet Douglas-Pennant, became a *cause celebre* and the subject of an official enquiry by a Select Committee of the House of Lords (Beauman, 1971; Escott, 1989). Under orders of Lord Weir of the Air Council, Brancker had to dismiss Douglas-Pennant. However, the 'bullying, blustering and contemptible manner' in which he did so surprised even Weir (Beauman, 1971: 21). Equally surprising, Brancker suggested that Emmeline Pankhurst, one of the nation's leading suffragettes, be appointed as Douglas-Pennant's replacement (Beauman, 1971: 22),[30] but she was overlooked in favour of Helen Gwynne-Vaughan. Brancker was, nonetheless, supportive of Gwynne-Vaughan, seeing her as a keen, efficient and sound administrator who made the WRAF 'the best disciplined and best turned-out women's organization in the country' (Brancker, quoted in Escott, 1989: 83).[31] She, in turn, praised Brancker for paying women the compliment of 'treating them like men'. For her: 'It was a great experience to serve with an officer who took for granted in women those qualities of steadfastness and good sense which the services require. One could not have wished for a better chief' (Gwynne-Vaughan, quoted in Beauman, 1971: 55).

Yet, Brancker brought none of this approach to commercial aviation. At ATT he did not hire women managers, totally dismissed the idea of female pilots,[32] but did employ a female secretary and a female clerical worker: this was in line with his view that women had a limited role to play, in stores depots and as typists, in any post-war women's air service (Beauman, 1971: 42).

In his dealings with men at ATT Brancker reproduced a RAF-style of leader–subordinate relations, where a close relationship between high ranking officers and those below them, particularly between pilots and their leading officers, was encouraged.[33] According to one subordinate,

> General Brancker had that magnetic personality which he radiated to all, revealing himself at once as a great chief and friend. After any particularly nasty flight, there was always awaiting his great hearty grip of the hand with a twinkling: 'Well done – Cheerio and stick it, old lad,' or a polite little note to that effect [...] His great secret was that he was *human* and showed appreciation for those who worked for him, and as a natural result received one hundred per cent unswerving loyalty and affection in return
> Bill Lawford, ex-RAF pilot, quoted in Pudney (1959: 55)

With the demise of ATT in 1920, Brancker's replacement in the new (Daimler) company was Colonel Frank Searle who brought a 'hard business mind' to the role of managing director (Pudney, 1959: 58), spending most of his time on safety and efficiency (Penrose, 1980b). At HPT Major Woods Humphery had an autocratic style; 'strong and severe, he was not so much liked as respected, and what he said went' (Bamford, 1986: 2). In contrast, his chief pilot, Major Herbert Brackley, a former bomber squadron commander, was both popular and trusted. He was 'the most gentlemanly of airmen, respected by all his crews and colleagues both for his flying skills and for his 'correctness' in every way' (Bamford, 1986: 5).

Airline culture and military camaraderie

Throughout the airlines, pilot recruitment was based on aviation skills, wartime heroism and air force experience, with many of those recruited having crossed paths at some point or other during the war.[34] The recruitment of air force pilots was not simply instrumental but was fostered by a strong ideological commitment on the part of those at the top of civil aviation. Sir Samuel Instone, for example, saw commercial aviation as building on the supposed gains of wartime flying. He felt that civil aviation provided 'openings for young men [offering] a fresh lease of life to pilots in the Royal Air Force when they have ceased to be of value flying' (Instone, 1938: 51–52). He also felt that civil aviation would contribute to an adequate reserve of officer pilots that would be needed 'in the next war' (Instone, 1938: 52), a view that was widely held among air force leaders (Penrose, 1973). Instone put this view into practice, beginning with Captain Barnard who, 'fresh from his war exploits' (Instone, 1938: 5), was hired as chief pilot.[35]

In a similar vein, Brancker, commenting in a post-war issue of the *Daily Mail*, expressed the view that: 'The War has bequeathed to us as a nation a great heritage in the air. Our pilots are the best, our designs the most efficient, and our industry the greatest in the world. Supremacy in the air is ours for the making' (quoted in Learmonth *et al.*, 1983: 34).

At ATT all the pilots who served under Brancker were recruited from the RAF, several of whom came from the wartime RAF Communication squadron at Hendon (Macmillan, 1935: 226).[36] Beyond the employment of a 'well-chosen team of pilots', Brancker organized the company on 'well-trained service lines drawn mainly from the air force. A brigadier was General Manager and Brancker's deputy. Majors and captains ran departments at headquarters. Eight of the pilots were lieutenants and two were captains' (Collier, 1959: 134–35).

Air force recruitment spread far beyond the ranks of pilots to include engineers, other ground crew and office staff,[37] and wartime experiences, like those of R. H. McIntosh, were not far from everyone's minds. McIntosh often marvelled that, as a commercial pilot, he was able to fly unhindered over places where previously he had been shelled from the ground during wartime bombing raids. Nonetheless, 'the scars of the Great War were [still] visible on the fields of France' many years after the First World War (McIntosh, 1963: 61).[38] Expressions of wartime camaraderie characterized British airlines at this time. Sir Alfred Instone contends that 'the atmosphere was permeated with much of the will-to-win spirit which followed from the war years' (quoted in Learmonth *et al.*, 1983: 42). McIntosh remembers 'a cheerful Service-like atmosphere' (McIntosh, 1963: 84),[39] and ATT Captain William Armstrong recalls 'the spirit and camaraderie of the war' that he and his fellow 'pilots, ground staff, mechanics, and office staff' shared (Armstrong, 1952: 77).[40]

Organizational discourse

Issues of survival, safety and service structured airline strategies and, in the process, images of manhood. In themselves these discourses are not specifically gendered but, on closer examination, there is evidence that they contributed to the exclusion of women from the industry and the construction of associations between forms of masculinity, categories of work and organizational rank.

Survival

In the first phase of civil aviation the industry offered little more than temporary work in an unstable operating environment. British airlines were in a difficult situation, having to compete with Dutch and (heavily subsidized) French airlines, as well as rail ferries, for cross-Channel passengers. By the end of 1920 all of the British airlines were in deep trouble – ATT went bankrupt and ceased operations, Instone suspended flying for the winter, and HPT greatly reduced its number of flights. The situation improved somewhat in the New Year with the introduction of government subsidies, but there remained an air of uncertainly among the surviving airlines. Some people left the business while others moved to different airlines in an endeavour to keep flying. Several of ATT's former employees, including Dorothy Young, went to work for KLM.[41]

Instability within the airlines, alongside a deepening problem of mass unemployment, was one of several factors that worked against the hiring of female employees at a time when women were being discouraged from working in well-established and relatively stable industries (Pugh, 1992). Airline companies preferred to recruit from the ranks of unemployed ex-service men than from the new generation of post-war women, with their 'bobbed hair, shortened skirts and shocking use of cosmetics' (Penrose, 1973: 213–14). It took a government inquiry, long-term government subsidies and the establishment of IAL to achieve a sense of stability and security in the British airline business.

Safety

From the beginning, commercial airlines had difficulty convincing people to fly. Pioneering and wartime aviation made flying appear dangerous, and the railway system and cross-channel ferries provided sound alternatives to passengers. Britain had the most extensive railway network in the world, on which passengers could travel in comfort, speed and relative safety to most parts of the country. For foreign travel airlines could not match ocean liners for distance and service. Even on the short cross-Channel crossing from London to Paris weather and technical problems sometimes meant that it could take longer to get there by plane, and was certainly less safe.[42] This encouraged airlines to spend time and effort publicizing service and safety.

Safety issues were translated into masculinity in at least three ways – references to wartime experience, aviation skill and technical knowledge, and male pride. The latter was part of the strategy of hiring cabin boys, whose presence, it was felt, would have a calming effect on passengers (Wright, 1985). The main effort, as discussed above, involved publicity built around the skills and heroism of the pilot. But this was also linked to engineering skills. References, such as those of Instone, to 'British pilots and British Machines' served to index notions of national superiority, wartime heroism and British engineering. Here reference was made to traditional practices of engineering recruitment and training. Passengers could feel safe knowing that the planes were built and maintained by British engineers. This was reflected not only in advertisements but also in recruitment practices focused on hiring from 'the older branches of engineering' (Instone, 1938: 170).

Service

In the immediate post-war era airlines were in direct competition with the railway/ferry services from England to the main continent of Europe. They were able to compete in terms of speed, successfully arguing that air services can get people to their destinations quicker, but they could not compete with the 'first-class service' that characterized rail and ocean travel. The upper-class traveller – the mainstay of the airlines' business – was used to service from a white-coated steward but the limited seating-capacity of planes made the hiring of in-flight crews prohibitive.[43] At best the airlines reproduced some of the personal touches to be found in railway and ocean-going travel, including chauffeur delivery to the airport and the use of 'passengers' affairs' agents to explain details of the journey to the passengers, check their luggage and passports, weigh them, and escort them to the aircraft or meet them on their arrival. Pilots often helped passengers with their luggage and assisted them from the plane (Penrose, 1980b), and, as we have seen above, there were limited attempts to introduce stewarding abroad planes.

These early attempts at airline service mimicked the practices of their competitors, utilizing not only the dress uniforms but also the practice of hiring only males in each of the positions. This was in line with the social values of the day, which frowned on women flying, but it is also a reflection of organizational isomorphism whereby a company copies the so-called best practices found in successful companies (DiMaggio and Powell, 1991).

Although organizational discourses and practices played a role in the gendering of organizational culture they need to be understood in the social context of the times, including social attitudes towards domesticity, entrepreneurship, the militarization of flight and the development of organizational forms and knowledge.

Domesticity and the workplace

In the first two decades of the twentieth century the social construction of female sexuality in Britain was influenced by several, often countervailing, trends. On the one hand, there was a discourse of domesticity, or 'domestic idyll' (Weeks, 1990), whose influence can be discerned throughout workplace practices and in associated statements on women and work. On the other hand, there was the impact of poverty, the women's movement and the First World War on changing attitudes and practices, but it would be inaccurate to characterize these latter two as strictly countervailing pressures to the domestic idyll. The women's suffrage movement and the First World War challenged some while confirming other discriminatory views on the role of women in society.

The domestic idyll

In Britain in the early part of the twentieth century dominant notions of masculinity and femininity were mediated through a powerful discourse centred on the family, or a 'domestic idyll', which placed value on 'the home', as a haven from the workplace, and 'motherhood', as a moral commitment (Weeks, 1990). It was primarily a discourse centred on female sexuality through an emphasis on women as home-based wives and mothers, but as such it also contributed to notions of manhood through an emphasis on the family provider. Developed and refined in the Victorian era, the domestic idyll served as a lens through which men were viewed as strong, unemotional, the family 'breadwinner' and protector, and women were seen as weak, emotional, delicate, pure, sexually timid, bearers of children.[44]

This notion of womanhood developed from a number of concerns and social developments, including inheritance rights and the legitimacy of heirs,[45] the sentimentalization of the home (with large numbers of middle-class wives staying at home), the 'non-working wife' as a visible symbol of status, laws restricting the use of child and female labour, and social pressures from middle-class reformers on working-class mothers to stay at home with their children (Anderson and Zinsser, 1988; Weeks, 1990).[46] These developments reinforced the idea among the middle and working classes alike that women should spend their time in the home as wives and mothers, sexually isolated and thus sexually pure. As increasing numbers of middle-class and working-class women began to stay at home necessity gave way to virtue and the notion of the male 'breadwinner' became an integral part of the emerging masculinities.[47] These decades were the formative years of the men who founded and led the early airline business, including George Holt Thomas (born in 1869), Sefton Brancker (1877), Frederick Handley Page (1885) and Hubert Scott-Paine (1891).

With the onset of the twentieth century, a falling birth-rate,[48] a renewed concern with 'respectability' and changing attitudes to childhood strengthened and refined the domestic idyll, placing an even greater emphasis on domesticity and motherhood: women were no longer simply the bearers of children but the guardians of the future, the guarantors of national and racial purity (Rowbotham, 1999). It was not only men who drew comfort from the ideal of 'hearth and home'. The 'non-working' mother was viewed by many women as a symbol of status and respectability and as an escape from the harshness of paid work (Roberts, 1988). Even leading suffragettes, such as Millicent Fawcett, argued that women should not be apologetic about domesticity and motherhood; that women should not become 'bad imitations of men' by denying or minimizing the 'differences between men and women' but should instead stress those differences because 'women bring something to the service of the state different from that which can be brought by men' (quoted in Pugh, 1992: 3).[49] Nonetheless, suffragette campaigns for the right to vote, entry into the professions, changes in property rights and tertiary education for middle-class women were helping to change existing notions of womanhood (and manhood).

Sexuality and the workplace, 1900–14

Despite a strong moral discourse about women's place in the home other forces were compelling women into the workplace. Poverty, for one thing, drove many women to seek paid employment (Roberts, 1988). With over one million more women than men, many women were forced to support themselves. The developing tertiary sector of the economy also helped to reshape the possibilities of women's work,[50] providing jobs that were seen as appropriate for women (Anderson and Zinsser, 1988). Middle-class women particularly benefited from the new work opportunities in teaching, nursing and clerical work (Anderson and Zinsser, 1988; Rowbotham, 1999).[51] Indeed, the expansion of office work saw the feminization of certain jobs as 'the male clerk began to give way to the female clerical worker and clerk-typist,' and wage rates fell (Anderson and Zinsser, 1988: 195).[52] On the other hand, a number of areas of women's work had been 'deskilled' (Braverman, 1974), with a loss of previously attained skilled jobs over the course of the nineteenth century (Roberts, 1988).

By 1911 more than 35 per cent of all women were involved in paid work and many others were engaged in some form of sale or trade from their homes (Pugh, 1992; Roberts, 1988). This represented a modification rather than a radical change in the idea of the domestic idyll. While the number of women in the workforce was increasing the proportion of married working women actually decreased[53]: upon marriage the great majority of women left the paid workforce, rarely to return. It was assumed that a woman's position as a wage earner was temporary, that she would give up work if and when she married (Rowbotham, 1999).[54] Despite some changes, women continued to face a limited range of jobs, and more than a third of all female workers were still employed in domestic service (Pugh, 1992; Roberts, 1988). Women's pay was still much less than that of men in roughly comparable jobs, and, to some extent, this was maintained by the ideological practice of 'the family wage' whereby a married man's wage supposedly reflected his need for sufficiency to support a family.

Thus, prior to the First World War attitudes to women's work were still framed by the narrow lens of a domestic idyll. Things were beginning to change. The women's movement was challenging some of the more egregious elements of the gender discourse and women were entering the new tertiary jobs in increasing numbers. It seemed to some that 'the opening of new work and educational opportunities to women of privilege was [...] a tremendous widening of women's previously restricted roles and functions' (Anderson and Zinsser, 1988: 196).

The First World War

The social upheavals of the First World War led to dramatic changes in the role of women and popular views of womanhood, but the outcomes were contradictory in many ways. At the onset of the war there was actually a fall in the paid employment of women, mostly from the clothing and luxury trades (Griffiths, 1991; Isaksson, 1988; Roberts, 1988), but this turned into a sharp increase from 1916 onwards. Initially large numbers of women were recruited to traditional female jobs in textiles and clothing, but then a number of so-called male occupations were opened up to women, including the metal industries, and the wood and aircraft trades where women eventually constituted one third of the workforce. The paid-work possibilities multiplied for privileged women during the War. Many of the jobs were at the clerk-typist level but represented real gains for privileged women (Anderson and Zinsser, 1988). Nonetheless, five-sixths of women workers continued to be engaged in traditional 'women's work' (Pugh, 1992); the entry of women into skilled jobs or classifications was resisted by the unions and upheld by the Government; the issue of equal pay was resisted by employers; and, ultimately, while six million women were in the work force by 1918 the majority (approximately 57%) continued to stay at home.

Despite expanded opportunities for women the war strengthened narrow images of femininity and masculinity, crystallizing 'conventional assumptions about the proper relations between the sexes [that image] man as fighter and woman as housekeeper' (Pugh, 1992: 12). In particular, the war, a severe staffing shortage and a falling birth rate focussed renewed attention on women as mothers, with numerous campaigns and policies designed to increase the birth rate.[55] There was also considerable moral panic at the start of the war concerning the prospect of 'war nymphomania' (Weeks, 1990), and in some instances military commanders placed evening curfews on the movement of women in their areas of command (Pugh, 1992).

The impact of the First World War on urban working-class women has been characterized as 'relatively minor [in comparison with] the improved standard of living, small family size, maternity benefits, protective legislation, unions, and new jobs [which] comprised the most important changes in [their] lives between the 1870s and the 1920s' (Anderson and Zinsser, 1988: 295). Indeed, it can be argued that the lives of working-class women changed very little, bringing 'only a temporary suspension of the normal conditions outside the home' (ibid.), with the one tangible change to survive the war being the advent of new white-collar jobs. Things were somewhat different for middle and upper class women who 'often reported that the war freed them from nineteenth-century attitudes limiting both work and personal life' (ibid.). Another important change in the lives of middle-class women began to take shape in the middle of the war with the opening of the military to female recruits and the establishment of the WRAF.

Womanhood and the armed forces

In 1916 the High Command of the British Armed Forces began to consider the recruitment of women to ancillary positions. This represented a sharp break with tradition as women had been excluded from the armed forces since the eighteenth century (Hacker, 1988), but it did not signal changing attitudes to women. Two years of warfare saw severe losses of front-line troops in battle, and a serious depletion of manpower (sic) (Escott, 1989; Pugh, 1992). Initially, women were employed as army clerks but with the establishment of the Women's Army Auxiliary Corps (WAAC),[56] in 1917, their role was expanded to include administrative and disciplinary positions – cooks, domestics, telephonists, telephone switchboard operators and drivers (Escott, 1989); these jobs , with the exception of driving, were mostly female in civilian life. The following year the Women's Royal Naval Service (WRNS) and the WRAF were established, but again women were largely confined to domestic chores (Escott, 1989).

The WRAF

The formation of the WRAF made history as the first women's military service to be established at the same time as its male counterpart, the RAF. Nonetheless, in common with the other branches of the military, the majority of WRAF recruits were assigned tasks that conformed to traditional views of women and female-typed employment. As the Air Ministry Weekly Order 1237 expressed it, 'women have been enrolled in the WRAF with the object of enabling them to assist in the war by releasing men for duty at home and overseas' (quoted in Escott, 1989: 34). More than 36 per cent of the WRAF were employed in a variety of domestic jobs, including cooks, laundresses, polishers, cleaners and waitresses; a further 44 per cent were assigned a variety of clerical tasks; and of the remaining 20 per cent, the majority were divided between work on dismantling wrecked aircraft[57] and as general labourers, packers, telephonists, tailoresses, shoemakers, fabric workers and nurses. Women were specifically excluded from combat roles and associated activities, so were not allowed to be pilots or even fly in air force planes as passengers (Bowen, 1980).[58]

The WRAF had its own female leadership but effective control lay with male officers.[59] There were numerous female officers at the lower levels of the WRAF but RAF Non-Commissioned Officers undertook many of the basic supervisory positions (Escott, 1989: 27–29). The WRAF's first Chief Superintendent, Lady Gertrude Crawford was placed under the direct control of a male officer and expected to act as little more than a figurehead (Escott, 1989: 74), having to gain prior permission to undertake even the most mundane tasks. When she complained she was promptly asked to resign.[60]

Violet Douglas-Pennant, the second woman to lead the WRAF, fared little better.[61] When she took over command in May 1918 she was given a small, dark attic room next to a men's toilet at the Head Quarters of the Air Ministry (Collier, 1959: 93). She had no Air Ministry pass and no clerical assistance, yet her [male] liaison officer, who was junior to her, had both. Her attempts to assume various responsibilities were blocked at every turn (Escott, 1989: 75–76). She concluded that the WRAF will never be on a 'sound footing unless the [WRAF leader] is treated with confidence and due respect' (quoted in Escott, 1989: 75–76). As a result her title was changed to Lady Commandant, with a rank equivalent to a Brigadier, and her powers and responsibilities increased. However, ten weeks later she was summarily dismissed for questioning recruitment practices. That her dismissal, at the hands of Sefton Brancker, was carried out in a particularly brutish manner did not help matters either.[62] Douglas-Pennant's replacement was Helen Gwynne-Vaughan[63] who remained in the post until December 1919.[64]

The WRAF was disbanded in early 1920, with a total of 32,000 women passing through its ranks, topping 25,000 at its peak (Beauman, 1971: xiv). Despite an overwhelming focus on domestic and clerical duties, a substantial minority of WRAF members worked in non-traditional jobs as drivers, aircraft repairers, welders, coppersmiths, tinsmiths, sheet-metal workers, turners, machinists, carpenters, painters and dopers, electricians, wireless operators, mechanics, upholsterers, draughtswomen, photographers, motor-cyclists, and even airplane mechanics (Beauman, 1971; Bowen, 1980; Escott, 1989).[65] Almost six hundred women served as WRAF officers at some point in the service's two-year history.

Not one of the former members of the WRAF, including those in clerical positions, ended up working for commercial airlines, even though airline recruitment and WRAF demobilization were occurring around the same time. This had much to do with attitudes within the new airlines but also with practices within the WRAF itself where traditional attitudes prevailed. In preparation for demobilization and a return to civilian jobs, the WRAF provided its personnel with short intensive training courses focused on dress-making, cookery, secretarial work, millinery, driving and foreign languages (Beauman, 1971: 45). Helen Gwynne-Vaughan went into politics, standing unsuccessfully as a Conservative candidate[66] and her boss, Sir Sefton Brancker, went on to run ATT.

The immediate post-war era

A confusing picture of advances and setbacks for women characterized the immediate post-war years (Rowbotham, 1999). The period was paradoxical in a number of ways. The press, which had welcomed women's involvement in the industrial war effort, now demanded that women return to 'the home'. Employers supported the call to replace female employees with returning service-men, and this had the full backing of the Government in the form of the Restoration of Pre-War Practices Act 1919. Not only did this lead to the dismissal of many women from occupations formerly held by men but also a number of positions that had not existed prior to the war (Pugh, 1992). While at least half of the women who had joined the war-time labour force withdrew voluntarily many others were dismissed, including the hundreds of women employed at National Aircraft Factory No. 1, which became Croydon Airport (Learmonth *et al.*, 1983). By the Spring of 1919 half-a-million women were unemployed and by 1921 there was actually a smaller percentage of women (down to 33.12%) involved in paid work than there had been ten years earlier.[67]

In 1918 a new Representation of the People Act enfranchised eight and a half million women, and granted the right of women to sit in Parliament. This political advance was tempered by two limitations. The right to vote was restricted to women aged 30 and above, and was tied to the rights of their husbands; to be eligible to vote women had to be on the local government register or married to registered men (Pugh, 1992; Rowbotham, 1999). Thus, while it represented a change in attitude to women voting it did not, according to some, represent a major change in perceptions of women and womanhood (Pugh, 1992: 39).

Also paradoxical was a widespread return to the practice of barring married women from paid employment despite the enactment of the 1919 Sex Disqualification (Removal) Act, which stated that: 'A person shall not be disqualified by sex or marriage from being appointed to or holding any civil or judicial office or post' (Pugh, 1992: 93). In 1921, two years after the Act became law, only 8.7 per cent of married women were in paid employment, a drop of almost one per cent since the pre-war years (Pugh, 1992). In fact, there were now two per cent less women involved in the workforce than ten years earlier. A series of others laws,[68] rooted in more traditional, pre-war notions of gender, nullified the impact of the Sex Disqualification (Removal) Act, and of 'the twenty pieces of legislation enacted between 1918 and 1927 and designed to improve the status of women, almost all were concerned with enhancing their position as wives and mothers' (Horn, 1994: 13–16).

All in all, the new legislation tended to reinforce pre-war notions of man as breadwinner and protector, and woman as wife and mother. These were social constructions built not only around notions of morality but also spatial location, with men associated with the 'public sphere' and women with the 'domestic sphere'. A woman's place was very much in the home, but when she did enter the workplace it was usually on a very limited basis, restricted to limited jobs, by attitudes, practices, legislation and marital status. Arguably, these factors had a bearing on the new commercial aviation business with its associations of danger and of unlimited horizons.

The aftermath of the First World War contributed to the paradoxes of the period. Traditional notions of man as warrior and woman as caregiver had been reinforced, yet also challenged. The war effort had taken centre stage, and armed conflict was associated exclusively with men; warrior-like images of masculinity were strengthened. Images of womanhood, however, were less sharply drawn. There was a heightened emphasis on the domestic role of women, as supporting wives and mothers, caregivers (e.g., nurses), providers of domestic services (at home, in the workplace and in the military) and 'stand-ins' for men at the front. But this changed the content of a woman's role and placed her in new and challenging roles in the public sphere, as large numbers of women entered the workforce and the new women's military organizations.

The War had the effect of unsettling the way the notions of men and women were understood and this led to considerable post-war debate. In particular there was concern about female sexuality and economic independence. Married working women were seen as a threat, not only to the jobs of men, but to the institution of the family itself, and this led to a series of legislative acts, enhanced by the onset of an economic slump in 1921, to restrict female employment.

Young, single women, particularly those from the middle class, were also the subject of media and legislative attention. Wartime losses meant that there were almost two million more women than men, and this raised political and social concerns about women and morality.[69] It was feared that women would attempt to seek permanent, long-term employment. Young, economically independent women found themselves vilified by the press as 'flappers', a term that came to denote self-absorbed and morally loose.[70] One critic warned that 'many of our young women have become de-sexed and masculinised', another argued that such women shun 'the servitude of household occupations [but] only at the expense of the integrity of [their] sexual organs'(quoted in Pugh, 1992: 78).[71] Sometimes concern with female sexuality took bizarre turns as in the attempt, in 1921, to amend the Criminal Law Amendment Bill to make homosexual acts between women illegal (as they already were between men). There were some fears that the excess of women over men and the new forms of womanhood would lead to lesbianism (Pugh, 1992: 79).

The media played a considerable role in the construction of images of womanhood in this period. Post-war women's magazines, such as *Home Chat*, not only encouraged a rediscovery of women as 'feminine' but, in contrast with the pre-war emphasis on the idealized wife, focussed on the *skills* of household management: domesticity had taken on a pseudo-scientific framework, linking the new 'science' of management to household chores.

Changes and stability in experiences of womanhood

There were a number of changes in the post-war era. A section of women had won the vote and, by 1918, were beginning to enter Parliament. The 1919

Sex Disqualification (Removal) Act permitted a number of middle-class women to enter the ranks of the higher professions, albeit in a small and uneven way. The percentage of women in the teaching and nursing professions fell from 63 per cent to 59 per cent, but the number in the higher professions rose from 6 per cent to 7.5 per cent (Pugh, 1992: 92). Despite an overall fall in female employment opportunities, women gained entry to some non-traditional jobs, including inspectors and foremen (sic), where the percentage of female employees more than doubled to 8.7 per cent, and new types of work, especially clerical and related jobs where they constituted 46 per cent of the workforce in the inter-war years (Pugh, 1992: 92)

The immediate post-war era can justly be described as 'post-Victorian,' particularly in relation to 'the sexual revolution' of the 1920s, with its relaxation of some sexual taboos: 'the new feminists spoke of sexual pleasure, birth control was more openly advocated, progressive intellectuals espoused sex reforms, while homosexuality caused a certain fashionable *frisson*' (Weeks, 1990: 199). If anything this was the era of the emancipated middle-class woman, fuelled by economic factors. The First World War had reduced the availability of potential husbands and a post-war slump made it more difficult for middle-class families to support their unmarried daughters, contributing to a new acceptance of the need for their daughters to find long-term work (Pugh, 1992).

Post-war changes were uneven. A large number of people continued to believe 'that a woman's place, especially a married woman's place, was in the home, not in the factory, shop or office' (Roberts, 1988: 72). As several commentators have observed, the period was marked by a 'full flowering of the domestic ideology', especially for working class women (ibid.). While women had, to some extent, improved their position in the labour force they had become more generally involved in marriage and motherhood than their Victorian predecessors (Pugh, 1992).

Homosexuality

Part of the outcome of an increasing emphasis upon the domestic idyll was a strengthening of the value of heterosexuality. As a powerful discourse of approved forms of sexuality the domestic idyll left little room for more than a narrow range of heterosexual images.[72] This may have made an important contribution to existing, but relatively vague, 'concerns' about homosexuality.[73] Nonetheless, the Law was very harsh on people associated with homosexual acts,[74] and was extended in 1912 to include acts of male homosexuality in private as well as in public.[75] Other than negative pronouncements, homosexuality was excluded from public discourse. At best homosexual activity was viewed as a disease and at worst a criminal activity. As such it had no part of the approved images of men and women that managers and other leaders wanted associated with their organizations. As we shall see later, narrow images of heterosexuality played a role in the construction of airline cultures for almost five decades.

Domesticity and the airlines

We can see the influence of the domestic idyll on the airline industry. Of the handful of women hired by airlines prior to 1924 – three were single (Young, Wyton and Liotard) and one widowed (Moore). One married woman (Didier) was possibly employed in a part-time capacity. The future Mrs Dorothy Young[76] was employed in clerical work at ATT until its collapse. She moved to KLM where, on her first day, she was 'asked out by George Young, the ground engineer' (Young, 1987). They were soon married and this 'effectively ended [her] career' (ibid.). Little is known of the future employment of ATT's Wyton or CMA's Liotard. Doris Moore – a young widow[77] when she began her working career in 1917, as a secretary to the Foreign Office and War Cabinet Secretariat[78] – joined Daimler Airways in 1922 and continued employment with IAL in 1924. As a widow she was not subject to the same pressures that single women faced (i.e., expectations of marriage followed by retirement from company employ), and she went on to a twenty-four year career in the airline business. Yvonne Didier worked alongside her husband, and General Manager, Jack Bamford as 'the third member of [CMA's] small office family' but it is far from clear 'whether she was on the staff or just helped her husband' (Bamford, 1986: 29). Nonetheless, Bamford remembers the 'chic, charming, very French' Didier as keeping the books, looking after the cash, doing the payroll and cooking 'meals for her husband and herself on a little stove in the corner of the office' (ibid.). Bamford's account conjures up domesticity not only in its confusion about Didier's status but also in the imagery that permeates the description of her workplace tasks. In early 1922 Didier left CMA to have a baby.

Masculinity at work

While images of femininity were largely viewed through the framework of domesticity, masculinity was developed through several reference points, including class, entrepreneurial activity, technical knowledge, nationalism, and the military and warfare.[79] These masculine images and experiences played a role in the development of the organizational cultures of the airlines and served to exclude women by creating associations between masculinity and a range of airline positions and tasks.

Class position afforded men the education and experience to acquire aeronautical knowledge. The men who made their mark in aviation – as inventor-entrepreneurs, airmen or both – were drawn from the upper and middle classes. These men had the education, financial resources, and time and energy to devote to airplane invention and development. George Holt Thomas, for example, was the son of a newspaper proprietor and was educated at King's College School.[80]

The very factors that helped these men were, for the most part, barriers to female involvement in aviation. The upper and middle classes made a virtue of domestic life and the notion of the genteel woman. Women were thus limited in their ability to gain technical knowledge and skills or to pursue entrepreneurial opportunities. Universities and other institutions of higher learning were highly restrictive, allowing very few women to enter and excluding them from technical spheres of education. Among the working classes very few women were employed in engineering concerns and were generally excluded from the skilled and semi-skilled engineering trades.[81]

Despite various prohibitions some middle and upper class women managed to become involved in aviation, usually through the encouragement of a male relative in the business, but their contributions were usually limited, ignored or marginalized.[82] The influence of male entrepreneurs, however, became embedded in the symbolism of flight, through the naming of engines (e.g., Rolls Royce), airplanes (e.g., de Havilland) and airline companies (e.g., Handley Page Transport).

The military

The class nature of the British military influenced the development of aviation by providing upper-class male leadership to the new air forces and restricting flying opportunities to a narrow group of middle and upper class men. Prior to the Second World War the British military establishment was the exclusive preserve of the upper-class (James, 1990) and the development of flying wings of the military services gave these men a unique opportunity to become associated with the development of aviation.

As a class the rulers of the military establishment inherited a domain that was exclusively male. Prior to the First World War there were no women in the army, the navy (Isaksson, 1988; Roberts, 1988) or the Royal Flying Corps (RFC). In line with older branches of the armed forces, RFC officer training was effectively restricted to the sons of the richer classes.[83] The typical air force officer was recruited from the Public Schools where, from early youth, 'they [were] taught self-confidence and initiative' (Captain Guy Pollard, quoted in James, 1990: 143). All RFC officers were required to learn to fly (James, 1982: 138), and this encouraged the development of a deep rooted attitude that the air force could only be commanded by pilots.[84] This ensured that not only were all officers pilots but that most pilots were also officers.[85] For ground crews the RFC insisted on the attainment of the School Certificate, effectively ensuring that the bulk of the RFC's skilled tradesmen and the majority of non-pilot ranks would be drawn at least from the lower middle-classes (James, 1990: 108).[86] These recruitment policies, which were carried on into the RAF, helped to establish the link between masculinity and aviation, particularly in relation to the specific skills of piloting and aviation engineering. Those links became indelibly stamped through the process of warfare.

The militarization of space

For the first decade of the twentieth century aviation became associated with the exploits of the inventor-entrepreneurs but by the end of the second decade flying had become associated in the popular consciousness with warfare and the military. The changing image of flying, from civil to military, strongly influenced gendered perceptions of aviation as a male pursuit.

Dramatic events such as the historic first flight by the Wright brothers in 1903, Alliott Roe's first British flight in 1908, and Blériot's cross-channel flight of 1909 helped to associate flying, danger and maleness in the public imagination. This was in large part due to the greater opportunities for men in aviation, but also in part because the efforts of women aviators were either ignored or treated with disdain.[87]

Women, nonetheless, were involved in ballooning, parachuting, and piloting.[88] From 1908 women began to make their mark in engine-powered aviation, in pioneering flight,[89] air races, long-distance records and titles, and aerial stunting and barnstorming.[90] Often these achievements were attained under difficult conditions in the face of aviation circles noted for their rough dealings with women (Lauwick, 1960: 33). The flying career of Matilde Moisant, for example, 'didn't last awfully long because in those days that was a man's work, and they didn't think a nice girl should be in it' (quoted in Cadogan, 1992: 49). In an endeavour that was already seen as masculine the establishment of the RFC and preparations for war made it far more difficult for women to become aviators.

Warfare and the air force

The onset of the First World War introduced the public to new (gendered) images of aviation. At first the army restricted the use of aeroplanes to reconnaissance, but that changed as the war progressed. Soon the RFC was producing armed aircraft to attack the enemy's reconnaissance planes, which, in turn, gave way to a strategy of producing fighter planes to defend the reconnaissance planes from attack. Eventually both sides were producing large numbers of fighter planes to patrol and sweep the skies. Meanwhile the air force wing of the navy, the Royal Naval Air Service (RNAS), was developing the strategy of bombing raids.

The changed use of aviation impacted on the public perception in at least two crucial ways. First, air raids on England dramatically altered the way that people viewed aviation: a raid by 18 German Gotha planes on London on 7 July 1917, for example, killed 57 and injuring almost two-hundred people. Second, the publicity given to the heroic exploits of individual flyers strongly associated flying with danger and masculinity. To a public numbed by the mass slaughter and the slow progress of trench warfare, aerial combat offered a new and exciting endeavour, or at least so the military and the press hoped. For an army needing to sell the idea of heroism to potential new recruits the air hero offered something of a godsend: the airman's exploits were easy to verify and could be quickly tabulated to feed a population thirsting for some good news from the Front. For example, 'a whole nation [...] rejoiced in the exploits of [air ace] Albert Ball. When he died, there was a far greater outpouring of genuine public sorrow than when 60,000 Englishmen [were] slaughtered in half an hour at the Somme' (McCaffery, 1988: 117). Warfare was turning perceptions of flight into images of threat, danger and heroism, and perceptions of the pilot into someone who was heroic and male:

> Flying was still new enough that civilians looked upon aviators with a certain degree of awe. It was assumed that you had to be something of a swashbuckler just to take one of those flimsy crates off the ground. To joust to the death in man-to-man duels above the clouds was something that staggered the imaginations of millions.
>
> McCaffery (1988: 117–18)

While the RFC, and other national air forces, provided flying experience to numerous men a generation of women flyers was effectively grounded.[91] Experienced women flyers, including Melli Beese in Germany, Nita Snook, Ruth Law and the Stinson sisters in the United States, and Hilda Hewlett in Britain, were all turned down by their respective air forces.[92]

Organizational linkages and influences

In the first two decades of the twentieth century a number of organizations came into being which influenced the gendered character of commercial aviation. Some of these organizations, such as the Aero Club, and the air races, such as the Schneider Trophy race, provided venues for male bonding, bringing together men throughout the various areas of aviation. The Aero Club, for example, founded in 1901, served as a meeting point for people in the aviation world, a flying school, and as an agency for the granting of pilot certificates of worthiness. Air races and displays, including the Schneider Trophy, provided other arenas at which the male aviation fraternity could meet and exchange ideas.

In short time, the Aero Club and the Schneider Trophy became institutions of male camaraderie, replete with gendered imagery. For example, the Schneider Trophy was by design a naked female form with the outstretched wings of a dragonfly diving towards the waves. This was meant to symbolize the command of aviation over the sea but Aero Club members were quick to grasp the sexual connotations of the Trophy, naming it the 'Flying Flirt'. Whenever the Aero Club had charge of the Trophy they would polish it to bright silver between the statuette's thighs (King, 1989: 243).

Various other organizations extended male control over aviation, and included the Society of British Aircraft Constructors (SBAC), the Air League of the Empire, the International Air Transport Association (IATA) and the International Civil Aviation Organization (ICAO).

Finally, the establishment of the RFC, RNAS and the RAF had a profound influence on the gendering of commercial aviation. For example, the RFC's command structure, ranks, uniforms, and recruitment practices influenced the recruitment practices and the symbolism of the post-war commercial airlines. RFC symbols taken up by the commercial airline business included the double-breasted 'Maternity Jacket' uniform, the flying badge, the rings of rank that were used on the jackets of airmen and even the air force moustache.[93] Various operational terms, such as 'on the strength', which referred to the number of recruits engaged by the air force, found their way into the language of the commercial airlines.[94]

Summary and conclusion

It was argued that to understand the absence of women in British airlines before 1924 we should examine the formative contexts in which the companies were formed, the formal and informal rules that constituted them, and the dynamics that developed within them. Analysis suggests that the key factors influencing the gendered character of post-war commercial aviation were class, warfare and, to a much lesser extent, the women's movement.

Class was influential in the development of warfare and the staffing of the upper echelons of the military, as well as government and business. Warfare was influential in shaping gendered notions of men and women and encouraging the fusion of a coherent group of upper-class men around the future of post-war aviation. The impact of the Suffragette movement was less direct. By challenging Victorian attitudes, the Suffragettes forced a rethink of women's abilities and political standing that likely accelerated the feminization of clerical work, influenced wartime attitudes to women's role in the military and the workplace, and encouraged post-war changes in electoral laws. However, because of wartime rationales (e.g., the temporary employment of women due to warfare) and anxieties (e.g., fears about falling birthrates and moral panic), the developing political and economic changes were not readily translated into practice until well after the First World War (Pugh, 1992).

Arguably, the existence of a rigidly defined class system in Britain shaped the war effort, the development of the air forces, and post-war commercial aviation. It was the narrow interests of the upper classes that shaped the factors that led to war, and consequently the discourse of warfare (Hobsbawm, 1994). The men of the upper classes broadly inhabited the same social and organizational milieu, and this process was exacerbated by warfare and the need for close cooperation between government, military and business. The men who established and ran the post-war commercial airlines were centrally located within the discourse of warfare. They came from the ranks of the wartime leadership, including military leaders, pilots, arms manufacturers, and high government officials. As such, they were part of the British upper classes who were committed to an 'Imperialist War', concerned with the division of world empires (Hobsbawm, 1994), the maintenance of economic, national and racial superiority (Said, 1993) and the retention of traditional views of gender and class (Rowbotham, 1999).

These men formed a cohesive group, who, for the most part, shared the same worldview. To them aviation and masculinity were inseparable. They came from a world where piloting, engineering and aircraft maintenance were male pursuits; where formal rules were built around rank and informal rules arose out of the camaraderie of air force experience. At a time of mass unemployment, few women in the transport industry as a whole,[95] and resistance to the feminization of clerical work in sections of industry,[96] commercial aviation managers were able to ignore the few experienced female pilots, the hundreds of WRAF women that had served in non-traditional and officer positions, and the thousands of women that had been employed in the Wood and Aircraft Trades industry during the war.[97]

The class dominance of the British airline industry can be contrasted with the more open and diverse class situations of the United States and Canada. In North America commercial aviation was far more disparate both in terms of the number of companies competing for business and the players involved.

In Canada commercial airlines did not develop until the end of the 1920s, before which most ventures were small-scale bush operations geared to mining and exploration concerns in wilderness areas. Canada boasted the most extensive railway system in the world, and successive post-First World War governments could see no need for commercial airways: apart from a few air-mail contracts, airlines were left to the devices of the so-called free market (Pigott, 1997). Bush operations were developed by a number of returning First World War airmen,[98] by mining, forestry and oil concerns, and by provincial governments.[99] James Richardson, a grain magnate, founded Canada's first commercial airline, Western Canada Airways (WCA), in 1926 and staffed it with former bush pilots and engineers.

The economic and social context of bush piloting shaped masculinity in the airways for years to come (Mills, 1998). Work was few and far between and competition for jobs was often sharp and 'cut throat' (Milberry, 1979). The social context of bush flying involved danger, isolation, uncharted and often harsh territory, and male dominated operations and communities (e.g., mining towns). In these conditions certain images of men and women came to dominate bush piloting and the communities they served and worked in. The archetypal bush pilot was seen as daring, heroic, tough, rugged, womanising and self-reliant (Henry, 1983; Shaw, 1964; Time-Life, 1983). The world of bush flying was very much 'a man's world'. In the isolated communities served by the bush pilots there were very few women apart from the wives of prospectors, and they were very much second class citizens (City of Yellowknife, 1984). Not surprising, there were virtually no women in the fledgling aviation industry,[100] and it stayed that way until the establishment of TCA in 1937. Nonetheless, the individualism of the industry allowed for individual decisions. When, for example, Stuart Graham, Canada's first bush pilot, set off on his historic flight his wife Madge, a landscape artist, was the navigator (Ellis, 1980; Pigott, 1997). When WCA was established, James Richardson appointed his wife, Muriel, as its vice president (Pigott, 1998).

In the United States military and wartime influences on aviation were diffused through a number of ventures and overtaken by discourses of cut-throat competition, entrepreneurship and corporate financing. A number of returning First World War aviators were engaged in small-time aviation ventures, but most failed in the face of fierce competition[101] and a lack of government subsidies. Ironically, the Air Mail Act in 1925, which established generous airmail contracts, killed off many of the remaining small-time air-lines as big business moved into, and consolidated, the industry (Williams, 1970). In the place of the pioneer operator 'there appeared a new breed: Wall Streeters' (Smith, 1944: 95). These men brought a new level of ruthlessness to the business: 'The holding company appeared, forcing out 'the little fellow' ruthlessly' (Smith, 1944: 130). Two powerful holding companies, Aviation Corporation (AVCO) and the Aviation Corporation of America (ACA), for instance, respectively established American Airways (American) and Pan Am. Aircraft builders Boeing and Curtiss-Wright acquired and consolidated several small airlines to establish, respectively, United Air Lines (UAL) and Transcontinental and Western Airline (TWA). General Motors established Eastern Air Transport (Eastern).[102]

By the mid-1920s military experience, disparate but small operations and cut-throat competition ensured that few, if any, women worked in commer-cial aviation. From the late 1920s there was a new breed of airline executive; men who competed furiously, but had their own camaraderie, fighting to the death to get routes but remaining friends at the end of the day – 'robber barons' (Smith, 1944), 'bar-room gamblers,' 'all boys together' (Sampson, 1984). As we shall see, this emerging form of masculine dominance contin-ued to exclude women from all but a few clerical jobs but, unlike their British counterparts, did open space for female flight attendants and, in at least one important example, a place in the higher ranks of Pan Am.

What this tells us about the gendering of organizational culture is that the strength of any masculine influence may depend on the extent to which var-ious cultural layers and dynamics (formative contexts, social class, organiza-tional rules, mimetic possibilities, social and organizational discourses, and the various actors involved) are mutually reinforcing, the centrality of the organization's cultural nuances to hegemonic forms of masculinity,[103] and the existence and relative strength of factors of resistance.

Although the different dominant forms of masculinity in British, Canadian and US airlines prior to 1925 had similar outcomes for female employment there were some differences in initial organizational culture development, the social construction of womanhood and long-term female employment. In the United Kingdom the powerful combination of class, warfare and the military had a powerful influence on the organizational cultures of British airlines. It would be twenty years before a woman was employed to a management position, twenty-one years before women moved outside of the ranks of lower clerical and secretarial work, and twenty-sven years before women were regularly employed as flight attendants. Notions of women were generally viewed through the lens of domesticity. In the United States, the military experiences of the flyers – coupled with the small-scale character of the enterprises – served to exclude women from the industry. By the mid-1920s a number of factors – including the passage of time, the character of the industry and ownership structure – ensured that military experience was only one of several influences on the development of commercial aviation. This meant that in time notions of womanhood were mediated through a more disparate lens that opened up some opportunities to women beyond that offered by British airlines. In the United States the domestic skills of women at work were emphasized in the employment of female flight attendants in the 1930s. In Canada the exclusion of women from aviation had as much to do with bush piloting as military experience. By the late 1930s, and some distance from the First World War, bush piloting had an important influence on the thinking of the men who established TCA and a very narrow framing of female opportunity – the range of female employment at TCA was less than in British airlines and flight attending was developed as a female-only job.

3
Thoroughly Modern Milieu:
The Feminine Presence in the Airways

> [The] middle-class woman's dilemma during the 1920s [was that]
> despite the increased scope of female employment, the prevailing
> philosophy remained that marriage was a woman's true vocation.
>
> Horn (1994: 61)

Introduction

From 1924 to 1939 commercial aviation in Britain underwent considerable
change. The Government intervened to encourage merger and to provide
funding, acquiring in the process more direct control. As a result a new, more
powerful, airline – IAL – emerged. Airplane technology improved greatly,
bringing an increase in passenger seating and operating range, allowing airlines to carry more passengers over greater distances. Trans-continental
travel was introduced and 'air stewards' became a standard part of the flight
crew. Competition sharpened with the development and growth of British
Airways Ltd (BAL) and a number of international competitors. Women
became an accepted part of the workforce but, with one or two exception,
were wholly employed in secretarial and clerical positions.

Looking back from the vantage point of 1939 it could be said that there
had been advances in the employment of women in commercial aviation
in Britain. From less than a handful in the whole business in 1924 there
were, by 1939, 500 women working for IAL alone. This number represented
nine per cent of IAL's total workforce (see Figure 1.1). The range of female
occupations had grown, from 4 to 24 distinct jobs over the period (see
Figure 2.1 and Table 3.1) but women were still a minority of employees,
confined to a range of support tasks, and absent from all of the airline's
central tasks of piloting, aircraft maintenance, stewarding and all but one
of the various positions of power and authority. There were, however, some
points of note. For brief periods in the 1930s two small airlines employed
the first female commercial pilots, and the country's first flight attendant,
and there were at least four women commercial airline operators. The end

Table 3.1   Male and female occupations in Imperial Airways, 1924–39*

Male-classified occupations and levels (122 categories)

Accountant	Flying establishment officer	Public relations officer
Administrative assistant grade III	Foreign public relations	Radio mechanic
Aircraft inspector	Foreman	Radio officer
Air superintendent	Foreman's clerk	Radio servicing improver
Assistant in buying deptment	General establishment officer	Reception officer
Assistant chief buyer	General manager	Records clerk
Assistant navigation instructor	Ground engineer	Requisition clerk
Assistant to ARP officer	Head kitchen porter	Rigger
Assistant to general establishment officer	House janitor and labourer	
Assistant to maintenance engineer	Improver	Riveter holdup
		Sales assistant
Assistant to ticket stock	Inspector	Section engineer
Auditor	Instrument maker	Senior accounts clerk
Barman	Instructor	Sheet mental worker
Booking clerk	Instrument repairer	Shop boy
Boy	Junior draughtsman	Shorthand typist
Bulletins clerk	Junior technical assistant	Signwriter
Cable messenger	Junior post clerk	Spray painter
Captain	Junior traffic clerk	Sprayer
Carpenter	Kitchen porter	Station officer
Cashier	Labourer	Steward
Catering manager	Land line switchboard operator	Stock keeper
Chargehand storekeeper	Launchman	Stoker
Clerical assistant	Maintenance engineer	Storekeeper
Clerk	Manager	Storeman
Cloakroom and lift attendant	Managing director	Stores clerk
Commissionaire	Marine officer	Technical assistant
Communications officer	Messenger	Technical clerk
Company secretary	Messenger boy	Ticket issuing clerk
Correspondence clerk	Metal worker	Trainee
Cost clerk	Metal worker semi-skilled	Upholsterer
Cost investigation clerk	Motor mechanic	Van boy
Coxswain	Night teleprinter operator	Van driver
Director	Night watchman	Victualling clerk
Divisional radio engineer	Office boy	Wages clerk
Electrician	Operations clerk	Watchman
Engineering establishment officer	Page-boy	Welder
Enquiry clerk	Painter	Wireless operator
First officer	Passenger clerk	Works foreman's clerk
Fitter	Porter	Works welfare officer
Fitters mate	Powers accountant	
Flight clerk	Probationary station officer	

continued

Table 3.1 Continued

Female-classified occupations and levels (24 categories)

Copy typist	Librarian	Stenographer
Deputy Section Leader	Personal stenographer	Supervisor
Deputy Supervisor	Powers operator	Telephonist
Filling clerk	Powers operator trainee	Teleprinter operator
Insprectress	Secretary	Touring representative
Invoice clerk	Senior filing clerk	
Junior filing clerk	Senior Powers operator	
Junior stenographer	Senior Section Leader	
Junior Tabulator Operators	Senior Tabulator Operators	
Lady Chef.		

Unclassified occupations and levels (4 categories)

Journalist	Machinist	Typist
Junior Clerk		

Source: Information compiled from internal company records and detailed reporting of recruitment in the company's internal newsletters and journals for the period 1924–1939.

of the era also saw the appointment of the industry's first female manager (at IAL).

In North America women played a smaller but more diverse role in commercial aviation for much of the era. In the United States women were not employed in any great numbers until the 1930s following the consolidation and growth of the airline industry.[1] For the most part women were employed as clerical workers but there were some interesting and important developments. In the 1930s UAL became the first airline in the world to hire female flight attendants, Central Airlines employed a female commercial airline pilot, and Pan Am hired the industry's first female Assistant Vice President. While flight attending became a female-typed job across the industry, female piloting was short-lived, and Pan Am's female Assistant Vice President remained an anomaly until well after the Second World War.

In Canada women were absent from the airline industry until the outbreak of the Second World War but again there were some contrasting developments. Prior to the establishment of TCA in 1937 the few women in the industry worked in secretarial and clerical positions in small airlines; usually they were the only female employed by a particular airline. However, in the late 1930s two airlines 'unofficially' employed female co-pilots. Yukon Southern Air Transport hired a female secretary, who also served unofficially as 'co-pilot or spotter for search and rescue and fire fighting missions' (Render, 1992: 51). Similarly, Ginger Coote Airways, a small bush operation, hired a female radio operator-cum-unofficial co-pilot. Ironically, her official title made her the world's first female airways radio operator (Render, 1992: 59).

Female flight attendants were introduced into Canada in 1938 by the newly established TCA, and from the beginning the airline saw this as a female-typed job. The only other female hires at this time were a housekeeper and two stenographers, and even though women constituted 6 per cent of TCA's workforce by the start of 1940 more than 90 per cent were flight attendants.

At this juncture: Inside Imperial Airways

IAL was formed from a merger of Daimler, HPT, Instone and BMAN, and began operations on 1 April 1924 (see Figure 1.1). The company stayed in existence until the end of 1939, when it was merged with BAL to from the British Overseas Airways Corporation (BOAC).

In its first year of operation the airline employed two hundred and sixty staff in a range of tasks from secretary to pilot (British Overseas Airways Corporation, 1946a). Most of the employees, particularly the pilots and ground staff, were hired from the merging airlines including Doris Moore, who was joined by a handful of women employed on clerical and secretarial tasks. Like other airlines, male directors, managers and supervisors ran IAL from top to bottom. Men occupied all core positions, such as piloting and engineering. But there had been a change from the previous airlines. There was an apparent willingness to hire women in the airline's offices. The initial female hires were small in number (less then 1% of the total workforce) and employed on a limited range of tasks, but this was a slight improvement on the previous situation.

Female employment

Although women were effectively excluded from piloting and ground crew positions in the merged airlines, this was based on informal practices rather than formal *written* rules. That changed in 1924 when the government established a national airline agreement that all IAL pilots and 75 per cent of the ground personnel, whether administrative staff or mechanics, must be members of the RAF, the Reserve, or the new Auxiliary Air Force prior to joining the airline (Penrose, 1980b: 37). As women were not part of these institutions, the rule, in effect, ensured that they were excluded from most of the airlines central activities, would be restricted to administrative positions and could not exceed 25 per cent of IAL's ground personnel.

Female employees were confined to clerical tasks in IAL's offices, which consisted of three converted army huts at Croydon Airport. One hut served as the Air Department, one as the Accounts Department, and one as the General Offices. Among the office staff was Doris Moore and five women who were new to commercial aviation, including Miss F. E. Claydon, who was in charge of the filing department, three office juniors (Peggy Russell, Margery Masters and Miss Dolamore) and a telephonist (Mrs 'Mac' McAtamney).[2]

Soon after the airline was established it opened its Head Office in a new building in London's Piccadilly. The building, known as Wolseley House,

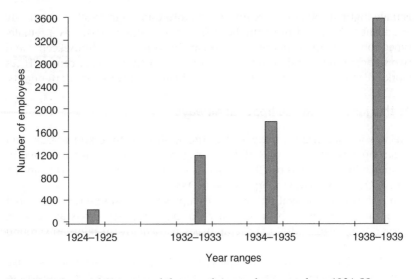

Figure 3.1   Imperial Airways and the growth in employee numbers, 1924–39

consisted of four rooms and a switchboard with three outgoing lines and ten extensions. Senior management consisted of Frank Searle (Managing Director), George Woods Humphery (General Manager) and S. A. Dismore (Company Secretary).[3] The office staff was made up of Doris Moore and Miss Dolamore, a statistics officer, two office juniors and an 'office-boy'. The female staff was expected to be flexible and to undertake various duties. Miss Dolamore, for example, acted as telephonist in addition to her other office duties and, at times, Doris Moore would answer passenger inquires (British Overseas Airways Corporation, 1949a).

By the early 1930s IAL had grown to twelve hundred employees (see Figure 3.1) but female employment had experienced limited growth (see Figure 3.2) and the narrow range of jobs open to women remained constant. Eileen 'Minnie' Mann, for example, was hired in 1930 as a 'floating typist'. Her job was to act as relief on the international telephone switchboard to give the regular operator a break, and to move from office to office depending on where the workload was heaviest.[4] Sheila Tracy joined IAL in 1931 as secretary to the Traffic Manager, and Frances 'Frankie' Probert was hired as a shorthand typist in 1934.[5] The only real change in women's work during this period occurred in 1930 when Doris Moore was transferred to a semi-professional position in the Traffic Department as 'touring representative' (British Overseas Airways Corporation, 1946g).

During this period women were employed in the Managing Director's office, the Secretary's Department, the Enquiry Office, the Wages Department, the Traffic Managers' Office (TMO), the Passenger Department, the Buyer's Office, the Accounts Department and the catering section. In 1935, the

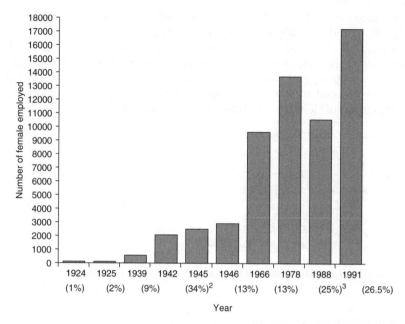

Figure 3.2 The number (%)[1] of females employed by British Airways and its predecessors, 1924–91

Notes:
[1] Percentages are rounded to the nearest whole number.
[2] The records refer to 'staff in various parts of the United Kingdom' (*BOAC Newsletter*, No. 32, September 1942). All other references include United Kingdom and overseas staffs.
[3] This is a combined total from BEA and BOAC.

appointment of a female Catering Superintendent added one new position to IAL's list of female jobs. Nonetheless, recruitment of female employees was very slow.[6] The first real explosion in female employment occurred between 1938 and 1939 as part of a rapid expansion of staff numbers as a whole (Imperial Airways, 1936d; 1939c).[7] In the process several new 'women's jobs' were added, including journalist, accounting machine operator,[8] statistical clerk, 'lady chef,' assistant chef, machinist, cloakroom attendant, invoice clerk, librarian and teleprinter operator. During this period women began to occupy a number of supervisory positions, including supervisor and deputy supervisor of the Typing Department, the supervisor of the Agency Department in the company's West End Office, senior section leader, and the women staff supervisor. In all cases these were positions of authority over other women.

With almost five hundred women working for IAL the Company hired its first senior female manager to be 'responsible for the engagement, training and administration of all women' employed by the company in the United Kingdom (Imperial Airways, 1939i). Mrs F. M. D. Henderson, MBE, was appointed on 1 March 1939, initially with the title of Women Staff Supervisor and then Women Staff Superintendent.

Almost all of the women supervised by Henderson were in female-only jobs but there were some clerical positions where a level of ambiguity existed, requiring gender-specific advertising, which was introduced in IAL towards the end of the 1930s when many offices were undergoing the feminization of clerical work (Lowe, 1987). Typical advertisements included:

> Clerk. A young man between 20–25 years of age is required.
> Imperial Airways (1938l)

> Man For Establishment Department. IA require a man for their Establishment (Staff) Department between 27 and 31 years.
> Imperial Airways (1939g)

> Receptionist (Male) Grade II Clerical
> Imperial Airways (1939f)

> Clerical Grade III. This post is probably especially suitable for women.
> Imperial Airways (1939e)

The advent of the air steward

By the 1920s the advent of large commercial aircraft made the employment of an in-flight attendant economically viable and socially desirable as airlines strove to compete with railway and ocean-going competitors where 'stewarding' was a male profession. The possibility of hiring women was so far removed from the thinking of those in charge that there was no need of official rules to formalize the exclusion of women.

In 1924, however, the International Commission for Air Navigation (ICAN), to which Britain was a signatory, decreed that commercial pilots 'must be of the male sex' (Cadogan, 1992: 72–73). The decision was made on 'medical advice', with doctors providing 'evidence' 'that women's menstrual cycles make then mentally unstable to fly' (ibid.).[9] The following year, at the eighth session of the ICAO, under the chairmanship of Sefton Brancker,[10] this limitation was extended to exclude women from 'any employment in such crews of aircraft engaged on public transport' (Penrose, 1980b: 43–44). It was argued that a female pilot and, by extension a stewardess, 'would have outraged the public' (ibid.).

In 1926 IAL introduced the Argosy, an aeroplane capable of carrying 28 passengers over a range of 520 miles. In April 1927 the company introduced its 'Silver Wing' flight from London to Paris, with passengers coached from London to Croydon airport, attended to by a uniformed pageboy. Once in the air a white-coated steward attended to their needs. Other airlines followed suit, including Lufthansa and Pan Am, and by 1930 air stewarding was firmly established as a male job throughout the world's airlines.

When the idea of hiring female stewards was first raised in the US airline, Boeing Air Transport (BAT),[11] it met with hostility.[12] The idea went against airline practices and conventional notions of the propriety of young women flying alone. Nonetheless, in 1930, BAT executives accepted the idea on an 'experimental basis', to encourage more men to fly, arguing that grown men would fly if a 'young girl' was seen to do so (Hochschild, 1983; Nielsen, 1982). To deal with the issue of propriety and develop a new marketing strategy (of in-flight medical care) the female hires were required to have nursing qualifications and were dressed in nursing uniforms during flight. However, from the beginning, the notion of attractiveness was introduced, with the stipulation that 'the girls had to present an attractive appearance'(Ellen Church quoted in Murray, 1951: 13). They had to be 25 years old or under, with a good posture, grooming and complexion, well poised, and no more than 115 lbs in weight and 5 feet 5 inches in height.

The BAT 'experiment' took hold as it became popular with passengers, and within a few years a number of other North American and European carriers followed suit, including Eastern (1931), American (1933), Air France (1933), TWA (1933), Swissair (1934), Western Airlines (1935), KLM[13] (1935), National Airlines (1935), Braniff (1937), Lufthansa (1938), and TCA (1938).[14] By the middle of the 1930s the female flight attendant was depicted in movies, including the *Air Hostess* (appearing in 1934); the *Flying Hostess*(1936), focussed on the training of TWA stewardesses; and *Love Takes Flight* (1937), concerning romance between a male commercial airline pilot and a female flight attendant.

Despite the steady growth in the number of female flight attendants in North American and European airlines commercial aviation in Britain remained firmly against the idea. For example, in a 1934 edition of the *Girl's Own Paper*, Captain W. E. Johns, author of the *Biggles* books, responded to a young women's enquiry about how to become an air 'hostess', telling readers, 'I'm afraid this young lady has been reading American air books, or perhaps she has seen *Air Hostess* on the films' (Cadogan, 1992: 213).[15] In 1937 there was a fleeting exception to the trend when the small, female-owned *Air Dispatch* hired Britain's first air 'hostess'.[16] This led to a warning in the *Girl's Own Paper* that, despite *Air Dispatch*, readers should not to send applications to British airlines 'for jobs which do not, *at present*, exist' (Cadogan, 1992: 214). Indeed, they certainly did not exist at IAL and when, in 1939, one young woman did apply to be a 'stewardess' not only was she turned down but also her letter of application was reproduced in the *Imperial Airways Staff News* for the amusement of the readers.[17]

The male character of the job was enshrined in the company's organizational rules. The 1938 '*Stewards Pay and Allowance (Regulations)*', for example, refers to the fact that: 'The company normally provides quarters for the steward when he is away from his base [but] when the steward's wife is accompanying him at the Company's expense, a gratuity may be paid [her] at the same rate as for the cabin steward, but no other gratuities will be allowed.'[18]

Comparative wage rates

Given the narrow range of jobs for women in IAL it is not surprising that there were considerable differences between the pay rates of women and men. Due to the segregated nature of most of jobs, direct wage comparisons are difficult but in cloakroom attending, where men and women were both employed, there is a clear gender gap, with men being paid almost double that of their female colleagues.[19]

In the late 1930s IAL's female staff earned between sixteen shillings (for trainee accountancy machine operators) and five pounds per week (for the most senior secretaries who had been with the company for 11 years or more) (see Table 3.2). In contrast, males earned anything from £3.5.0 (for a first year steward) to £14.8.0 (for a senior captain).[20] Only the most senior, long-term secretaries, of which there were very few in 1938, could match the incomes of some male colleagues.

Certainly the jobs of males and females were far from comparable, with the more lucrative flight and ground crew positions reserved for men. The privileging of the male employees was also embodied in company rules and regulations. Regulation 10(c) of the *Flight Clerks Pay and Allowances, 1938*, for example, sets out conditions for when 'the Flight Clerk's wife is accompanying him' (Imperial Airways, 1938e). Similarly, the *Radio Officer Pay and Allowances, 1938* states that the Company 'will bear the cost of the transport of wives [...] of staff proceeding overseas or returning home on contract leave' (Imperial Airways, 1938k). Members of the on-duty traffic staff were required to 'address their seniors and the navigating officers as "sir". Staff of equal rank and subordinates should be addressed as "Mr" ' (Imperial Airways, 1938g).

Power and authority

Prior to 1938 the most important female position in the airline was that of secretary, defined as someone whose job involved work for 'Managers, Heads of Departments, and other senior officers' (see Table 3.2).[21] Beyond the actual job title, a secretary gained status depending on the office holder that she worked for. Doris Moore, for example, was one of the more influential secretaries at IAL in 1924 due to her role as secretary to the managing director.

Very few formally designated positions of authority were assigned to female staff but they were low-level ranks involving supervision of a small number of female employees. Miss Claydon, who ran the Filing Department in 1924, was the first woman to occupy a formal position of authority but it was a while before other women occupied supervisory ranks. One important change occurred in 1935 with the appointment of Marguerite Mundy as

Table 3.2 Female office staff salaries, Imperial Airways, August 1938

Scale	Position	Pay scale
A	**Secretaries**	
	1st Year	**£3.5.0**
	4th Year	**£4.0.0**
	11th Year	**£5.0.0**
	Scale A only applies to 'authorised secretaries' posts, i.e., secretaries to Managers, Heads of Departments, and other senior officers'	
B	**Personal Stenographers**	
	On appointment at age 21–22 or with less than 2 years experience	**£2.10.0**
	2nd year, or on appointment at age 22 and below 24, and accepted as having 2 years previous experience	**£2.15.0**
	5th Year	**£3.5.0**
	11th Year	**£4.0.0**
	This scale applies to stenographers who work for Assistants to Managers and Heads of Departments and whose duties indicate a certain amount of secretarial work but who are not graded as secretaries under scale A	
C	**Pool or General Stenographers**	
	Senior Filing Clerks	
	Teleprinter Operators	
	Telephonists	
	On appointment at age 21–22 or with less than 2 years experience	**£2.10.0**
	5th Year	**£3.5.0**
	7th Year	**£3.10.0**
D	**Junior Stenographer**	
	1st Year	**£1.15.0**
	4th Year	**£2.10.0**
E	**Filing Clerks**	
	Typists	
	Junior Clerks	
	1st Year	**£1. 5.0**
	7th Year	**£2.10.0**
F	**Powers Accounting Staff**	
	1. Trainees (punchers and checkers) 1st Year, on appointment at age 15–16½	**16.0**
	After 3 months	**18.6**
	5th Year	**£1.15.0**
	2. Deputy Section Leaders	**£2. 0.0–£2. 5.0**
	3. Section Leaders	**£2. 5.0–£2.10.0**
	4. Junior Tabulator Operators	**£2.12.6–£2.15.0**
	5. Senior Tabulator Operators	**£3. 0.0–£3.10.0**
	6. Deputy Supervisor	**£3.10.0–£4.10.0**

Source: Imperial Airways internal document, issued August 1938 by the Staff Manager's Office.

Catering Superintendent, who was given broad responsibility for buying the food, wines and tobacco for IAL, with all the catering staff and the male flight stewards under 'her care' (British Overseas Airways Corporation, 1940f). In the late 1930s female supervisors were appointed to some sections, including the Agency[22] and General Typing[23] departments. The other turning point was the 1939 appointment of Florence Henderson to a senior management position, albeit in charge of all other female employees.

Professional jobs for women were also few and far between. The promotion of Doris Moore to the new post of 'touring representative' in 1930 was probably the first of its kind. In the mid-1930s Mrs Lovelands was employed as an 'inspectress' at the company's Hythe works, Miss J. Carter joined Head Office as a journalist in March 1938, and Miss Packard was employed as a librarian in 1939.

As with its forerunners, power, authority and professional status at IAL were dominated by men. Sir Eric Geddes was the company's first 'chairman', serving from 1924 to 1937. He was succeeded for a short time (1937–38) by an interim chair, Sir George Beharrell who then handed over to Sir John Reith (1938–40). None of these men had any previous background in commercial aviation prior to joining IAL. The airline's first Managing Director was Frank Searle (1924–25), followed by George Woods Humphery (1925–38) and then Sir John Reith, who held the post of Managing Director alongside that of Chairman. Men held all other leading positions, including the Board of Directors. Women were, however, shareholders and, from 1927, began to appear at the Annual General Meeting of the company.[24] Nonetheless, there is no evidence that any of these women had a direct influence on company policy.

Men were in overall change of every single department until the mid-1930s when small changes in female dominated areas took place. Men filled all engineering and flight crew positions as well as a range of other skill and professional status jobs (see Table 3.1). Women were almost entirely hidden from the view of the public – typing, computing, tabulating, invoicing and filing in one or other of the company offices. Men, on the other hand, were visibly involved in every aspect of passenger travel, including travel enquiries, booking, coach travel to the airport, baggage handling and the flight itself.[25]

Imaging women

Glimpses of corporate attitudes to women and men can be seen in the various company documents produced over the period. From the beginning, the new airline generated a wealth of documents for internal (e.g., memoranda, in-house newsletters)[26] and public (e.g., advertisements, annual reports, in-flight magazines and films) consumption.[27]

One thing is immediately clear. In comparison with male employees, very little attention is given in the annual reports and in-house newsletters to the activities of female staff. In the Annual Reports for this period there are numerous references to individual men and groups of male employees but none to women.[28] The in-house newsletters include only curt references to female employees when they join the company, become part of a social club, marry and/or leave the company.[29] Even the departure of Miss F. E. Claydon only warranted two lines, informing staff that she had 'for the past seven years [...] been in charge of the filing department at Head Office' (Imperial Airways, 1931d). One small exception was coverage of Doris Moore who, in 1931, became the first female employee to be referenced in the *Imperial Airways Staff News*, when it announced that, as IAL's new 'touring representative', she had 'been touring England visiting agents and distributing literature in hotels'(Imperial Airways, 1931a).

Classes of female employees (e.g., secretaries) were rarely discussed and then only in a negative or frivolous vein. For example, in 1931, when few women worked for the airline a spoof ad appeared in the company newsletter mocking the notion of female hires to the publicity department:

> We regret to have to state that so far all applicants for the post of *Pub* and *Licity* have proved unsuitable [...] All applicants should be:
>
> 1. Confirmed women haters.
> 2. Of the male sex.
> 3. Have a very low milk consumption per mouse, imbued with a strong sense of property.
> 4. The hunting cry shall not extend beyond the range of middle c.
>
> Imperial Airways (1931b)

Not surprising, it was 1935 before a woman was recruited to the Publicity Department.[30] In a slightly different vein, a 1939 article on typists praises their hard work but characterizes it as low-status and unskilled by comparing it with the work of navvies:

> A typist in Imperial Airways has asked us to put it on record that, according to scientific tests, typists work harder than navvies.
>
> We are always anxious to show appreciation of the work of our lady typists, and we can only hope that they will derive unbounded satisfaction from the following scientific pronouncement, which, it need hardly be added, comes from America.
>
> When the effort required to strike a typewriter key is multiplied by the thousands of key depressions per day, the total effort is actually greater that that required in eight hours of ditch digging.
>
> Imperial Airways (1939b)

But the most enduring trend was to characterize female staff in terms of their beauty rather than skills. In a report on the employees of the 'West End

Office', for example, the metaphor of flowers is used to focus on feminine beauty:

> There has been a subtle change in the appearance of the Agency Department in the last few days. This has been caused by the eagerly awaited arrival of several spring visitors. The hyacinths, for such they are, have been nurtured by the female staff of the department under the supervision of Mrs. Spence and the flowers are beginning to make a pretty show.
> Imperial Airways (1938a)

Female beauty, passivity and lack of skill are reinforced in those few newsletter articles that mentioned female passengers. Women and fashion was the single-most point of discussion of femininity, as in a report on 'Ladies Only', which noted that 'On arrival at Croydon recently of the regular afternoon Paris shopping service, it was noticed that the twelve passengers were all ladies. This is only another indication of the fascination that flying has for women, and the increasing popularity of the Paris shopping service' (Imperial Airways, 1927). Increasingly, as the number of female employees grew, articles and jokes characterized women as technically backward and ignorant, as in the following story:

> The following story says a correspondent is true,
>
> First Old Lady: 'Look, dear, that's the new Imperial Airways building.'
>
> Second Old Lady: 'Really. But won't it be very dangerous when the aeroplanes land? They might come down in Victoria Station by mistake.'
> Imperial Airways (1938j)

The only article of any length on women and aviation appeared in a 1936 issue of the *Imperial Airways Weekly News Bulletin (1936a)* under the title, 'Feminine Influence in Air Transport Progress'. It refers to a group of male transport officials who, 'discussing the progress of civil aviation', paid 'warm tribute [to] women in the development of civil aviation' (ibid.). The article makes no mention of female aviators or any of the women of IAL, instead praise is limited to the role of the female passenger who, in the early years of commercial aviation, 'braved the inconvenience' of cramped quarters and deafening engine noise. These pioneering female passengers were said to 'have encouraged other women to fly, especially those who follow their husbands to the "far-off territories" who no longer need to feel that sense of isolation which used to weigh upon them so heavily' (ibid.).

If one were to use corporate materials to construct an identity-kit image of women in IAL of the time, there would be little to go on. We could surmise that the average female employee was single, relatively young, joined the company until she married, occupied a limited range of clerical positions and tended to stay with the same position for the duration of her time with the company. Indeed, approximately eighty per cent of IAL's female employees were single and never married, and of the remaining number several were widows. Very few women changed jobs or experienced promotion. Drawing on the social attitudes of the day, we might infer that women lacked technical skills, had only a limited role to play in the workforce, were employed primarily as support to male employers and office holders, and that their main role in life was to look good and get married.

Imaging men

Unlike their female colleagues, male employees were constantly the focus of reports, applauding their contributions to IAL and society in general; images that painted positive pictures of masculinity in various forms. In particular, dedication, rationality, knowledge, skill and professionalism were seen as masculine traits and highly desired employee characteristics.

Dedication and long-term commitment

Throughout IAL's corporate materials the efforts of male employees are reported as a means of stressing loyalty, long-term commitment and hard work. This style of reporting is evident from the earliest days, when IAL Chairman Sir Eric Geddes paid 'Tribute to Staff' at the 1927 Annual General Meeting, singling out 'the continued record of safety and of improved regularity [which] reflect very creditably on the engineering staff and [...] pilots'. He also praised 'the untiring energies' of the traffic staff who 'greatly improved traffic receipts' (*The Times*, 1927). Similar sentiments are contained in Geddes announcement of the death of Captain Frank Barnard, whose 'skill, ability and personality were outstanding and the company lost in him a very valued and loyal servant and a magnificent pilot' (ibid.). Over the years Geddes continued to focus on loyalty and devotion to duty, singling out pilots, 'technical personnel' (Imperial Airways, 1929) and navigating officers (Imperial Airways, 1937d). The latter were seen as role models to whom the company looked 'for the guiding of junior officers in the earlier stages of their career' (ibid.).

Speaking to the Bulawayo Rotary Club in 1937 Captain G. I. Thomson outlined the type of characteristics required to be an IAL employee. They must be young men who have a sound education to 'cope with the organization work which, sooner of later, they may find themselves called upon to perform. Most of all, perhaps, they must be willing – whether pilots, engineers or members of the ground staffs – to set off quite cheerfully, at a moment's notice, to any part of the globe where operations may call for their services' (Imperial Airways, 1937f).

Loyalty and long-term commitment were enshrined in IAL's rules. Each pay scale, whether for men or women, set out a rate of income for each of the number of years of service. The longer the years of service the higher the pay.

But whereas women were expected to resign from the company if they married, the rules stipulated that married men would receive higher rates of pay. In some cases, however, male employees, as in the case of First Officers, had to obtain the company's prior permission to marry.[31]

Rationality

Unlike the informality of its forerunners, IAL introduced a series of formal rules and developed a bureaucratic structure. Against that background, rationality was seen as an important requirement of IAL's employees in the performance of their duties, but again this quality was valued through male associations. This took the form of valuing calculation over emotionality, science over superstition, seriousness over frivolity, and work over domesticity. In particular, discourses of business and bureaucracy intertwined to create new images of valued masculinity. These discourses were enshrined in the stated 'original aims of the company to do justice to national aims and also to provide a satisfactory investment for the public' (Imperial Airways, 1926). To that end, the four airlines, involved in the merger, 'had to be welded into an efficient single organization; repair shops and stores were centralized [and] regularity and reliability [were] the first considerations' (ibid.). The importance of rationality and its link with masculinity is captured in a number of articles on managers and male employees over the years, as exemplified in a profile of Captain H. J. Horsey. In the article, 'Veteran Civil Airman's 1,100,000 miles of flying', Horsey is asked 'what adventures he had met with in the air?'

> 'Adventures?' he replied. 'Would you ask the driver of an express train whether he had met with any adventures on one of his runs? Of course you wouldn't. You'd know that a modern railway service operates as a matter of routine, eliminating anything in the nature of unusual happenings. And nowadays, believe me, it is precisely the same with an airway. We air-captains fly to our schedules, day in and day out, in exactly the same way as boats or trains operate to their regular timetables.'
>
> Imperial Airways (1937e)

The melding of rationality and masculinity was also shaped through a series of comparisons between men and women and between 'white' British men and 'non-white' foreigners. For example, the newsletters often characterized men as travelling for adventure or business and women travelling to shop or to join their menfolk. Heralding that 'Men Lead The Way', one IAL newsletter argued that 'In these days of "female emancipation", it is refreshing to know that in some matters men are still in the lead. Men are in the majority of passengers on Imperial Airways European services [and] they are substantially more "air minded" ' (Imperial Airways, 1938i).

Racial contrasts also served to stress the superiority of rationality over emotionality and, with it, white over black. Newsletter reports from the company's foreign stations in Africa and Asia carried stories of black male employees that were designed for the amusement of the white British reader.[32] In every case black employees are shown as illiterate, superstitious, emotional and irrational, in contrast to the white reader who, by definition, is assumed to be well educated, scientific and rational. In the following example, a letter from a 'former hangar boy' to the Germiston Station Master (South Africa) is reproduced by the editor of the newsletter because it may be 'amusing' to the readers:

Sir, I have the honour to beg, unto thee, and pray Good master Forgive me from disturbing thee, Sir, please gentlemaster. I am begging thee sir, to increase thy poor servant's wages. I am under thy employer since 1927, Still, I, M, getting very less Salary. For that cause, pray, pray, Goodmaster do kindly attend to thy poor servants' beseech favourably. I am waiting for thy kindly reply, I beg to remain, I, M, thine Capable Servant, Sixpence Kapande.

Imperial Airways (1935)

Superstition is the focus of the 1932 'Story From the South Africa Division', which also serves to naturalize the control of African people by white Europeans:

Some native labourers were quietly washing down the City of Basra [plane] under the watchful eye of the 'Baas' (Zulu foreman) when the actions of one Alexandra Sefuti (who was cleaning the fuselage close to the saloon door) aroused suspicion. On getting a closer view the 'Baas' discovered that Alexandra was busily scratching with his finger nails the jewels out of the crown in the Royal Mail sign. In response to a stentorian cry as to 'what he thought he was doing' Alexandra turned around and blushed [...] Prolonged cross examination elucidated the fact that all the members of the cleaning gang (who are descendants of King Setuwago) had drawn lots to see who should steal the jewels off the crown and it had fallen to Alexandra to perpetrate the crime. The latter having been suitably dealt with the 'Big White Baas' appeared and after sticking a piece of paper in the fuselage tore this off, and hey presto! left behind a brand new crown and marvelous glittering jewels, and was promptly awarded the first-class Order of Witch Doctors by the assembled multitude.

Imperial Airways (1932d)

Knowledge, skill and professionalism

In a number of ways IAL's corporate imagery impressed on its readers a firm association between various forms of knowledge and masculinity. In particular piloting skills and engineering knowledge were highly prized as central requirements of the organization. Service professionalism was later added with a growing focus on the work of the airline steward. Images of the pilot were often overdrawn and idealized in such claims that 'no body of men in the world have won greater genuine admiration [...]. In physique, in ability and in sheer knowledge of every aspect of flying' (Harper, 1930: 36). Readers of the *Imperial Airways Weekly News Bulletin* were nonetheless informed that in addition to the abilities of the individual pilot 'the reliability of the modern air-liner is ensured [by] a unique ground organization of maintenance and overhaul, expert engineers and mechanics'(Imperial Airways, 1937c). Then there is the Reception Officer who 'is a mine of information on air travel topics. He knows all there is to know about making air journeys across Europe' (Imperial Airways, 1937b). Behind it all are the men who build the great aeroplanes that make it all possible:

> In a great factory beside the river Medway at Rochester, Kent, a row of huge metal-built flying boat hulls are now rising on their stocks like the hulls of ships. In vast sheds men are fashioning the wings which are to lift these great leviathans from the water to the air [...] More than 3,000 men are now busy of the great undertaking – the most remarkable of its kind in the annuls of the air.
>
> Imperial Airways (1936g)

That technical knowledge was somehow a masculine (and Caucasian) quality was reinforced through a number of gender and race contrasts. On occasion in-house newsletters would make fun of women's lack of technical ability. On other occasions IAL's technical superiority was demonstrated through contrasts with various people of colour. The theme was invariably the same, the modern airline versus the traditional backward lifestyle of colonial peoples. An example of this can be found on the front cover of a 1937 issue of the *Imperial Airways Staff News* which shows a group of Arab men in traditional dress (described as 'local inhabitants') sitting along the banks of the Sea of Galilee watching an IAL plane landing. In another, more directly gendered, image the naked bodies of a Black African woman and child are used to frame the image of the all-important aeroplane.[33]

The association of technical knowledge with masculinity served to privilege masculinity over femininity in the construction of hegemonic masculinity (Connell, 1987). However, the various ways that expectations of 'knowledge' were attached to different roles served to create different forms of masculinity with somewhat different meanings in the social construction of engineering, piloting and stewarding.

The ground engineer

The masculinity of the engineer at IAL was established through numerous references to safety and reliability. Unlike piloting where the skills of the individual pilot were of immediate importance to the passengers, engineering was characterized as a collective effort whose outcome ensured the overall safety of the aircraft. Thus, it was the collective rather than the individual engineer who received attention in corporate advertising. When the newsletters discussed engineering it was usually in the context of the work of a given department or section of engineers. Here the focus was on skills that were exercised as part of a team effort.

The pilot

In the early airlines masculine images of the pilot were built around danger, heroism and skill and reinforced by the wartime feel and symbolism of the airlines themselves. Nonetheless, it was recognized that the problem of attracting sufficient customers was due to perceptions of commercial aviation as unsafe and unreliable; perceptions that were not entirely helped by the image of the heroic pilot.

IAL set out, from the beginning, to create a new perception of the pilot, which emphasized science, experience and coordination. The individual pilot was still singled out but it was less as the heroic flyer as the skilled professional who is part of a wider team effort. The practice of providing passengers with signed photographs of the pilot, complete with brief biography was continued by IAL. By designation, the 'Captain' was in charge of his aircraft and responsible for the lives of his passengers. Once airborne he was expected 'to hand over the controls at some stage on a trip, and come back into the cabin to chat to some of the passengers'(McIntosh, 1963: 107). But beyond the individual element IAL tended to cast the pilot as part of a well-organized team, combining with scientists, designers and engineers 'in a splendid form of teamwork' (Imperial Airways, 1936e).

The changing masculine character of the pilot is evident in the following descriptions of pilots in the mid-1930s. In 1934 Gordon Olley (1934: 229–30) described pilots as men of the new age of the air, 'all extremely matter-of fact. Flying is their job, and they thoroughly enjoy it. But they object to be regarded as heroes. Each [...] is a master of his craft. Not only [do they have] brilliant records and long flying experiences, but they are licensed only after rigid medical, flying, and technical tests'. Two years later, in a newsletter focus on pilots, the contrast of the new scientific era with the old days of adventure is even more striking. Here it is argued that in the early days, before 'air-liners were organized scientifically', every flight was apt to be an adventure (Imperial Airways, 1936f) but now, thanks to the pilots 'who sit at the controls of the Company's air-liners', the passengers are inspired with confidence. These men 'do not care to talk about themselves [or] their own exploits' but rather wish 'to sink their own identity in the general progress of the movement they have at heart. It is their endeavor to convince the public, by the smooth precision of their flying, that air travel has left the era of experiment far behind, and is now [...] a swift, dependable, ever-ready method for expediting the transport of passengers, mails, and freight' (ibid.).

The 'science of flying' and the 'dedicated team work' was being achieved through training, standardized equipment and uniforms, careerism, rules and regulations, and a rigidly enforced timetable. The establishment of IAL with guaranteed government funding for at least a decade facilitated the development of careers for commercial airline pilots that had not existed previously. Initially training was done outside of the company and relied to a large extent on the recruitment of former RAF pilots but in 1935 Imperial Airways developed its own training school.

The air steward

Over the years a discourse of service developed through IAL's efforts to attract and keep customers by selling luxury, comfort and attentiveness. To this end, the company promoted the ideal steward who was able to achieve all of those things well. Thus, the readers of the *Imperial Airways Gazette* were informed that the typical steward is 'a man experienced in the art of pleasing and giving attention, [and is enthused with] the human spirit of service and understanding'(Imperial Airways, 1938b). The Company depicted their stewards as 'men on a new calling', who were keen judges of character, displaying 'deft artistry' in their provision of catering service, methodical, proud, but small, agile and quick-moving and 'ready to play his part in the smooth and efficient working of a modern air-line' (Imperial Airways, 1936c). The requirements that the steward be short and light weight were dictated by cramped galley conditions and fuel efficiency.

Organizational growth and social life

Between 1924 and 1939 IAL experienced tremendous growth, going from 260 to 3600 employees (see Figure 3.1). With growth came the introduction of in-house newsletters and the development of various social activities. For example, an annual dinner and dance was instituted, and marriage announcements were often marked with informal social gatherings, especially when it meant the departure of a female colleague.[34] By the mid-1930s a Sports and Social Club had been established.

As the new social and sporting events developed women played a role alongside male employees, including the organization of the annual dinner and dance, and in the swimming and table tennis divisions of the 'Sports and Social Club'. This provided women with an entrée into organizational leadership that was otherwise closed off to them in the official channels of IAL. Nonetheless, women's leadership and organization roles were limited. In areas of joint male and female activities men were in overall charge,[35] and women were excluded from clubs based on male pursuits (e.g., rugby, rambling, football). In three cases women lead a social club – Table Tennis, where Minnie Mann shared the organizational leadership with a male colleague; the Aeronians Dramatic Society, where, in the late 1930s, Miss Newman became the first woman to attain sole leadership of a club; and Women's Hockey, which was established by women who were 'discontented' at being excluded from the existing hockey club (Imperial Airways, 1939d).[36]

Organizational discourse

IAL was dominated at the top by a Board of Directors led by Sir Eric Geddes: one nominee from each of the four merged airlines – Sir Samuel Instone (Instone), Lieutenant-Colonel Frank Searle (Daimler), Lieutenant-Colonel John Barrett-Lennard (HPT) and Hubert Scott-Paine (BMAN) – Sir George Beharrell (Geddes' financial advisor), Lord Invernairn and two government appointees (Sir Herbert Hambling and Major John Waller Hills). The operation of the new airline was effectively in the hands of Geddes and Beharrell, along with Searle as Managing Director and George Woods Humphery as General Manager. Major H. Brackley was appointed the Air Superintendent and S. A. Dismore, the Company Secretary. These men contributed to the culture of the airline over the next decade through their leadership style and through the lens of bureaucracy and imperialism.

Leadership style

The new breed of business leaders put their stamp on the culture of IAL. They established leadership style that was authoritative and authoritarian in tone. The influence of these men was felt through a series of disciplinary rules and regulations but also through dint of personality. This was particularly the case of Sir Eric Geddes, who ruled the company from 1924 to 1937, George Woods Humphery, the company's managing director from 1925 to 1928, and Frank Searle, IAL's first managing director (1924–25).

Geddes, who had a 'meteoric official career' (Macmillan, 1935: 103),[37] was the head of the Dunlop rubber company when he took over IAL in 1924.[38] Although formerly designated the 'part-time' chairman, for the next thirteen years, until his death in 1937, Geddes ran the airline with 'an iron will and a strong prejudice' (Penrose, 1980b: 30). Friend and foe alike characterized him as a strong-willed leader. To Beharrell, he was a great leader and a wise counsellor, but to others Geddes was 'a driver of men' (Penrose, 1980a: 155), a 'lofty figure' (Collier, 1959: 176) who did not suffer fools gladly, with 'a reputation for impatience, particularly with human foibles' (Jackson, 1995: 48). His hard nosed business approach can be seen in his attitude to the pilots, 'who he regarded as no different from the engine drivers in his employ when he ran the North Eastern Railway' (Jackson, 1995: 32), and to his employees in general, who he regarded as 'mere cogs in the machinery' (Penrose, 1980a: 194–95).

Geddes management style led to a number of high profile disputes with employees, including struggles with ground personnel in 1924, wireless operators in the 1920s and 1930s, and pilots in 1924 and 1936. At the very founding of IAL, Geddes took on the pilots. When it was announced that IAL's terms and conditions for pilots would involve greater flying hours and less pay than they were used to they formed a union to negotiate different terms. The two sides were on a collision course. Faced with management 'who were domineering and overbearing in their treatment of the pilots' (McIntosh, 1963: 93) a strike ensued. It seemed to some that Geddes had consciously chosen the 'very moment of [the company's] inception [...] to crack the whip'; a decision that 'was ill-timed and the terms much too harsh' (Armstrong, 1952: 82). Geddes, not one to be intimidated by the pilots, laid plans to bring in strike-breakers before the problem was eventually resolved through mediation. Shortly after the strike the now disgruntled wireless operators formed a union but Geddes refused to recognize it, ignoring it for eight years. By 1936 pilots were once again troubled by the way they were being treated. Many felt that salaries were low and that they were too often forced to fly under adverse conditions against their professional judgment. Things came to a head at the company's Annual General Meeting when Geddes announced that the shareholder dividend was to be raised and Director fees doubled. The following summer the pilots formed the British Air Line Pilots' Association (BALPA). Management responded by firing the leaders. A subsequent enquiry blamed Woods Humphery for the handling of the dispute but at least one important commentator – Charles Grey, the editor of *The Aeroplane* – had little doubt that the problem lay in 'the shadow of Sir Eric Geddes,' whose outstanding successes were built from 'a system of almost inhuman mechanical efficiency' (quoted in Jackson, 1995: 131–32). According to Grey, IAL employees viewed Geddes as 'a machine to be feared rather than a human being to be loved and followed. Even many of those who admired him, because of the outward efficiency which he forced on to other people, could never bring themselves to regard him as a human being (ibid.)

Geddes leadership indelibly stamped the style of management throughout the company. Frank Searle, for instance, was also a 'hard-headed' business type and focussed IAL on high efficiency,[39] but his strong-minded approach led to a clash with Geddes and he was forced out of IAL in 1925 (Pudney, 1959: 58). George Woods Humphery, whose style of management was very much to the liking of Geddes, replaced Searle as Managing Director – a post he held until 1938. Woods Humphery's job 'was to execute in an impersonal manner the orders of [Geddes] with the full authority of his own technical and operational experience' (Penrose, 1980a: 195). Woods Humphery's style of management is evident in the two major pilots' strikes and an incident that led to the resignation of a senior pilot. The pilots abhorred Woods Humphery's authoritarian style of management and opposed his initial appointment as General Manager. It was felt that at HPT and Daimler he had pressured pilots to fly against their better judgment. Geddes backed Woods Humphery who, meanwhile, issued a writ for liable against the pilots and put plans in place to employ strike-breakers. Following mediation the residual hostility between Woods Humphery and the pilots remained.

In 1927 Captain McIntosh, a senior pilot, took a one-month's leave of absence in order to attempt a pioneering Trans-Atlantic crossing. Delays held up McIntosh's plans so he wrote to Woods Humphery for an extension of unpaid leave. McIntosh was bitterly disappointed at the 'stiff and uncompromising' reply which demanded that he return 'by the date specified [or] we must ask you to resign from Imperial Airways' (McIntosh, 1963: 125). He had known Woods Humphery for many years, worked with him at HPT, and had 'offered to work for nothing when we were in a sticky time with the old company' (ibid.). It was a 'bitter blow' and McIntosh resigned as a result (ibid.).

Woods Humphery also played a key role in the antagonisms that led to the establishment of BALPA and the second major pilots' strike in 1937. He responded harshly, firing the union leaders, who subsequently sought redress from Robert Perkins, the Conservative MP for Stroud. Raising the issue in the House of Commons, Stroud noted that director's fees had been sharply increased for two years in a row while pilots' wages were being cut. Stroud argued that the pilots had tried to negotiate but had the door 'slammed in their faces' and their leaders victimized (quoted in Jackson, 1995: 121). He concluded with a call for a public investigation that led to the establishment of a public enquiry under Sir John Cadman.

The Cadman Report made far-reaching recommendations and soundly criticized the style of management at IAL, particularly that of George Woods Humphery. The Report called for the appointment of a new, full-time, chairman whose close intervention 'would be immediately necessary to restore the mutual confidence and goodwill which have been seriously prejudiced' (quoted in Cluett, Nash, and Learmonth, 1980: 74). Cadman concluded that 'the management of Imperial Airways ... has been intolerant of suggestion and unyielding in negotiation. Internally its attitude in staff matters has left much to be desired [...] and there should, in our opinion, be an immediate improvement in these respects and this may well involve some change in the direction of personnel' (ibid.).

The government accepted the recommendation and duly appointed Sir John Reith, the head of the British Broadcasting Corporation (BBC) as IAL's Chairman. Reith's position as full-time chairman incorporated the duties of the managing direction, leading to Woods Humphery's resignation.

From military to bureaucratic ethos

In a number of ways military experience influenced the development of IAL's culture, from the various military leaders, pilots and ground crews that it inherited from the merged airlines to the new recruitment rules (see above). Piloting, in particular, remained a bastion of former wartime flyers and continued to do so over the life of the airline.[40] These men were under the command of former airmen George Woods Humphery, Major H. G. Brackley and S. A. Dismore,[41] and prominent wartime military officers who sat on the IAL

Board over the years.[42] Nonetheless, while wartime camaraderie lingered within IAL the influence of military experience was tempered through the demands of a new breed of hard-headed business leaders, government involvement, and the process of merger and organizational growth.

One major change was a lessening of the air force leadership. Six of the nine directors were entrepreneurs and business leaders, who set out to ensure that IAL operated on sound business practices. This was evident in the government's appointment of Sir Eric Geddes, who 'knew nothing of aviation', but 'whose wide knowledge of existing transport could be particularly applied to the economic and commercial problems that were certain to arise in the new chapter of air travel' (Sir Samuel Hoare, quoted in Pudney, 1959: 89). Geddes was not only different in experience and temperament to the old air force types but was often at odds with their viewpoint.

Like his struggle with the pilots, Geddes' clash with Searle arose out of his hardnosed view of business. Searle's emphasis on balancing safety and efficiency was constantly challenged by the 'non-aeronautical members of the Board, notably the chairman, Sir Eric Geddes, [who was] more concerned with attracting revenue and cutting down expenses to show that the business is a commercial success' (*London Evening News*, quoted in Penrose, 1980b: 42). This caused a split in the Board and Geddes asked Searle to resign. Searle had little doubt that it was the new business philosophy that had forced him out. For Searle, the Board consisted of 'very successful men who know the danger of trusting the unknown, but none of them had successfully operated any new form of transport' (quoted in Penrose, 1980b: 42–43).

The new business philosophy, with its emphasis on efficiency, was giving shape to a new dominant form of masculinity. In part, this was due to the fact that all the company's business leaders and managers were men. But it was also due to various others factors that privileged commerce over domesticity, rationality over emotionality, impersonality over closeness and objectivity over subjectivity. This was largely achieved through the development of a bureaucratic set of values and practices.

Certain rules and regulations were gendered in that they excluded women in direct (e.g., ICAN and ICAO rules against female crew), or indirect (e.g., the national airline agreement requiring air force training), and subtle (e.g., references to the 'employee's wife') ways.

Formally, women were expected to resign once they married. Those who did not marry and stayed at IAL rarely rose about their original work level. Mary Peters, for example, retired from the airline in the late 1940s as a clerk after 20 years employment.[43] The fact that women were hired in the first place may be due to the feminization of clerical work and government involvement in IAL.

The fact that the government was *the* major employer of female office employees in Britain at the time may have had some bearing on IAL's employment practices, although there is no evidence of any direct government intervention in that regard. It is more likely that government influence on the bureaucratization of the airline, and the need for increasing numbers of administrative personnel, encouraged the employment of female staff. Arguably, at the very least, government involvement in the airline may have tempered some of the more discriminatory attitudes.

In the all-male piloting and stewarding professions manhood was, in large measure, associated with the characteristics of the job. In the case of the pilot, wartime associations with flying were becoming a distant memory and the associated symbolism was rapidly disappearing. Wartime aerodromes, planes and outfits had given way to new commercial airports, airliners and uniforms. Haphazard and dangerous flights had given way to a regularly scheduled and safe service. The individualism of the pilot had been curtailed by training and a series of rules and regulations. The notion of the heroic flyer gave way to an emphasis on professionalism. References to heroism gave way to flight-time experience, individualism gave way to rule-bound behaviour, and danger gave way to stability and regularity. Initially, there was some resistance to the new practices. Some pilots resented 'being kept to a fairly rigid time-table in order to create efficiency'(Higham, 1960: 78). Nonetheless, although many found the work 'boring, miserable and routine' it offered new career opportunities that eventually encouraged a 'a very different atmosphere in flying' (Armstrong, 1952: 87). The pilots went from

'a jumpy and excitable bunch of fellows [to] a stable, serious, responsible body [...]. They were embarked on a career [with] a strong sense of security [because] the Government had given Imperial Airways a grant of a million pounds to be spread over the years and come what might, [the pilots] felt secure for that period.

(ibid).

Pilot Armstrong (1952: 87–89), for example, felt that 'the security which Imperial Airways supplied was comforting' and, in his early years with the company, he began to see 'the possibility of nailing down security' for his family and for himself'. Similarly, pilot McIntosh (1963: 107–08) felt 'well content', seeing his future as 'reasonably secure', with a fair salary and 'a better standard of life than in the early uncertain and impecunious days of the business'.

Although the masculine image of stewarding initially owed much to isomorphic influences (DiMaggio and Powell, 1991) this too was tempered by bureaucratic demands as the airline strove to develop the 'service orientation,' professionalism and dedication of the air steward.

Imperialist discourse

Before the end of the First World War it was a dream of many in the British High Command to develop aviation as a way of uniting the British Empire

(James, 1990; Sampson, 1984). This view was shared by the British Government who, in 1923, legislated for the establishment of a new airline that would act as 'the chosen instrument' of government imperial policy. In line with that intent, the new airline was named Imperial Airways. For the next 15 years the airline took an active interest in the Empire that influenced notions of manhood and womanhood through contrasting images of white British rulers and non-white colonial peoples (see above).

At the time of the merger none of IAL's forerunners had provided services beyond Europe but this changed with the development of larger aircraft capable of travelling longer distances and by 1938 IAL was operating nearly 70 aircraft to over 30 countries in various parts of Europe and the British Empire.

The notion of imperialism and empire ran deep in IAL. It had an 'empire mission', 'Empire routes' (i.e., to British colonies and protectorates) and 'news from the imperial outposts' (i.e., reports from its African and Asian stations). Staffs were encouraged to 'think imperially',[44] and the newsletters constantly reported on the ethnic origins of IAL's passengers.[45] Outlining the airline's 'empire mission', Sir Eric Geddes told successive annual meetings that it was a guiding principle aimed at 'linking up the various parts of the British Empire with each other and ultimately these with the rest of the world' (Imperial Airways, 1934). For Geddes 'the future of civilization depend[ed] upon the spreading of a closer international understanding ... between the Commonwealth of Nations, the British Empire and between nation and nation' (Imperial Airways, 1934).

Racial imagery and gendered subjectivities

At IAL the discourse of imperialism engaged the thinking of the white, largely British, staffs throughout the company's employ. In part the national airline agreement helped to ensure that most of IAL's staff were white by recruiting from former members of the air force, with its requirements that airmen be of 'British birth and pure European descent' (James, 1990). Later, when the airline recruited stewards they extended the practice of employing only white, British men (Hudson and Pettifer, 1979).

In the so-called 'outposts' the airline rarely if ever employed non-whites, and when it did it hired male workers for largely menial tasks.[46] It was also rare for white British women to be hired at any of the Empire outposts. While young men, such Commercial Trainee Geoffrey Pett, were sent over-sees to the company's African bases it was unthinkable to send female employees.[47] The few women who were employed in the colonial regions were drawn from the white middle classes of the metropolitan areas in which they were employed.[48]

The discourse of Empire contributed to two major archetypes of masculinity and the almost total subjugation of femininity. One prominent masculine archetype is that of the white adventurer – active, civilized, developed, modern, while the other archetype is that of the black 'boy' – passive, primitive, backward, archaic (see Table 3.3).

The association of masculinity with Empire was achieved through a discourse in which travel, empire building, and 'foreign parts' were associated with a mixture of danger, militarism, and adventure. The non-white countries of the British Empire were seen as exotic, unstable and uncivilized, and, thus, no place for a woman. It was for male explorers, soldiers and missionaries to discover, conquer and civilize. This was the stuff of fiction and of fact.

IAL's depiction of non-white colonial peoples, reflected in its hiring practices, exemplifies Said's (1993: ix) analysis of 'European writing on Africa, India, [and] parts of the Far East, [that are] part of the general European effort to rule distant lands and peoples'. The 'mysterious East' and 'darkest Africa' were never far from the pages of IAL's corporate imagery. When, for example, IAL began to fly to the African continent it was said, 'Africa became civilized', the scheduled flights lit a light in 'darkest Africa [...]; the lamp of civilization [...] in the last stronghold of the unknown' (Imperial Airways, 1932c).[49] The 'darkness' of Africa conveyed a sense of backwardness and danger that reflected on the African people, who were portrayed in IAL advertisements and newsletters as primitive, superstitious and unintelligent.[50] The main descriptors of non-white employees diminished any sense of

Table 3.3   The hierarchical system of colonial binaries

West	Non-West
Active	Passive
Center	Margin/periphery
Civilized	Primitive/savage
Colonizer	Colonized
Developed	Backward/undeveloped/ underdeveloped/developing
Fullness/plenitude/completeness	Lack/inadequacy/incompleteness
Historical (people with history)	Ahistorical (people without history)
The liberated	The savable
Masculine	Feminine/effeminate
Modern	Archaic
Nation	Tribe
Occidental	Oriental
Scientific	Superstitious
Secular	Nonsecular
Subject	Object
Superior	Inferior
The vanguard	The led
White	Black/brown/yellow

Source: Prasad (1997: 291).

masculinity through such terms as 'boy', 'peon', 'coolie', 'natives', 'servants', 'custodian', 'native labourers' and 'Zulu foreman'.[51]

In contrast, there were numerous images of IAL's overseas white, male employees as dedicated and adventurous, bringing civilization and modern technology to backward regions. These images strengthened the prominence of masculinity within the airline, and privileged the associated characteristics of bravery, exploration, rationality and scientific knowledge.

Symbolism

In contrast to previous years, and the dominance of wartime military imagery, symbolism in IAL was diverse, often subtle and not always clearly indexed to masculinity. The subtler referencing of masculinity arose out of the burgeoning bureaucracy – rules and regulations, standardization, uniforms, and so on. These served to reinforce particular aspects of masculinity in the broadest sense, such as rationality, technical knowledge, and professionalism. Other symbolism was drawn from the company's imperial project and was often more overt in its imaging of contrasting forms of masculinity. The mimetic symbolism associated with the steward, on the other hand, indexed a masculine type that was familiar in other organizational settings.

More direct attempts to link masculinity with airline travel can be found in the company's advertising practices, which, for the most part, were aimed at the male business traveller.[52] Advertisements often utilized the symbolism of the white-coated steward, the experienced pilot, or even images of the male traveller, to sell seats (Morris, 1989).

A less intended, yet nonetheless gendered, aspect of company symbolism was the naming of individual aeroplanes. Originally the company named its planes after cities (e.g., City of London) but after 1930 named them after real and mythical heroes, including Scipio (a 'brave Roman Warrior'), Satyrus ('a distinguished comic actor'), Hannibal ('one of the greatest generals that the world has ever seen'), Heracles ('the most celebrated of all the heroes of antiquity') and Hanno the Great ('so-called for his military successes in Africa').[53] When, in a few cases, the names of female mythological figures were used, they were chosen for their reference to beauty and male patronage (e.g., 'the daughters of Zeus' – Atalanta, Astraea, and Helen 'a surpassing beauty'), rather than the action and achievement associated with male figures.

Social discourse

The suffragette movement before the First World War and the war itself contributed to new images of women that continued into the post-war era. Between 1919 and 1939 the idea of women as sexually and economically independent flourished in various degrees as it vied with a renewed concern with domesticity.

In the inter-war era there was a shift in people's attitudes to women working. Many women were reluctance to give up the economic independence they had enjoyed in the war years. With the onset of recession, many – mainly middle-class – fathers encouraged their daughters to work to take a financial burden off the home. The loss of so many men during the war meant that a large number of women were unlikely to ever marry and would need the security of economic independence (Horn, 1994: 55).

Signs of changing attitudes could be found in such things as the advent of 'the flapper', a small but significant development among a section of upper- and middle-class females, the extension of the vote in 1928 to women under 30, and the entry of women into Parliament.[54] On the domestic front, there was a decline in the birth rate that affected all classes of society. From a peak of 25.5 births per 1000 of the population in 1920, the rate fell to 18.2 per 1000 in 1925 and 16.3 per 1000 in 1929 (Horn, 1994: 116). Between 1910 and 1930 the average age at which a woman gave birth to her last child dropped from 30 to age 28 (Halsey, 1978: 101). Over the same period the percentage of couples with five or more children fell from 27.5 per cent to 10.4 per cent and those with only one or two children increased from 33.5 per cent to 51.1 per cent (Weeks, 1990: 202). These various changes were not, however, reflected in the workplace.

Alongside broadening images of womanhood the domestic ideal still loomed large and, arguably, formed the framework in which ideas of gender were contested. Shifts began to occur within the women's movement from an emphasis on equality to an emphasis on women's difference. This 'new feminist' perspective developed within the National Union of Societies for Equal Citizenship (NUSEC), where it was argued that 'women's interests were best served by recognizing gender differences' (Rowbotham, 1999: 128–29). Feminists debated these issues against a social backdrop in which women's domestic role was a constant focus of concern. In the 1930s a number of issues, specifically mass unemployment and the threat of war, combined to encourage a 'counter-revolution' in gender thinking (Millett, 1971), with 'the overt demands for women's emancipation in terms of political and economic change [going] into retreat' (Rowbotham, 1999: 172). A new 'cult of domesticity' was evidenced in newspaper articles and a spate of new magazines devoted to motherhood and mother craft, including *Women's Own* (introduced in 1932), *Women's Illustrated* (1936) and *Woman* (1937). These magazines had mass readerships and contributed to modern images of women in the home, viewing female housework as a craft, aided by modern appliances.

Women and work

In a number of ways IAL's hiring practices mirrored broad economic practices but in some regards it was slower to hire women, particularly in regard to clerical staff and married women.

Following a sharp decrease at the end of the First World War, female employment steadily climbed throughout the 1920s, yet barely reached pre-war levels by 1931. Working women – representing one-third of all employment-aged women – constituted fewer than 30 per cent of the workforce as a whole but around 40 per cent of Greater London, the home base of IAL. Compared with 1911, there were slightly more women over 35 in the workforce (up from 24% to 26%), and slightly more married women at work (up from 14% to 16%) in 1931. The narrow *range* of jobs available to women had not changed much since the pre-war era but the types of job did. Throughout the 1920s women's work in manufacturing industry declined from 26 per cent to 22 per cent, but work in shops and offices sharply increased (Horn, 1994). In the latter case the number of female clerks increased from 560,000 in 1921 to around 650,000 (or 46% of all clerical workers) in 1931 (Halsey, 1978: 26).[55]

Over this period IAL's female employees barely exceeded two per cent of its workforce and, in common with the Civil Service and many other occupations, operated a marriage bar. Unlike the General Post Office (GPO), which was by far the largest employer of female clerical staffs, IAL was more in line with the Great Western Railway (GWR), which was one of the slowest to hire female clerks.[56] The reasons may not be hard to decipher. To begin with, IAL management did not seem to share the changing view that clerical work was more suitable for women[57] and continued to hire a number of male clerks. If anything, Geddes, a former railway manager,[58] shared the more backward view of female employment that was prevalent in the railway industry.[59] Indeed, prior to taking over IAL Geddes had chaired a government committee that recommended women be cut from the police force as a cost saving measure. The recommendation earned him the ire of feminist groups and two female Members of Parliament.[60]

A comparison of the different structures of the Post Office and the railway industries suggests that capital-intensive firms 'can offset the costs of more expensive male clerks through savings due to new technologies and lower raw material and capital equipment costs. [While] employers in white-collar industries, [where], clerical labour is their major overhead cost, [...] will be more responsive to cheaper sources of labour' (Lowe, 1987: 18). IAL was something of a hybrid between the two extremes. It employed expensive technology in the form of aeroplanes but needed to employ a large number of people to provide a commercial service and administration. At the capital-intense end of the business they only hired men, with women hired in purely administrative jobs. Another explanation is that women were only employed where their presence did not bring into question the masculine character of certain jobs. Feminization is also due to the development of large-scale routines and mechanization that allowed employers to routinize clerical work and thus do away with expensive, specialized labour normally done by men (Lowe, 1987; Roberts, 1988). At IAL women undertook the most routine work and we see a growth in their employment as machine operators (e.g., powers machines) in the late 1930s.

Beyond the ranks of office and factory worker there were few women. In 1931 less than 2.5 per cent of all female employees were in the 'managerial category', the great majority of who were in female-typed work in charge of female employees. This was the case at IAL and the employment of Mrs Florence Henderson.

The average earnings of women in Britain were well below that of men. This was often justified on the grounds that work is temporary for women but long-term for men (and the maintenance of their families). Between 1931 and 1935 the average women's wage across all industries as a percentage of that of men fell from 48.3 per cent to 48 per cent (Pugh, 1992: 96). The wage rates at IAL are not easily comparable as most men occupied skilled, managerial and professional posts while women were confined to routine clerical tasks. However, there is strong indication that men were paid more than women and that, while the only pay differential for women was based on time served, for men it was based on time served and marriage, with married men were paid more than single men (see Table 3.2).

It has been suggested that a series of protective labour laws in force at the time contributed to workplace inequity (Horn, 1994). By excluding women from certain dangerous tasks and from night-work employers could claim that women were unable to work on terms that were strictly equal with men. This was very much the case at IAL where much of the important work depended not only on dangerous and night-work but also on extensive periods away from home.

Women and aviation

Prior to the First World War a number of pioneering female flyers had taken to the air and made their mark but the war closed all doors to women pilots. Organizationally, women were excluded from piloting. Imaginatively, the image of flying was indelibly associated with masculinity. Following the war, women were still excluded from air force piloting and to this was added commercial airline flying. Nonetheless, flying had inspired a new generation of women who were interested in aviation but very few would make it.

The life of Amy Johnson captures sometime of the flavour of women and aviation during these times. Johnson, 'an ingenuous, provincial version of the flapper' (Smith, 1988: 55), was born in Hull in 1903 and, like many of the young women at IAL, came from a middle-class background, was well educated,[61] yet ended up working in a series of secretarial and sales positions.[62] Nonetheless, in 1928, she took flying lessons, studied for an aircraft ground engineer's licence,[63] and began to establish aviation records, including the first solo flight by a woman from England to Australia. But her achievements were hard won[64] and, despite her fame, she found it impossible to obtain a serious flying job. At IAL, for example, the response of senior management to Johnson's Australia flight was not so much admiration as bemusement, arguing that 'if a woman can do this, why not Imperial Airways?' (Penrose, 1980b: 64).

A number of other women made their name in aviation in the same era as Johnson, including, Adrienne Bollard, Lady Sophie Heath, Lady Mary Bailey, Elsie Mackay and Amelia Earhart.[65] Reaction to the achievement of female flyers was mixed. They were applauded in the media, became instant celebrities and were often hired by advertisers to sell their products. But, by and large, they were still seen as *women* flyers. Writing in a 1929 issue of the North American Review a male pilot characterized female pilots as 'impulsive and scatterbrained' (quoted in Corn, 1983: 76). British attitudes were not far behind. After Amy Johnson made her historic flight she was constantly referred to as the 'typist who became an airwoman' (Cadogan, 1992: 113), and when Amelia Earhart made a solo crossing of the Atlantic in 1932, Charles Grey commented that 'Mrs. G. P. Putnam, known professionally, or for purposes of publicity, as Miss Amelia Earhart [has proven] that in 1932 with a modern aeroplane, a modern engine, and the latest navigational instruments, a woman is capable of doing what a mere man did in 1919, but in three hours less than the man's time' (quoted in Lovell, 1989: 217). Similarly, a US aviation writer contended that Earhart was 'only an average flyer who had pushed herself to the front by following the tactics of the feminists [...] Using a man-made perfect machine, tuned by men mechanics, trained by men flyers, [and a] course laid out by a man, by a lucky break she just managed to make the hop' (quoted in Lovell, 1989: 217).[66]

Despite some of the more negative attitudes, women continued to make their mark in aviation throughout the 1930s. In 1932 Winifred Drinkwater made history of a different kind when she became the first female commercial airline pilot in Britain and probably the world, flying for Midland and Scottish Air Ferries (Simons, 1993: 112).[67] By 1933 there were at least four women operators in the aircraft transport business, including Pauline Gower (who ran a joy riding operation), Constance Leathart (Cramlington Aircraft Ltd.), Mrs A. L. Patterson (Patterson Air Traders Ltd.) and Mildred Bruce (Air Dispatch). It was Bruce's airline that, in 1937, hired the first female flight attendant in Britain and, a year later, employed at least one female commercial airline pilot (Curtis, 1985: 37).[68]

In Britain, as the 1930s came to a close, women flyers were making their mark, yet, with the exception of Winifred Drinkwater and Grace Brown, none had been hired as commercial airline pilots. When Air Dispatch was taken over by the Government in 1939 Grace Brown was out of a job and it was 30 years before another British airline hired women pilots. Apart from Air Dispatch's other short-lived experiment, there were no female flight attendants in Britain until after the war; IAL remained steadfastly against the idea. But, in some respects, things were changing. In October 1938, fearful about the coming war, the British Government established the Civil Air

Guard (CAG) to encourage the training of new pilots. Remarkably, the scheme was open to men and women, leading Charles Grey to comment that; 'the menace is the woman who thinks that she ought to be flying a high-speed bomber, when she really has not the intelligence to scrub the floor of a hospital properly'. Despite this viewpoint, 1000 women were among the 10,000 new pilots who were in training, and several of these women were to play an important role in the war.

The gendering of Imperial Airways

In the first few years of IAL men constituted 99 per cent of all the employees, and all positions of power, authority, profession and skilled work. In building an airline these men also built a culture. Male dominance of an organization provides an explanation of how its culture reflects masculinist values (Kanter, 1977), but this is only a starting point: there are numerous examples of male dominated work, including stewarding in the United States, which were feminized. An important clue to the masculine character of IAL lies with the leadership, the configuration of the men involved (their personalities, experiences and skills) and the demands of the organization.

With the founding of IAL the leadership of commercial aviation shifted away from wartime military to hardnosed business experience. In the absence of any widespread social change the changing face of leadership simply imposed a different form of masculinity on the organization, one based on rationality, calculability and authoritarian leadership. To understand why this did not open up more than a few clerical jobs to women we need to look at the central jobs involved and the men who occupied them. Piloting and engineering jobs, as we have seen, were almost exclusively filled by former airmen. To introduce women into either range of jobs would have presented a challenge to the deep-rooted masculine character of the work, whose associations were rooted in broad socio-economic collectives of men in aviation and engineering. But such a notion was unthinkable at that time, engineering and commercial piloting being viewed as men's work. Stewarding was different, relying as it did on mimetic isomorphism. This work, although associated with men in other aspects of service (hotels, railways, ocean liners), was not rooted in particular notions of masculinity and was potentially more susceptible to feminization. The fact that at IAL stewarding remained steadfastly male may have had more to do with the resistance of pilots to females joining the aircrew, and a formative context in which British upper-class sensibilities continued to frown on the notion of young women as air 'hostesses'. The only crack in IAL's gender gestalt was due in large part to the fact that the feminization of clerical work had already moved at a pace and was supported by changing social attitudes to young women and work.

It took a radical change in the formative context for women to be accepted into the workplace in great numbers with the onset of the First World War.

The immediate aftermath of the war and gender anxieties provided another powerful context in which workplace decisions were made. But by the mid-1920s Britain had settled into the post-war era and gender attitudes had, for the most part, settled into a period of compromise – a modified domestic idyll in which young women were encouraged into the workplace until they married. Despite the fact that IAL was a quasi-government agency there was no pressure on management to employ women to anything but routine clerical jobs. Indeed, much of IAL practices, including the marriage bar, were in line with certain government institutions.

In contrast, US airlines, with the exception of Pan Am, went beyond clerical and secretarial roles in the feminization of flight attending. In Canada, on the other hand, the continued dominance of bush flying helped to ensure that few women joined the industry until the establishment of TCA, but even then hiring was limited to flight attending.

Pan Am

Pan Am, originally the brainchild of a group of army officers,[69] was established in 1927 with backing from financiers but was rapidly taken over by one holding company – AGCAL, and then merged with another – ACA, headed by Juan Trippe. Trippe was named President and General Manager of Pan Am and, drawing on government support and anxieties, quickly established the airline's presence throughout South America. By 1929 Pan Am was a major international airline, with the largest route system of any carrier in the Americas, linking a total of 23 countries and colonies across the Caribbean and Central America, and as far down as Montevideo. Building on government fears about the encroachment of German airlines south of the border, Trippe gained substantial financial support in the form of airmail subsidies, and political support in the form of assistance to develop a near monopoly over the region, and quasi-official status as the 'chosen instrument' of the government's foreign policy in South America (Bender and Altschul, 1982; Sampson, 1984).[70]

At the end of 1927 Pan Am hired its first steward, a young Spanish-speaking man from the hospitality business.[71] Unlike IAL's racial hiring restrictions, many of Pan Am's early stewards were Hispanics.[72] However, Pan Am did not hire stewardesses until 1943. It took a war and a shortage of manpower (sic) to encourage the airline to hire female flight attendants. Part of the reason lay with the company's operations in South America, with its long-distances over dangerous terrain and its associations with machismo forms of masculinity. Part lay with the role of competition; while US domestic airlines began to mimic UAL by hiring stewardesses, Pan Am's direct competitors in the international field, including IAL, retained a stewards-only policy until the late 1930s and beyond.[73] And part was almost certainly due to Trippe, who ran the airline as a benevolent ruler for much of this era. He has been described as a robber baron, ruthless and unscrupulous (Bender and Altschul, 1982), a 'latter day conquistador, immensely aggressive' (Josephson, 1944: 89). A man of few words, 'approval was inferred from his lack of commitment for a project' (Bender and Altschul, 1982: 462). As late as February 1941 the airline's official view was that Pan Am 'has stewards rather than stewardesses [because]... the Clippers make long flights over isolated territory, and the job has already been considered too strenuous for a young woman' (Pan American Airways, 1941).

An exception to Trippe's apparent lack of interest in the promotion of women was the hiring of Anne Archibald. Originally employed by Pan Am as a secretary in 1928, Archibald's Latin American experience[74] and lobbying skills were noticed by Trippe and she was promoted to manage the Washington office, where her major role was lobbyist for the airline.[75] So spectacular was her success in this role that Trippe promoted her to Assistant Vice President in 1939. Yet, it was 'strange that a woman ran his Washington office,' because 'Trippe displayed little interest in women,' rarely speaking to them at social functions or showing any 'prurient interest' (Daley, 1980: 351).[76]

TCA

In Canada bush piloting continued to dominate aviation in the 1930s and, coupled with the Great Depression, posed insurmountable obstacles for women flyers. Bush airlines were small operations, flying in wilderness conditions that were seen unsuitable for women. The fact that two women did pilot for bush companies, and in an unofficial capacity, is likely due to the so-called rugged individualism that characterized the industry (Henry, 1983; Time-Life, 1983).[77]

Towards the late 1930s the Canadian government, concerned to build a single national airline, established TCA as a wholly owned affiliate of CNR.[78] Three differing forms of masculinity – technocracy, cut-throat competitiveness and rugged individualism – influenced the new company. The first group consisted of the railwaymen who ran the board and privileged technical knowledge in their hiring decisions. The second group consisted of a group of men, including Philip G. Johnson, who were recruited from the cut-throat US aviation business to run the company and who expected efficiency, discipline and competitiveness. The third group consisted of the bush pilots and crew who operated the service, establishing an esprit de corps around the manliness of working under harsh conditions. The end result was a mixed response to the hiring of women and narrowly constructed images of women. After 15 months of operations the first women to be employed were 'stewardesses'. Successful recruits were expected to 'combine the comeliness of Venus with the capabilities of Florence Nightingale'[79] (Collins, 1978: 8).

The decision to hire female flight attendants was primarily influenced by mimetic isomorphism (DiMaggio and Powell, 1983). US domestic airlines, including those that flew into Canada, had already feminized the work; and Phil Johnson, the operational head of TCA had been part of the management team at BAT when the very first female flight attendants were hired.

4

Their Finest Hour: Mrs Miniver and the World at War

> Back to normal. No, thought Mrs. Miniver, standing by the window and looking out into the square, they weren't quite back to normal, and never would be [...] Clem had gone off with his Anti-Aircraft Battery, and Vin had been sent up to Quern, and the children's day school had been evacuated to the west country, and the maids had gone down to Starlings to prepare it for refugees, and she herself, staying at her sister's flat, had signed on as an ambulance driver ... .
>
> Jan Struthers, *Mrs. Miniver* (1942: 155–57)

Introduction

When Britain declared war on Germany, on 3 September 1939, IAL was in the process of merging with British Airways Ltd (BAL) to form the British Overseas Airways Corporation (BOAC). Both the war and the merger had a profound impact on commercial aviation in Britain. With war came renewed pressures for women to join the workforce in increased numbers, and with the merger came state control and extensive reorganization.

The war period (1939–45) saw tremendous changes in the gendering of the airline's culture as women were hired to a range of previously men-only jobs and the percentage of female employees climbed to 34 per cent.[1] At the upper levels, one woman joined the board and four others were appointed to senior management. A small group of 'female stewards' were employed for selected flights to neutral countries, and several women served as pilots in BOAC's aircraft ferrying service.

The Second World War also had an effect on the gendering of airlines in North America. Canada entered the war shortly after Britain in September 1939, and the United States entered the war following the Japanese attack on Pearl Harbor in December 1941. In each case TCA and Pan Am greatly increased the number and range of their female employees as replacements for men called to the armed forces. Apart from Pan Am's Anne Archibald, neither airline elevated women to management positions, but Pan Am hired stewardesses while TCA hired its first stewards.

At the juncture: Inside BOAC (1940–45)

In November 1938 the British Government announced that it was acquiring the undertakings of IAL and BAL and over the next year tremendous efforts were made to create one new airline from two disparate companies. Against a background of major reorganization there were several changes at the top of the airline, including the appointment of new directors, a fairly rapid turnover of leaders, and the appointment of the first female board member.

BOAC officially began operations on 1 April 1940 with 5500 employees, including 500 women and a new 'Chairman,' Clive Pearson.[2] Before the year's end significant changes occurred as the company recruited women to replace men and the newly established Air Transport Auxiliary (ATA), under BOAC control, hired a small group of female pilots. In 1943 Pauline Gower, the commandant of ATA's female flyers, became the first women to be appointed to the airline's board following the resignation of Clive Pearson and three board members[3] over a dispute with the government about the future of BOAC. Pearson was replaced with Viscount Knollys (Chairman).[4] By the middle of the war, the absolute number of female employees grew almost five-fold, and much of the leadership of the company's social organization was under female control. For the first time ever the company newsletter regularly carried items on female employees.

The female employee

By the summer of 1939 the threat of war was encouraging a return to old gendered scripts of man as combatant and woman as domestic help. In a directive on *'National Service. Essential Staff in Time of Emergency,'* for example, male employees were assured that after a period of mobilization to the armed forces the company would endeavour to re-engage them (Imperial Airways, 1939a). Women were informed that the airline wished 'to retain as many of the secretaries and personal stenographers as possible. Certain others would be needed either in their present capacities as clerical staff, stenographers, telephonists or cable clerks, filing clerks and powers operators, or else as replacements for men in the clerical grades' (ibid.). Similarly, a memorandum on 'compensation for war injuries', classified employees into six categories that portrayed men as either 'civil defence volunteers' or 'gainfully employed persons' and women as either 'widows' or 'persons [who] perform household duties' (British Overseas Airways Corporation, undated). A civil defence notice, posted throughout the airline's Grand Spa offices in September 1940, warned that in the event of an emergency staff should

> assemble in the passages [with] women on the left and men on the right [...] All women will proceed to shelter through the Ballroom entrance. Men will proceed to the far staircase of the shelter by way of the front or back of the building, keeping close to walls for protection. Should there be gunfire the wardens on duty at the doors may instruct men to proceed under cover through the Ballroom after the women have reached shelter.
>
> British Overseas Airways Corporation (1940d)

Wartime changes

At the beginning BOAC characterized the 'normal' employee as male. Company documents were directed at male rather than female employees, with most job descriptions continuing to refer to the employee and his 'wife'. Applicants for the post of engineer officers and technical assistants, for example, were asked: 'If married, nationality of wife before marriage' (British Overseas Airways Corporation, 1940i).[5]

Married men were privileged over all other employees, as witnessed in cost of living bonuses, which were the highest of any employee (British Overseas Airways Corporation, 1940c),[6] and their allowances for working in London, which were double that of 'single men and all women' (British Overseas Airways Corporation, 1941e).

As the war progressed changes occurred in the recruitment of female employees. By 1942 BOAC's UK staff of 5800 included 2000 women (British Overseas Airways Corporation, 1942e), a four-fold growth over 1939 to a point where they constituted over a third of the airline's UK employees. The growth was mainly in clerical work, where women continued to undertake a range of administrative support roles. This was particularly evident among the company's Head Office staffs where, by 1944, women made up 48 per cent of the 3000 employees. But women were also filling a number of more traditionally male jobs. In the summer of 1940, in recognition of the growing number of female staff, the company appointed female doctors 'to carry out the examination of women staff' (British Overseas Airways Corporation, 1940g). However, over the following years, wartime exigencies led to the appointment of Miss Vicary as a 'salaries accountant', and several other women to be hired as traffic assistants and in other male-associated jobs.

Jakey Adams was among the first women to be employed as a traffic assistant. Prior to the Second World War Adams had been engaged in secretarial work in the United Kingdom but 'always found it boring, not to say frustrating'.[7] At the outbreak of war she 'went to Egypt with a small volunteer unit of ambulances, [...] attached to the British Army' but in 1941 applied to BOAC. She heard that the airline's Traffic department was finding it 'increasingly difficult to find new male staff, most of whom by then were in the Services [and, as a result,] was taking on women'. The airline was looking for women for various postings around the Middle East so were 'anxious to employ girls from [Adam's] unit'. Adams, along with four or five other women, was hired. Taken on in Cairo, she was sent to Baghdad where her job was 'to handle reservations' and to undertake all manner of clerical and secretarial duties when needed. Nonetheless, she 'was delighted to find a job with a little more scope and which carried a certain amount of responsibility as well as being full of interest'.

By June of 1942 the airline was employing 'two women architects, one woman barrister, twenty draughtswomen, one women computor, ten women traffic clerks, three hundred waitresses, a large number of transport drivers, canteen workers, secretarial staff, and several hundred factor workers' (British Overseas Airways Corporation, 1942h).

Like Jakey Adams, many of the women entering male-typed jobs at BOAC came from traditional middle-class female employment. Mary Baynham, for example, was a matron's assistant at a girl's school prior to becoming a BOAC transport driver, while her colleague, Pamela Battson, had been a riding instructor at a livery stable. Miss Chivers, their boss, was employed by a fashion house before she took charge of BOAC's 34 female drivers.[8] In the buying department assistant buyers Winifred Williams and Jane Fryer were among the first to be promoted out of the airline's own clerical ranks, both had spent several years at IAL and BOAC as stenographers. Nonetheless, they pledged to 'be stenographers again when the war is over,' because they didn't 'want to take jobs away from the men – even if such a thing was possible' (British Overseas Airways Corporation, 1942g).

Not all female recruits came from traditionally female employment. Mary Reade, who headed up BOAC's Cable Department, for example, was a barrister by profession;[9] Hilda Langdon, the company's only female computor,[10] previously worked in a government income tax department; and Miss Halliley, the airline's first ever woman ground engineer, served her apprenticeship with the de Havilland aircraft company.[11]

Factory work also provided a welcome change for some women. Miss Lewis, a former bar maid, found satisfaction in 'the comradeship of factory life' at the BOAC works in Wales, and Margretta Williams, a former domestic worker, felt 'happier than she had ever been before'. Mrs Iles, 'a soldier's wife', got 'lonely at the weekends and could hardly wait for Monday to get back to the bench' (British Overseas Airways Corporation, 1942g).

Senior management

Despite the numerous changes in women's employment the representation of women in management changed very little. In 1940 Florence Henderson, as the Women's Staff Superintendent, was the highest placed woman in BOAC and by the war's end there were only three other women in senior staff positions – Mrs Thorley, Miss Edwards and Miss Turner, who were part of the Personnel Officers and Administrative Assistants group. Below them a small number of women filled supervisory roles in female-dominated areas, including Mrs 'Mac', the Senior Telephone Supervisor and 'unofficial liaison officer' whose job was 'to know the whereabouts of all the directors and heads of departments' (British Overseas Airways Corporation, 1942d).[12]

Piloting

Although a thousand women underwent training in the Civil Air Guard immediately prior to the Second World War commercial and military aviation steadfastly refused to recruit female pilots. At the beginning of the war the Government established the *Air Transport Auxiliary* (ATA) to be responsible for the transport of dispatches, mail, news, medical supplies, civil authorities, medical officers, ambulance work and the ferrying of military planes. The ATA was placed under the umbrella of BOAC, with Gerard d'Erlanger in charge. Women were excluded. ATA requirements stipulated that pilots should be male, between the ages of 28 and 50, with a minimum of 250 flying hours' experience.

As early as 1937 Amy Johnson, Dorothy Spicer and Pauline Gower had floated the idea of female wartime ferry pilots (Beauman, 1971: 63), and Lady Bailey suggested that women should be allowed to become air force combat flyers. These ideas met with open hostility. Lord Londonderry argued that Britain 'had not yet accepted the principle that women should be exposed to fighting risks,' but he did concede that experienced women pilots might be useful for other tasks in the event of an emergency (Curtis, 1985: 11). Charles Grey was less gracious in contending that women insist on flying jobs 'which they are quite incapable of doing' (quoted in Curtis, 1985: 13).[13] He need not have worried; the Air Council was categorical in its opposition to female air force flyers and rejected the idea of 'a flying section of the WAAF' (ibid.).

In the changed conditions of warfare, however, it soon became clear that there were not enough men to staff the piloting needs of the RAF and the ferrying work. Thus, training was stepped up and a move was made to recruit female ferry pilots. Press reaction was generally unfavourable,[14] and the RAF refused to employ women in their ferry pools or to undertake conversion training at the air force's Central Flying School. The government, nonetheless, agreed in principle that women pilots could join the ATA but would not be 'enrolled unless they [came] up to the required standard'.[15] Recruitment was restricted to eight women.[16] Despite the stipulation that the terms and conditions of employment were to be identical to that of male pilots, the women were paid 20 per cent less than a man of similar grade (Curtis, 1985: 16).

With the fall of Dunkirk, and the Battle of Britain underway, the government realized that it was desperately short of fighter pilots so agreed to increase the number of female ATA pilots, from 26 by the end of 1940,[17] to 166 in 1945.[18] Within the ATA there were numerous biases to be overcome, not least of which was a lack of facilities for women and a serious restriction on the types of plane that the women were allowed to fly. When the Under Secretary of State recommended a female section of the ATA he doubted whether the women would be 'capable of flying all types of aircraft' (Curtis, 1985: 7). This was translated into a firm rule and caused frustration among the female flyers and problems for the ATA. The restriction initially halted the expansion of female recruitment, as there were not enough planes for women to fly and angered existing female pilots who witnessed the recruitment of less experienced male fliers to pilot a range of aeroplanes.[19] The situation was such that Amy Johnson, out of work but desperate to find 'a serious flying job,' was reluctant to join the ATA because 'the prejudice against women pilots is still very strong' (Smith, 1988: 344). She saw the female section of the ATA as 'a team of women [who've been] given the crumbs to keep them quiet' (ibid.). Gower shared Johnson's opinions and successfully pressed the ATA to allow female pilots to fly a range of planes comparable to their male counterparts.[20]

The women's section of the ATA was the closest that BOAC ever came to having female pilots under its broad remit and then only for a short while. Soon after its establishment BOAC came under the control of the Air Ministry, where it was treated very much as a junior arm, used largely for transporting troops. In the fall of 1942, it was decided that administrative matters affecting the ATA should be the subject of direct discussion between the Ministry of Aircraft Production (MAP) and the Commanding Officers of the ATA, that it should have its own administrative headquarters and should be directly accountable for financial matters (Curtis, 1985: 54). These factors put ATA beyond the control of BOAC. BOAC's role in transportation was further diminished in 1943 with the creation of the RAF's Transport Command. This caused tensions between the Government and the BOAC Board, which led to the resignation of all but d'Erlanger. Although a number of male pilots flew for BOAC and the ATA,[21] no female flyers (ATA or otherwise) ever flew for BOAC.

Stewarding

Despite the exigencies of war and the feminization of stewarding in North America and part of Europe, BOAC continued to resist hiring female flight attendants. Instead the company announced that 'owing to a shortage of man-power in war-time', it was hiring boys, aged 14 to 16, to be trained as stewards (British Overseas Airways Corporation, 1942i).

However, the company did make some small but significant changes in the middle of the war. Perhaps as a nod to the North American environment, in August of 1942 the company's Baltimore office employed a 'Passenger Hostess', dressed in a US style stewardess uniform, to 'minister' to Boeing passengers and crews (British Overseas Airways Corporation, 1942g). A more important development was the 1943 hiring of six female 'stewards' on the airline's services from Croydon to Madrid, Lisbon and, later, Paris and

Stockholm. Even though the female stewards were continually employed until 1946 the scheme was viewed as a limited experiment, rather than a permanent shift in hiring policy. The women were dressed in a 'masculine style' uniform, consisting of 'navy blue serge suits [with] pleated skirts and double-breasted jackets with brass buttons'[22]. For serving passengers they had to wear a white tunic with brass buttons and epaulettes, and 'stout brogues' (ibid.). They found that 'discipline was strict and departure and destinations had to be kept secret for security reasons,' and there was 'nothing glamorous about the job' (ibid.).

At the war's end, at a time when most world airlines were recruiting female flight attendants, BOAC wound down their employment of women and prepared for the future with the recruitment of a new generation of male stewards, recruiting two hundred 17- and 18-year-old boys from the Air Training Cadets (British Overseas Airways Corporation, 1946b). Ironically, the description of the new stewards' duties mirrored expectations 'normally' associated with women at that time. The young men were expected to

> be able to cook, clear and lay tables, and wash up [as well as] look after the comfort and welfare of passengers, give them advice on what to wear in the different countries visited, and provide the answers to questions on the route, the stopping places, and almost anything that interests passengers by air
>
> (ibid)[23]

Internal social organization

Throughout the war years various sports and social clubs flourished within BOAC and women played a central role across a range of activities. By late 1941 there were women's sections of the previously all-male cricket and rifle clubs,[24] and the Hockey Section, the subject of gender controversy before the war (see Chapter 3), now had both separate and mixed sections. Only two associations were female dominated – the knitting group, and the previously male-dominated drama club; and one was male dominated – the Staff Association, established in November 1945. Other associations were 'mixed', both at the level of activity and in the composition of their committees, with women playing a leading role in a number of cases.[25]

Imaging female employees

Although women constituted one-third of all UK-based staff during the war, in contrast to their male colleagues, they received little coverage in the company's newsletters and none in the annual reports. In the latter case individual male leaders and employees serving in the armed forces were singled out for attention.

The *BOAC Newsletter*, established in February of 1940, recorded the involvement of female employees in social activities, but rarely went beyond listing names. The reports were usually framed by the war and imbued with very definite attitudes about the role of women and men at work. Two constant and related themes revolved around women's support of men in their central wartime roles and women's abilities to undertake that supporting role. In an article on 'Our "Women at War," ' for example, female employees are viewed as 'Back Room Girls,'[26] who are

> doing jobs which women have never done before. Some are wearing uniforms. Some work in mechanic's overalls, others in ordinary clothes. But just as the W.A.A.F. exists in order to help the R.A.F., so these 1,800 women are all working hard behind the scenes to help not only the men of the Merchant Air Service but also the R.A.F. and the Ministry of Aircraft Production.
>
> British Overseas Airways Corporation (1942h)

As the number of female employees grew, the newsletter assured (male) readers that women were not only helpful, but 'definitely capable of undertaking a man's job efficiently and well' (British Overseas Airways Corporation, 1941a).

Innumerably, gendered descriptors were used to characterize female employees, such as reference to one female supervisor as 'charming' and 'capable' (British Overseas Airways Corporation, 1941a) and another as 'dividing her time between [work] and her two children' (ibid.).[27] A story that typifies this approach was on Mrs Butler, a 'Leading Hand in the Airscrew Factory', who is described as 'well over 60 [...] dressed in her khaki overalls with a red collar, set off by grey hair and a pair of long earrings'; a woman who before the war was not 'accustomed to hard work' yet now worked 'five days a week from 8 a.m. to 6.30 p.m., and on Saturdays from 8 a.m. to 5.30 p.m.'. (ibid.). Butler is quoted as saying, 'Before the war I spent most of my time at bridge parties. Nowadays I feel that it is the job of every women, young or old, to help kill Germans. That is why I enjoy working in the factory, although I do get rather tired. I nearly always spend my Sundays in bed to make up for the hard work during the week' (British Overseas Airways Corporation, 1941a). This description of the attitudes and class origins of Mrs Butler very much mirrored that of the then popular fictional character of Mrs Miniver, the subject of a best selling novel and movie during the war years.

A notable feature of the newsletter in this period was the increased use of photographs,[28] which, for the most part, helped to visualize the storyline, but an element of gendered composition and accompanying text was also apparent. When, for example, uniforms were first introduced for female staff in 1940 one of the younger women was photographed to show 'how smart our girl road transport drivers look in their nice uniform' (British Overseas Airways Corporation, 1942c). The notion of (heterosexual) attractiveness became an overworked theme that was highlighted through announcements of engagements, marriages[29] and births, and various news snippets. The text accompanying a photograph of a 'group of women members of the Airways House Traffic Staff', for example, points out that 'the two married members of the group are those who, having obeyed the photographer's injunction, are looking at the camera. The two single members are those looking elsewhere. The fact that a company of Irish Guards was at that moment passing Airways House is of course, without any significance in this connection!' (ibid.)

Unlike their male counterparts, individual female employees were rarely the subjects of extended coverage; however, on occasion they were singled out for their (long-term) contribution to the company and/or to the greater war effort. A December 1940 article on Marguerite Mundy combined both these elements. Mundy, a catering superintendent since 1935, had been granted a commission in the Auxiliary Territorial Service (ATS)[30] and consequently resigned from BOAC. Her resignation was greeted, unusually, with a lengthy article, suggesting that she was an unsung pioneer whose title belied her more senior-level responsibilities. Nonetheless, this characterization was framed by underlying notions of domesticity, with references to her responsibility 'for the feeding of all along the routes' and the various staff 'under her care' who she ensured 'got new uniforms,' were 'kept well,' were 'inoculated' and 'were happy in their job' (British Overseas Airways Corporation, 1940f).

Mundy was the first of many female employees to join one of the women's military organizations but the others were either ignored or received scant attention in the newsletter. Thus, for example, when a former employee returned to the airline after serving in the ATA it was simply noted that, 'Miss M. Mann (previously employed at Croydon) had returned to the Corporation' (British Overseas Airways Corporation, 1942b). In fact, Minnie Mann had served with IAL and BOAC since 1930, playing an active role in the social life of the airline (see Chapter 3).

The only other recognition of note was an article on Mrs H. McAtamney, as part of a series celebrating the airline's milestones and achievements. Of the various articles on individual managers and employees, McAtamney, one of the company's longest serving employees at the time, was the only woman to receive attention. Under a photograph of 'Mrs. Mac,' she is reported as joining the airline as a telephonist in 1924 and being 'one of the first youthful enthusiasts who saw a future in aviation and watched with interest the development of Imperial Airways' (British Overseas Airways Corporation, 1942d).

The curt and infrequent attention given to female employees nonetheless marked a change from previous eras when women had been totally ignored. There were other changes too that would have an impact on female employment in the post-war era. Women were now occupying a range of job previously associated only with men and were in a number of job categories and departments where they constituted a majority.

Organizational discourse

BOAC was different from IAL and BAL in at least five crucial ways. First, it was now a state-owned airline. Second, it was constituted out of a combination of former IAL and BAL employees. Third, there were a series of leadership changes. Fourth, there was an extensive turnover in personnel as increasing numbers of women replaced men who had joined the armed forces. Fifth, the airline experienced a period of sharp growth, which added to the changed character of the airline's personnel. Existing scripts were broken and it was left to a diverse group of people to establish new ones – arguably, opening the door for changes to gendered scripts and the gender gestalt (Kohler, 1961).[31]

Restructuring

Sir John Reith began the process of internal reorganization in 1938, setting out on a path 'of almost ruthless reconstruction' (Pudney, 1959: 132) that followed the 'basic principle of organization [as] functionalism tempered by a considerable measure of regionalism' (Pudney, 1959: 138). In contrast to the previous ethos of private enterprise and the 'dividends motive,' Reith was committed to a 'public services motive' (Pudney, 1959: 132) and a 'non-commercial constitution' for the airline (quoted in Pudney, 1959: 137). He argued that that a massive injection of state capital was needed to replace IAL's aging fleet and to attain greater efficiencies. To that end, he proposed the merger of IAL and BAL and their transition from private enterprise to State control, creating in effect 'one large nationalised air corporation' (Jackson, 1995: 140), with a very different operating philosophy.[32] The outbreak of war accelerated the process of nationalization that had by now been agreed between all relevant parties.

With the war underway, Reith left and was replaced by Pearson, Head Office was moved to Bristol, and the Department of Civil Aviation, under the Air Ministry, was the sole arbiter and initiator in all matters of air transport policy. The new Corporation had little 'initiative and responsibility' (Pudney, 1959: 205) but as a government agency may have been expected to apply appropriate guidelines for the recruitment of women. How far that was actually the case would be hard to identify as the war intervened at the very point that BOAC came into being.

Changing personnel and leadership

Many of BOAC's top positions went to former members of BAL, including Clive Pearson (as Chairman) and Gerard d'Erlanger (in charge of ATA).[33] The highest ranked former IAL officer at BOAC was Colonel H. Burchall,

Assistant Director General for the eastern hemisphere. Major Brackley remained with BOAC but in a reduced role.[34] In the middle ranks Commander B. W. Galpin (who joined IAL in 1931) became BOAC's Chief Secretary, and Mr. A. J. Quinn-Harkin (IAL's Chief Accountant, 1924–40) became the Administration Director.[35]

Personalities

Unlike previous eras, the gendered character of the airline at this time had more to do with the wartime context than the strength of the personalities involved. For one thing, there were at least two situations of leadership in such a short space of time – the Reith/Pearson era (1940–43) and the Knollys era (1943–46). In both cases the leaders had to cope with the development of a new airline that was subject to rapid and dramatic change under wartime conditions.

Much of the increase in female employees was due to the needs of the airline rather than the inclinations of those in charge.[36] The company faced the dual requirement of replacing many of the male employees who left to join the services, while also needing to recruit extra staff to cope with growing needs.[37] In less than three years the airline grew from around 4000 to more than 14,000 employees; little wonder that BOAC felt the need to employ greater numbers of women.

Nonetheless, those in charge made an impact on the airline culture. The Reith/Pearson era, for instance, was characterized as rule by 'men of dependability, with enough imagination to have a healthy and active forward look' (Thomas, 1964: 276). The Knollys's era, on the other hand, was marked by a country club atmosphere. Both eras were projections of different forms of masculinity (Collinson and Hearn, 1994), each, in its way, promoting different types of men to positions of authority. Pearson preferred quiet business types but Knollys was seen as a Parkinsonian figure, 'creating posts for executive assistants to himself [and] assistants to executive assistants' (Thomas, 1964: 276).[38] Knollys's board consisted of 'mostly large, ebullient gentlemen who were first class golfers [and] hail-fellow-well-met, husky types'[39] whose deliberations 'usually ended in a kind of relaxed compromise in which a programme of action was invariably missing' (Thomas, 1964: 274). Criticism of the Knollys' Board was fairly widespread,[40] and more than one employee used the columns of *The Aeroplane*, rather than internal newsletters, to complain about the new leadership. In one case the writer expressed fear that his viewpoint would get him in trouble with the airline but pointed out that *The Aeroplane* offered the only channel for employees to present their case. He expressed bitterness and bewilderment at 'the steady flow into B.O.A.C. of Marquesses, Group Captains and Wing Commanders and first-class golfers, commencing in the highest grades and at salaries that we, after 15 years of hard work, mainly overseas, still dream about'. (quoted in Pudney,

1959: 209–10). The writer went on to complain that employees

> find themselves unwanted, often unknown to our new masters, and our wide and varied experience apparently rated as of little or no value [...] Today we feel that the new régime controlling B.O.A.C. would be only too glad to see the last of us go and may even have decided to do so.

(ibid.).

Images of warfare and gendered practices

Warfare dominated the first six years of BOAC's operation and contributed to specific images of men and women within the organization. In July 1940 the airline's operating capacity, compared with IAL, reached its lowest level ever when 'the entry of Italy into the war and the collapse of France dislocated the services both in Europe and through the Mediterranean' (British Overseas Airways Corporation, 1941b). In 1940 Head Office was moved from London to Bristol and, under section 32 of the British Overseas Airways Act, the Secretary of State exercised his right to have the whole undertaking of the Corporation placed at his disposal. The airline was by now very much an arm of the air force and included the ATA under its command. On 21 December the company's London office – Airways House – was badly damaged when a heavy bomb exploded nearby, but there were no casualties. A further raid in April of the following year saw further damage and this time there were four casualties. By now many of the official memoranda were directed at wartime contingencies such as recruitment for 'national service' (June, 1940), the establishment of a 'watch-keeping system' (July, 1940), 'compensation for war injuries' (August, 1940), air raid procedures (September, 1940), the issuance of identity cards (November, 1940) and the establishment of 'station welfare committees' (March, 1941).

Much of the copy of the internal newsletter was geared to the war effort, with the focus on the 'heroism' of male employees and the 'support' role of female employees. From the beginning the *BOAC Newsletter* carried regular columns on the activities of male employees that had joined the armed forces, including 'Awards for Gallantry,' 'Roll of Honour' (listing former employees killed in wartime service) and 'Keeping in Touch' (correspondence from male employees serving in the armed forces). Readers could 'learn with pride [...] the distinguished part which our pilots now with the R.A.F. are playing in the air war' (British Overseas Airways Corporation, 1940b); that 'First Officer A. J. Lilly, a Canadian who was in our School when war broke out, is now Chief Flying Instructor in the Royal Canadian Air Force training base at Moncton, New Brunswick' (British Overseas Airways Corporation, 1940a); or, sadly, that former trainee 'Pilot Officer P. Montague-Bates [was] killed in action' (British Overseas Airways Corporation, 1942f).

Women's names did not appear in the 'Roll of Honour', nor the 'Awards' column, and the only correspondence from female writers to 'Keeping in

Touch' were letters from grieving widows giving thanks for condolences. Women's national service was rarely mentioned, and then in general terms, such as reference to the 'more than 150 men and women [of the ATA who] have been lost in this valuable service' (British Overseas Airways Corporation, 1945b); little was made of the fact that 12 women ATA flyers were killed, which included Amy Johnson and Margaret Fairweather. Even a regular column on 'Passengers of Note' rarely included mention of any female passengers. Yet the role of the female employee was not entirely ignored. As if casting around for an appropriate point to stress their importance, the newsletter focussed on women as the all-important replacement staff.

Organizational commitment and longevity

In the midst of the wartime drama BOAC worked to build a sense of organizational history that spanned two decades, with stories celebrating pioneering flights – '25 Years Ago – Our First Air Service' and pilots – Captain O. P. Jones celebrates '25th year in aviation,' (British Overseas Airways Corporation, 1944b).

Throughout the war a number of male employees were singled out for long service to the airline. Typical was the coverage given to L. Malabbot who, despite employment with three different airlines (HPT, IAL and BOAC) is applauded for his 'Twenty-one Year's Service' to the company. This is described as a seamless process, in which Malabbot 'joined Handley Page Transport [in 1919] as a maintenance foreman until the merger. [In 1928 was] appointed Engineer Superintendent of the Mediterranean Division. [And in 1940] took up his present appointment in Lagos' (as Engineering Superintendent).

Other features appeared on the Chief Secretary, the Chief Accountant, the Public Relations Director, the Administration Director, the Deputy Director General and various other male employees. But, as we have seen above, two women – Marguerite Mundy and Mrs Mac – were also singled out for their contribution to the airline.

In October 1944 the airline threw a party to honour 'all members of the staff serving at home, having twenty years' or more service with the Corporation and its predecessors' (British Overseas Airways Corporation, 1944a). Among the 67 people honoured that evening were two women – Doris Clayton, and Miss M. V. Masters. Eighteen months later the company instituted 'The 25 Club' to formally recognize the service of long-term employees. The inaugural membership consisted of 18 men. There were no women members. Arguably, a discourse of long-term service served to emphasis organizational commitment and longevity as male qualities.

Race and empire

Throughout the war severe labour shortages in 'the colonies' encouraged BOAC to increase the number of non-white staff at its 'outposts' but still mostly men and mostly in menial jobs. Few people of colour, however, could be found in the ranks of the airline's UK employees, and piloting and stewarding were still restricted to white, British-born nationals (Hudson and Pettifer, 1979). Despite dropping 'Imperial' from the airline's name,[41] BOAC continued IAL's practice of imaging non-white colonial peoples in a negative light, using demeaning terms (e.g., 'boy,' 'coolie')[42] and making fun of their supposed ignorance.[43] It was always made clear, either by inference or in the following direct fashion, that British official was the natural ruler of non-white peoples, as in the case of 'parts of the Sudan [where] the natives have not yet been trained to the standard of efficiency required of them by the white man' (British Overseas Airways Corporation, 1941f).

Social discourse

The changing gender composition of BOAC mirrored changes within British society. In the inter-war years women experienced a number of significant political, legal and social changes as well as new employment opportunities in the growing fields of shop, office, and light industry work. Whereas before the First World War the dominant socio-legal characterization of woman was as an appendage of man, by the 1930s the notion of womanhood, although still subordinate to manhood, was more complex. The 'cult of domesticity' was decidedly different from the 'domestic idyll' of two decades earlier. In the latter discourse 'domesticity' was more a *state of being*, the notion of woman was interchangeable with the functions she was expected to perform; women were viewed as almost entirely subordinate to men, with few rights and privileges. In the newer discourse 'domesticity' was more about the *relationship* between women and men, women were defined through their supposed relationship to men – as wives and mothers; but now women were also viewed as citizens with a number of rights both within marriage and society generally.

Compared to the previous world war, women began the Second World War as citizens who expected to play a fuller role in the war effort than they had done in the past. Indeed, the experiences of the previous world war contributed to a greater acceptance of women's involvement in a range of wartime activities and the implementation of policies designed to aid women's contribution, including the provision of milk and school meals, the establishment of day nurseries and the introduction of an emergency hospital service (Pugh, 1992: 264).

The discourse of warfare

The character of the Second World War encouraged women to play a greater part in the war effort than they had done previously. The anti-fascist war aims were more encompassing, more complex than the more narrowly focussed, masculinist aims of the First World War. It was hard to ignore the reality of modern warfare that involved the bombing of civilian populations. There was a tremendous shortage of labour, and with most of Britain's former European allies under German occupation, there was a need to utilize as many people as possible for war work. In any event, twice as many women were mobilized for the the Second World War than had been in the First World War, reaching a peak in 1943 with 7,250,000 women employed in industry and the armed forces: 30,000 women were enrolled in the Land Army, 375,000 in civil defence and 470,000 joined the armed forces (Pugh, 1992: 264–65, 274).

Gender and the 'People's War'

Unlike the First World War, with its imperialist war aims (Hobsbawm, 1994), the roots of the Second World War lay in a series of ideological debates and conflicts over the nature of democracy and freedom that led to a questioning of established socio-economic values and beliefs. Challenges to the existing dominant (western) worldview was evidenced by and through a series of events that included the Irish Easter Uprising (1916), the Russian Revolution (1917), the British General Strike (1924), the election of the Labour Party to office in 1924 and in 1929, the rise of fascism in Italy and Nazism in Germany during the 1920s and 1930s, the Spanish Civil War (1936–39) and numerous other political upheavals of the times. Challenges to the character of fascism and Nazism almost inevitably raised questions about the alternatives and encouraged discussion among people about the war aims, leading one historian to characterize the era as 'the people's war' (Calder, 1969). While this did not radically alter debate about the role of women in society it did lead to a 'revival of interest in the woman question, because many aspects of life which had been regarded as individual assumed a social significance and became the business of government and policy-makers' (Rowbotham, 1999: 224). Various women's organizations pressed the government for equal treatment for women (Pugh, 1992: 275) and within this context it was more difficult, than it had been a generation earlier, to view women simply as producers of the next generation of (racially pure) Britons. Now the wartime struggle was not simply for nation but a better, more democratic sense of nationhood in which men and women had a role to play.

The reality of total war

If ideological issues were not enough, the character of modern warfare was evidence of the need to involve large numbers of women in the war effort. From the onset of the 1930s it was becoming increasingly clear that not only would there be another world war but that it would be a 'total war' involving large numbers of civilian casualties. Civil wars in Ireland, Russia and Spain had revealed the potential of modern warfare to engulf whole populations. But it was the aeroplane that portended the greatest threat to civil populations, witnessed in the First World War and then in the Japanese attack on Manchuria (1931), the Italian bombing of Ethiopia (1935) and the bombing of civilian populations during the Spanish Civil War. Added to this there was an imminent threat of invasion. Unlike the First World War when men went off to fight on distant battlefields, the new world war blurred the distinctions between the battlefront and the so-called home front. Indeed 130,000 civilians were killed or injured during the Second World War and no fewer than 48 per cent were women (Pugh, 1992: 264).[44] In March of 1941 Britain became the first country to conscript women for the war effort. All women between the ages of 19 and 40 were required to register at employment exchanges to be directed to essential war work.

Women and organization

In the inter-war years large numbers of women established and played a role in various organizations, including the Women's Institutes (WI), the WRAF Old Comrades' Association (OCA), the Women's Legion, the First Aid Nursing Yeomanry (FANY), the Emergency Service and the Auxiliary Territorial Service (ATS).

One of the paradoxes of the 'cult of domesticity' was the development of the Women's Institutes. Founded in 1915, the WI brought together numbers of women in local branches throughout Britain to discuss ways of improving domestic work. In a very real sense the WI contributed to the ideology of home and family, yet it did so in a way that involved hundreds of thousands of women in organized activity outside of the home. By 1919 there were more than 1000 WI branches with 50,000 members throughout England and Wales. By 1937 this number had grown to 5534 branches with 318,000 members.

With the threat of war on the horizon a number of women's organizations were revived or came into being to prepare women for the war effort, including the Women's Legion, which eventually became the Emergency Service, and then, through amalgamation with FANY and the women's Motor Transport Section of the Army Council, the Auxiliary Territorial Service (ATS).[45] The new ATS served the Regular and Territorial Armies as well as the RAF but remained civilians under the strict control of male military officers, leading Dame Helen Gwynne-Vaughan to protest that women 'were back at the beginning of auxiliary services as though the experience of their use in war had never been' (Beauman, 1971: 60).

Women and aviation

With war looming many female flyers and former WRAF leaders were anxious to ensure that women would be mobilized for the range of military aviation tasks, from clerical to piloting. As a result of their efforts two women's organization came into being – the Women's Auxiliary Air Force (WAAF) and the women's section of the Air Transport Auxiliary (ATA). In both cases women were accepted to undertake a range of aviation activities within organizations that were more or less integrated with their male counterparts. But in both cases the women were viewed as 'substitutes' for men.

The ATA

Over its five-year existence, 166 women were hired as ATA pilots. Despite initial restrictions, women came to fly various planes but with one important exception – the flying boats. Here only a limited number of pilots were required and it was the one area where there was not a shortage of male pilots. This restriction had ramifications for post-war flying as BOAC relied heavily on flying boats for many of its transcontinental flights. Once they had overcome initial hostility and resistance women pilots came to be an accepted part of the ATA, to the extent that some had 'the feeling of working in an integrated, close-knit community [where] the 'boys' couldn't have been kinder or more helpful' (Curtis, 1985: 239, 110). Indeed, the ATA 'did not seem to breed the frustrations which in so many small communities lead to jealousies and disharmony' (Curtis, 1985: 109–10). This attitude extended to situations where men found themselves under the command of a female officer. For example, when Margot Gore, an ATA flyer, was promoted to Captain the men under her command 'cheerfully' accepted her leadership (ibid.).

The ATA women's section consisted of many of Britain's leading female flyers, but also several from other countries, including Canada and the United States who were excluded from their own country's military flying activities.[46] For the most part male attitudes to the women flyers were positive[47] but they were often couched in terms of the their ability to release male flyers for air force combat. Thus, although they were viewed as highly competent and skilled, female flyers were ultimately seen as 'filling in', doing men's jobs for the war effort.

The ATA's acceptance of female flyers barely extended to other skilled ranks such as flight engineering. Of the 151 flight engineers recruited by the ATA only four were women. Clearly, the fact that any woman was hired to this branch of the ATA signalled a breakthrough, but a limited one because women constituted less than 3 per cent of flight engineers compared to nearly 13 per cent of ATA pilots.

When it came to future generations of military and commercial aviation personnel the ATA (in line with the RAF, the Air Fleet Arm and the commercial airlines) looked to boys and young men. The Air Training Corps (ATC), for instance, was a training ground for boys interested in aviation, and they received aviation training, including flying experience, through the ATA. As a result, several ATC cadets went on to obtain commissions in one or other of the military air forces as aircrew. At the end of the Second World War BOAC hired some sixty ATC cadets as flight stewards. There were no such opportunities for future generations of women. Indeed, by September 1945 the women of the ATA had already become 'forgotten pilots' (Curtis, 1985).

Addressing an Air Display and Pageant that month, Lord Beaverbrook bid a fond farewell to the ATA and asked the audience to remember the pilots who were killed in action as, 'the men who were too old to fly and fight, but who were not too old to fall' (quoted in Curtis, 1985: 281–82): the 12 women flyers who were killed on duty did not rate a mention.[48]

The WAAF

Recruitment to the ATS was so popular that the Territorial Units to which they were affiliated suggested that the London branches be attached to the RAF's No. 601 Squadron and the Balloon Squadrons at Kidbrooke. Jane Trefusis-Forbes, who had been the chief instructor with the Emergency Service, was made Commanding Officer of the new No. 20 RAF (County of London) Company of ATS at Kidbrooke. In this embryo stage the WAAF resembled its forerunner, the WRAF, in recruiting women to a limited range of jobs. Among the first five trades open to ATS recruits were those of Drivers, Cooks, Clerks, Mess Orderlies and Equipment Assistants. Fabric Work became the sixth trade and by the time the WAAF was established on 28 June 1939, Teleprinter Operator, Telephonist, Plotter, and Radio Operator tasks were added. Jane Trefusis-Forbes was by now the WAAF's first Director.

The WAAF was also similar to the WRAF in so far as many of its members met with initial hostility and amusement from male RAF colleagues and they were forbidden to fly in air force planes, even on duty. But there were some significant differences. To begin with, the WRAF was formed toward the end of the First World War, while the WAAF was established prior to the onset of the Second World War. The number and range of trades undertaken by members of the WAAF were initially much less than the 5 officer branches and the 53 'airwomen trades' of the WRAF but this changed quite rapidly. By the end of the Second World War there were 24 officer branches, 19 'airwomen only trades,' and 74 trades for airmen and airwomen alike (Beauman, 1971: 286–87; Escott, 1989: 298–99). Even the hostility appears to have been limited and short lived. Instead of outright rejection each new proposal to extend the range of airwomen trades was classified 'an experiment' and thereafter accepted. The women were often 'treated as "one of the boys", particularly in engineering trades, with no privileges, but with fierce protection against outsiders' (Escott, 1989: 100). From the beginning members of the WAAF were given the same uniform and badges of rank as the RAF and, on 25 April 1941, the Defence (Women's Forces) Regulations ensured that WAAF members were no longer civilians in uniform but Members of the Armed Forces of the Crown. WAAF Officers were now officially commissioned and all WAAF members operated under the Air Force Act. The one area where WAAF members fared less well than their WRAF counterparts was in regard to flying. While it took a matter of months before the ban on WRAF members flying while on duty was rescinded it took three years, until 1942, for the ban to be lifted on WAAF members. Compared with the peak of

25,000 women who served in the WRAF, recruitment to the WAAF peaked in 1943 at 181,835–16 per cent of the total RAF numbers and 22 per cent of the RAF in Britain.

As with the women's section of the ATA, WAAF members became accepted by their male counterparts as competent and skilled personnel. But also like ATA female flyers, WAAF members were ultimately viewed as 'substitutes' for men.[49] Thus, new trades for airwomen were introduced as 'experiments' before being officially instituted. For example, on 1 February 1941 a letter was sent to all Commands, Groups and Stations, asking for suitable air-women to be recommended for police duties in the WAAF 'for a trial period'. The notion of 'substitution' was embedded in official policy and practice, to the extent that the RAF established a Substitution Committee to decide where best to employ female labour to 'ease the manpower shortage' (Escott, 1989: 104–05). The one area where substitution was most resisted was in the area of link-trainer instructor. Three WAAF members with pilot certificates were assigned to this post but found that some would-be male pilots objected to being taught by women.

At the start of the war WAAF 'women replaced men in a ratio of three to two, then later one for one in some trades,' and by the end of the Second World War approximately a quarter of a million women served with the WAAF. Official 'post-war calculations suggest that without WAAF support, the RAF would have needed about 150,000 extra men' (Escott, 1989: 96).

Despite the fact that women were deemed 'good substitutes' they were paid less than the men they replaced. WAAF members' pay, for instance, was two-thirds of their equivalent rank in the RAF. It has been suggested that while women endured this discrimination they never inured to it. In the conditions of warfare women grumbled about the situation but let it pass, but 'such treatment was to fuel the civilian equal pay lobby after the war' (Escott, 1989: 169).

Race

At the onset of the Second World War Britain was still very much an imperial nation, with an empire spread out over much of the globe. The character of the war, unrest in many of Britain's colonies and the increased need for recruits provided a challenge to some of the more outmoded attitudes of imperial dominance, but many of the stereotyped images of non-whites continued.

Throughout the 1930s Britain's imperial attitude to its colonial peoples was aptly, if not a little crudely, captured in a series of movies that portrayed the British as a good and civilizing influence in their Empire.[50] Production of such films continued well into the war with films such as *Stanley and Livingstone* (1939), *The Sun Never Sets* (1939), *Safari* (1940) and *Sundown* (1941). However, by 1943, agencies overseeing film production – including the British Ministry of Information (MoI) and the United States Office of War

Information (OWI) – were concerned that 'in the midst of a "people's war" there was no place for films that would send the wrong message about Britain and her war aims,' and Empire films were put on hold for the duration of the rest of the war (Glancy, 1999: 192–93).

This concern did not extend to the redress of domestic racist attitudes, particularly armed forces recruitment. The United States developed a crude system of segregated army units, separating Black and White soldiers into separate army units, which lasted until 1945. This policy of segregation was maintained even when the troops were sent abroad. In the United Kingdom the Cabinet upheld their US allies segregationist practices on British soil.[51] British recruitment practices were little better. From the Land Army, through the armed forces,[52] to the ATS applications from people of colour were rejected (Bousquet and Douglas, 1991; Rowbotham, 1999). Black men were characterized as having a 'negro character,' composed of a 'simple mental outlook' (Major General Dowler, quoted in Bousquet and Douglas, 1991). Black women, on the other hand, hardly rated official comment.

The ATS was one of the few military organizations to change its policy, albeit in a limited way, to allow the recruitment of women of colour. The question of race came to the fore in a number of ways, not least of which was recruitment of women in the Caribbean to serve with the British military mission in the US capitol. Partly for their own deep-rooted discriminatory attitudes and partly to avoid upsetting the racial sensibilities of their US allies, the War Office avoided sending women of colour. As Brigadier Alan Piggot expressed it, the War Office 'are quite prepared to accept any suitable European woman from the Colonies for enrolment in the ATS [but] I must emphasise that this applies to European women only and that we cannot agree to accept coloured women for service in this country' (quoted in Bousquet and Douglas, 1991: 100). In the meantime the War Office was embarrassed when it initially accepted the application of a woman – Mrs L. Curtis from Bermuda – it assumed was white but in fact turned out to be black. Interestingly, when the War Office subsequently attempted to block Curtis' application Lord Knollys, the governor of Bermuda, protested that the rejection would be understood as racial discrimination and cause resentment in the Colony. Eventually, through the 'strategic needs of a deepening war [and] a Colonial Office that argued for black recruitment for its own internal reasons' (Bousquet and Douglas, 1991: 82), the War Office agreed to accept a token force of some 30 black women from the West Indies (including Curtis), who arrived in Britain in October 1943. At BOAC there were not the same pressures for change, and publicly expressed attitudes were more similar to those of the War Office rather than the Colonial Office.

Class

Social class continued to influence organizational practices throughout the war years. The new light industries provided opportunities for working class women while the burgeoning clerical work attracted women from the better-educated working class, and the middle class. Professional opportunities for women, such as they were, were almost exclusively the preserve of middle and upper class women. There was also a social hierarchy in the development of women's organizations. The WRNS maintained an upper class image and consisted exclusively of volunteers, each of whom had to provide three references (Bousquet and Douglas, 1991: 26). Similarly the WAAF and the ATA tended to recruit upper and middle class women of 'excellent character'. The ATS, the civil defence services, the Auxiliary Fire Service and Air Raid Precaution, the Women's Timber Corps and the Land Army became, on the whole, preserves for working class women. In all cases, however, upper-class women tended to dominate the leadership positions.

While working class women in their millions played a role in the war it was the image of upper-middle class womanhood that served as an icon of women's efforts. In popular fiction and the movies this image was exemplified in the character of Mrs Miniver. In women's war service organizations the image was captured in reports on the efforts of women such as Dame Helen Gwynne-Vaughan (ATS), Jane Trefusis-Forbes (WAAF), and Pauline Gower (ATA). At the movies wartime audiences flocked to see Greer Garson as Mrs Miniver while at BOAC women, like Mrs Butler, were singled out for their Miniver-typed qualities.

The gendering of BOAC

In 1939 IAL's gender gestalt included a largely invisible female workforce that constituted around nine per cent of the workforce. These women were absent from the structures of power and authority and did not appear on any organizational charts. Their jobs were literally in the background, away from the eyes and ears of the public. They did not appear in advertisements of annual reports and were virtually absent from the pages of the in-house newsletters and the in-flight magazine.[53] By 1945 the gender gestalt had been disturbed, women not only constituted one third of the workforce but were foregrounded in a number of places, including several areas of public visibility, in several new areas of the workplace, and in the storyline of a number of newsletter items.

A number of major changes occurred to the ongoing sense of organization (Weick, 1995) but of these the formative context of war seems to have been the major influence on the institutional and imaginative arrangements within BOAC. The war led to manpower (sic) shortages that necessitated the recruitment of women to the airline but it was also the character ('people's war') and impact ('total war') of the conflict, recent experiences of world war and the development of a number of mainstream women's organizations that influenced decisions to expand women's work in the airline. Speculatively, in the absence of warfare, the airline may have witnessed an increase in the use of female labour because it became a government employer. In all likelihood this would not have led to the rapid growth of female employment or its diffuseness across the airline. And there is little to believe that the changed leadership would by itself have led to real change in female employment. What it may have achieved, however, was the creation of a new discourse of masculinity built around 'government service' (as opposed to hardnosed business practices) that ultimately provided fertile ground for future female employment. On the other hand, warfare renewed the image of man the warrior, which had particular resonance in a company built from military roots, deepening the idea that certain jobs (i.e., piloting, stewarding and leadership) were masculine.

As in the First World War, women were portrayed as 'substitutes' for men at work but there were two crucial differences at BOAC. First, a large number of women were already occupying 'women's' (clerical) jobs and were not clearly substitutes. Second, with warfare literally on the doorstep, women workers were also seen as home-front activists – Mrs Minivers. Unlike the First World War, women were conscripted into industry and the armed forces (Braybon and Summerfield, 1987), and were portrayed as more directly involved and part of the war. This had consequences for the post-war era.

TCA

The war years saw rapid changes in TCA's top leadership. Phil Johnson, Vice President of Operations, resigned in 1940 to take up the post as president of Boeing: he was succeeded by D. B. Colyer (1940–41), Ted Larson (1941–44), and Bill English (1944–47). Sam Hungerford, President of CNR, retired in 1941 and was replaced by Herb Symington, who held the position until 1947. There is little evidence to suggest that the new leadership had a significant impact on the gendering of TCA during the war years. For one thing Colyer, Larson and English were in place for so little time. For another thing they were all insiders and carried on much in the same vein as Johnson.[54] Like BOAC the war context was a more powerful influence.

TCA hiring practices were similar to BOAC in a number of ways, and by the middle of the war women constituted over one-third of the employees of each airline.[55] But TCA also differed from BOAC in viewing stewarding as a female job (see Chapter 3), resisting the appointment of women managers, being reluctant to hire female clerical staff, presenting an ambiguous view of women's long-term employment, and projecting a narrower image of female sexuality.

Much of TCA's approach to female recruitment is rooted and reflected in its pre-war corporate imagery, focussed on youth, glamour, and sexuality as defining characteristics of TCA's female employees. This was in large part due to the marketing of the stewardess but was extended to other female employees. Marriageability and attractiveness were constants in references to female employees, as in the announcement that '11 more attractive young ladies stepped behind airport counters at the conclusion of the seventh Personnel Training School in Winnipeg' (Trans-Canada Air Lines, 1943b). This is in marked contrast to BOAC that had ignored female employees until the war but them made a conscious effort to explain their presence by focusing on wartime contributions. Here the imagery was informed by the existing masculinity, the 'quiet' feminine presence, and the impact of blitzkrieg warfare. Unlike in Canada where men were portrayed as quite literally 'going off to war,' the bombing of British cities meant that BOAC's female and male employees were both, in a very real sense, 'frontline workers'.

While BOAC made much of women as substitutes, to be returned to the domestic front at the war's end, TCA presented a divided viewpoint. At times it was made clear that women's employment – 'to release men for war service' (Trans-Canada Air Lines, 1942) – was 'limited to the duration of the war' (Trans-Canada Air Lines, 1943a). Yet, on occasion, it was reported that female employees are 'doing an excellent job, and there is every indication that many of them have already won a permanent place in our industry' (Trans-Canada Air Lines, 1943d).

In comparison to BOAC, TCA's initial slowness to employ female clerical staff may be explained, in part, to the respective histories of government practices in the United Kingdom and Canada, which we might expect to have had some influence on the state-owned airlines (DiMaggio and Powell, 1983). While sections of the UK civil service, particularly the Post Office, had pioneered female clerical work (Cohn, 1985; Lowe, 1987), in Canada government departments, including the Post Office and the railway, resisted hiring women (Morgan, 1988).[56] Indeed, while the percentage of female clerks in government employ rose steadily in Britain between 1914 and 1936 (Cohn, 1985: 26) there was a decrease in Canada in 1921 to 1925 to accommodate a flood of veteran's appointments and again in 1932–35 due to the Depression (Morgan, 1986: 7).

Finally, in the midst of the war, TCA introduced stewards to fly military missions over the Atlantic. Like BOAC's employment of stewardesses, this was an experiment but one that would be extended into the post-war era.

Pan Am

For a brief part of 1939 the Pan Am Board stripped Juan Trippe of his control and replaced him with Sonny Whitney, the director with the largest investment in the airline. Trippe 'continued as president and general manager' (Bender and Altschul, 1982: 297), but Whitney, the chairman of the board, was named chief executive officer (CEO). A growing financial concern was laid at the feet of Trippe and his 'eccentric management' style, with an inability to delegate authority and leadership by bulletins and circular rather than 'personal contacts' (Bender and Altschul, 1982: 295). But Whitney proved unable to run the company effectively and, in January 1940, in the absence of any real alternative, the board voted to reinstate Trippe as president and CEO.

The Second World War had an impact on the operations of Pan Am, but wartime preparations and critical disruptions in the services of European competitors added to its fortunes (Josephson, 1944),[57] and the company grew almost fivefold between 1940 and the end of 1941.[58] Nonetheless, it was not until the United States entered the war in December 1941 that the airline began to change its hiring policy on women.[59] Over the next two years the airline experienced a tumultuous growth, employing approximately 88,000 persons (Pan American Airways, 1943a), while losing a large number of existing male employees to the armed forces.[60] To meet the challenge Pan Am was forced to look beyond its traditional labour pool and hire women. Thus, it was, for example, that the 'rapid expansion of the Miami base' (to over 3000 people) was achieved with the recruitment of 449 women, 'who filled many positions formerly handled by men, e.g., chemist, Link trainer operator, baggage clerk, ground station radio operator, map plotter, stockroom and code clerk' (Pan American Airways, 1943b). Unlike BOAC, Pan Am did hire a substantial number of female mechanics that were imaged more in line with 'Rosie the Riveter', the US icon of the female war effort, than Britain's Mrs Miniver.[61] But like BOAC (and TCA) Pan Am made it clear that female recruits to non-traditional (i.e., men's) jobs would only be filling in for the duration of the war. Employees who left to join the armed forces were granted 'a leave of absence,' but this rule was also applied to women as well as men.[62] Nonetheless, in numerous ways the company made it clear that the women were joining a man's world. Thus, when a woman joined one of the teletype sections she was reported as joining 'Fred Gardner's harem in Teletype [...] not to be confused with Fred's Cafeteria harem (you can hardly see Fred for all the pretty girls)' (Pan American Airways).

Yet it wasn't until the end of 1943 that Pan Am felt compelled to employ female flight attendants (see Chapter 3). Citing the exigencies of war,[63] the airline reluctantly recruited existing female staff to take on the role of 'air stewardess,' to fly the company's Nassau, Havana, Mérida (Mexico) routes (Lester, 2000). But the airline quickly adapted to the new reality by switching from a 'quasi-military rule' and imagery to one of selling 'attractiveness,' (Lester, 2000: 41–42). To that end, the 'ideal stewardess [was] blue-eyed, with brown hair, poised and self-possessed, slender, 5 feet 3 inches tall; [weighed] 115 lb, was 23 years old, actively engaged in some particular sport, an expert swimmer, a high school graduate, with business training – and attractive' [ibid.].

While the number of female staff grew apace Ann Archibald remained the sole female in senior management, and, despite the role of the Women's Airforce Service Pilots (WASPS) during the Second World War, female flyers in were not even considered for employment.[64] Under the leadership of Juan Trippe and André Priester, the chief engineer,[65] Pan Am continued to privilege 'men's men' for positions of authority, running the business as an old boys club, with only necessary concessions as wartime conditions dictated.

5

Angels With Dirty Faces: Strategies of 'Normalization' and 'Equity' in the Immediate Post-War Era

[The] suppression of sexuality is one of the first tasks the bureaucracy sets itself [...] Moreover, in modern times, individual organizations inaugurate mechanisms for the control of sexuality at a very early stage in their development [...] Today we are presented with a situation in which human features such as love and comfort are not seen as part of the organizational life [...] Human feelings including sexuality have gradually been repulsed from bureaucratic structures [...] The desexualization of labour, for this is what is entailed, involves the repulsion of many human feelings out of the organization and out of its sight.

(Burrell, 1992: 73–74)

Introduction

A major restructuring of BOAC, sweeping leadership changes and rapid growth dramatically changed the face of Britain's airlines in the post-war era and influenced their gendered character. Restructuring saw the airline divided in two, with the separation of European and transcontinental routes, respectively, to a new British European Airways and a truncated BOAC.[1] In both airlines senior management positions changed hands over the next five years before a pattern of leadership was established. Rapid growth saw BOAC grow from just under 19,000 at the war's end to around 25,000 by 1947. BEA, in the meantime stood at close to 6000 employees, as many as were employed by IAL and BAL combined in 1939 (see Figure 5.1) (British European Airways, 1947a; British Overseas Airways Corporation, 1950a).

As these changes were unfolding, BOAC employees prepared for a return to the pre-war status quo, with management making clear that most wartime female hires would be replaced by returning (male) veterans.[2] At the war's

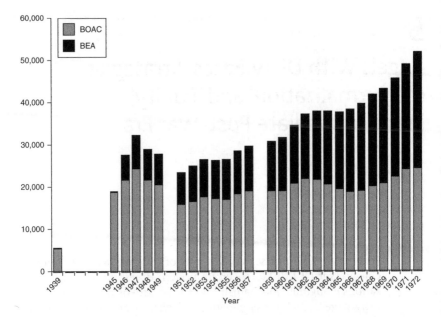

Figure 5.1   Total number of employees in BOAC–BEA, 1939–72

Note: In 1949 BSAA was merged and incorporated into BOAC but the total number of employees in the restructured company was drastically reduced through lay-offs.

end, there was a rapid fall in the percentage of female employees, a continued ban on female pilots, stewards and engineers,[3] and, with the retirement of Pauline Gower, the absence of women on the Board.[4] Nonetheless, there were some important changes in female employment practices. First, women retained many of the areas of work that they had moved into during the war. This was especially the case with a number of routine traffic and counter positions. Second, the actual *number* of female employees continued to rise, from 2000 in 1942 to just under 2900 in 1946: it was rapid growth and a large-scale recruitment of returning servicemen and male recruits, rather than a diminishment of existing female numbers, that reduced the percentage of female employees. Third, a dramatic turnaround in policy led to the recruitment of female flight attendants in BOAC in 1946/47,[5] and this was coupled with an unprecedented equity policy. Fourth, women retained much of the visibility they had acquired during the war, occupying jobs that dealt directly with the public but also receiving increased attention in the pages of the airlines' in-house newsletters. However, there were some distinct differences in the recruitment and imaging of female employees in BOAC and BEA. The percentage of women at BEA was roughly double that at BOAC, yet, if anything, BEA's corporate imagery was more sexualized, focused on female bodily beauty.

Exhibit 5.1 TCA Supervisor, Phil Helms talks with a female passenger, early 1960s

Similar stories were unfolding in TCA and Pan Am, where the respective percentage of female employees fell dramatically at the end of the war,[6] as women were replaced by returning veterans. Unlike BOAC, however, the actual number of female employees in TCA and Pan Am also fell.[7] Piloting and engineering remained male preserves,[8] and for several years women were not to be found above the ranks of supervisor (see Exhibit 5.1). However, the role of stewarding was changing in both airlines. TCA hired stewards and Pan Am (like BOAC and BEA) normalized the hiring of stewardesses.

At this juncture: Inside BOAC/BEA (1945–50)

BOAC began peacetime operations with an enlarged number of female employees many in non-traditional female jobs, including customer-contact positions. For the next few years those in charge of the airline's recruitment, training and corporate communications struggled to make sense of the changed reality.

Female employment

In July 1945 the great majority of BOAC's female employees were located in the United Kingdom, where almost three-quarters worked at the Head Office and constituted almost 50 per cent of the staff. A further 21 per cent worked

Table 5.1 Number of males and females employed in the divisions and departments of BOAC, 31 July 1945

Divisions	Non-departmental		Medical		Publicity and liaison		Training		Admin		Commercial — Traffic		Catering		Technical — Engineering		Operations		Finance and accounts		Total	
	M	F	M	F	M	F	M	F	M	F	M	F	M	F	M	F	M	F	M	F	M	F
Head office	64	64	3	7	12	6	6	4	199	237	149	78	62	35	26	24	51	99	30	39	602	593
Regions:																						
European	147	30	14	14	0	0	33	0	722	384	156	14	108	163	2128	238	910	126	135	185	4353	1154
(i) UK																						
(ii) Overseas	67	0	1	0	0	0	0	0	686	0	220	0	505	0	278	0	77	0	80	0	1914	0
India and Burma	127	10	2	1	0	0	3	1	1029	17	85	1	771	5	402	0	216	9	70	7	2702	50
Middle East	304	46	4	0	0	0	5	1	1362	44	494	42	328	9	1783	11	287	43	119	22	4684	217
South Africa	60	15	2	0	0	0	5	1	351	34	131	17	127	28	581	18	126	28	46	29	1429	147
West Atlantic	39	13	0	3	0	0	2	1	179	28	30	16	59	58	180	30	170	46	18	38	677	233
Personnel Awaiting Posting	8	0	0	0	0	0	0	0	5	0	13	0	5	0	14	0	17	0	1	0	63	0
Total	816	178	26	25	12	6	49	6	4533	744	1278	168	1965	275	5392	321	1854	351	499	320	16424	2394

Source: Adapted from the BOAC Handbook, 1945.

Table 5.2 Number of males and females employed in the divisions and departments of BOAC, 30 April 1946

Divisions	Non-departmental		Medical		Publicity and liaison		Training		Admin		Commercial				Technical				Finance and accounts		Total	
											Traffic		Catering		Engineering		Operations					
	M	F	M	F	M	F	M	F	M	F	M	F	M	F	M	F	M	F	M	F	M	F
Head office	64	64	3	7	12	6	6	4	199	237	149	78	62	35	26	24	51	99	30	39	602	593
Head Office	112	81	7	12	16	11	7	6	273	323	324	160	164	38	51	34	47	130	59	66	1060	861
European Regions (i)UK	104	38	14	15	0	0	31	0	976	335	254	64	240	212	3214	292	1182	169	254	241	6269	1366
(ii)Overseas	91	0	2	0	0	0	1	0	624	0	329	0	527	0	286	0	51	0	100	0	2011	0
India and Burma	165	11	0	1	1	0	0	0	1364	24	79	3	740	5	458	2	263	9	88	12	3158	67
Middle East	163	22	8	2	0	0	9	1	1413	69	591	49	306	4	1292	16	269	42	126	23	4177	228
South Africa	79	15	1	0	0	0	5	0	357	26	146	19	81	4	612	14	121	21	71	34	1473	133
West Atlantic	30	11	1	2	0	0	5	2	143	36	62	21	46	16	154	17	194	35	28	45	663	185
Personal Awaiting Posting	5	0	0	0	0	0	0	0	8	0	15	0	3	0	72	0	35	0	0	0	138	0
Total	749	178	33	32	17	11	58	9	5158	813	1800	316	2107	279	6139	375	2162	406	726	421	18949	2840

Source: Adapted from the BOAC HandBook, Part II Current, June 1946.

at the UK-based offices and counters of the European region (see Table 5.1). Outside of the United Kingdom there were sharp regional differences in the airline's employment of female employees. This ranged from the West Atlantic (i.e., Canada and the US) and South African regions, where women constituted 25 per cent and 9 per cent of the respective staffs, through to the India and Burma, and Middle East regions, where female employees constituted between two per cent to four per cent of the respective workforces.

By the end of June 1946, the employment landscape remained fairly stable for female employees (see Table 5.2).[9] The great majority of women were employed in clerical work. The largest concentrations of female labour were in Administration (29% of all female employees), Operations (14%), Finance and Accounts (15%) and Engineering (13%). In three areas women constituted a significant presence, including Medical (approx. 50%), Publicity and Liaison (39%), and Finance and Accounting (37%). The lowest concentration was in Engineering where women constituted less than six per cent of employees. In all other departments women constituted between ten per cent and eighteen per cent of all employees (see Table 5.1).[10]

Betty Paige – one woman's story[11]

Betty Paige was serving in the WAAF[12] at the end of the Second World War and, wanting to 'keep going with aircraft', applied to BOAC for a job. She was initially rejected – her application addressed to 'Mr. Paige' – but her brother, an RAF pilot, 'had a word with the Personnel Director' and within a week she was called for interview, where she was 'confronted by quite a large board of people'. Asked whether she could type or do various other clerical tasks she answered 'no' and was surprised when, a week later, they offered her the job.[13] Hoping to be employed in a more 'glamorous' uniformed job, Paige ended up in a 'very monotonous job', in a 'dreary room' doing telephone reservations. She was told that she was placed in reservations because it was like the job she was doing in the war. Yet 'it was absolutely nothing like' her exciting wartime work that involved accurate plotting of aircraft that meant life and death to the pilots involved.[14]

Paige worked as part of a group of six men and women in an office 'doing the overseas bookings', but while the women stayed put the men rose through the ranks, including an ex-wing commander who 'soon sailed up into greater heights' of the airline: according to Paige, in 'those days it was considered, quite rightly, [that men] had to have the jobs – they had families and so on. That's the way it was'. Paige continued in reservations until 1949 and then worked on the counter at BOAC's Regent Street office with five other uniformed staff.

Although she didn't enjoy the work she kept going because she needed a job and had begun to make friends. Sustained by the 'thought there were better things around the corner, that always something better would happen', Paige eventually became 'truly entrenched' in the job and knowing 'jolly well that [she] couldn't leave it'. She was 'hooked' and felt that she 'just wasn't trained to do anything'.

In the early 1950s Paige became engaged to a BOAC sales representative and followed him when he was sent to the company's Singapore office. They were married in Singapore six months later. Like many women she left the airline's employ once she was married, but felt that she was still contributing to BOAC by serving as a hostess for her husband, 'entertaining anybody who came along, from the visiting farmer to various airline managers coming out from England; shopping for various social events; being present at all the occasions; and organizing the inevitable cocktail parties'. Early in 1954 her husband was killed in the first ever crash of a jetliner, the Comet, so Paige (now Mrs Hill) returned to England and resumed her employment with BOAC, where she asked for a job in sales. Informed that sales was not a job for women,[15] she returned to 'good old Reservations' – a job she did for the next seven years.

Not only sales work was closed to women, there were very few opportunities for women in British airlines at this time. The highest placed female at this time was the Customer Relations Manager and below that there were female duty officers in the traffic department. For Hill, this was something that 'you accepted. You didn't really anticipate anything. You were jolly lucky to have a job'.

Betty Paige's story is interesting in a number of ways. To begin with her self-perception as a woman is influenced by post-war discourse on the gendered status of work, particularly notions of skill and technical knowledge. At several points Paige characterizes herself as being unqualified to do much, despite the fact that she was involved in ground control during the war. To a certain extent, she appears to accept the notion that job experience is something that only a man has. Her notion of self is also influenced by a post-war stress on the importance of the male as breadwinner, and the need for female employees to take a back seat to returning servicemen. But she also seems to recognize, however implicitly, that notions of men and women were rooted 'in the times', that were social constructions. We see this in several of Paige's comments about the status of female employees at BOAC over time. For example, she calls the company's argument against the hiring of female sales staff as 'trifle theories', arguing that she 'was born too early and, of course, going in at a time when jobs were at a premium and there obviously weren't going to be the opportunities for promotion because there were many men to take the jobs so couldn't entirely blame management for that'. BOAC 'thought that women would get married and push off so what's the use of giving them a promotion'.

Employment rules and piloting

Despite the fact that women had performed valiantly as pilots with the ATA, and as stewards on the UK–Portugal route during the war, BOAC prepared for a return to the status quo at the war's end. The company's written policy in 1945 simply stated that, 'recruitment for aircrew is mainly from two sources: (i) R.A.F. on secondment, and (ii) civilian ex-R.A.F., A.T.A., or 45 group'[16] (British Overseas Airways Corporation, 1945a). Co-pilots and second officers were limited to 'a maximum age for engagement of 25', with 800 solo hours of flying 'including 250 hours on representative types' of aircraft. Senior captains were required to have '3000 hours in command of transport aircraft in circumstances deemed comparable to BOAC service' (British Overseas Airways Corporation, 1945a). These requirements excluded all but a few women who had served with the ATA, and recruiters made it quite clear that piloting was strictly limited to men. This policy was continued in BEA. For example, when a former ATA pilot applied for a piloting job with BEA she put her initials, rather than her full name, on the application form. Her resume was impressive and she had the requisite skills and flying hours. Not realizing that the application was from a woman, she was accepted subject to a successful medical examination. When she arrived for the medical exam the male doctor informed her that he was 'not doing stewardesses today'. When he found out that she had arrived for the pilot's medical he refused to deal with her. She later received a terse letter from BEA., stating that 'it is not the policy of the company to employ women as pilots'. (Simons, 1993: 112). A similar story is told of BEA's rejection of a woman 'with six years' of experience of flying fare-paying passengers with other airlines' (May, 1971: 94). BEA's response was that, 'We don't employ girl pilots because we don't think they do the job as well as men and many people would not be prepared to get on a plane if they knew a woman was at the controls. We know of no big international airline which employs women on any scale' (quoted in May, 1971: 95).

Equity and the female steward

Following the Second World War BOAC recruited a large number of young men for training as the next generation of air stewards and BEA prepared to follow suit. But changes in the operating environment encouraged the airlines to consider hiring stewardesses, at least on the North American route (Bray, 1975: 120).

A new generation of faster, long-range airlines was now available (thanks to the wartime development of long-range bombers) and made the North Atlantic routes both possible and commercially viable. In Britain businessmen (sic) replaced the upper-class elite as the majority passenger, and in North America a new generation of demobilized, air-minded soldiers became an important part of the airline market. Passenger numbers had grown rapidly since the pre-war days and international air travel was very competitive.[17] There had also been a major change in airline recruitment policies over the years, with flight attending becoming a female occupation in a number of the world's airlines, including BOAC's closest competitor on the Atlantic, Pan Am.[18]

In 1946, under some pressure from its New York sales office and competition with Pan Am, BOAC decided to employ a group of female flight attendants on its North Atlantic route on 'an experimental basis' (Edwards and Edwards, 1990; Wright, 1985). The airline was initially reluctant to hire stewardesses due to concerns of impropriety, worrying that the British public would be appalled at the idea of glamorous young women flying to faraway places without a chaperone. To overcome these concerns the airline played down any hint of glamour or sexuality, stressing instead the exacting nature of the work involved.

The women were to be British, 'preferably light-weight,' and aged between 23 to 30 years (Edwards and Edwards, 1990: 59). It was stressed that 'the girls must have a good education, poise and tact. Glamour girls are definitely not required, but patience, a pleasant charming manner are great assets. Training in simple cookery and the service of meals is given to all candidates' (BOAC, quoted in Wright, 1985: 6). The new hires were called 'stewardesses'[19] and dressed in a uniform similar to that worn by male stewards.[20] Both male and female stewards wore a collar and tie, and a dark blue uniform. The main difference was that the female uniform included a skirt rather than trousers (see Exhibit 5.2). To avoid a 'tarty' appearance, the uniform hem lengths of stewardesses were strictly controlled and kept to well below the knee close to ankle-length. Blouses had an extra long shirttail to tuck into skirts so that

Exhibit 5.2 BOAC Stewardess uniform, late 1940s

when stewardess had to bend for any reason she wouldn't expose 'any entic-ing flesh' (Wright, 1985: 7–8). Stewardesses were sent on a ten-week training course at the airline's Catering Training School, where they learnt the 'duties required of them as waitresses and elementary first aid'.

An apparent equity between male and female flight attendants was rein-forced in a number of ways. A newsletter article on 'the art of the steward', for example, refers to the ten-week course at the Aldermaston Training School where 'pupil steward and stewardesses learn the practice and theory of the catering art [...], elementary medical training [...], 'catering documen-tation' and 'voyage procedure'' (British Overseas Airways Corporation, 1947b). And, in a rare mention of female employees, the 1949 BOAC Annual Report recorded that 'the high standard of service given by BOAC stewards and stewardesses was favourably commented on by many passengers' and warned that 'Any sense of unfairness or instability engendered among the men and women employed by BOAC would inevitably react to the chronic disadvantage of the Corporation in efficiency' (British Overseas Airways Corporation, 1949b).

BOAC continued to recruit large numbers of stewardesses over the next 15 years, in part to equal the number of stewards and in part to keep up with the large turnover generated by a company rule requiring stewardesses to retire if they married.[21] It also continued to employ a large number of stewards and by 1960 was recruiting almost equal numbers of male and female flight attendants.[22]

The newly formed BEA also wrestled with the idea of employing female flight attendants, especially in light of BOAC's change of policy. Ironically, Railway Air Service (RAS), that was taken over by BEA, introduced 'stew-ardesses' around the same time as BOAC,[23] but BEA's senior management 'thought of substituting the steward, boy instead of girl' before deciding to hire stewardesses (British European Airways, 1947d). They reasoned that the 'steward is another hard worker, with lots of training and experience, as well, usually, as an RAF background, but there's no doubt that his lady colleague has stolen the market for the time being. So we're keeping him in cold stor-age' (British European Airways, 1947d).

BEA valued RAF-experience but was willing to give in to market pressures. What is interesting is that, by inference, they were willing to admit that female flight attendants were equally hard working although, presumably, lacking in training and experience. Having made the decision to hire female 'stewards' BEA recruited women between 25 and 30 years old, maximum 5 feet 8 inches tall and eight-and-a-half stone (119 lbs) in weight, with good English and one other European language, and past experience of personal service, particularly nursing (Wright, 1985: 5). Nonetheless, like BOAC, the airline was keen to dissociate the image of its new flight attendants from any notion of glamour. The women were called 'stewards' and, as with BOAC stewardesses, were dressed in a military-style uniform similar to that of male

Exhibit 5.3 BEA female stewards' uniforms, 1946–48

stewards; the men wore a naval officer-style hat and the women wore a tri-corn hat similar to that worn by WRNS (see Exhibit 5.3). Publicity releases stressed that the female steward was a hard working member of the flight crew (British European Airways, 1947d). The policy was explained to employees through the *BEA Magazine* in an article with the ironically misogynous title, 'We had to kill the stewardess':

> We launched the slogan 'Glamour is Out'; we even de-sexed her by knocking the -ess off her title. Picture Post did us proud over the whole thing, showing the intelligence and hard work that goes into making a good stewardess: foreign languages and training in first aid and navigation, apart from the expected ability to serve hot coffee and administer air-sickness pills.

The 'equal work' focus also appeared in BEA's discussion of steward selection:

> We had twenty-eight vacancies this year and wanted a predominantly female recruitment. Our policy is 'half male, half female' but the female element was below strength [...] In the past we have carried only one steward on each aircraft. Our girls were the first of any airline [...] to earn as much as men – they did the same job, so they were paid the same money. Periodically, we ran polls to see which the public preferred. The last of these showed that 55 per cent were in favour of men and 45 per cent for girls.

Table 5.3   BEA flight attendants, 1952–56

Year	Total number of flight attendants	Men	Women
1952	245	107(44%)	138(56%)
1953	256	106(41.5%)	150(58.5%)
1954	249	108(43.5%)	141(56.5%)
1955	273	114(42%)	159(58%)
1956	371	147(40%)	224(60%)

> Policy for the new aircraft – which will require two stewards – is therefore clear; one man and one girl – to please, we hope, everyone.
>
> (Gibbons, 1950)

BEA also recruited a large number of female stewards to equal the number of male stewards, and this target was met by 1950 and exceeded over the next few years (see Table 5.3).[24]

Becoming a stewardess

At British South American Airways (BSAA) one of the early recruits was Priscilla Vinyals, who became a stewardess in March 1947. BEA's first female steward was Helen Wigmore who had started as a secretary at BOAC's Head Office during the war and had been awarded a certificate of commendation for her wartime efforts. BOAC's new stewardesses included Viva Barker, Janet Huntley, Mary Cowper and Felicity Farquharson. Barker had been one of the six stewardesses employed by the Corporation during the war. Huntley was the first of the new hires to be employed – serving on the airline's Constellation flight from London to New York on 28 November 1946. Cowper had been with the government Code and Cypher School during the war, then joined the WRNS and served as a radio mechanic with the Fleet Air Arm before joining BOAC in September of 1946. Farquharson joined BOAC as a traffic clerk in 1945 before becoming a stewardess the following year.

By 1948 there were stewardesses on many of BEA's European routes and BOAC's North American routes and the anti-glamour attitude was still in evidence when BOAC recruited women as stewardesses for its flying boat services to Africa and Asia. Betty Chapel joined the airline at this time and from the beginning found it to be 'very much a male orientated world'.[25] To her mind, BOAC had always used stewards on its flying boats but 'they thought they'd try having stewardesses because it gives a little confidence to the passengers seeing a woman around [...] We were all rather guinea pigs'. Chapel was one of eighty women called for interview on the same day, in 1948, at BOAC's London Headquarters. They were kept waiting in 'two or three big rooms, [with] everyone looking very, very, glamorous'. Nonetheless, Chapel felt that her work experience gave her an edge over the other female candidates:

> 'I'd been a stewardess on a ship so I think that sort of helped a little bit because they knew that you wouldn't be all glamorous. They knew that if anyone was ill or sick, or things went wrong – so often they did – you would be able to cope and not put [up] your hands in horror and say, 'whatever shall I do'. You've just got to get on with it'.

Candidates were called into the interviewing room alphabetically, where they faced a barrage of questions from a Selection Board, composed of ten 'rather somber men' and two women, who sat behind a huge table. For Chapel it was 'most alarming, terrible, intimidating [...] Then they fired questions at you, each one, you know, like a firing range, making you feel smaller, and smaller, and smaller. The women were quite pleasant [though] I got more and more nervous'.

Despite trepidation, Chapel did well. That day, she was called back for a second interview where she was told that she 'might be good at being a stewardess but didn't radiate a great deal of confidence'. She responded, saying that

> 'if you were in my position sitting here [having had a number of people firing questions at you] you'd feel [a lack of confidence]. They thought that was a great joke. They said, "right, you're in".' Chapel was one of a small group of women who were hired, all looking 'reasonably neatish and tidyish; not too going to Ascot sort of thing'.

Once accepted, Chapel and her cohorts discovered other aspects of the 'male orientated' culture of BOAC. To begin with, Chapel felt that her acceptance letter was 'rude', by saying such things as 'you will be subject to this. You will do this. You will do the other'. It was also evident that the company was not used to employing women in certain capacities: 'All our contracts, you know, had to be crossed out' with 'he' replaced by 'she' throughout. Uncertainty over the employment of female stewards also meant that the new recruits were given contracts that were renewed annually. As for the job title, 'there was always a little controversy. The Pan Am girls, and the glamour girls on other airlines, were hostesses but we were actually stewardesses and don't you forget it'[26].

Equity: Myth and reality

Despite a very public emphasis on equity the reality was far from the projected idea. For one thing the female uniform, although modified later, was modelled on that of the male steward. Even the name (steward or stewardess) referenced the male character of the job. Initially, male and female stewards received the same training but on BOAC flights the stewardess was not allowed in the galley or on the flight deck; she was seen as an assistant to the male steward, helping the sick and feeding babies.

At BEA the female steward 'seemed more like a housekeeper in the air – tending to all the housekeeping arrangements for the journey, washing up, and ensuring that crockery is stowed away. During the flight she would change into a white mess jacket, prepare and serve a light meal' (Wright, 1985: 6–7).

Despite the gap between myth and reality the myth had been woven. BOAC and BEA, for the first time in a long line of predecessors, had adopted a recruitment policy with attendant publicity that gave the appearance, and even a measure, of equity to males and females doing the same work.

Power and authority

In the immediate post-war era Florence (now Lady) Henderson was the only woman in a management position.[27] When she retired in 1947 a male colleague replaced her and, with Pauline Gower's retirement, there were also no women on the Board.[28]

Male dominance also extended to the various clubs that made up the social life of the airlines, with many existing groups reverting to male leadership and a number of male-only groups coming into existence.[29] For example, in 1945 the British Airways (UK Staff) Friendly Society was one of several clubs that went from female to male leadership, and the newly formed Staff Association saw the election of a male 'chairman' and an all-male committee.[30] Nonetheless, women continued to take part in numerous committees including the Bristol dance committee, the Bristol Brains Trust, the Hurn Badminton Club, the BOAC Speedbird Club, the Hythe Sports Club and various other committees.[31]

Leadership

The men who headed up BOAC and BEA brought new and varied leadership to the airlines, with different impacts on notions of masculinity and femininity.

BOAC

Between 1945 and 1950 three men headed BOAC – Lord Knollys (1943–47), Sir Harold Hartley (1947–49) and Sir Miles Thomas (1949–56) – who, along with other company leaders,[32] brought with them military, especially air force, experiences. Hartley, a former Brigadier General, was an air force observer during the First World War. Sir Miles Thomas and Lord Knollys were ex-RFC/RAF pilots.

Nick Georgiades, who later became Head of Human Resources for BA, remembers the period as a time when the airline had its pick of the best wartime pilots, navigators and flight engineers: 'The attitudes were military. "Don't do as I do. Do as I say". It was a case of "Biggles joins BOAC" '. (quoted in Hampden-Turner, 1990: 84–85). Military references permeated the organization. A number of job titles, for example, ended in the word 'officer' and the chief executive was referred to as CX. All canteen facilities were referred to as the 'mess', including the Senior Manager's Mess on the fourth floor of the airline's Head Quarters (Smallpiece, 1980: 36). When Sir Miles Thomas was appointed to BOAC in 1949 he used his RFC experiences to 'establish common ground' between himself and the Minister of Aviation, Lord Pakenham (Thomas, 1964: 269). The same air force experience helped to establish a bond between Thomas and Sir Basil Smallpiece who succeeded him as Chair of BOAC. When Smallpiece joined BOAC in 1950 he 'took an immediate liking to Miles Thomas, with his Royal Flying Corps tie' (Smallpiece, 1980: 24).

The air force culture was very much in evidence when Prinny Sherwin joined BOAC in September of 1946. She was interviewed 'in a disused R.A.F. caravan', along with a 'motley crew [...] all newly back from the forces'. Her unit comprised of 'ex-RAF, Navy, Fleet Air Arm, WRNS, WAAF and one sole Marine'. Sherwin had been in the WRNS where she had spent two-and-a-half years as an Air Mechanic with the Fleet Air Arm. At the war's end she applied to work at BOAC in the Traffic Passenger Service. She began work as a shift leader in load control but on 'a lower pay scale than the males of the shift'.

Military attitudes were evident in workplace practices, leading trade union officials to complain that airlines should 'promote amongst their minor officials an active desire to consult with workers' representatives', noting that 'at present the attitude of such officers is sometimes adversely affected by previous military experience' (Trades Union Congress, 1949: 217).

Despite the strong military presence the post-war leadership of BOAC differed somewhat from that in commercial airlines following the First World War. If nothing else it was tempered by different experiences that gave the airline a hybrid feel of part military, part business, part government agency. The men who ran the Corporation during this period brought together a range of experiences from the military, government,[33] the trade unions,[34] civil aviation and private industry.[35]

At a time when the government of the day was faced with economic difficulties the airline's leadership emphasized efficiencies and productivity. Between 1945 and 1950 the state-owned airlines, run for the most part by businessmen, entered into a discourse of bureaucratization, efficiency and professionalism. When BOAC recorded a loss of £8 million for the fiscal year of 1946–47 the press were quick to round on the company's 'Parkinsonian' leadership (Thomas, 1964: 276). When a House of Commons Select Committee was established to examine the administration of Civil Aviation Lord Knollys took this as a reflection of his leadership and promptly resigned effective 30 June 1947.

On 1 July 1947 Sir Harold Hartley, 'a man of ripe experience in transport',[36] took over as Chairman of BOAC and 'inherited a financial disaster' (Penrose, 1980b: 153). Placing the airline on a 'sound financial footing' (ibid.), Hartley began a series of cost-saving exercises, including extensive staff cuts, which saw an immediate drop of just under 11 per cent in employees numbers, and a further 5.5 per cent the following year (see Figure 5.1).

Accounting practices reflected the drive for greater efficiency, by linking *individual* performance to profitability. Prior to 1947 the main gauge of 'output' was a formula called 'capacity ton mileage' (c.t.m.), which measured the number of aircraft operated and the number of hours flown by each. This measurement was not directly linked to any assessment of profitability and only indirectly linked performance to the efforts of employees *as a whole*. For example, the annual report for the fiscal year 1945–46 reports c.t.m. as increasing by 26 per cent and the staff are 'given great credit [...] for the way in which they have overcome the considerable difficulties encountered during the year' (British Overseas Airways Corporation, 1946d).

In the post-war era the airline began to collect data on 'load ton miles' (the load actually carried for each ton mile), 'load factor' (the ratio of the load carried to capacity offered), 'passenger miles' (the total number of passengers multiplied by the number of miles they travel), 'service aircraft miles' (the total amount of revenue-earning mileage flown) and 'net route mileage' (the total mileage of all routes, counting once only stages common to more than one route). Most of these statistics link performance to employees in a very general way. In 1946 the airline began to link outcomes (e.g., sales, revenues, etc.) to the average *individual* performance of employees, by dividing the c.t.m. by the total number of staff. In 1947 it was able, for the first time, to argue that the 'Corporation as a whole produced 2,422 capacity ton miles per employee, while the Atlantic Division with a staff of 1,493, equipped with fourteen aircraft [...] operating with high utilisation from well-equipped bases at Dorval and Baltimore, produced 6,493 capacity ton miles per employee' (British Overseas Airways Corporation, 1947c: 16).

This new formula was prominent in subsequent reports. By 1948 it was now stated that 'the comparison of the capacity ton miles produced per employee gives a good indication of improving administrative economy within the Corporation' (British Overseas Airways Corporation, 1948c: 16). The Annual Report of that year also included a diagram linking 'the progressive decrease in numbers of staff [with] the increasing number of capacity ton miles per month' (ibid.). Sir Harold Hartley used the new accounting procedure to argue that, 'progress has been made during the year in securing great efficiency and economy' (British Overseas Airways Corporation, 1948c: 30).

Hartley retired from BOAC in 1949 after 15 years in the airline business – 13 years with RAS, a few months as head of BEA and two years with BOAC. But his tenure had been marked by a reluctance to hire female employees. As the head of RAS he had been slow to employ female labour – hiring female traffic assistants in 1944, three years after BOAC (Stroud, 1987: 75–76). As BEA's first 'chairman', he reluctantly presided over the employment of female flight attendants, being concerned about how it would look to the public. Some of Hartley's concerns about public perceptions are perhaps explained by the fact that 'he had a complete phobia for the published word' and shunned publicity (Thomas, 1964: 264).[37]

Hartley's successor, Sir Miles Thomas, brought to BOAC his vision of a commercial venture.[38] He 'had a highly developed commercial sense [and] did not tolerate ineffectiveness, which is why some people did not get on with him' (Smallpiece, 1980: 30). One of his ambitions was to end the airline's reliance on Government financial support as soon as possible (Smallpiece, 1980: 31). Through a series of measures, including re-organization and lay-offs, Thomas encouraged a strong discourse of 'commercialism' within the airline. He impressed on everyone that although the airline was state-owned the only way employees could keep their jobs 'was by making the Corporation a commercially viable and profit-making enterprise' (Thomas, 1964: 274). He stepped up the process of cuts initiated by his predecessor, seeing them as a necessary process of lopping 'several extraneous branches from the overburdened vine' (Thomas, 1964: 276).[39] In the next two years Thomas cut the staff numbers from 20, 655 to 16, 000, including 84 executives that he personally sacked.[40] He also cut the directors' salaries in half, and extricated the Corporation from a number of non-airline ventures, including, for example, a plastic glasses production concern.

As part of his vision of management, Thomas created an 'economical and well-balanced structure' built around 'the principle of clear-cut objectives and more precise definition of duties [to be] followed' (quoted in Penrose, 1980b: 165). To this end, he adopted a process of close consultation with the leaders of the 17 unions representing members throughout BOAC;[41] initiated a philosophy of 'management by walking around', feeling that one of the problems with British management was that they were too far removed from the productive process; made certain Directors of the Board were responsible for designated areas of the airline's business;[42] closed the gap between aircrews (the *corps d'elite*) and the administrative executive' (Thomas, 1964: 280); placed executive control of operational and commercial activities in the hand of a small group of leaders;[43] and moved senior executive offices closer to the shop floor, in a new hangar block at London Airport, to allow senior management to be able to just walk out of their offices to see what was being done.[44]

Thomas's ethos of 'commercial realism' was much in evidence when Basil Smallpiece joined BOAC in 1950. To Smallpiece, one of Thomas's 'great contributions to the building up of BOAC was that he gave us a united sense of purpose and made us into a team. He also gave BOAC back a healthy sense of commercial purpose and profit justification, which had been lost during the war years' (Smallpiece, 1980: 36).

Gender and the commercial ethos

In many ways the commercial ethos lent itself to more ambiguous, paradoxical constructions of gender. Although piloting, engineering and managing continued to be associated with masculinity, the masculine reference points had changed. Warfare had renewed the associations of piloting and the military but was mediated through a series of bureaucratic and professional rules that began in the late 1920s, which were developed through the air force and were stressed in the post-war BOAC. Managing was becoming detached from qualities of military leadership and the control of men (sic), and more associated with the office and the implementation of rules and regulations.[45] The gendered character of engineering, with its associations of skill and masculinity, remained relatively unchanged.[46]

Stewarding underwent the most gendered change with the recruitment of women. Unlike piloting and engineering, with their respective masculine reference points in danger and skill, stewarding 'was influenced by institutional practices rather than broad social practices and, as such, had a far weaker link to established' notions of masculinity (Mills, 1998:185). The image of the steward continued to draw on male reference points (e.g., the uniform, the title) but the qualities associated with the job, such as attentiveness and service, were readily transferable to women. In the recruitment of stewardesses the company 'insisted on service before sex', stressing that being 'a stewardess on BOAC is very hard work indeed' (Thomas, 1964: 284–85). In the stewardess Thomas sought 'competence, not glamour'; loudly praising 'the way in which [...] those girls helped to bring up the operating prestige of British airlines' (Thomas, 1964: 284–85).

The emphasis on efficiency and profitability had a paradoxical impact on the rest of the employees. On the one hand, people were increasingly judged on what they produced rather than their assumed biological capabilities. In the past, anything not deemed operational was lumped together as 'administration' and considered dead weight. Thomas changed that by insisting that clerical staffs be productive (Smallpiece, 1980: 36). Thus, female (as well as male) staff was judged in terms of efficiency, hard work and competence – terms previously not used in characterizing the work of female employees.[47]

On the other hand, notions of efficiency and productivity were mainly associated with the male-dominated operational side of the airline business and much less so with the female-dominated administrative side of the Corporation. Thus, arguably, a stress on efficiency and productivity tended to privilege masculinity. Also the divide between operational and administrative staff had become ghettoized. There was now a permanent place for female employees but that place was generally in an office and confined to a limited range of administrative support roles. In the process women's work was linked to feminine-associated characteristics, and served to inform differing notions of job efficiency. Miles Thomas, for example, draws on RAF experiences when describing the characteristics of a good aircrew as 'dogged dependability'. On the other hand, he references gender when describing the efficient secretary as a woman with 'poise, interest, experience, a good memory and, above all, patience,' and the good stewardess as a 'girl' who has a high standard of education, knows something about nursing, has one language apart from English, is attractive in appearance, but above all is psychologically stable and physically fit (Thomas, 1964).[48]

British European Airways

The leadership of BEA was similar to BOAC and included a mixture of businessmen, RAF-leaders and government appointees. Indeed, several men played key roles on both Boards, including Sir Harold Hartley, Gerard d'Erlanger and Lord Douglas. d'Erlanger took over from Hartley in 1947 but resigned two years later over a conflict with the government and was replaced with Douglas who served as BEA's 'Chairman' for the next 15 years.

As at BOAC, military experience made a strong impression on the emerging culture of BEA, with many at the top, including d'Erlanger and Douglas, bringing air force and wartime flying experiences to the job.[49] Indeed, air force connections ran deep. During the Second World War the European Division of BOAC, which formed the basis of BEA, was operated by 100 Wing, 46 Group of the RAF. BEA's base of operations was at Northolt, the former RAF aerodrome. These military experiences contributed to an air force ethos where comfort levels were judged by the number of aircraft on the ground rather than in the air.[50]

BEA's leadership also stressed efficiency and productivity but tempered this with appeals to public service and metaphors of family. Hartley set the tone in a Christmas message to the staff, in which he stated, 'I don't like the word "organization". It sounds mechanical and soulless, and I want BEA to be a living organism. I want it to have the sensitive co-ordination of the parts of the living body' (quoted in May, 1971: 146). His successors, d'Erlanger and Douglas, rooted notions of efficiency in a discourse of public and national service, marking it out from BOAC's ethos of commercialism. d'Erlanger 'never believed that it was the Corporation's job to make profits. The Corporation was there to support the British aircraft industry and to develop routes around the world' (quoted in Sampson, 1984: 88). When Douglas took over from d'Erlanger his message to the staff was that BEA needed to be run 'as economically as possible consistent with efficiency' (British European Airways, 1949c) and that 'stringent economy and hard work must be our watchword' (British European Airways, 1949b). As a socialist Douglas saw economy and efficiency as means to serve the public interest better.

The biggest challenge faced by the leadership was to develop a cohesive sense of organization out of disparate factors. The core to the new company was staff from BOAC's European Division,[51] but they were joined by a large number of employees from RAS and nine other smaller airlines (see Figure 1.1) as well as a large number of new recruits. This contributed to a mishmash of planes, routes, personnel and cultural values. Much of the first four years was taken up with dealing with the different elements of the new company and the associated problems. The take-overs themselves and the way they were handled led to anger and sadness among many of the staffs of

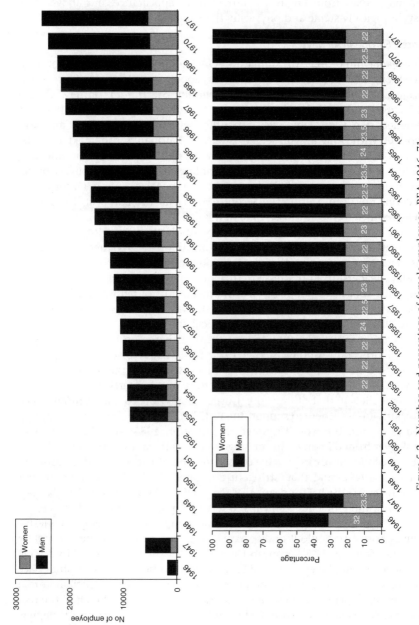

Figure 5.2 Number and percentage of female employees, BEA 1946–71

the airlines involved,[52] and rapid growth meant that three-quarters of all staff consisted of people that did not have any previous experience of civil airline work,[53] presenting a considerable problem for management to weld them into 'a proficient unit' (British European Airways, 1947a).

From the beginning, women constituted around a quarter of BEA's workforce and stabilized at that level for the rest of its existence (see Figure 5.2).[54] This may have influenced the normalization of female labour, as women – most of them experienced in airline work – were a large part of the organization at its inception.

However, the containment of female labour to a narrow range of jobs needs some explaining.[55] The answer may lie in a combination of the military ethos; job loss among a number of senior men and those from the smaller airlines; the problems of welding together disparate airlines; and the absence of established leadership at the top who were able and willing to introduce radical changes. Of note, however, is that the percentage of female employees remained stable even during period of deep cuts.

Organizational discourse and imagery

The imaging of men and women in the corporate documents of BOAC and BEA drew on a number of dominant discourses, including commercialization (BOAC), organization building (BEA) and wartime experience. The military theme crisscrossed both airlines, as did an ambiguous discourse of feminine beauty and desexualization.

At both airlines military experience was privileged in the pages of the respective newsletters. Warfare and masculinity were strongly linked and influenced recruitment practices. In the first annual report of the newly established BEA, for example, much was made of the fact that almost 70 per cent of the staff had been recruited from the services:[56] the remaining third, the great majority of whom were women, were described as 'civilian' (British European Airways, 1947a). For its part the BOAC applauded the 'men who came back' to the Corporation after doing service in the armed forces; men who 'left the Corporation as messenger boys, junior clerks, or apprentices, [and] have come back as R.A.F. Wing Commanders or Squadron Leaders, Naval Commanders, or Army Lieutenant-Colonels and Majors, and in lesser commissioned ranks [...] They have grown into men with experience of the world' (British Overseas Airways Corporation, 1946f).

When it came to female employees both companies fell back on domesticity and beauty to deal with the permanency of women in the airline business. The feminine presence in the airlines was glimpsed through photographs (often without accompanying text), various references to subordinate position,[57] and regular features on engagements, marriages, births, and physical characteristics that reference marriagability.[58] The increasing use of photographs served to simultaneously represent the female employee while obscuring her workplace role through a focus on her attractiveness, and references to the marriage of a female employee invariably reported her retirement from the company. Even rare reports on women in skilled or supervisory positions tended to focus on gender rather than work characteristics,[59] stressing the novelty and hence temporary nature of women in these positions. A report on BEA's 'Staff Travel Office Chief', for example, refers to her as 'tall [with a] slim figure' (British European Airways, 1949d). Similarly, BOAC's *only* woman engineer', is described as 'slim with dark curls', married with a five-year old daughter and of the opinion that she is 'a better housewife than an aircraft engineer'[60] (British Overseas Airways Corporation, 1947f).[61] Uniqueness was also the sub-text in items devoted to the retirement of selected women with long-term service. When BOAC paid tribute to two veterans of the company much was made of 'Major' Brackley's war service (British Overseas Airways Corporation, 1946c), but the main references to 'Mrs.' Doris Clayton are her widowhood in 1916, her marriage in 1937 and her husband's profession (British Overseas Airways Corporation, 1946g). While Brackley was profiled for his important contribution to the airline, Clayton was written up because of her retirement from the airline after 24 years.[62]

Symbolism

Military-style uniforms, complete with rank,[63] dominated the post-war air-lines but the era began to see the influence of women's fashion. Earlier every attempt was made to ensure that uniformed female staff, in particular stew-ardesses, were dressed in a similar fashion to their male colleagues. This soon gave way to pressure from the women themselves who did not want to look like men and male managers who felt that the women should reflect stan-dard notions of femininity. This led to a gradual change in female uniforms and their presentation, shifting gradually from a work uniform to a fashion statement. Redesigned women's uniforms were launched, in fashion-house style, in September 1946, amidst a 'fanfare of trumpets' at the Orchid Room of London's Dorchester Hotel (British Overseas Airways Corporation, 1946f). The 'attractive', modern and streamlined uniform was heralded as typifying 'the spirit of the new air age' in meeting the practical requirements of airline personnel while being designed for 'a woman's build [which is] entirely different from a man's' (ibid.) Thus, 'Miss B.O.A.C. wears a uniform designed from the start for women' (ibid).

Gender and the discourse of race and empire

In the immediate post-war era many of the old imperial themes were still evident in BOAC's corporate imaging, with the British white man central to stories from the 'outposts'. Once again whiteness and privileged forms of masculinity are equated with rationality, intelligence, modernity and civi-lization, and are achieved through contrasts with so-called non-whites in

Britain's colonies. The cruelest example of this is a letter of application to the Lagos Station Master, which was reproduced in the *BOAC Newsletter* for the amusement of the readers. In the letter the applicant, 'a mechanic by trade,' respectfully pleads for 'any kind of work', citing poverty and 18 months of unemployment (British Overseas Airways Corporation, 1945b). Yet the newsletter's only comment was that the 'Station Master did not enclose a copy of his reply, which, we have no doubt, was expressed in the same philosophical strain' (ibid).

The 'savagery' and 'primitive' character of the African is highlighted in several in-house news items over the next few years,[64] including a report from one of the airline's flight operations officers on tour in Africa, where we gain an image of Africans as a simple, primitive people in contrast to the modern, technologically advanced British man and his 'wife'. Travelling through 'Darkest Africa', the author encounters pygmies and 'distributes the usual gift of cigarettes' in return for a 'bow and four arrows' but is convinced that the 'raw natives [...] had never seen either white men or motor cars there before, and [wished that] he had had a radio fitted, for it would have been interesting to see their reactions' (British Overseas Airways Corporation, 1950d).[65]

Race and femininity

The first mention to any women of colour in BOAC's corporate documents appeared in 1946 with a simple reference to an Egyptian employee's membership of a basketball team.[66] The following year a story on a female Thai station assistant – 'Jan, of Bangkok' – draws on several layers of gender and racial reference points to create an image of Asian women as exotic, pleasing, caring and sexually alluring (British Overseas Airways Corporation, 1948b). Described as 'Pearl (as the travel agents say) of the Orient, one of the Corporation's most popular girl station assistants in the Far East', a poem dedicated to her by a grateful passenger is reproduced in the *BOAC Newsletter*:

Lost your ticket? She'll help you through.
And, 'spite your failings, she'll smile at you.
Feeling lousy? Are things going against the grain?
The cure's quite simple – you turn to Jane!
She never fusses, she's always neat;
In fact the lady's extremely sweet!

Pause for a moment and count the cost –
Could you conceivably feel more lost?
Just supposing you had to forego
The aid of the lady who helps you so?
I think it would be the ached pain
To stay in Bangkok and not see Jane!

(ibid.)

The same themes were evident when BOAC recruited 'local girls' on selected routes. From 1949 the company began to hire women from Hong Kong, India and Pakistan as 'assistant stewardesses' and ground staff. The women, who were usually shown being trained by white British stewardesses,[67] were often referenced through their exotic 'national dress' rather than their skills or experiences. For example, an article on five female receptionists at Karachi station includes a picture of one of the women in a Sari-style uniform, showing 'a touch of "local colour" ' (British Overseas Airways Corporation, 1950b).[68]

UK-based women of colour, on the other hand, were not generally part of the airlines' staffs and so not referenced in any of the corporate materials. This did not begin to change until the mid-1960s despite massive efforts by the British government to recruit hundreds of thousands of people from the so-called non-white Commonwealth to work in the United Kingdom.[69]

Women's work in post-war Britain

The immediate post-war era witnessed anxiety about population levels and the post-war role of women as wives and mothers; labour shortages; debate about equal pay; rapid change in the character of employment in Britain; and the growth of the Welfare State.

Motherhood and the birth of a nation

During the Second World War public debate on the future of the family was dominated by fears of a falling birth rate (Lewis, 1992) and in 1944 the Government established a Royal Commission on Population. Concerns with motherhood and the birthrate were very much in evidence in a range of new welfare initiatives introduced by the post-war Labour Government. The notion of 'the stay-home mother' was at the heart of a number of welfare provisions that were introduced throughout the latter part of the 1940s. The Beveridge Report, for example, argued that in 'the next thirty years housewives as Mothers have vital work to do in ensuring the adequate continuance of the British Race and of the British Ideal in the world;' therefore the 'great majority of married women must be regarded as occupied on work which is vital but unpaid, without which their husbands could not do their paid work and without which the nation could not continue' (quoted in Pugh, 1992: 294).

The powerful image of the stay-at-home mother differed in a number of ways from the old pre-war image of motherhood. A number of women 'greeted peacetime with a profound sense of relief; both wanting and expecting to return to normal family life' (Pugh, 1992: 284), but their image of womanhood had undergone change during the war years. Social democracy and the election of a majority Labour Government represented the aspirations of large sections of the British people for progressive change. Many of those changes focussed on improvements in family life but it was a progressivism that also envisioned a continued role for women in paid employment, working on the same terms as men (Riley, 1987). Changing social attitudes and the widespread use of birth control meant that young women could anticipate fewer pregnancies than their mothers and grandmothers and, consequently, greater time for home life and a potential return to the labour market once their children were of school age (Lewis, 1992; Pugh, 1992).

Loves labour lost: Labour shortages and the demand for female employees

As much as renewed attitudes to motherhood, family and population encouraged women to leave the workplace, post-war labour shortages and the changing character of British industry encouraged them to remain in the paid workforce.

Between 1945 and 1948 there was a shortage of labour in a number of sectors of British industry, particularly in nursing, midwifery, teaching, and clerical and administrative work,[70] leading the Trades Union Congress (TUC) to express concern that, 'At the present time, most of the peacetime industries of this country are suffering from a severe lack of women workers' (Trades Union Congress, 1946). The government – facing a massive loss of earnings from foreign investments and visible exports, and a serious balance of payments problem – began an official campaign to get more women back into the workforce,[71] particularly those in the 35–50 age group, including married women who had worked during the war (Pugh, 1992: 286–87).[72]

The post-war demand for labour, government campaigning and a shift of the economy towards the feminized clerical, administrative, commercial and lower professional areas[73] (Pugh, 1992) brought a number of women back into the workplace after the initial post-war downturn. Further, the long-term buoyancy of certain industries in the Midlands and the South East of England – including aircraft, light engineering and railways – was already providing steady employment opportunities for women. By 1948 there were 350,000 more insured women workers than there had been immediately prior to the war, including 65,000 women in the motor vehicles, cycles and aircraft industries (Trades Union Congress, 1946: 167).[74] By 1951 only a third of female employees were under 25 years, and the remainder were evenly drawn from those in their thirties, forties and fifties, while the percentage of married women in paid employment had risen to 22 per cent (Pugh, 1992: 288).[75]

Many of the jobs available to women were sex segregated and low-paid, and included many of those who had remained in the workforce only to find themselves 'squeezed out of their wartime roles into lower level jobs designated as "women's work" ' (Pugh, 1992: 286). A limited attempt by the government to introduce equal pay to local government and civil service grades where men and women did comparable work was ended with a general pay freeze in 1948 (Rowbotham, 1999: 244–45).[76]

As state-owned enterprises, BOAC and BEA were included in changes to the public sector, which may explain, in part, why the new female flight attendants received the same pay as their male colleagues. Arguably, the new post-war job opportunities signalled a shift in attitudes to women and work, with developments pointing 'strongly to the collapse of the traditional ideal of the non-working wife amongst both middle-class and respectable working-class families'(Pugh, 1992: 289). However, this did not mark a radical shift in thinking about the primary role of women as wives and mothers. Government attitudes to female employees reflected a concern with democratization and progress that was, nonetheless, rooted more in the interests of state and nation than in the needs of women as individuals (Lewis, 1992: 25). Any shift in the attitudes of employers can be explained through changes in demand and supply. On the one hand, the occupational structure was marked by a rapidly expanding service sector which made a particular call on women's labour 'because of profoundly gendered ideas as to what kind of work is appropriate to women' (Lewis, 1992: 68). On the other hand, women themselves were influenced by wartime experiences, 'increasing educational attainment and changing expectations about the balance of activities they might hope to attain in their adult lives' (ibid.).

Many of the workplace trends of 1945 to 1950 are evident in BOAC and BEA. The increase in female labour after 1946 was due, not so much to changed attitudes within management ranks, but to the fact that the airlines were in an expanding industry that relied heavily on the employment of great numbers of clerical and administrative staffs. The major difference to workplace trends was that the growth of male clerical and administrative staffs initially exceeded that of female staff. The airlines also followed the trend of displacing women from traditionally male jobs while retaining large numbers of female employees in segregated work. The general trend may have reinforced such ideas rather than supplied them. Both BOAC and BEA retained married female employees but encouraged the idea that women should resign upon marriage. Thus, while it had become acceptable to retain married women among the staff it is still evident that female employees felt some pressure to leave at the time of their marriage.

Social discourse and desexualization

The airlines' concerns with 'desexualization' were informed by a number of factors that informed notions of sexuality during the immediate post-war era. Those factors included austerity, bureaucratization, welfarism, changing family values and the influence of popular culture.

The discourse of desexualization

During the war women's work had been presented in public discourse as the result of women's 'collective heroic capacity' but, nonetheless, work done by women, 'permeated by the gender of its performers, and consequently' temporary to the real role of wife and mother (Riley, 1987: 260). The critical economic situation following the war and the government's campaign to recruit more female workers recreated the notion of women's work as temporary and 'for the duration only'. The result was a powerful image of work as unglamorous but necessary, leading one feminist historian to summarize the situation as one where 'rhetorically, women were overpersonified as mothers and desexed as workers' (Riley, 1987: 261). It was in this framework that BOAC and BEA emphasized the professionalism rather than the sex of the new stewardesses. The stress on professionalism fit nicely with the bureaucratization that was occurring throughout the industry, and the austere dress and moral code fit well with the cost-conscious, efficiency drive that marked the airlines at the time.

Austerity

The austerity of the times discouraged all but a few businesses to trade on glamour. It was a time of rationing, food shortages and long-line ups for even the most mundane goods and services. Even airline seats were rationed and priority was given to those travelling on essential business. In this context it was not surprising that airline management deemphasized the glamour aspects of commercial flying that were being sold by US airlines in a very different market to that being experienced in Britain.

Bureaucracy, sexuality and the rise of the welfare state

The immediate post-war era, with austerity, the expansion of government ownership and the establishment of a system of welfare agencies saw a strengthening of bureaucratic control of industrial and social life.

With the rapid growth of the Welfare State new layers of bureaucracy proliferated around notions of family and motherhood. Most, if not all, of the new welfare policies had particular notions of the role of men and women at their core. The idea of married women as 'dependants' (of male earners) was, for example, at the core of the Beveridge Plan. Under the National Insurance Act of 1946 married women were treated as if their 'normal' state was non-working and dependant.

Meantime the functioning of the government bureaucracies was informed by a need for greater efficiency and professionalism, discourse which highlighted traits primarily associated at the time with men rather than women (Ferguson, 1984).

The airline industry, which was undergoing a period of restructuring and government regulation, was caught up in the spirit of the time, and Lord Knollys, BOAC's Chairman, informed staff that the keynote for the financial year is 'Economy through Efficiency', and all staff had to 'organize their work so that it can be done with greater efficiency by fewer personnel' (British Overseas Airways Corporation, 1947a). This was coupled by constant references to the airline as 'a family',[77] with BOAC described as 'the mother company' and BEA as 'the child' (British Overseas Airways Corporation, 1946a).

Popular culture and images of sexuality: A night at the movies

A focus on traditional themes of motherhood and domesticity was very much to the fore in the cinema of the 1940s. Popular films of the time tended to portray females as 'wholesome' girls (*Courage of Lassie, Little Women*), or traditional *wives* and mothers who keep the family together (*Best Years of Our Lives, Life with Father*). Women who 'stray' from their traditional roles were often portrayed as troublesome and doomed to failure (e.g., *Brief Encounter, Forever Amber, Samson and Delilah, The Woman in the Window, The Postman Always Rings Twice, Mildred Pierce*.[78]

The gendering of BOAC and BEA

That the female employee became a permanent feature of BOAC and BEA was due to a combination of factors, including the wartime employment of women coupled with post-war labour shortages, government restructuring, increased bureaucratization and the continued feminization of clerical work. These factors contributed to a break in the existing ways of working, forcing a rethink of some labour practices and the consolidation of the airline as a government agency, making it at least more difficult to avoid the hiring of female clerical staff. On the other hand, the aftermath of war provided a strong formative context in which associations between masculinity and piloting and allied tasks were strengthened. This influenced both airlines.

The major change was the employment of stewardesses after decades of management resistance. It might have been expected that warfare would have strengthened the link between masculinity and stewarding. That this was not the case is likely due to market pressures and the fact that unlike piloting, stewarding was not linked to any deep-rooted layers of masculinity. Austerity, and a stress on desexualization, allowed the airlines to overcome any potential objections to the hiring of stewardesses.

At Pan Am a few women remained in non-traditional jobs – including Ann Archibald, and Kay Keener, a company solicitor; at least two women were in supervisory roles,[79] and one woman was named editor of the Pan American Clipper. Stewarding, however, was the major change at Pan Am and at TCA. This involved regularizing of the hiring of female flight attendants at Pan AM and the hiring of male stewards at TCA.

From boys to men: Stewarding and Pan Am

The introduction of stewarding into the airline business owed more to mimetic isomorphism (DiMaggio and Powell, 1983) than any embedded notion of masculinity. Pan Am recruited 'attentive and good looking youngsters' (McLaughlin, 1994: 5), and often stressed their youth more than their masculinity. Candidates for the job had to be male, American citizens, no older than 32 years of age, between 5 feet 5 inches and 5 feet 9 inches in height, no more than 150 pounds in weight, experience in the first class hotel or restaurant business, a high-school graduate, with three languages (McLaughlin, 1994: 5). The early stewards were often as young as 17 and were often praised for their boyish enthusiasm. A local Miami newspaper described Pan Am's stewards as 'American boys born of Cuban parents' and suggested that the reason why there were more applicants for stewardships than there are places to fill is because 'young men are willing to take the job for nothing, almost, just for the fun of going back and forth in the air between Miami and Havana' (Herald Telephone, 1930).[80] References to stewarding itself was largely descriptive (e.g., serving passengers a light supper) but often implied an intuitive knowledge – the boys 'know what a steward should do' (ibid.) because 'you can't stump a good steward', who is even capable to quieting a baby in flight (Pan American Airways, 1932). Behind the intuition the 'boys' lived by the mantra of 'Service, Tact, Efficiency, Wisdom, Ability, Responsibility, Dependability'[81] (McLaughlin, 1994: 5).

The hiring of female flight attendants in 1943 was problematic not only because it meant accepting women as part of the flight crew but also the threat to male jobs and the masculinity of the men involved. Thus, it was cast as 'a departure from [...] custom', due to wartime necessity (Pan American Airways, 1944). The title 'stewardesses' referenced a female in a male job but it also became a fixed rank, with only stewards being promoted to purser (Pan American Airways, 1946c).[82]

Following the Second World War and the regularization of the stewardess role, there was an increased emphasis on the beauty and marriagability of the occupant and a corresponding emphasis on the professionalism of the male purser. For example, while the first group of stewardesses were 'given the same two-month intensive training as the stewards' (McLaughlin, 1994: 85), post-war training included a heavy emphasis on beauty techniques and preparations (Pan American Airways, 1948). Soon various articles focussed on the attractiveness of the stewardess, both in terms of her sexual appeal and as an explanation of her job skills. Thus, for example, it was said of one stewardess that 'no one could be better qualified than she due to her genial, even disposition' (Pan American Airways, 1945b). Requirements of the job included languages and high-school graduation but also focussed on age and looks. Stewardesses had to be US citizens

21–27 years of age at time of employment; between five feet three inches and five feet seven inches tall, and her weight must be in proportion to her height [however] the most outstanding requisite required of a flight stewardess is her ability to be a gracious hostess, alertly anticipating her passengers' needs and providing the necessary services in an attractive and efficient manner.

Pan American Airways (1956b)

To ensure this mystique the airline required stewardesses to resign upon marriage (Pan American Airways, 1947a).

Gender realignment at TCA

TCA's steward recruitment issue was the reverse of Pan Am's but the strategies employed were very similar. Anxious to attract men, TCA had a problem in that it had overly focussed on the glamour and attractiveness of their female flight attendants to the extent that it appeared to be a female job – involving 'care for the comfort of passengers' (Trans-Canada Air Lines, 1938a), 'gracious and personalized service' (Trans-Canada Air Lines, 1940), and efficiency and charm (Trans-Canada Air Lines, 1938b). Thus, the airline was at great pains to construct the image of the male flight attendant as markedly different from his female counterpart. Much was made of the fact that all the men in the first graduating class of stewards were 'ex-service men' (Trans-Canada Air Lines, 1945). The new purser-steward was not as 'a mere adjunct to the present four-man transatlantic crew, but rather an integral part of a five-man team' (ibid.). And for TCA, it was 'no exaggeration to say that on the performance of these young men will be based many an evaluation of our national worth' (ibid.).

This image stands in sharp contrast to that of the stewardesses, who were viewed as subservient to and dependent on male members of the crew: required to 'address flight officers as "Captain" or "Mr.", other employees as "Mr." or "Miss". Stewardesses will be addressed as 'Miss'. It is to be appreciated that the stewardesses have had practically no aviation experience and will have to rely on other personnel for assistance from time to time' (TCA memo, 1939, quoted in Smith, 1986: 79). [In practice male flight attendants were appointed at the distinctly higher rank of 'pursers'[83], were paid higher wages ($180 per month compared to $150 for stewardesses), and were given oversees assignments (while stewardesses flew mostly the so-called 'domestic' routes) because of the rigours of transatlantic flights were assumed to be too much for 'the gentle sex' (Smith, 1986: 81). Thus, unlike the situation at BOAC, the employment of male flight attendants reduced the opportunities for women at TCA.

6

The Invasion of the Body Snatchers: The Jet Age and the Eroticization of the Female Employee

Sex was becoming more overt: women were ready and raunchy, aggressive and yet yielding in 1960s advertisements. Male fantasies came out from under wraps and pleasure beckoned. Images of femininity were communicating blatantly opposing messages of freedom and subordination. Young women confronted forms of feminine representation which were sexually reductionist while signaling infinite expansion of one's consciousness. Moreover, these images were dissolving and reforming in constant flux before one's eyes.

Rowbotham (1999: 361–64)

Introduction

When stewardess Janet Huntley flew from London to New York on BOAC's Constellation service during November 1946 she wore a military-style uniform, similar to that worn by her male colleagues. Symbolically, Huntley was the very image of the Corporation's anti-glamour/equity policy. Twenty years later, when stewardess Pat Bleasdale flew BOAC's Caribbean to New York flight she was dressed in a paper mini-dress. The dress – white with cerise and purple flowers and green leaves, and a hem that, at most, ended three inches above the knee – was a far cry from the uniform wore by Janet Huntley (See Exhibit 6.1). In many ways, Bleasdale epitomized the marketing strategy of selling female sexuality not only of BOAC but also of airlines across the globe, including Pan Am and, to a much lesser extent, TCA (Newby, 1986), as 'beautiful young women became marketing tools' for a range of companies to promote their products and services (Omelia and Waldock, 2003: 76).

At a facile level, it would seem that BOAC had simply caught up with the times, that the economics of jet travel had forced the airline to use female sexuality to sell tickets in order to compete. Certainly the jet age had

(a)

(b)

Exhibit 6.1   Changing images of the stewardess, 1948 and 1968

'transformed both the economics and the sociology of air transport, making travel not only faster but more reliable and cheaper and opening it up to a mass market' (Sampson, 1984: 105). The new jets, specifically the Boeing 707, 'sacrificed lounges to provide more revenue-generating seats; marketing based on comfort disappeared' (Omelia and Waldock, 2003: 76). In response the 'airlines focused on their flight attendants [...] themed around the attractiveness of their female cabin crew. Stewardesses became the product used to sell the airline and were repackaged, that is, dressed in alluring new ways' (ibid.). However, this does not explain how BOAC and BEA went from the 'desexualized' professional stewardess (as the embodiedment or an equity strategy) to the sexy air hostess in less than two decades. In this chapter we explore that transformation and what we can learn from it.

At this juncture: Inside BOAC/BEA (1960–69)

Throughout the 1960s BOAC and BEA underwent a number of dramatic changes. BOAC was led by Sir Gerard d'Erlanger (1956–60), Rear Admiral Sir Matthew Slattery (1960–63), Sir Giles Gutherie (1963–69) and Sir Charles Hardie (1969–70). BEA was led by Lord Douglas (1949–64) and Lieutenant Commander Sir Anthony Milward (1964–71).

Elsewhere the public face of the airlines was also undergoing considerable change. The image of the flight attendant had changed the most, with the marketing of female bodily sexuality. The airline continued to recruit male stewards but flight attending was marketed as primarily a female job. Female recruits had to be of 'good appearance [with a] pleasant personality [and] high physical fitness' (British Overseas Airways Corporation, 1959g). Recruitment practices differed in regard to male and female flight attendants. BOAC, for instance, stressed that all recruits had to be at least 21 years old, but women could not exceed 28 years of age, while men could be as old as 38. Men were expected to have 'hotel or restaurant experience', while women needed 'nursing or catering experience' (British Overseas Airways Corporation, 1959g). The old anti-glamour publicity had entirely given way to focus on female beauty. BEA was now claiming,

> The job of an airline stewardess is generally regarded as one of the 'glamour' occupations ... [Any] girl who does the job is on show and has to look her best for a considerable period of time – and an airline passenger can be very critical indeed. Women by pulling something to pieces or by slightly envying their turnout, men by being pleased at having an attractive young woman to look at.
>
> British European Airways (1969)

Similarly, BOAC was stating that it always endeavours 'to ensure that our female staff are the smartest – and the most feminine – in the world' (British Overseas Airways Corporation, 1962f).

The focus on glamour and female bodily sexuality was extended to most of the female staffs of BEA and BOAC and this was evidenced throughout the in-house newsletters, with increasing numbers of photographs of female staff in bathing suits with little or no purpose other than to show off the respective women's bodies. For example, a *BOAC Newsletter* article on the Lebanon included a photograph of a female employee in a two-piece bathing suit, with the caption: 'Beirut boasts such lovely potential damsels in distress as Miss Raymonde Kouyoudjian, a telephonist at our Beirut office' (British Overseas Airways Corporation, 1961a).[1] The other main change was the recruitment of women of colour as flight attendants. The women were recruited from those countries into which BOAC flew and they served, under white stewardesses, on the routes to and from their homeland. In each case the women wore a uniform that supposedly typified their 'traditional dress' (e.g., a Japanese woman in a kimono – British Overseas Airways Corporation, 1962f). Influenced by events outside of the airlines, many of the changes were nonetheless rooted in developments within BEA and BOAC in the decade leading up to the 1960s.

Female employment

Between 1946 and 1969 the number of female employees in BOAC and BEA grew at a tremendous rate. While there were just over 2800 women employed in the old BOAC in 1946 (see Table 5.3), by 1966 there were just under 5000 women working for BOAC and a further 4500 working for BEA. In both cases this signalled a greater acceptance of the female employee, with the range of female job titles growing considerably since the pre-war era. On the other hand, the 'normalization' of female labour had its boundaries, with much of the work basically ghettoized. The vast majority of male employees worked in engineering and maintenance and the vast majority of women were employed in administrative support roles,[2] with nearly all female supervisory positions confined to female dominated work. Men held virtually all the senior positions until the mid-1960s. Piloting remained closed to women but stewarding, along with signals, information handling, personnel and finance were equally staffed by men and women (British Overseas Airways Corporation, 1966d, 1966b). It was a very similar division of labour at BEA.[3]

Apart from flight attending, there was little or no change in female employment until the onset of the 1960s when women attained comparable rank to their male colleagues and moved into new areas of male-dominated work (see Tables 6.1 and 6.2).

In a number of ways the gendered division of labour was explained, and to some extent legitimized, through corporate discourse. This occurred through various recruitment practices, training, advertising and reporting of the activities of male and female employees through associations of maleness with experience, skill and knowledge, and womanhood with either personal characteristics or physical appearance. In two consecutive *BOAC Newsletters*, for example, a male Purchase Controller is reported as having '40 years in aviation', including time served with the RNAS in First World War (British Overseas Airways Corporation, 1957c), while a female telephonist is referred

Table 6.1   Male and female-typed Jobs in BOAC, 1946–69

1 Jobs solely or primarily occupied by male employees (118 categories)

Accounts supervisor	Electrician	Postal supervisor
Admin. Director	Engine fitter	Premises officer
Aero engineer	Engineer	Progress assistant
Aircraft production officer	Engineering apprentice	Project engineer
Apron control	Engineering instructor	Purchasing controller
Apprentice	European sales representative	Radio maintenance engineer
Architect	Field stores auditor	Radio officer
Assistants groundsman	Financial comptroller	Regional sales manager
Assistants line engineer	First officer	Reservations clerk
Assistants load control super.	Fitter	Reservations officer
Assistant manager	Flight administration officer	Rigger
Assistant technical development director	Flight engineering superintendent	Route inspector
Cabin services director	Flight manager	Sales manager
Cabin services officer	Flight navigation supervisor	Sales officer
Captain	Flight superintendent	Schedules reproduction
Careers officer	Foreman	Seaman
Catering apprentices	HO drawing officer	Section leader
Chairman	HO Staff superintendent	Security officer
Charge hand	In charge of engineering aircraft instruction	Security warden
Chartered architect	In charge of engineering instruction	Senior first officer
Chef	Inspector	Senior captain second class
Chief medical officer	Inspector of accidents	Senior flight foreman
Chief executive	Insurance clerk	Senior medical officer
Chief instructor	Leading hand	Senior planning engineer
Chief of security	Loader	Senior steward
Chief photographer	Maintenance foreman	Senior supplies officer
Chief pilot	Maintenance staff	Senior foreman
Communications officer	Manager	Staff appointments superintendent
Cost accountant engineering	Manager no. 5 line	Standards engineer
Coxswain	Managing director	Station supervisor
Crane driver	Navigation officer	Superintendent of technical requirements
Deputy chief reservations officer	Navigator	Supplies superintedent
Deputy flight engineering supervisor	Oarsman	Technical manager
Deputy flight manager	Officer i/c training	Traffic movements controller
Deputy flight navigation superintendent		

continued

Table 6.1 Continued

Director of conference and interline activities	Operations clerk	Traffic officer
Director of medical services	Pilot	Training steward
Driver	Pilot instructor	Welder
Duty officer	Planning engineer	Works foreman
Economic statistics officer	Planning engineer in charge	

2 Jobs occupied by male and female employees (17 categories)

Advertising assistant	Receptionist	Senior steward/ess
Billeting officer	Reservations assistant	Steward/ess
Catering officer/supervisor	Reservations officer	Storekeeper
Chief air steward	Sales apprenticeship	Traffic clerk
Flight steward/ess	Sales rep/salewoman	Waiter/ess
Manager	Staff supervisor	Work measurement officer

3 Jobs solely or primarily occupied by female employees (62 categories)

Account equipment supervisor	Establishment assessor	Secretary
Admin. Assistant	Flight cabin services officer	Selection officer
Admin officer	House supervisor	Senior computor
Advertising officer	Marketing intelligence officer	Senior physiotherapist
Air traffic clerk		
Aircraft catering attendant	M.C.A. telecommunications	Senior traffic clerk
Audit clerk	Matron	Shift supervisor
Booking clerk	Medical sister	Singnals supervisor
Booking officer	Microfilm operator	Special events repre- sentative
Business travel officer	Nurse	Station assistant
Canteen worker	Nursing sister	Station clerk
Cargo reservations clerk	Operations statistician	Stenographer
Cargo sales officer	Passenger relations officer	Stock records clerk
		Stock inspector
Chief signals supervisor	Personal secretary	Supervisor, post & telex section
Chief telephone supervisor	Personnel assistant	Switchboard supervisor
Clerk	Personnel officer	Tailoress
Computor	Personnel supervisor	Telephonist
Convention manager	Powers operator	Teleprinter operator
Copy typist	Post & registry supervisor	Traffic receptionst
Deputy flight stewardess	Premises equipment officer	Traffic shift supervisor
Distributions clerk	Registry supervisor	Translator
	Sales development assistant	

Source: Information compiled from internal company records and detailed reporting of recruitment and job activities in the airlines newsletters and journals of the period.

Table 6.2 Male and female-typed Jobs in BEA, 1946–69

1 Jobs solely or primarily occupied by male employees (53 categories)

Accountant	Draughtsman	Pilot
Airline loader	Driver	Postboy
Apprentice instrument repairer	Engineer	Printer
Apron control	Engineer in charge	Radio officer
Area manager	Engineering apprentice	Receptionist
Assistant station controller	Fitter	Route service officer
Cadet pilot	Flight catering officer	Second officer
Captian	First officer	Senior captain second class
Catering manager	Freight handler	Senior first officer
Central personnel office psychologist	General manager staff and services	Senior link training instructor
Chairman	Grindstone operator	Senior steward
Chef	Instrument engineer	Shift inspector
Chief accountant	Loader	Station engineer
Chief engineer	Manager	Supervisor booking office
Chief executive	Marketer	Supplies manager
Chief pilot	Officer in charge of training	Timetables assistant
Controller	Operations controller	Traffic dispatcher
Dispatcher	Pay officer	Traffic director
		Training sales instructor

2 Jobs occupied by male and female employees (12 categories)

Air traffic controller	First class steward/ess	Station clerk
Catering apprentice	General apprentice	Steward
Board member	Official-in-charge	Traffic clerk
Booking clerk	Station assitant	
Clerk		

3 Jobs solely or primarily occupied by female employees (31 categories)

Cashier	Secretary	Telephone operator
Catering staff	Senior accounts clerk	Telephone sales operator
Junior clerk	Senior traffic clerk	Teleprinter operator
Nursing sister	Senior welfare officer	Teletype operator
Office typist	Sister-in-charge	Traffic officer
Operator in charge, powers dept	Supervisor, typing bureau	Training supervisor
Packer	Staff sister	Typing bureau supervisor
Passenger handling	Staff travel office chief	Typist
Passenger officer	Stenographer	Welfare officer
Reservations sales clerk	Technical librarian	Women's personnel officer
		Women's staff advisor

Source: Information compiled from internal company records and detailed reporting of recruitment and job activities in the airline's newsletters and journals of the period.

to as having a 'most pleasing telephone voice [...] of bell-like resonance', and 'to compound her listener's pleasure [is] a slim blond with dancing blue eyes' (British Overseas Airways Corporation, 1957d).

On occasion the supposed 'natural' characteristics of women and men were used to privilege certain work as either female or male. Explaining the post-Second World War shift from male- to female-dominated signals and telephone work, BOAC explained to employees that this was due to the fact that women are 'psychologically [...] far more suited to be telephonists than men [because] they display more patience [...] and are better intermediaries between the correspondents using the phone' (British Overseas Airways Corporation, 1966b).[4] On the other hand, the work of BOAC's Supplies Provisioning Branch has to be undertaken by 'men [who] must be trained engineers [with] the right temperament – they must be able to look ahead, and, as a result of experience, know where to anticipate possible trouble in new design' (British Overseas Airways Corporation, 1957b).[5]

Imaging masculinity and femininity

As we saw in Chapter 5, following Second World War it was relatively easy to image the male employee through references to wartime experiences, skill, knowledge and leadership. Danger, bravery, adventure and manhood became intertwined in the notion of piloting and provided the contours of a desired form of masculinity in the post-war airlines. Similarly, the male engineer gained in prominence as much was made of the wartime role of aircraft maintenance. The association of management with masculinity drew on references both to wartime military and business leadership. If there were any problem areas it was in those ranks in which women had become a stable, and even a dominant, part. Stewarding, for instance, had undergone a transformation since the onset of Second World War, with the hiring of boys and then large numbers of women. However, it was well into the 1960s that the masculinity of the male steward became problematic for the image-makers.

Imaging women was far more problematic for the airline bosses, editors, copywriters, trainers and recruiters. While men were defined through their work, women were initially defined through broad notions of domesticity (Feldberg and Glenn, 1979), focussing on their assumed roles as wives and mothers. Youth and marriageability were emphasized throughout internal documents, and women were expected to give up their jobs when they married. Yet where certain feminine characteristics were seen as threatening to the good name of the company the imagery was 'desexualized', as in the case of the work of the stewardesses. Eventually, those very characteristics would overwhelm all others in the imaging of female employees at all levels.

Masculinity

The shifting nature of female sexuality was not unrelated to shifts in masculine imagery in British airlines during the period in question.[6] Analysis of corporate imaging of the pilot, the steward and engineer suggest that different forms of masculinity were at play that influenced or were influenced by shifting female imagery.

The pilot

Piloting retained its associations with maleness primarily through the exclusion of women from commercial flying. BOAC and BEA steadfastly refused to employ female pilots. The existence of all-male air forces and their involvement, from time to time, in warfare, helped to maintain associations of flying with bravery and masculinity. However, the association of commercial flying and maleness was largely achieved through the exclusion of women. While the job of piloting remained a male pursuit the flight crew as a whole had begun to lose its masculine associations with the introduction of stewardess in 1946. Over time the masculine image of the pilot was achieved through references to the supposed characteristics of the male pilot, assumed problems with would-be female pilots, contrasts with the experiences and practices of the stewardesses, and, eventually, sexual co-option of the stewardess's glamour image.

The pilot was defined in terms of his training, experience, professionalism, career path and organizational commitment. These characteristics took on more masculine associations when the issue of female piloting was raised. While in the pre-war era emotional instability and menstrual periods were referenced to exclude women from piloting, now economic factors were to the fore, in the argument that the huge costs of pilot training prohibited the hiring of women because they would leave the airline to marry and have children.[7]

The masculine character of piloting also emerged through constant contrasts with the feminization of stewarding.[8] Piloting was imaged as a career involving high levels of skill, responsibility and professional objectivity. In contrast, the evolving (female) role of stewarding was viewed as temporary, involving care, attentiveness, appearance and emotional labour (Hochschild, 1983). In time the juxtaposition of pilot and stewardess took on new meaning as corporate images increasingly used femininity to frame images of pilots (and managers), with pictures of men surrounded by female staff. In many cases the women were superfluous to the story and seem to have been included to highlight the importance of the male subject.[9] In a similar vein, newsletter cartoons presented images of 'sexy' stewardesses attracting and distracting pilots. In one, for example, a 'shapely' stewardess is being observed by two pilots, one of whom is pointing towards the woman and saying to the other pilot: 'That's the one Fred – they had to take her off flying duties 'cos the passengers couldn't stand the vibrations' (British European Airways, 1965b).

The steward

During Second World War the masculine image of stewarding was fundamentally altered as boys replaced men. Following the war the recruitment of a number of females made it difficult if not impossible to re-establish any sense of masculine identity with the role of the steward. Initial post-war images seemed poised to rescue the steward's masculine image through references to sexual dynamics. For example, under the title of the 'B.O.A.C. Harem', a 1947 newsletter showed a photograph of a BOAC steward surrounded by eight stewardesses from other airlines (British Overseas Airways Corporation, 1947e). This type of imaging was short-lived and the steward was put in the back ground in the practices and publicity of the airlines, with the stewardesses taking a more public role in aircraft service and news features. Psychologically the airlines had begun to trade on the idea of the 'pilot as father [and] the stewardess as mother, waiting on her children hand and foot, listening and watching to see if one is crying and unhappy, always at hand with comforting words and an understanding smile' (Hudson and Pettifer, 1979: 157). Arguably 'a steward cannot have this function. He is no more than an airline servant in uniform, and his usefulness is limited to efficiency' (ibid.). The publicity afforded to the stewardess also helped to create a public image that associated the role with glamour and femininity. This may explain why, in later years, male flight attendants were sometimes stereotyped as homosexual in popular culture.

The engineer

The image of the ideal-typical aviation engineer gained in prominence in the corporate materials of BOAC and BEA in the post-war era. The image has several masculine reference points, specifically skill and technical knowledge. These characteristics were stressed time and time again through numerous images depicting white-coveralled engineers working on one machine or another. It was as if the images served to reinforce the associations of manliness and engineering.

Like the piloting, the skills associated with engineering are not inherently gender specific. The First World War had brought a number of women into engineering work and it took widespread displacements of those women in the post-war era to re-establish engineering as male work. Similarly, during the Second World War women were brought back into engineering jobs and in the period following the masculinity of engineering was asserted through the further exclusion of women,[10] the restriction of apprenticeship schemes to boys, and corporate imagery which emphasized women's ignorance of technical things, while stressing male power and control over machinery.

At its crudest, images of female stupidity appeared in cartoons designed to laugh at women's lack of technical knowledge. For example, in one cartoon a 'shapely' woman is shown crossing an airfield, with the wind blowing her dress up. The caption reads: 'Dumb Types – the girl who thought the ''prop wash' was something you did in the garden on Mondays' (British European Airways, 1949b).[11] At a more subtle level a series of corporate photographs contrasted men and women with machinery. On the one hand, images of male engineers working *on* large machines served to emphasis male control over powerful engines. On the other hand, photos of women *inside* or *beside* large machines served to emphasis female vulnerability and frailty. For example, in one picture three BOAC stewardesses are shown inside an aero engine. The photograph is titled 'The Big Beautiful World of 747' and the accompanying text states that 'it is a beautiful sight. Three lovely girls smiling gracefully from an engine intake of the world's largest carrier' (British Overseas Airways Corporation, 1968b).

Femininity

Following the war there was a return to the generalized notion of women as periphery to the workplace, only this time it was more graphically expressed through two major images – the young maiden and, to a lesser degree, the loyal spinster. The young maiden captures the notion of the woman who spends her time in employment until she marries and has children. She is assumed to have no long-term interest in employment, but in the short term she works through economic necessity to help her family. Thus, in-house newsletters usually only referred to young female employees through references to their marital status (i.e., 'Miss'), suitability as a potential wife (e.g., 'available'), and notices of marriage and births.[12]

The loyal spinster image served to explain the woman who does not marry but continues her career with the airline over a lifetime. A classic example was a report on the retirement of Vivien 'Mick' Smithers, who 'joined Imperial Airways in 1926 as 'a temporary', and somehow no-one ever got around to telling her her time was up' (British Overseas Airways Corporation, 1964d).[13]

At first the in-house newsletters did little more than report the comings and goings to female employees. On occasion photographs of female staff were used to report trends in female recruitment. However, it was becoming evident to those in charge that men *and* women now permanently peopled the airline companies. The old military metaphors began to give way to notions of the company as 'a family'. But, in the early post-war years, there were some differences between BOAC and BEA in the way the metaphor of family was understood. BOAC considered itself the direct successor of the old BOAC and IAL before it. There was a sense of establishment and tradition within BOAC and a certain tendency to look down on the newer BEA. At BOAC there was a greater sense of formality and this was reflected in the in-house magazine reports.

BEA

To build solidarity in the new company, BEA's General Manager (Staff and Services) determined that the *BEA Magazine* would 'devote more space to articles on the work, hobbies and social activities of the staff and less to matters of external interest' (British European Airways, 1947c). This encouraged more coverage of female employees but did not lead to any greater discussion of the various roles and workplace activities that women performed. Instead, an increasing number of items reflected not on what women employees *do* but on the problematics of women *as* employees.

Reports on younger female employees and even some of the older female employees referred to personality and bodily appearance. Sometimes female beauty was referenced in a direct way, as in a photograph of 'attractive BEA telephonists, celebrating the opening of their new exchange' (British European Airways, 1949a)[14]; sometimes the allusion was less direct, as in a story praising the female traffic clerk as the Cinderella of the airlines – perhaps in contrast to her more glamorous stewardess colleagues (British European Airways, 1948e).

Humour in the form of cartoons, headlines and quips often reflected traditionalist masculinist notions, and anxieties about the role of women in society. An example of the former is a photograph of two women in bathing suits that the newsletter editor explains (to a supposedly male audience) he has had on 'his desk for the last two months but now thinks that it is only fair that the rest of the staff should have a chance of seeing it' (British European Airways, 1948a). An example of the latter is a cartoon depicting two male helicopter pilots flying over a nude female swimmer who is partially hidden by bushes. One pilot is saying to the other: 'Come on Henry, old chap – concentrate on the mails – not the blinking females' (British European Airways, 1948b).

BOAC

BOAC's family metaphor was very much subordinate to the notion of the organization as a team. In his 'New Year Message' in January 1948 Sir Harold Hartley told staff

> the essence of good team work is mutual confidence and understanding. Now let me say at once that we have found in B.O.A.C. a fine team and a fine team spirit [...] We have the finest human equipment of any airline in the world to-day. We are a big family because our task is worldwide.
>
> British Overseas Airways Corporation (1948d)

Like BEA, BOAC's in-house newsletters restricted reportage to the appointments and marriages of female employees. However, in contrast to BEA, BOAC tended to avoid comments on appearance or personality, and more reports on the achievements of female staff. In particular there were reports on the number of times that certain stewardesses had flown the Atlantic, including an item on 'seven air stewardesses [who] have between them made 430 crossings of the North Atlantic since November 1946' (British European Airways, 1948b).

If BEA's version of the young maiden bordered on the notion of the wench, BOAC's version was more the dutiful daughter. BOAC restricted its referencing of sexuality to the use of photographs. On a number of occasions the *BOAC Review* and *BOAC News* included photographs of female staff as a means of making the page more visually interesting. On a rare occasion when comment was made on a woman's appearance it was much more understated than BEA's more overt attention to sexuality. Often the focus was more on age than appearance, such as that of a newsletter front cover photograph of 'The Two "Babies" ', which referred to 'twenty-year-old Sheila Bevin, youngest station clerk at London Airport [making] friends with a four-month-old panther cub' (British Overseas Airways Corporation, 1948e).

Organizational discourse

Unlike any other era in the history of British airlines gender, specifically female sexuality, became a key part of organizational discourse. It began with debates about glamour and moved steadily towards issues of eroticism. Within this broad context issues of race and ethnicity were primarily depicted through a gender lens.

Glamour

Initially BEA and BOAC were concerned to avoid 'glamorizing' their front-line female staff. Closer examination of this concern suggests that airline managers feared having their company associated with the *wrong* feminine image. Glamour, to these men, was associated with frivolity. The notion of the 'glamorous hostess' conjured up images of the carefree middle-class socialite with nothing better to do than to entertain, a notion that was both counter to the austerity and socialist concerns of post-war Britain. Glamour was also associated with a measure of female sexual independence that exacerbated deep-rooted concerns about the role of women as wives and mothers in the post-war era (Lewis, 1992; Pugh, 1992; Weeks, 1990). A focus on the hard-working efforts of uniformed female staff served to deflect certain notions of glamour but can be read as part of a broader discourse on appropriate images of sexuality.

The concern with glamour was not just confined to male managers but was shared to some extent by male and female employees. Nonetheless, the suppression of glamour per se did not fully accord with the aspirations, or the notion of glamour, of some female employees. Like many women of the time (Rowbotham, 1999), there were those within the airlines who longed for individuality, for leisure, for adventure and for glamour and where better to find it than in the role of stewardess. Thus, despite the best efforts of airline management a number of women saw the role of stewardess as glamorous. Jeannie Lardner, for example, was set to work as hotel management secretary when she read an article in a French women's magazine about an 'air Stewardess with Air France'. This encouraged her to apply to BOAC and she was employed as a stewardess in May 1952.[15] For Anne Redmile, who became a BOAC flight attendant in 1968, the job offered 'the glamour of unattachment' with the ability to travel to exotic places and meet people without the usual 'pressure on partnerships' (quoted in Petit, 1991). Helen Long, one of BEA's first female stewards, found that although there was not 'so much glamour' on the short-haul routes the job was 'the next best thing to being a film star or model' (quoted in Wright, 1985: 11). Not insignificantly, just after the Second World War, being a stewardess on the transatlantic routes afforded the opportunity to purchase, without ration coupons, items that were otherwise difficult to find in the United Kingdom.[16]

Some tension between management's notion of glamour and that of the aspiring stewardess was evident in the widening gap between corporate recruitment practices and the tremendous growth in applications. A 1946 BEA press release, for example, admitted that 'hundreds of applicants are received every week from girls from all walks of life who are anxious to travel, meet the famous, do a job that is 'different''. But it warned that 'glamour girls need not apply for jobs as stewardesses [who] are employed by British European Airways are paid on an equal basis with an expectation to do the same work as stewards' (*The Star*, 1946).[17] Nonetheless, between 1950 and 1960 the airlines' notions of glamour steadily changed and were reflected in their uniforms, training and recruitment policies.

Uniforms

Initially stewardesses were required to wear uniforms based on the masculine military look, to 'salute senior officers, (and) forgo nail polish' (*The Star*, 1946). Jean Lardner remembers the 'terrible brogues' that stewardesses were required to wear and the uniform, which 'was very much a throw back from the forces'.[18]

> [Uniform] regulations were very strict and woe betide any one who stepped out of line. [A stewardesses] wore collar and tie, there were brass buttons on the jacket which had to be cleaned regularly. [She] was required to have 'short hair, off the collar, no earrings, no jewelry at all, just a watch. [And] wasn't allowed to be seen without her hat unless she was seated at a table having a meal.
>
> (ibid.)

For Lardner, this was not only 'utterly ridiculous' but worrisome because 'everybody wrote reports' on those who failed to wear the uniform in the correct manner.[19] BEA took a similar approach, arguing that the 'B.E.A. mädchen in uniform [...] besides being expected to look pleasant and attractive, has to conform also to very strict rules as to smartness and the wearing of her uniform' (British European Airways, 1954).

Concern with the masculine nature of the uniform contributed to a feminization of airline uniforms over time. Gladys Godley, a BOAC stewardess in the 1950s, took it on herself to try to change the hat she was supplied with. She had a tailor in India refashion it so that instead of the forage style which sat on the head it fitted around the back of the head. It was with 'fear and trembling [that] she showed the result to the catering bosses in London and they approved it' (Wright, 1985: 7). Emboldened, on her next flight to India she had the same tailor round the edges of the jacket to 'make it more feminine', and this was also approved by the catering management (ibid.). Similar disquiet among BEA's stewardesses led to the replacement of the unpopular tricorn hat in April 1950 (British European Airways, 1950b). Eventually, the airline began to listen to suggestions from individual flight attendants and then from the unions involved. By the early 1960s, for instance, many of the modifications made to the airlines' uniforms were 'suggestions by the wearer' (British Overseas Airways Corporation, 1966e). Nonetheless, changes to the uniform were a long time coming. In BOAC, for example, female criticism against wearing a collar and tie 'reached its exasperation peak by 1949 [... but] only finally achieved victory, by transition through a placatory soft-collar stage, in 1952' (ibid.).

Many of the changes accorded with the interests of senior management who wanted their female staff to have a professional but feminine image. In 1958 BOAC hired Norman Hartnell to design a more overtly 'feminine' uniform, and by the end of the decade the airline was boasting that its 'uniformed women are so universally admired for their well-groomed elegance' (British Overseas Airways Corporation, 1966e). Changes included,

> an off-white rayon blouse, replacement of the brass buckle with three pairs of neat buttons, and a redesigned jacket in a non-fluff wool material, waisted and tailored in a simple classic design, with slit pockets slanted downwards and outwards to give a slimmer hipline, worn over a slim pencil-line skirt.

> (ibid.)

Further changes followed, with

> a rounding of the bottom of the jacket, a more pleasing line for the collar and lapels, a more 'open' neckline to the blouse and the attainment of a

Exhibit 6.2   Changing stewardess uniform, 1940s to 1980s

lighter, more flattering shade of navy blue [...] High-heeled court shoes was allowed to oust the unflattering 'flatties' from the aircraft cabin.

(ibid.)

By the early 1960s skirt hemlines were just above the knee, moving to well above the knee by the late 1960s (see Exhibit 6.2). In 1968 the 'official ruling' was that hemlines should not go higher than three inches above the centre of the knee (British Overseas Airways Corporation, 1967b).

There was less concern with the male uniform because it was felt that 'men's fashions change more gradually'. Pilots' uniforms, for example, were seen as 'purely functional dress [that have] to be adaptable to all climates and at the same time project a favourable 'image' of the operator to the peoples of the world' (ibid.).

Training

When BEA and BOAC first hired stewardesses the new recruits underwent training alongside their male counterparts. BOAC, for example, sent stewards and stewardess for an 11-week training course at its catering school where they learned the preparation and service of food and drinks, medical training and first aid, passenger welfare, tropical hygiene, route geography, care of equipment, the organization of the aircraft catering service, aircraft cleanliness, fire precautions, passenger psychology and the folding of clothes (British Overseas Airways Corporation, 1950c). By the time Gladys Godley and Jeannie Lardner joined the airline in the early 1950s things were beginning to change. BOAC management was developing a certain image of femininity that stewardesses would be required to project. To that end, the Corporation employed Elizabeth Arden consultants to help groom stewardesses. According to Godley, stewardesses were provided with Elizabeth Arden toiletries and the consultant 'would peer at our face for blackheads, our legs for hair, our shoulders for dandruff and nails for cleanliness' (Wright, 1985: 7). Lardner found that the trainers were all men who didn't 'teach the women much about the technical side of flying'.[20] Her training included a day at Elizabeth Arden, day nursery experience, classes on aviation medicine, a fire fighting exercise and a visit to a decompression chamber. Stewards and stewardesses had similar duties on board an aircraft but the stewardesses were primarily responsible for looking after the children.

When Francine Carville joined BOAC in 1960 she found that the training had become even more segregated and only 'stewards were trained on aircraft documentation, on bar, on currency [...] on difficult and more responsible courses'.[21] By 1964 the airline had a fully segregated training pro-gramme for stewardesses, colloquially known as 'the charm school,' consist-ing of an eight-week course on preparation and presentation of meals, food values and special diets, cocktail mixing, beauty care, deportment, care of children and invalids, and the complexities of the many documents, which surrounded international travel (British Overseas Airways Corporation, 1964b). There was also a much more segregated division of labour between stewards and stewardesses.[22] In flight the stewards were more involved in the background running of the service while the stewardesses were involved in direct passenger service (Wright, 1985: 6). In Carville's day,

> [stewardesses] never did any work in the galley, or we never did any bar work in that sense. We were always out with the customers, chatting to them. Obviously, you'd greet the passengers. The stewards would prepare the drinks and you would dispense the drinks. And you'd look after the mothers and babies. And you'd give out the meal trays and you'd collect them in. But what I'm saying is that the hard graft behind the scenes was always done by the stewards.
>
> (ibid.)

In the early 1960s Jeannie Lardner became an instructor at the training school but this reflected the nature of the segregated training rather than a simple advancement of women's roles in BOAC. At this time there were two male instructors and two female instructors: 'the men concentrated on the bar and the galley and we did most of the customer services and more with the stewardesses – customer relations, looking after children, babies, special

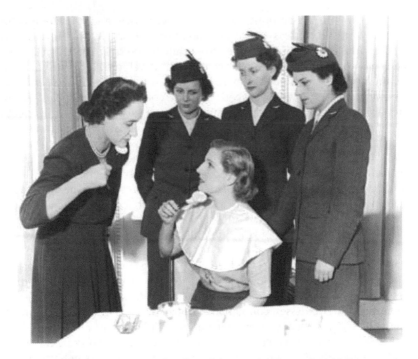

Exhibit 6.3   BEA stewardess 'learn' the art of make-up, late 1940s

care, young people, currency, time schedules, uniform regulations'.[23] Elizabeth Arden consultants still came to the school 'to advise on make-up and hair' but Lardner took over teaching of deportment, previously done by the London School of Deportment (ibid.).[24] BEA also introduced beauty classes in the late 1940s (see Exhibit 6.3) and a gendered division of in-flight practices. Segregated training was extended in 1968 when the airline decided 'that the new entry of stewards [...] should still learn the full technical duties of an aircraft, whereas stewardesses would concentrate on those subjects which were more realistic with their duties' (British European Airways, 1969).[25]

Recruitment

Youth was always an issue in the recruitment of stewardesses: BEA recruited women aged between 25 and 30 but later changed this to 21 and 27 years of age; BOAC required female recruits to be between 23 and 30 years old but reduced this to between 21 to 28 years of age in the late 1950s. Both airlines had higher age limits for stewards. It was taken for granted that men would make stewarding their long-term career and that women would see it as a short-term route to marriage.

In the early 1950s only a marriage bar restricted a stewardess's potential length of service[26] but this changed shortly after Jeannie Larder joined BOAC, when the company introduced contracts, requiring stewardesses to retire from flying after ten years. Stewardesses who became 'too old' to fly or who married ended up being transferred to BOAC's reservations staff (British Overseas Airways Corporation, 1958b).[27] Ten-year contracts eventually gave way to age-specific contracts, with stewardesses being forced to retire from flight crews once they were in their early 30s: older stewardesses were often referred to as 'trolley dollies'.[28] The airline 'wanted to keep the stewardesses [young], to give them a kind of young look'.[29] Lardner suggests that this may also have been due to flight crew concerns because in the 'mid-1950s there was a big intake of second officers and they were often the youngest' crew members, creating a situation where some stewardesses were older and more experienced airline personnel than the pilots (ibid).[30]

In addition to youth, there were also height and weight restrictions for stewardesses. Weight had long been a concern with airlines because of issues of fuel cost and aeronautical balance,[31] leading them to hire boys and relatively small, lightweight men as stewards. Similarly, the first female flight attendants were required to be no more than 5 feet 4 inches and less than 115 pounds (Omelia and Waldock, 2003), but soon these requirements took on different, gendered, meanings when applied to men and women. Following Second World War, and in line with most airlines, BOAC and BEA insisted that stewardesses should have 'a reasonable proportion between height and weight'. This soon came to mean that the women had to have an attractive appearance, and weight requirements for male stewards were far less stringent.

Concern with the ideal weight of the stewardess was the beginning of a growing interest in appearance and bodily looks. Despite the concerns with 'glamour' and 'desexualization', there was always an assumption that stewardesses would be 'attractive girls all anxious to create a good impression' (British Overseas Airways Corporation, 1953).[32] Even though the direct link between an individual's weight and the balance of an aeroplane had long since diminished, between 1951 and 1961 BOAC and BEA decreased by 20 pounds the maximum weight requirement for stewardesses – bringing it below 120 pounds.

Over the years the airlines' notion of attractiveness changed to reflect both their needs and the changing gender discourse of the time. At first this involved an emphasis on passenger service, and, in spite of equity claims, BOAC told its recruiters to describe the work of the stewardess 'as similar to that of a domestic servant' (Edwards and Edwards, 1990: 59). Men were always in charge, from the pilot to the chief and senior steward. For Jean Gordon, a flight attendant from 1947 to 1956, 'the Captain was, of course,

God. He was always "sir". All the other [male crew members] in front of the passengers was referred to as "Mr" '. (quoted in Petit, 1991). Gordon felt that the task of the stewardesses was 'a cross between a governess and a nanny' (ibid.). A decade later Anita Hughes (BOAC stewardess, 1958–60) was 'taught that the passenger was king' (ibid.) and that the company was 'looking for the well-bred young English girl,[33] someone who would be a cross between a governess and a nanny' (ibid.).

When Jeannie Lardner joined BOAC the glamorous stewardess featured in company publicity, and Lardner herself was featured in women's magazines. Stewards, meanwhile, were being pushed into the background and out of the public limelight, causing tensions in the ranks: 'Whenever there was publicity it was always the stewardess who got it. The Royal flights, the VIP flights, it was always the stewardesses [in the spotlight]'.[34] Lardner sensed that 'some of the stewards didn't like [stewardesses] at all [because of] fear of their jobs. [They felt that] these girls coming in could take over' and were also concerned that if more girls were taken on their jobs would disappear' (ibid.).

A decade later Francine Carville felt that, 'there was a different caliber of female employed to the male at that time, in the sense that the stewards didn't have to have the same qualifications'.[35] The company churned 'out stewardesses, and the idea was to keep a flow of young [...] females, who were literally cheap labour' (ibid.). Although stewardesses were not given enough responsibility Carville sees this as 'a two-edged sword,' because 'stewards were always in the background, always doing all the hard work, always having to do all the bars, all the documentation of the aircraft [while] stewardesses had no responsibility all together other than being nice to the passengers'(ibid.)

In 1961 BEA celebrated the recruitment of its 1000th stewardess by announcing new criteria, and a changed attitude to glamour and sexuality, signalling that British airlines had moved away from their anti-glamour stance:

> For the past fifteen years, pretty girls have been leaving their typists desks, hospital wards and a host of other professions to don a BEA uniform [...]
>
> [In the period 1948–61] although the basic educational qualifications were the same [as now], the age limit for the girls was between 25 and 30 and we accepted them up to 9 1/2 stone in weight providing they were no more than five feel eight inches tall. The weight limit was politely reduced to 8 1/2 stone, and at present the vital statistics are trimly and diplomatically defined as 'a reasonable proportion between height and weight'. Age limits too are now between 21 and 27 [...]
>
> British European Airways (1961)[36]

Eroticism

In the early post-war years, while the formal policy of BEA and BOAC was to desexualize the image of their female employees, a series of informal practices began to undermine the official view of the airlines, turning attention away from personality towards physical attractiveness. The most glaring of these informal practices was the development of beauty contests, but was matched by use of female sexuality in the pages of the in-house magazines of BEA and BOAC.

'Beauty' Contests

In early 1948 BOAC supported the newly developed 'Miss Airways' contest but stressed that it was a competition focussed on personality rather than (physical) beauty, and its report on the winner was matter-of-fact: 'Miss Eileen Danten (of material records) was chosen from among twenty competitors as 'Miss Airways'' (British Overseas Airways Corporation, 1948a). Similarly, when BEA was 'invited to enter an international airline contest to find the Perfect Airline Girl', it stressed that this was 'NOT a beauty competition. The accent will be on charm, personality, poise and professional competence' (British European Airways, 1950a). Nonetheless, it added, 'BEA is lucky in having so many attractive girls' (ibid.).

In rapid order the number of such contests proliferated[37] and any attempt to disguise them as anything other than 'beauty' contests receded, that by the mid-1950s they were advertised as 'bathing beauty contests' (British Overseas Airways Corporation, 1955a),[38] with the full support of senior management. When, for example, a BOAC stewardess was crowned 'Queen of the Air' in 1955 Sir Miles Thomas sent her an official cable, stating 'your success is a great tribute to British girlhood' (British Overseas Airways Corporation, 1955b).[39]

In-house newsletters

In various ways the in-house newsletters of both airlines shifted attention away from personality to physical attractiveness. By the late 1960s the young maiden had given way to a new feminine archetype of the sexually available woman. Over time the notion of men as technical and women as non-technical took a new turn, with men being cast as the 'real' workers and women as largely decorative. The latter was achieved in a number of ways, including photographs of female staff with animals and senior managers, and as 'pin-up girls'. From around 1948 onwards in-house newsletters used animals to frame the physical beauty of young female staff, including Siamese cats, raccoons, baby kangaroos, lion-cubs, baby crocodiles, turkeys and baby chimpanzees. In this vein, a picture of a woman and an elephant was titled, 'beauty and the beast' (British Overseas Airways Corporation, 1949c).[40] Attractive young women were also used to frame the authority and importance of managers and pilots, including pictures of stewardesses 'assisting' BEA's chef (British European Airways, 1960a); pilots flanked by grass-skirted Hawaiian women (British Overseas Airways Corporation, 1962d); an airline Vice President 'escorting two glamorous stewardesses' (British Overseas Airways Corporation, 1963b); and an airline captain flanked by 'six dolly birds' (British Overseas Airways Corporation, 1966f). The use of the pin-up appeared in 1951 when the front cover of *BOAC Review* featured a 'cover girl' – a stewardess holding a baby (British Overseas Airways Corporation, 1951). By the mid-1950s BOAC was regularly featuring 'a cover girl' on its front page, and in 1958 introduced a 'Picture of the Month' feature (British Overseas Airways Corporation, 1958c); purporting to feature some aspect of work activity all the photographs, with one exception, were of young, 'attractive' females. In contrast, the series was replaced with 'Job of the Month', which focussed on the work of male employees, beginning with a profile of a male-only battery shop (British Overseas Airways Corporation, 1959f).

BEA was slower to develop pin-ups (introducing 'cover girls' on the back pages of its in-house magazine in 1963), but more advanced in its eroticism of women. *BEA Magazine* took the cover girl analogy furthest with the introduction in 1967 of a series that featured female employees as 'Miss January', 'Miss February' and so on.[41] From the beginning BEA Magazine focussed on women's physical characteristics, through cartoons, caricatures, photographs, and descriptors – depicting the ideal woman as young, voluptuous, full bodied but perfectly proportioned. This archetype of the sexually alluring woman was achieved through concerns with women's weight, contrasts between seemingly ugly and attractive women, and a focus on nudity. For example, in one cartoon fun is made of an overweight passenger (British European Airways, 1948c) and in another a male manager says to a supposedly overweight secretary: 'an' we must get our waste down – er, nothing personal, of course, Miss Elphin' (British Overseas Airways Corporation, 1962e). The notion of the ideal woman is pursued through a series of cartoons featuring the curvaceous 'Andya Ticketover' and her unnamed but 'ugly' female colleagues. One cartoon shows a group of very plain women with ill-fitting uniforms, one of whom is pointing to Andya, whose shapely body is barely contained by her uniform, saying: 'And here, girls, is Miss Andya Ticketover to show us how we shall all look in our new uniforms'. In another cartoon Andya is shown with large breasts but not wearing a bra under her blouse. Two 'ugly' stewardesses are commenting, 'I wonder what she'll forget next' (British European Airways, 1960b).

Cartoons also introduced female nudity to *BEA Magazine* in 1948, with a drawing of a naked female swimmer who is strategically covered by bushes (British European Airways, 1948b). By the 1960s cartoons were portraying full frontal nudity, complete with drawings on nipples and buttocks, including one of a 'shapely' woman shown in the airline's uniform section complaining that nothing fits (British European Airways, 1962) and another featuring three naked stewardesses outside of the uniform store, complaining to a pilot that 'They could only fit us with hats and shoes' (British European Airways, 1968). In a similar vein both airlines used a series of photographs of women in bathing suits, often under the guise of employees pictured on holiday.

Descriptors of female attractiveness gradually crept into stories throughout both airlines' in-house newsletters. First they were focussed on overall beauty (e.g., 'pretty', 'charming', 'attractive') and then on more specific areas of anatomy (e.g., 'curvaceous', 'blond', 'flashing eyes'). In one example, a woman is referred to as 'petite, blue-eyed, silver-haired [and] prettier than a walking encyclopedia has any right to be' (British Overseas Airways Corporation, 1960a), and in another example the reader is informed that a photograph of two women in bathing suits is of, 'stewardess Miss Marion Prosser [...] 22, auburn-haired 38–25–37 and [...] Miss Joy Thorpe, a blue-eyed blond with a 38–25–38 figure. Joy was also equipped with a Bermuda sun-tan' (British Overseas Airways Corporation, 1962b).

Other stories linked female sexuality directly to promiscuity and/or male fantasies, including an in-house competition that invited (male) readers to match pictures of women's faces with pictures of women's legs, asking 'Have you seen legs so deliciously displayed [...] We're sure you'll have fun matching the right face to the right legs' (British European Airways, 1967).

In the mid-1960s the airlines began to use female sexuality to sell their product. One pictured a 'sexy, seductive' woman with the caption, 'there is always time for a new experience [...] Triumphantly swift, silent, serene. The BOAC VC10' (British Overseas Airways Corporation, 1965a). This was followed four months later with a picture of a bikini-clad model on top of a VC10 and another focussed on the mini-skirted legs of an unknown woman that asked 'Should BOAC stewardesses wear the mini-skirt?' Drawing heavily on sexual innuendo, BOAC answered its own question, replying 'all our jets are now equipped with the[most luxurious seats ever designed. So[...]who needs mini-skirts?' (British Overseas Airways Corporation, 1967a). Three months later BOAC introduced 'the mini-dress' for all stewardesses on BOAC services between New York and the Caribbean.[42]

Race, gender and sexuality

In the 1950s Britain was adjusting to the new post-colonial realities,[43] and a 'long boom' in the economy and subsequent severe labour shortages that led the government to embark on a policy of widespread recruitment in the Commonwealth countries (Ben-Tovim and Gabriel, 1984). Nonetheless, despite gradual changes in hiring policy it was a long time before British airlines depicted people of colour as 'normal' members of their company's community of employees: men and women fared differently in the process.

African men were still depicted as backward and incapable of self-rule. Paradoxically this characterization appeared in a BOAC report on its 'Africanisation' Policy, designed to groom 'Africans of high education [...] so that they eventually may be suitable for consideration for senior appointments in the Corporation' (British Overseas Airways Corporation, 1954b). The report warned, however, that the process would not be easy because in 'some instances an imperfect command of the English language causes communication of abstract ideas to be difficult' and there is 'the problem of the disciplining of Africans by Africans within the framework of airline organization' (ibid.).

Indian and Pakistani men fared a little better in the pages of the newsletters. They received slightly more coverage and came to be associated with technical and clerical jobs, and with long service. However, such reports were usually curt, and failed to provide any details of the subject's experience or work. For example, a reference to Mabud Mirza states that he has 'been with the BOAC Accounts department at Karachi for [...] three years [...] and is an outstanding hockey player'. Similarly a report on the fact that 'Mr. Julius E. Kantharia – engineering staff, Bombay' – had become one the newest members of the company's '25 Club' tells us nothing about his job, background or history with the company (British Overseas Airways Corporation, 1958a).[44]

From the late 1940s to the early 1960s the more enduring images of people of colour were focussed on Asian female employees, especially flight attendants, as part of a marketing strategy. BOAC began to hire Chinese, Indian, Pakistani and Japanese stewardesses to serve specific routes from their country of origin (see Exhibit 6.4).

Images of the exotic were evoked through the use and descriptions of 'national dress,' including the use of Saris, 'traditional kimonos' and the cheongsam. The outfits constituted an important break with the military-style uniform worn by British stewardesses and were seen as 'eye-catching, publicity winning innovation(s)' (British Overseas Airways Corporation, 1962f). Much of the so-called traditional dress was used to suggest the subservience[45] and, on occasion, sexuality of Asian women. While Indian and Pakistani women were imaged as attentive and servile, 'it was the Chinese girls in their side slit cheongsam that sent male passengers' pulses racing. *The Financial Times* was always being dropped in the aisle so the girls had to bend down and pick it up to the men's delight. The girls had, of course, been well trained in this' (BOAC trainer, Gladys Godly, quoted in Wright, 1985: 8). References to the 'mysterious east' added an air of sexual intrigue but also served to privilege 'westerners'. A story about a new service on the San Francisco–New York sector, for example, traded on the imagery of (US-born) Chinese stewardesses (dressed in 'dark-blue Mandarin-style overcoat[s]'), with the heading 'East Goes Further West' (British Overseas Airways Corporation, 1961f). A story entitled 'East meets West', pictured a group of women from Japan, Ghana, Nigeria and India who were training to be flight attendants at London Airport;' the newsletter describes them as 'a regular glamour league of nations' (British Overseas Airways Corporation, 1961g).

Exhibit 6.4 The training of Indian, Pakistani and Chinese stewardesses

Source: Photographs courtesy of Jeannie Sutherland. She is the trainer at the centre of all these pictures.

(c)

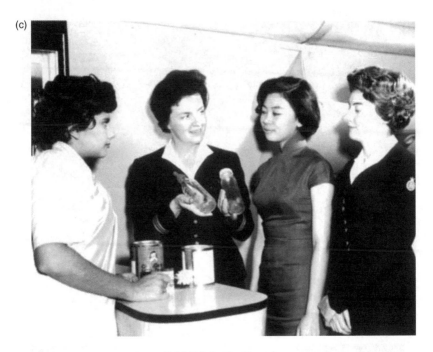

Exhibit 6.4   Continued

Afro-Caribbean women were virtually absent from the newsletters until the mid-1960s[46] and then were typecast as pleasantly jolly, as in a report that 'five sunny Jamaican girls' were hired to work 'alongside British stewardesses' on BOAC's Caribbean–New York route (British Overseas Airways Corporation, 1965c).

In the United Kingdom itself only a few people of colour were employed at BOAC during the first two decades of the post-war era,[47] to the extent it made news when they were hired. Thus, for example, when Shirley Shen – 'a 26-year old Hong Kong girl' – joined BOAC's flight operations in 1960 she was heralded as the 'first Asian girl to enter the highly skilled field of flight operations' (British Overseas Airways Corporation, 1960c).[48] Seven years later there was still some fascination with the employment of Chinese women in the United Kingdom, when it was reported that 'Pricilla Chan, Chinese stewardess, has been appointed station clerk at Heathrow' (British Airways, 1967).

In contrast to BOAC, *BEA Magazine* had few images of people of colour. A rare exception was in a book review contrasting Western women with those of the East. The review argued that 'in this age of emancipation of women it brings one to a halt with a jolt to realise that the women of the East do not have the same freedom which we in the West are accustomed' (British European Airways, 1965a). The difference between the two airlines may be due, in some small part, to the fact that BOAC served Commonwealth countries while BEA served European countries.

From desexualization to eroticization: Organizational and social influences

As airlines moved into 'the jet age' they were under increasing pressure to sell airline seats. Airlines, with a greatly increased number of seats to fill and several competitors vying for available passengers, needed to find ways to attract passengers and this led to limited price wars but also moves to sell airline *service*. In the latter regard, advertising increasingly focussed on the sexuality of the female flight attendants. In the United States the problem was exacerbated in the early 1960s by the Civil Aviation Board's (CAB) granting of an unprecedented number of new routes to encourage further competition. Airlines with identical routes and fares focussed on making their service and thus their service providers – the stewardesses – more distinctive (Kane, 1974).

In Britain the need to be competitive had come from other types of pressure. Both BEA and BOAC were government-owned airlines and to some extent free from the economic problems of attempting to make a profit. Nonetheless, they were under considerable political pressures to become and remain economically viable. BOAC's Sir Miles Thomas, for instance, worked to make the airline a profitable concern by, among other things, developing marketing strategies and making a series of deep cuts in the number of employees. In 1955 BOAC felt considerable economic pressure when Pan Am purchased twenty Boeing 707 Stratoliners and twenty-five Douglas DC-8s. This was the most expensive purchase ever made by an airline and had far-reaching effects, with few airlines being able to stand the competitive pace of having to reequip on such a scale (Penrose, 1980b). Prohibited from developing and purchasing state-of-the-art planes, BOAC was left 'flogging the air with aircraft which, if not out of date, certainly soon would be', with international competitors 'getting newer and faster and more economical aircraft' (Thomas, 1964: 344). In the meantime, while pressing government ministers for permission to help develop a new aircraft (the Comet), BOAC put much of its efforts into its cabin service, including the strategy of hiring of 'local' women as stewardesses from the countries served by the airline. (Thomas, 1964: 344).[49]

Government ministers were reluctant to support Thomas's call for the development of a new Comet aircraft and on 8 March 1956 he placed his resignation before the Board. Gerard d'Erlanger, who returned to the airline business from banking and African land interests, succeeded him but over the next four years fought the same political battles before retiring in 1960.

On his last day as Chairman he reported that the airline had made a small profit, despite the fact that Pan Am and TWA had established a traffic growth on the North Atlantic routes more than five times greater than that of BOAC. He handed over to Rear Admiral Sir Matthew Slattery.

The 'Permissive Society'

Erotic images were not out of place in the Britain of the 1960s. Although the label of 'permissiveness' glosses over a number of social contradictions (Weeks, 1990), there were several changes in the way that sex and sexuality were viewed, with women experiencing 'the most obvious sexualization'. The changing roles and sexual imagery of women was at the root of a number of legal changes, including abortion and divorce reform, family-planning legislation, and reform of the obscenity law (Weeks, 1990: 256).

A number of factors contributed to this changing image of female sexuality, including an increased role for women in the workforce as 'a vital element in the expansion of the consumer economy', and the increasing utilization, stimulation and reshaping of female sexuality to the demands of mass marketing (Weeks, 1990: 257–58). Some of the newer journals aimed at women (e.g., *Cosmopolitan*) were redefining female sexuality in terms of its possibilities for pleasure and enjoyment 'unbounded by the old exigencies of compulsory childbirth or endless domestic chores' (ibid.). The female body was being constructed as 'sensitive and sexual', capable of stimulation and excitation, and 'therefore demanding care and attention if women were to be sexual and sexually desirable to men' (ibid.). In short, 'Women were asserting their own perceived sexual needs, though largely within a heterosexual framework and in the terms allowed by commercialism' (ibid.).

At the movies the 'sex kitten' and the 'sex bombshell' became new popular images of women and female desirability. Audiences – especially male audiences – were lured by a new female icon – exemplified by Marilyn Monroe in *The Seven Year Itch*, Ursula Andress in *Dr. No*, Jane Russell in *The Paleface*, Carroll Baker in *Baby Doll* and Brigitte Bardot in *And God Created Woman*.

The stewardess and popular culture

In the workplace the stewardess became the icon of changing images of sexuality. In the pre-Second World War era movie images of the stewardess dealt with such issue as training (e.g., *Flying Air Hostess*)[50] and romance (e.g., *Flight Angels*)[51]. These story lines continued in the early post-war years and included the 1953 British film, *Innocents in Paris*, which featured BEA but by the early 1960s the stewardess role had become eroticized with movies such as *Come Fly With Me* (1962) and *Boeing Boeing* (1965). In these later two movies stewardesses were portrayed as having an active and promiscuous sex life in their search for a husband. The sexual adventure of stewardesses, thereafter, became a cliché in movies and was furthered by such films as the *Stewardess* (1970) and *Coffee, Tea or Me?* (1973). Romance, glamour and sexual promiscuity were among the themes pursued in several *Airport* (1970, 1975, 1977 and 1979) movies, *Flying High* (1975) and the comedy *Airplane* (1980). Similarly, 'the sexy stewardess' became the subject of product advertising, novels and popular books such as *Coffee, Tea, or Me?*[52]

Coffee, Tea, or Me? was one of a long line of books on the role of the stewardess. While earlier books emphasized technical training and education, later books focussed on glamour and beauty. In 1951 Mary F. Murray's[53] career handbook for airline stewardesses warned potential recruits that 'being an airline stewardess involves a lot more than an interest in flying and a pleasing personality. It is a serious career for which applicants today are carefully trained' (Murray, 1951). Appearance was important and 'any physical disability or noticeable scar will cause the applicant to be disqualified' (Murray, 1951). The training of successful candidates included a wealth of technical detail, including airline codes, the work of the flight crew, how an airline operates and the workings of an airliner. Thus, recruits had to meet fairly high educational standards, with 'at least two years of higher learning [in courses that] included study in history, geography, rhetoric, sociology, elementary psychology, physical education, literature, world affairs, and English' (Murray, 1951: 46). Murray noted that the 'general trend today seems to be a return to the original term, stewardess' and away from the notion of the air hostess (Murray, 1951: 64).

Two decades later things were very different. Keith Saunders's[54] career advice, for example, stressed that 'being an airline stewardess has long been considered one of the most 'glamourous' professions open to young women and, if anything, it is still more glamourous and exciting in today's jet age' (Saunders, 1968: inside cover). Outlining the requirements to be a stewardess, Saunders focuses on age (young), height (relatively small), weight ('well distributed'), vision (no eyeglasses), education ('a high school diploma or better'), languages ('a reasonable command of English'), health (physically fit), marital status (single) and appearance ('neat, natural, well-groomed, clear complexion') (Saunders, 1968: 13).[55] Unlike Murray, Saunders depicted a trend back towards the notion of the air 'hostess,' seeing it as

> more closely descriptive of the function of the cabin attendant [...] who welcomes the airline's guests (the passengers) into her home (the aircraft cabin) and who strives to put them at ease and make them comfortable, who converses with them and caters to their normal needs and whims.
>
> Saunders (1968: 13)[56]

Compliance and resistance

Despite British airlines' anti-glamour stance women were attracted to flight attending because of the supposed glamour of the job. Jean Lardner, for example, wanted to be a stewardess because 'it was one of the ten top jobs for girls'.[57] Similarly, Francine Carville followed 'every girl's dream to be an air stewardess'.[58] She had completed nurses' training but wanted to see the world and felt that the best way to do so was as a flight attendant. That was the early 1960s when, according to Carville,

> a girl who came out of a high school either wanted to do teaching or stew-ardessing, there weren't that many jobs open to women. It was a job where within eighteen months [you could be] totally independent, away from you parents. Although you couldn't afford a flat to buy you shared flats with other stewardesses and were given the total freedom of the world. So it was an attractive occupation, so [the airline recruiters] could afford to be choosy.
>
> (ibid.)

Indeed, airline recruiters were choosy and many of their choices revolved around the looks and 'pleasing personality' of each candidate. The glamour of the stewardess role and its attraction for young women was often captured (or reproduced) in the pages of the in-house magazines. One cartoon that exemplifies this depicts a woman and her 'attractive' daughter in the office of a psychoanalyst. The mother is saying: 'I thought I had better bring my daughter along to you ... [as] she doesn't want to be an air stewardess' (British European Airways, 1952a).[59]

For many recruits the airlines' introduction of make-up consultants and deportment training played to their own notions of glamour. In the words of one former British stewardess, the make-up courses 'enhance the girls' natural loveliness. Airlines and the bachelors enjoy similar taste' (quoted in Petit, 1991). There is no evidence, at least prior to the 1960s, that stewardesses were, on the whole, opposed to such things as make-up classes. When problems began to surface it was with such things as the relative lack of responsibility, short-term contracts, and the fact that the training over-emphasized looks and appearance at the expense of other forms of training given to the stewards. Jeannie Lardner, for example, felt that her training 'didn't relate much to the job at all' and that consequently 'stewardesses were always bottom of the list'.[60] Nonetheless, when a group of stewardesses formed a union Lardner would have nothing to do with it. For her 'it was too much, well, burn your bra types. But in all fairness, the majority of us were happy. It was just a few who thought if they formed an association they would get better, but it didn't work out' (ibid.).

Francine Carville was more ambivalent about some of the aspects of the training. In her opinion the emphasis on youth and the consequent age contracts was 'such a waste of good people' and probably accounted for the fact that the airline found it hard to find female managers with the right experience. In her opinion stewardesses were trained to exercise little authority and responsibility once they graduated. On the one hand, she felt that this wasn't entirely a bad thing: 'You could have a very nice life actually in that sense' (ibid.). On the other hand, she recognized that this was a barrier to promotion, that 'once there was equal opportunity you could do anything on the aircraft. It was the barriers you had to break down' (ibid.). Unlike Lardner, Carville felt that unionization helped the stewardesses to improve their position. When she joined the airline a closed shop agreement had been signed with the unions. A union representative would 'come in on the first day of training and make every person in that room join. That is how [the airline] became strongly unionized and got very much better conditions for cabin crew' (ibid.). Eventually, with everybody 'employed under the same conditions, same pay ... stewardesses had to be retrained of stewards' responsibilities, and for that you had to take responsibility for your own promotion and becoming part of this workload. It took us not a long time for that to bed down' (ibid.).

One of the glamour stereotypes surrounding the role of stewardess was its association with 'good marriage opportunities'. In Francine Carville's experience many stewardesses married long before they reached the tenth year of their contracts. Some stewardesses saw marriage to a pilot as a prime example of the good marriage opportunities afforded by the job and thus tended to socialize with the pilots (ibid.). A 'lot of the girls went for the flight deck. They were impressed by the stripes' (stewardess quoted in Petit, 1991). Opinions on the marriage opportunities of the stewardesses were reinforced through numerous announcements, of the engagements and weddings between pilots and stewardesses, in the pages of the in-flight magazines. In particular both BEA and BOAC made much of the high turnover of stewardesses, which they linked to high rates of marriage.[61]

The association of the stewardess role with glamour and marriage may, in part, help to explain the acquiescence of some to a corporate focus on female youth and attractiveness. For one thing, an emphasis on glamour and marriage helped the airlines to attract the 'right type' of recruit, that is women who would understand and accept the need to look young and attractive, undertake training in deportment and make-up, and retire on marriage, attainment of an age limit or completion of a limited number of years of service. In many ways this image of the stewardess accorded with the growing tensions within an evolving social discourse of sexuality. On the one hand, there was still very much an emphasis on wife and motherhood as the primary roles of women. But on the other hand, there were various signs that the young women of the day also envisaged some measure of economic and sexual independence before marrying (Lewis, 1992;

Rowbotham, 1999). In many ways the image of the stewardess reconciled some of the tensions between glamour and marriage, offering a period of independence, travel and social opportunity unrivalled by any other jobs for women, followed by 'a good marriage' which afforded the possibility of continued glamour within marriage. Where acquiescence tended to break down was over the requirement to resign on marriage. A number of stewardesses were already objecting at having to give up such a relatively good job just because they were married. Some of these formed an association to press for better conditions but were initially unsuccessful. Others eventually saw the stewardess image itself as the problem, because 'glamour is a strange commodity, and you have to be in a particular state of mind to experience it' (Kane, 1974: 48). For former stewardess Pauline Kane, the glamour 'myth only substituted for Victorian prudishness and subjugation a kind of impersonal body worship of women – women who were unblemished, girlish, passive, obedient picture postcards, women who were the playthings of the elegant rich and powerful and creative. Airline stewardesses were selected to play that role' (Kane, 1974: 29). Similar attitudes had emerged in British airlines.

Flight attending in North America

Changes in female imagery over the same period were less dramatic in TCA and Pan Am, more differences in magnitude than in kind. When TCA hired stewardesses in 1938 the profession was already undergoing a change throughout North America. The focus had shifted from flying 'nurses' in functional outfits to glamorous 'hostesses' in uniforms that were 'more feminine and fashionable' (Omelia and Waldock, 2003: 27). Wartime encouraged airlines to play down glamour and emphasize duty, patriotism and service, leading to more professionalism in appearance and even in unionization (Newby, 1986).[62] It was at this point that Pan Am introduced female flight attendants and positioned them as wartime replacements rather than permanent glamour girls.

In the post-war era there was something of a return to glamour but, as Murray (1951) reflects, this was tempered by a move away from the hostess-style of imagery to 'the image of the perfect wife. They wore shapely but demure uniforms and were shown in advertisements to be as adept at warming a baby's bottle as mixing a martini' (Omelia and Waldock, 2003: 50). This was very much the image of Pan Am, with constant news stories of stewardesses leaving to get married.[63] The link between stewardesses, glamour and marriage is exemplified in a 1950s cartoon of a large, unattractive woman who is standing behind a pilot, and he is saying to an airline recruiter: 'She wants a job as a stewardess ... says she is not likely to leave to get married' (Pan American Airways, 1953a). It was the same story at TCA. Many of the early post-war issues of *Between Ourselves* were adorned with pictures of stewardesses[64] performing various services, including assisting children, dealing with animals, serving passengers and accompanying various men in a variety of pursuits. The one major difference between the two airlines in this regard was that Pan Am stewardesses wore a stylish, feminine-looking outfit while those of TCA were dressed in more of a military-style uniform.

In almost identical language, both TCA and Pan Am imaged their stewardesses as glamorous but hardworking. At TCA it took 'more than glamour and the right qualifications to become a TCA stewardess', it took hard training (Trans-Canada Air Lines, 1950). At Pan Am 'the trim young woman who smiles prettily at you as she walks down the aisle of a PAA Clipper high in the skies has earned the job through study, training and hard work' (Pan American Airways, 1951). Nonetheless, a focus on bodily attraction and sexuality was not far from the surface. Like their British counterparts, the physical attractiveness of the female body was celebrated in a series of cartoons, photographs, descriptors and innumerable 'beauty competitions'. However, unlike British airlines, such imagery was not in sharp contrast to official policy.

Large breasted women featured in several Pan Am cartoons, including one where a young woman is told to take the week off so as not to distract the men while they are 'trying to win the Safety contest' (Pan American Airways, 1954: 12).[65] Such cartoons were absent from TCA's newsletters but often carried line drawings of women in bathing suits and, in at least one case, a naked woman – shown hiding her private parts with a towel as she answers the telephone (Trans-Canada Air Lines, 1949a: 19). From around 1947 onwards, both airlines' newsletters featured numerous photographs of women in bathing suits[66] sponsored by 'beauty competitions' (e.g., 'Miss Pan American,' 'Miss TCA'),[67] pictured female employees as pin-ups or 'cover girls'[68] and used almost identical language to describe female employees according to desirable bodily looks. Pan Am, for example, described an employee in the communications department as 'a new acquirement – a luscious six-foot blonde named Willa' (Pan American Airways, 1947c). TCA, meanwhile, presented a 'Five Year Pin to luscious Marion McPhail' (Trans-Canada Air Lines, 1949b).[69] And both airlines had a thing for showing off women's legs by reference to their nylons, with TCA picturing a group of stewardesses 'demonstrating their nylons' (Trans-Canada Air Lines, 1946a; see Exhibit 6.5). and Pan Am showing a male employee holding a measuring stick to the leg of one of two women showing off their nylons (Pan American Airways, 1946b: 3).[70]

With the onset of the 1960s the archetypal western woman moved from wife and mother to someone who was 'free-spirited and independent, to the Pill, and liked being single. The sexual revolution had arrived', (Omelia and Waldock, 2003: 76) and airlines, including Pan Am and to a lesser extent TCA,[71] were among the first to adapt (if not invent) this image to sell airplane seats. Much of the imagery was built around the stewardess' appearance

Exhibit 6.5   Those fabulous *nylons*!

but also advertising campaigns that traded heavily on sexual innuendo. But this was not a stretch for Pan Am and TCA who had been using similar imagery in much of their newsletters, including a Pan Am headline that read 'Our Girls Can Say 'No' in 20 Different Languages' (Pan American Airways, 1957b: 8),[72] and a TCA story stating that 'one reason why the New York load factors are so high is Irene Kendall, stenographer' (Trans-Canada Air Lines, 1959: 7). Not insignificantly, the main differences between the 1960s and the 1950s were that the sheer number of pictures of women in bathing suits increased substantially, the poses were sexually suggestive, there were a number of overtly erotic imagery (e.g., a TCA stewardess straddling a plane) and female uniforms were made to reproduce the image of the sexually independent woman of 1960s popular culture. The only major difference between Pan Am and TCA was that the Canadian airline avoided the more overtly 'sexist advertising' that was common in the United States (Newby, 1986: 58); this might be explained by TCA's dominance of the Canadian market and the relative lack of competition on its domestic routes, although its competitors did resort to cheap measures (including flimsy outfits and dancing girls – Newby, 1986). Nonetheless, on 1 January 1960, in keeping with the new emphasis on female youth and sexuality, TCA announced that the maximum age for stewardesses was to be dropped to 32 years old, claiming that those older than this were 'often the ones least able to meet the standards of appearance and personally which the public expects of a stewardess' (quoted in Newby, 1986). Likewise Pan Am sought young women between 5 feet 3 inches and 5 feet 9 inches with a 'pleasant personality and appearance' (Pan American Airways, 1969).

Summary

The change from desexualization to the eroticism at BOAC and BEA had several roots. There were conflicting notions of glamour that eventually encouraged a new discourse on sexuality. There were the official concerns of senior management to avoid the wrong image but the unofficial sense of traditional notions of womanhood. And there was, of course, the aspiration of female employees whose sexuality was framed by male images and anxieties. There were conflicting practices. While official rules encouraged a public image of equity – supported by such things as nomenclature, uniforms and equalized training – informal rules encouraged an exploration of beauty and glamour. Then there was the issue of masculinity and femininity. If we accept the argument that 'masculinity and femininity are socially constructed within a historical context of gender relations' (Kimmel, 1987: 14), what part did the changing presence of female employees play in the corporate imaging of men and women? Arguably as females became a permanent feature of the airline and, as a result, were redefined as women so men faced the problem of displaced masculinities. Multiple masculinities are evident in the post-war era and each fared differently in the face of changing female employment. Piloting and engineering prospered as masculine projects, while that of stewarding receded, suggesting that not all masculine types are resilient to and have dominance over forms of femininity.[73] Nonetheless, on reflection, male-domination of piloting, engineering and management was not, on its own, enough to retain a strong masculine image. There needed to be a repositioning of masculine identity and perhaps that explains, at least in part, why a stress on male virility and an eroticization of the female body developed when it did.[74] Female resistance also played a role in the documented changes. Throughout the post-war era female employees effected a number of changes, contributing to changing notions of fashion and glamour but also the range and levels of jobs that a woman could do. At first the changes were small and piece-meal but a level of dissatisfaction with the male status quo was growing and on the political arena the new women's movement was about to explode on to the scene. Male angst about both sets of changes is reflected in a 1966 cartoon in *BEA Magazine*, which shows a stewardess standing by a plane advertising the 'world's first ladies only service'. The caption reads: 'Suffra-jet'. As we shall see in Chapter 7 the various seeds of a new more equitable workplace had long taken root by the onset of the 1970s.

Finally, it would appear that airlines followed broad cultural changes as societies became characterized as 'permissive'. As Rowbotham argues (in the chapter's opening quote), the notion of the sexually liberated young woman was more reflective of social tension than resolve as females struggled between new freedoms (from pregnancy, marriage, etc.) and new constraints (type-cast as sexually free and available). The question remains, however, as to how far certain airlines such as Pan Am, TCA, BOAC and BEA followed the social mores of the time and how much did they actually construct those times. There are a number of feminist scholars who argue that organizations are 'inevitably shaped by a wide variety of social forces, gender notably amongst them' (Witz and Savage, 1992: 57). On the other hand, there are those who argue that social discourses develop, are maintained, and are questioned in social 'places' or enduring bounded networks of social interactions, such as organizations. These feminist scholars contend that organizational arrangements contribute unique variants of gendered relationships that may have implications beyond the bounds of a particular set of organizational relationships (Burrell, 1984; Ferguson, 1984; Kanter, 1977). In short, as we explore developments within BOAC and BEA we need to examine the extent to which, as peculiar bounded networks, they can be said to have *reflected* or *created* public discourse on gender.

7

Close Encounters of the Third Kind: Towards an Employment Equity Discourse

> [The] workplace equality movement is essentially contradictory. On the one hand sex equality is a demand women make on their own behalf … . On the other hand it is a policy introduced into organizations by owners and managers 'on behalf of' women. Though some employers are genuinely concerned with justice, often it is transparently clear that it is organizational ends they have primarily in mind. They aim to improve recruitment and retention of women whose qualities they perceive themselves as needing. Or they just want a good public image.
>
> Cynthia Cockburn (1991: 16)

Introduction

In 1974 the British Government merged BOAC and BEA to form British Airways (BA), which began operations with just under 59, 000 employees, of whom approximately one in four were women. The airline had one female board member but very few female managers, and most female employees continued to be ghettoized in the clerical and support staff sections. Strong barriers remained against the employment of female pilots and engineers. Corporate imagery of the female employee continued to focus on physical attractiveness, and the 'sexy stewardess' remained a central theme in advertising campaigns. Yet beneath the advertising image of the new airline things were beginning to change. The percentage of female employees was growing, with women entering jobs and ranks previously confined to men. When, in 1991, BA announced that it was taking part in *Opportunity 2000* – an initiative aimed at improving the number of women at all levels of management – it was reflecting the momentum that had already taken hold in the company. How that momentum got started and how it was mediated by competing discourses of culture change, merger and privatization is the subject of this chapter.

In the United States the momentum started earlier, with the passing of the Equal Pay Act in 1963, and the Civil Rights Act the following year. Flight attendants were among the first to test the new laws – 'challenging discriminatory policies based on gender, race, age, weight, pregnancy and marital status' (Association of Flight Attendants – CWA, 2005). Throughout the industry airlines were beginning to investigate equity issues, including Pan Am, which established 'affirmative action' and 'opportunities for women' programs in the early 1970s, and, albeit slowly, women were being hired as commercial airline pilots[1] and promoted to senior management positions.

In Canada, preoccupation with nationhood meant that on the legal front things were slower than in the United States, with the Employment Equity Act becoming law in 1986. Nonetheless, at Air Canada in the 1970s equity debates went to the forefront, the airline introduced employment equity policies, and women won the right to become pursers, move into senior management positions and be hired as pilots.

At this juncture: Inside British Airways (1970–91)

In 1991 women constituted one third of BA's employees (see Figure 3.1). At the top there were no female board members but the company had just appointed its first ever female executive – Gail Redwood – as Company Secretary (British Airways, 1991).[2] Below her, women made up around 20 per cent of the airline's managers (ibid.), appearing on the organizational charts of all but two key departments[3] – Flight Crew and Engineering. Yet even in these latter areas changes were underway.

Since 1987 the male dominated Flight Crew Division had been recruiting female pilots. That year Lynn Barton, an experienced pilot with another airline, began her career with BA as co-pilot of a Boeing 747, gaining the distinction of being not only BA's first female pilot but also the first female pilot in Britain to be licensed to fly 'jumbo' jets.[4] By 1991, although still a woefully small number, there were 267 female commercial airline pilots in Britain – many of them flying with BA.[5] In Engineering, as part of new equity initiatives, women were being hired as 'foremen' and the Director, Alistair Cummings, was publicly committed to further improvements in the number of women (and people of colour) at all levels of the Division.

It is also noticeable at this time that management training opportunities, through specially designed higher education courses, were opening up to female staff. The Diploma of Business Administration (DBA) and Masters in Business Administration (MBA) courses, for instance, included various women who went on to make their mark in management.[6]

Employment Equity Policy

BA, responding to legislative changes, introduced an equal opportunities policy in 1984, but it was not until 1991 that the airline made a public and detailed commitment to far-reaching changes in hiring and promotion of women and people of colour. That year Sir Colin Marshall, 'Deputy Chairman' and CEO of BA, joined the Conservative Government's *Opportunity 2000* initiative, which brought together leading members of the business community to investigate how women could advance to the top ranks of industry and commerce. With a 'greater awareness of the many issues surrounding equal opportunities' (British Airways, 1991), Marshall initiated a series of management workshops that led to the formation of an Equality Steering Group (ESG), consisting of departmental 'champions', and a number of key recommendations, including commitment to:

1. Ensure top-level support for employment equity initiatives;
2. Clearly establish the airline's position on employment equity and how it will be handled;
3. Develop and promote relevant employment policies;
4. Make equality of opportunity part of the airline's culture;
5. Introduce pre-selection training prior to job applications where appropriate;
6. Remove any inadvertent discrimination from recruitment/selection procedures;
7. Become much more involved in the local community;
8. Communicate ongoing progress (British Airways, 1991).

John Watson, the Director of Human Resources and Information Management, headed up the new ESG and Eva Lauermann was given HR responsibilities for equal opportunities. Lauermann was one of five women on the fourteen-person committee,[7] which introduced several initiatives, including 'a revision of the Corporate Employment Equity Policy, the development of a range of flexible employment contracts, and examination of [BA's] recruitment and test procedures' (ibid.). Watson, saw the major task of the ESG as to ensure that progress is 'seen to be made', announcing that: 'When we are clear what the priorities are, we will harness line managers to achieve them. Human Resources will provide a support role to them, giving guidance and advice when required and providing the tools needed to remove discriminatory practices' (ibid.). Targets were established for improving the percentage of female employees and managers, respectively to 35 and 23 per cent by 1995 and 42 and 27 per cent by the year 2000. Over the same period the aim was to increase the percentage of 'ethnic minority' employees to 13 per cent by 1995 and 15 per cent by 2000, with 'ethnic managers' increasing to 3 per cent of management by 1995 and 5 per cent by 2000.[8]

As part of the new campaign several top managers publicly voiced their support, including Sir Colin Marshall, John Watson, Alistair Cummings, Gail Redwood, Derek Stevens (Chief Financial Officer) and Robert Ayling (Director of Marketing and Operations). Much of the rhetoric, however, was couched in terms of benefits to the company. Sir Colin Marshall, for example, was interested in removing 'any remaining barriers preventing talented people from advancing in their careers', but this was clearly linked to a concern to ensure that the airline remained at the forefront of British industry (British Airways, 1991). That business concerns took priority over issues of natural justice can be seen in Marshall's declaration that 'advancement in the airline must depend on individual merit for a particular job. Positive action may be needed to help some members of the minorities and other individuals, but there can be no question of positive discrimination' (ibid.). Marshall went on to state that 'in this often difficult area, where no ideal solution has yet to be found, we will always accept people on *the sole criterion of what they can contribute to the success of British Airways*. This approach should become part of our everyday culture, making the term 'equality of opportunity' redundant within the airline' (ibid., my emphasis).

Similarly, other senior managers saw employment equity as 'critical for [...] business' (Lauermann), leading to improved customer service (Watson), better decision making (Cummings) and other benefits from diversity (Stevens) (British Airways, 1991). This corporate case is reflected in the airline's 'policy of equal employment opportunity', which:

- Reflects the corporate goals of being a good employer and a good neighbor.
- Improves staff quality by removing barriers to recruitment and advancement of talent.
- [Encourages] employees [to] stay with the company longer, reducing recruitment and training costs.
- Improves our ability to understand and satisfy customer needs through a workforce which more accurately reflects the world we serve.
- Creates a diverse workforce which aids competitive advantage through diversity of problem solving.
- Brings cultural understanding, improving relationships between employees, their colleagues and customers.
- Generates public relations spin-offs. Companies with good equal opportunity practices are publicly perceived as considerate, caring and committed to change (British Airways, 1991).

Of the management group only Redwood and Ayling focused on the benefits of employment equity for the individuals involved. Redwood hoped that the initiative would 'enable more people to feel more confident of their ability to achieve at work' (ibid.). Ayling embraced the new initiative saying,

It is a happy coincidence for me that my new job allows me to put into practice my strong views in the equal opportunities area. We made good progress on EO issues during my time as Director of HR and I am determined that the momentum continues with Marketing and Operations taking a key role.

(ibid.)

BA's approach to employment equity was not untypical of companies at that time (Cockburn, 1991b). For those concerned with workplace discrimination it was a mixed blessing. Corporate commitment to employment equity was an advance on what had existed before, but it came with a cost. The underlying rationale served to weigh the value of women, people of colour and employment equity, itself, against the corporate 'bottom line:' while individual men have always been judged on their ability to contribute to efficiency and productivity, men as a class have not had to justify their place in the workplace. Further, it was clear from the various statements by BA senior managers that women and people of colour would have to fit in and be judged by existing (male-associated) standards of business efficiency. Debate around the hiring of female 'foremen' provides a useful example. Against those who saw this as 'yet another stake into the heart of the dedicated and loyal engineering staff' (British Airways, 1990c), and demanded that women go through the same promotion process as male engineers, were those who argued that *'fellow* [engineers] have nothing to fear from the ladies [because they] are of a very high caliber and indeed a pleasure to work with' (ibid.).[9] This latter viewpoint is shared by Alistair Cummings, who argued that 'women in Engineering [...] is a culture shock', but he was frankly 'delighted with the quality of those [women] who have joined us' (British Airways, 1990c). Cummins' defense of equity initiatives, however, served to reinforce the idea that under-qualified female applicants were promoted for the good of the company's bottom line. Dealing with the charge that women were given 'special' rather than 'equal' opportunities, being promoted 'without aircraft maintenance licences and time-served experience' (ibid.), Cummings responded that 'while all foremen's jobs require leadership skills ... not all of them need a licensed engineer's background' (British Airways, 1990b). For Cummings, it was an absolute necessity for BA 'to attract enough talented people into our very demanding profession' (British Airways, 1990c) and to improve 'the quality of decisions [...] with a more balanced workforce' (British Airways, 1991).

Part of the danger of a business justification of employment equity lies in the fact that the link between diversity and productivity is far from proven (Prasad and Mills, 1997). Perception was a large part of the appeal. The idea of being seen as a good corporation – 'considerate, caring and committed to change' – was an important aspect of BA's equity statement. Whatever the specific reasons, it was not management decision-making alone that led to the onset of an equity discourse at that time, it was a number of events that contributed to the ongoing and sensemaking 'shocks' that preceded it (Weick, 1995).

Towards an equity discourse (1960–70)

After a period of normalization that stretched roughly from the end of the war until the early 1960s a number of supervisory positions and jobs, hitherto male preserves, began to open up to women. Almost all the supervisory positions were in female dominated jobs (see Figures 6.1 and 6.2) but the main job advances were in stewarding and sales, and elsewhere the ground was also being laid for female advances into piloting.

Stewarding

The first significant breach had been the employment of stewardesses just after the war but promotion was a long time coming. Women were not appointed to the rank of senior stewardess until 1961 and 'chief air stewardess' until 1964.[10] Announcing the appointment of Joy Henderson as the company's first Chief Air Stewardess, BOAC management stated that this was due to an increased 'awareness of the advantages of employing a woman in an administrative position where her feminine influence and practical experience will be reflected in the cabin service BOAC provides for its passengers' (British Overseas Airways Corporation, 1963a).[11] Nonetheless, Henderson's position was not considered at par with her male counterparts, and it was not until 1974 that women achieved the same status as male Chief Stewards.[12]

Sales

The next major area to be breached was that of sales. When BOAC introduced a sales apprenticeship programme in 1960, like its many other apprentice schemes, it was only open to male applicants, and the first class of 17 young men graduated in October of 1960. However, it was becoming 'apparent that in order to serve [the increasing number of] women passengers efficiently it is necessary to have the feminine view-point represented in the airline sales staff' (British Overseas Airways Corporation, 1961d).[13] With 'this in mind [...] BOAC [began] offering some places to female sales apprentices' in March 1961 (ibid.).[14] Over the decade other sales opportunities opened to women, including sales development assistant in 1962, cargo sales officer in 1964, and business travel officer and marketing intelligence officer in 1969.

Things moved much slower at BEA where there was greater male resistance to female sales representatives, and it was not until 1970 that the first woman – Betty Wright[15] – was hired in that capacity.[16] She was met with a variety of reactions 'ranging from ' thank God – a woman' to a very 'anti' attitude – from another woman' (ibid.). She felt that she 'had to prove, even more than a male rep, that [she] really knew her job' (ibid.). She recalled one particular customer who, when she first called him, 'really put [her] through it until he was satisfied that [she] *did* know what [she] was fully about' (ibid.). Wright survived in the job by trying 'to remain as feminine as possible,' fearing that if she didn't she would 'lose a certain advantage' (ibid.): being treated as a woman 'in this man's world of sales reps' she was 'not so likely to get the door shut in [her] face' (ibid.).

Piloting

In 1947 BOAC and BEA established a joint flying club for employees. The Airways Aero Club was open to all employees and provided an opportunity for them to learn to fly at their own expense. A number of women joined, including 'Miss' Albrechtova, an airline clerk, who was the first female BOAC employee to gain her wings.[17] In 1955 Silvia Buscall, from the General Accounts Department, became BEA's first female employee to gain her wings through the flying club. Between 1948 and 1957 at least one in twelve of the Club's 123 licensed pilots were women, including Muriel Adnams, a BOAC traffic receptionist, and Nellie Tucker, a BOAC duty officer, both of who went on to play key roles in the British Women's Pilots Association (BWPA), an organization dedicated to 'promote better opportunities for women in aviation, offering scholarships and awards for feminine achievements' (Adnams, quoted in British Overseas Airways Corporation, 1961c).[18]

Other female pilots among the ranks of BOAC and BEA employees learned to fly through outside organizations, including Yvonne van den Hoek, one of three BOAC stewardesses who joined the RAF Volunteer Reserve to train for commercial pilot licences,[19] and Marlene Black, a BOAC typist, and B. M. Hook, with BEA's Personnel Department, who learned to fly with the Women's Junior Air Corp (WJAC).[20]

Despite the growing number of female pilots among their ranks both airlines continued their policy of only hiring male pilots, although the Airways Flying Club hired a female pilot – Joan Hughes – as its assistant chief flying instructor in 1961. The idea of women commercial pilots remained an enigma to those in charge of pilot recruitment. Women pilots were first and foremost *women*. Thus, when Joan Hughes, a pilot with over 10,000 flying hours to her credit, was featured in *BOAC News* she was described as 'a petite brunette who is certainly one of the most experienced women pilots in Britain' (British Overseas Airways Corporation, 1969).[21] Similarly, when Sue Firmin gained her wings the news report referred to her as 'the jet-set hostess with more than a pretty face. A stewardess with BOAC's VC10 fleet to New York, she also pilots a light aircraft' (British Overseas Airways Corporation, 1968c). News of the activities of female pilots were often accompanied by comments casting doubt on their viability as commercial airline pilots, leading the BWPA to lament that, 'To most people the thought of a woman commanding an airliner – or even occupying the right-hand seat – would probably be dismissed as a pipe-dream' (British Overseas Airways Corporation, 1961c). Airline companies feared that 'the large costs which they incur in converting newly engaged pilots to a modern commercial airliner will be wasted when a young woman marries and takes on family responsibilities' (Jackson, 1975: 78–79).

British airlines made it clear that commercial flying was the preserve of men. When BOAC stewardess Yvonne Sintes joined the Airways Aero Club the airline was advertising 'openings for suitably qualified young men who wish to be airline pilots' (British Overseas Airways Corporation, 1952). Shortly after Silvia Buscall and Betty Dillon-Trenchard joined the flying club, BEA announced that, as the normal supply of air force pilots had dried up in 1953, it would 'look for newcomers in a completely different category of pilots [including] flying clubs or small charter companies' (British European Airways, 1956a), but foresaw that the largest percentage of recruits would be ex-national service members of the RAF. Things had not changed when Muriel Adnams gained her pilot license, and BOAC advertised for 'well-qualified men' who were required to serve as engineering flying officers (British Overseas Airways Corporation, 1957d).

By the end of the 1950s, in the face of severe shortages of air force pilots, BOAC and BEA established a joint College of Air Training (at Hamble), where 'pilots of the future will be recruited from among boys in their late teens and early 20s and [...] trained 'from scratch'" (British Overseas Airways Corporation, 1959d). Far from opening opportunities to women, the new school reinforced the practice of male only recruitment, instituting a nation-wide recruitment campaign directed at 'suitable young men through schools and youth organizations' (British Overseas Airways Corporation, 1965b), aimed at 'the rising young men [who] one day ... will be taking over command' from 'the men who are kings in the air' (British Overseas Airways Corporation, 1968a; 1971b).[22]

Despite the intransigence of BOAC and BEA other British airlines and flying clubs began to recruit female pilots in the 1940s. Monique Agazarian, a former ATA flyer,[23] was one of the first women in post-war Britain to become a commercial airline pilot, serving as Managing Director and Chief Pilot of a small Heathrow-based airline called Island Air Services during the 1950s, and went on to hire other female pilots. By the 1960s Morton Air Services, Dan Air and the Autair/Court Line[24] were also hiring women pilots, including Yvonne Sintes.

In 1964 Sintes, who obtained her pilot's licence from the Airways Aero Club,[25] was recruited by Morton Air Services to fly freight and then as a co-pilot on scheduled passenger routes. She was fired shortly after during an industrial relations dispute between the airline and the British Air Lines Pilots Association (BALPA), of which Sintes was the only female member.[26] She was then hired by Dan Air as a First Officer and observed that although generally 'there was prejudice against women pilots [there was] very little within Dan Air,' who had been hiring female pilots since the mid-1960s (Sintes, quoted in Simons, 1993: 119): there 'never was an official policy about employing women pilots within the company – if they needed a pilot and a qualified woman was available, they hired her – it was as simple as that' (ibid.).[27] In the mid-1970s Sintes became a captain on Dan Air's BAC I-11 fleet, making her 'possibly the first woman in Europe – certainly the first in the United Kingdom – to command a pure-jet airliner' (Sintes, quoted in Simons, 1993: 119).[28] By now 'the mould of male only flight-deck crews had been well and truly broken' (Simons, 1993: 118). BALPA and the Guild of Air Pilots and Air Navigators both 'accepted women members and they were entitled to hold office' (Jackson, 1975: 79).[29]

The bastions of male domination

While doors were opening to female employees the three most crucial areas of the airline's operation remained firmly closed – piloting, engineering and management. Piloting, as we have seen, was opening up in other airlines but not engineering and management.

Engineering

Attitudes at BOAC effectively discouraged women from applying to become engineers. Apprenticeship training, for example, was only open to boys, and parents were advised, 'If your boy is 14, now is the time to start thinking. If he is 16, now may be the time for action' (British Overseas Airways Corporation, 1962c). The link between masculinity and engineering was maintained through several layers of discourse. At its most obvious the innumerable images of engineers – whether through advertising, annual reports or articles on the workplace – were always of men. While custom and practice restricted recruitment to men,[30] imaging served to legitimize and reinforce the association between engineering and masculinity. Virtually all discussion of engineering within BEA and BOAC referenced 'skill', 'technical competence', 'knowledge' and 'experience', which were usually symbolized through images of an engineer working on an engine of some type or other and dressed in white coveralls. The masculine image was also achieved through contrasting images of machinery with the bodily size or physical appearance of women, and their supposed lack of technical knowledge, with numerous photographs of women either sitting in or by machines or being shown how to operate them.[31]

When Carole Waddle set out to be an engineer in the mid-1950s she found 'an attitude that was unfavourable to women' (quoted in British Overseas Airways Corporation, 1967b) and it had not changed five years later when, having obtained her National Certificate in Aeronautical Engineering, she found work at Hawker Siddeley. Discouraged, Waddle left engineering and became a BOAC stewardess, but even here she experienced 'wisecracks from engineering staff [about her] early ambition' (ibid.).

Women were not entirely excluded from engineering;[32] most were employed as secretaries and clerical staff but there were a number of female operatives. While the work of male engineers of all grades and skill levels were praised and profiled in corporate materials, female operatives were almost totally ignored.[33]

With the onset of the 1970s the airlines remained slow to change their practices. They were not alone. With the introduction, in 1970, of the Equal Pay Act the Engineering Employers Federation was to the fore in resisting the new legislation. A confidential memorandum advised members that they could avoid paying equal pay by introducing labour saving machines, job evaluation and strict segregation of the sexes at the workplace (Rowbotham, 1973: 99).

Management

Women, as we have seen in earlier chapters, were excluded from management positions in the airline industry for a variety of reasons, including issues of leadership, experience, technical competence, professionalism, ownership and control.

Prior to the 1960s, airline managers were appointed on the basis of (male-associated) job characteristics (e.g., industry experience), technical qualifications (e.g., pilot licence, engineering certificate, etc.) and wartime experience.[34] The association of management with maleness was so ingrained that the airlines easily referred to such things as 'the boss and his secretary' (British Overseas Airways Corporation, 1968d).

For most of this post-war era BOAC's most senior female staff member was Sheila Portch, the company's Passenger Relations Officer, which, in 1964, was 'the highest office' of any woman at BOAC (British Overseas Airways Corporation, 1964a).[35] Other women were beginning to move up the ranks. Betty Paige, for one, had moved from reservations to the Tours Department where, in the late 1960s, she became 'the first woman to be promoted to being a Supervisor on telephone sales'.[36] After a few years the airline decided that perhaps she 'could look after the counter downstairs. A sort of a manager but the overseer of the counter downstairs in the airways terminal (ibid). Then it was decided that 'perhaps [she] could go even further,' so she was appointed manager of the Regent Street office (ibid.). A contemporary of Paige was Della Head, who was promoted to Personnel Officer in BOAC's Flight Operations Department. This was the first time that a woman had been promoted to that position, and she was 'administratively responsible for all the women staff in the Department' (British Overseas Airways Corporation, 1962a). Within four years Head had been promoted to Assistant Welfare Superintendent and then to Personnel Superintendent with the 'task of assisting the Personnel Manager' (British Overseas Airways Corporation, 1966d). That same year Joan Harrison became BOAC's first and 'only Market Intelligence Officer' (British Overseas Airways Corporation, 1966a).

At BEA Catherine 'Kitty' Macpherson, who was in charge of the tiny airport of Barra in Scotland, was the airline's 'only permanent female Station

Superintendent' (British European Airways, 1955a), managing the airport 'entirely on her own, dealing with all the paper work [...] and [dealing] with not only commercial traffic but also the air ambulance service'.[37] She had inherited the job after her father, the previous station manager, died and her brother, who took over for a while, found 'it was not to his liking'.[38] In 1969 Macpherson was awarded the M.B.E. for her services and was still being described as 'BEA's only woman 'official-in-charge' (British European Airways, 1969).[39] She was still running the operation in the early 1990s, by which time 'the regular and ambulance services [had] since been handed over to other operators' (ibid.).

The one major advance in this era was the appointment of Alison Munro to the BEA Board. Munro was the first female board member in BEA's history and the second woman to ever serve on the board of a state-owned British airline – exactly 20 years after Pauline Gower retired from the board of BOAC. Like her predecessor, Munro's wartime experience was referenced as an important quality for board membership, joining the airline 'with a wealth of experience gained in the Ministry of Aircraft Production during the war and recently as Under-Secretary, Overseas Policy Division, Ministry of Aviation' (quoted in Cadogan, 1992: 222).[40] Such was the novelty of female airline executives that forgetting Pauline Gower, some commentators described Munro as the first woman to be appointed to the board of any state-owned airline in the world (ibid.).

Despite the promotion of Hill, Head, Harrison, Macpherson and Munro the number of women in administrative and managerial posts in BOAC and BEA was well below the national average of 14 to 16 per cent in the period 1951 to 1971 (Halsey, 1978).

Compliance and resistance

Towards the end of the 1960s there were evident signs of grumbling among a section of female employees. Jeannie Lardner notes that 'some of the girls had formed their own [...] union, but it didn't really take off [because] it was too much [...] burn your bra types'.[41] Lardner's characterization of female union activists references the growing influence of the new feminist movement of the 1960s and female resistance to discriminatory practices at all levels of work and society. It also indicates that other women often rejected such resistance.

When Francine Carville joined the airline she noted a number of things that irked her. She felt that it 'was quite scandalous' that stewardesses were forced to resign when they married and contributed to a situation where, when the airline 'went to try to find female managers there weren't that many; they'd lost a lot of people that had the background'.[42] In a similar vein, Annie Redmile, a stewardess from 1968 to 1973, felt that the airlines missed out by not using flight attendants in higher positions such as marketing and senior management (quoted in Petit, 1991).

Glamour also became an area of contention. Sometimes a stewardesses' notion of glamour coincided with that of management. For example, management's concern with physical appearance often gelled with a particular woman's desire to look 'stylish and attractive'. Stewardess Roz Hanby, for example, felt that 'because of the limited time [stewardesses] were allowed to fly, women regarded the job less as a career and more as a [...] finishing school' (ibid.). This was hardly surprising given the use of glamour in airline recruitment and in popular culture. Sometimes ideas of glamour were independent but supportive, for example, where an attraction to travel coincided with the needs of the stewardess role. Francine Carville saw the job as a chance to be 'independent, away from your parents and [...] the total freedom of the world',[43] and Anne Redmile saw it as the 'glamour of unattachment' (quoted in Petit, 1991). Sometimes, however, ideas of glamour came into conflict where the airlines equated 'attractiveness' with being single and when they insisted on the production of a consistent performance of friendliness, subservience and attractiveness for hours on end (Hochschild, 1983; Kane, 1974). When Sue Smith joined the airline in 1972 stewardesses 'were grounded at thirty-five' years of age. Smith was trained to 'look as good when [she] got off the plane as when [she] got on' (quoted in Petit, 1991).

Some stewardesses resisted the corporate glamour image by confronting the comments of male passengers and, covertly, by evaluating passengers behind the scenes. For example, one stewardess speaks of how she responded to the oft-used phrase by male passengers, 'Give us a smile'. 'I said, 'I will if you will'. He did, and I said, 'Right, hold it there for twelve hours' (quoted in Petit, 1991). This type of resistance challenged pre-conceived notions of the ideal-typical stewardess, and expectations of the stewardess as subservient and 'the passenger as king' (ibid.). Anne Redmile and her colleagues coped with judgements of their *appearance* by engaging in evaluations of individual passengers' *behaviour*: 'Often passengers weren't aware of how they were being judged behind the galley curtains [...] People weren't evaluated on why they were, what they were, but how they behaved' (ibid.). Others adopted an exaggerated style of attentiveness, similar to 'the camp behaviour of some of the gay stewards. It was a kind of protection, a sort of cloak against the world. A good sort of protection because no one can get through the barrier' (ibid.).[44]

Other forms of resistance involve rule manipulation in situations, such as uncertainties over delays and bad weather, where the stewardess can gain some control over her work. Under the tight control of schedules and rosters, delays provide the stewardess with a measure of control as to whether she will accept revised duties:

> It's the one time she has a choice. Most times she doesn't have a choice in what she wants to do, she is totally powerless. But occasionally she does get the opportunity and some girls like the idea of being able to [...] get an immense kick out of saying 'stuff it, I'm not going to do it'.
> O'Brien (1983: 8)[45]

In the United States stewardesses took action through pressure groups,[46] demonstrations, court challenges and unionization. In June 1966, one of the first acts of the newly founded National Organization of Women (NOW) was a demonstration against airline rules requiring stewardesses to leave when they reached a certain age. In 1968, prompted by the complaints of ex-stewardesses, the Equal Employment Opportunity Commission (EEOC) looked into the airlines' age restriction rules and declared them to be in violation of Title VII of the Civil Rights Act of 1964. The courts were slow to act, however, and in 1970 twelve Trans World Airline (TWA) stewardesses filed a multi-million-dollars suit against the airline. Eventually TWA drew up new long-term retirement rules for its female flight attendants. Within the unions there were also struggles. For years stewardesses constituted a separate division under 'the guidance and control' of the pilots' union, whose leaders did all the negotiating. From the early 1960s through to the late 1970s there were numerous internal battles before stewardesses were able to free themselves from male dominant union control (Nielsen, 1982).

In Britain, by the time Francine Carville joined the airlines there was a

> stewardess' union as well as a very mild male union. Stewards had their own union and that was affiliated to the Transport and General Workers Union. Stewardesses were not allowed to belong to it. It was called a stewardesses union but if there were any problems they took them to the stewards union.[47]

Nonetheless, male and female flight attendants did eventually join together in the same union and pressed BA to establish a 'closed shop'[48] for the cabin crews. From then on, 'a union rep who would come in on the first day of the training course and make every person in that room join. That is how it became strong unionized and got very much better conditions for cabin crew' (ibid).

War of the words

With the onset of the 1960s and the development of the new women's movement various signs of gender angst appeared in the in-house newsletters. Numerous articles expressed concern (and sometimes joy) over the employment of women in new endeavours. Thus, for example, it was seen as a sign of a 'woman's world' when two female employees 'invaded Judo' by joining BOAC's judo club (British Overseas Airways Corporation, 1959e) or when some male jobs, such as commissionaire, were dying out (British Overseas Airways Corporation, 1967c). On the other hand, when female flight attendants won the right not to wear stiff collars and tie BOAC celebrated these 'women in a "man's world"', who won the 'freedom to be feminine' (British Overseas Airways Corporation, 1962f). Numerous other headlines (e.g., 'Four Men on Top of the World', 'The Men Who Are Kings Of

The Air', etc.) reminded readers of the power and influence of men through-out aviation.

Designed to represent the views of senior management and the general interests of the company, the newsletters did not provide space for discussion or debate,[49] but reflected the concerns of the male editors and writers.[50] However, in the mid-1960s, following a company-wide survey of employees, *BOAC News* was revamped and opened to a small measure of employee dialogue. Among the various letters of reminiscences, complaints began to appear from male employees angry about female advancement, including one man who wrote in to complain about the class and gender bias of the newsletter, arguing

> BOAC News is a publication for the glorification of the few. I've yet to see an article on, say, the labourer who has devoted 25 years to the cause of BOAC; the write-ups seem to go to those departments whose majority are men with 'old boy' accents or dolly girls with empty heads.
>
> British Overseas Airways Corporation (1970c)

But soon women were writing to complain about the gendered nature of the airline's recruitment processes. In one case a female employee complained that a number of 'plum positions' were going to new recruits who were under forty years of age. In her opinion, the fault lay

> with those who select. In the main they are MEN, many of them over 40 themselves, who can't resist a younger face or a younger shapely leg [...] They forget the old-stagers – the faithful, hard-working females who have devoted a good many years to BOAC. I expect the answer to this will be, 'Ah yes, but they've got qualifications'. I'm sure some have very good qualifications. Nevertheless, we 'old-timers' have got experience of work within BOAC, so why not some promotions on merit?
>
> British Overseas Airways Corporation (1970b)[51]

Over the next decade *BOAC News* reflected the discourse of 'women's liberation'. A particularly telling example is a story of a female passenger who complained about a 'family excursion' deal that offered 'full fare for the father, half fare for his wife and so on' (British Overseas Airways Corporation, 1971a). The 'indignant' passenger asked 'why not full fare for the wife and half for the husband?' (ibid.). The newsletter responded that

> this women's lib business has gone as far as it can go. [It] was greatly pointed out to [the female passenger] that the full fare was normally applicable to the head of the household – and that was a matter for domestic assessment. [The airline] did think of asking: who's paying

for the flight anyway? But, with admirable restraint, [...] resisted the temptation.

British Overseas Airways Corporation (1971a)

But soon protests from female employees began to fill the letters columns of the newsletters, including angry reactions to a cartoon that showed two pilots speaking about a pregnant stewardess. One is commenting: 'Copped it at the family day, they reckon'. In another newsletter the issue of women's liberation surfaced during an interview with Grace McCoy, a promotional Material Superintendent, who was retiring after twenty-seven 'very happy' years. Commenting that she was 'strongly against bra-burning women's lib and believes emphatically that women should always retain their femininity,' she went on to 'plea' for the airline to 'give women a chance' and to encourage women to 'have more faith in their capabilities, and realize that they need not always be content with being the power *behind* the throne' (British Overseas Airways Corporation, 1973). Expressing the hope that

> perhaps one day British Airways may have a woman member on the Board', McCoy concluded that, 'the airline business is very much a man's world [...] yet there are many jobs in this world that a woman can do equally well, and often better than a man. But, it is a hard fight. A woman has to be twice as good as a man in any job in order to prove her worth.
>
> (ibid.)

In December 1973, *BEA Magazine* and *BOAC News* were replaced by *British Airways News*, which was dedicated to 'creditable communication between management and staff [within the constraints] of good taste and common-sense' (British Airways, 1973). In that first issue good taste and common-sense included several references to female staff as 'girls', a woman's 'happy smile', the virtues of belly dancing and two items on 'Miss Speedbird'. Gender angst and the debate with 'women's liberation' were evident in an article on cost cutting that 'allowed' female staff to wear trousers, prompting the headline 'Girls Can Wear the Trousers Now' (ibid.).

Over the next decade the newsletter continued to reflect the gendered angst of management and employees as they faced new and changing realities. It was a time of several 'firsts' in the hiring and promotion of women to management positions,[52] including Jennifer Tanburn who joined the Board of British Airways. Early in 1974 the rank of 'Chief Stewardess' was instituted for the first time, and Jennifer Clay made airline history with her appointment to the post of Sales Training Manager. Clay's promotion was met with a now typical response from the newsletter. Referring to her as 'bright, beautiful and the boss', it called the promotion 'another victory for the feminist camp' (British Airways, 1974a). Clay, an honors graduate from the University of Wales and a Fulbright scholar, had joined BEA in 1970 as a

Senior Language Training Officer. The newsletter asked her how people reacted to 'such a young, beautiful and highly intelligent lady boss?' Clay responded, 'People are naturally suspicious of a female manager. But generally they are looking for technical efficiency and once they see that you know what you're doing they become more confident about your all-round ability.' Meanwhile a headline on a departmental weight-watchers club – 'Watch it girls, you're losing' – seemed designed to reference the broader issue of women's liberation.

But some things remained static. For example, Peggy Ward's promotion to engineering inspector was hailed as the airline's 'only woman engineer' (British Airways, 1974b)[53] and when Court Line went bankrupt BA recruited the entire complement of stewardesses but failed to employ its female pilot Elizabeth Overbury.

Organizational change and employment equity

By the mid-1970s the face of British Airways was changing in a number of ways, including far reaching technological changes and the introduction of employment equity and anti-discrimination legislation. Throughout the 1980s the airline went through a widespread process of culture change.

Technological change

Jet travel and computerization had important, but different, impacts on gendered relationships throughout the airline industry. Airline responses to jet technology contributed to a weakening of the ideal of the 'air hostess', and encouraged unionization and other forms of resistance. Responses to computerization, on the other hand, led to a new emphasis on technical skill and knowledge that strengthened associations with organizational power and masculinity.

The introduction of the jumbo jet in 1969 brought tremendous changes in the working conditions of flight attendants, with fewer stewardesses and greater numbers of passengers on each aircraft. Technological change, coupled with political (i.e., the 1973 oil embargo) and regulative (e.g., US deregulation policies) changes, forced airlines into price wars and cost cutting exercises, including speed-ups (with one flight attendant doing the work previously done by two); the reintroduction of short-term (5–10 years) contracts; and the employment of a large number of part-time employees (Gil, 1990).[54] Stewardesses were beginning to redefine their job as a flying waitress. Gone was the intimacy of travel that characterized the past. In many ways stewardesses felt themselves to be part of a flying bureaucratic workplace, losing the respect of the public that they once had. Francine Carville, felt that 'toward the middle of the 70s respect for the stewardess changed because the job wasn't as attractive to them, there was other competition out there, women were doing different things'.[55]

With the growth of mass tourism, the changing demographics of the airline business, encouraged airlines to rethink their service strategy, replacing the older generation of senior managers with men like Colin Marshall (BA) and Jan Carlzon (Scandinavian Airlines System – SAS) from successful service enterprises. Carlzon and Marshall saw a need for a new, all-embracing service strategy which involved cost-cutting and the extension of emotion work from the stewardesses to all employees. Both SAS and BA put their entire staff through a culture change program based on emotion management. While this new strategy was mediated by an elaborate series of bureaucratic rules (Carlzon, 1987; Corke, 1986; Hampden-Turner, 1990), female sexuality was retained as an important element. Stewardesses, for example, continued to be judged in terms of age and attractiveness. As BA Chairman, Sir John King, expressed it: 'We give 'em five year contracts and after that we take a look at 'em and see what they are like'(quoted in Sampson, 1984). Nonetheless, while female flight attendants were still expected to 'display' a certain appearance, much of the requirements of overt sexual display had been shifted to the check-in operations 'where it was cheaper to maintain and may have a greater impact, especially in crowded airports' (Gil, 1990: 328). Now female ground staff was trained to smooth over problems between the customer and the airline, to a point where,

> Passengers checking in at the airport can't fail to have noticed the warmth of welcome from the smiling BA girls behind the desks, and the freshness of their looks, their complexions smooth, their make-up alive with colour and gloss. If – heaven forbid – there should be a delay or baggage hold-up, the girls are all smiling efficiency and sympathy.
>
> from *BA News*, quoted in Sampson (1984: 221)[56]

Computerization, on the other hand, was changing the basis of expertise and authority within the airline. Computerization was introduced into the airline business in Britain in the 1950s, expanded rapidly in the 1960s and was consolidated as a key aspect of operations in the 1970s (Lansbury, 1978). This led to significant changes in management personnel. Until the 1970s senior managers of BEA and BOAC were 'predominantly middle-aged, were without formal qualifications, and had spent most of their working lives in the airline' (Lansbury, 1978: 20–21). By the time of the merger 'specialist personnel employed in the management services department – considered part of the 'guiding intelligence' of the airline – tended to be young and highly qualified, with experience of at least two or more previous employers; most had joined the airline fairly recently' (ibid.).

The development of management services played a key role in the shift from a culture based on air force experience to one based on information control and this shifted the dynamics of gender ideal types and the gender gestalt of the airline, with women yet again faring badly because of the relative lack of female graduates. While the percentage of female employees in BA as a whole was around 21 per cent, the percentage in management services was 14 per cent, most of whom were employed in lower-paid computer functions (Lansbury, 1978: 72).

Employment Equity Policy

In 1975 the Labour Government introduced a series of ant-discrimination laws, including the Equal Pay Act, the Sex Discrimination Act and the establishment of an Equal Opportunities Commission (EOC). In preparation for the new legislation BA commissioned an equity study to examine 'existing staff regulations' (British Airways, 1976c), and declared that it was 'determined to meet to the fullest extent its statutory obligations to ensure equal opportunity in employment to all staff regardless of sex or marital status' (British Airways, 1976d). Managers were encouraged to 'prepare, and where possible, implement plans to recruit and train women in those employment areas where they are currently not to be found' (ibid.). But obvious areas of scepticism remained, with 'sex equality' questioned in *BA News*. In one case the editorial focussed 'the spotlight on two women who didn't need the law' but attained senior positions 'long before 'women's lib' became fashionable' (British Airways, 1976a).[57]

Within the female-dominated cabin crew services Training Manager Jill Parker was publicly arguing that there should be more women in the management structure (British Airways, 1976b), while in the letters column of *BA News* battle was raging on the issue of childcare, uniform ranks and the use of the term 'girls;' arguing for crèche facilities,[58] a change in 'the rank markings for women so that they are as prominent and easily recognizable as those worn by men' (British Airways, 1977d),[59] and an end to the constant reference to female employees as 'girls'. In the latter case, describing herself 'proud to be a woman' and not a 'bra-burning women's libber', the woman expressed her anger at 'the paper's constant throwback to the dark ages' when describing women (British Airways, 1977b). A male colleague, however, wrote in to say that the argument was frivolous, that 'girls will be girls' (British Airways, 1977a).

The equity discourse raged through the pages of *BA News* for some time into the future. David G. Lindsay, one of BA's Senior Solicitors, for example, was taken to task by female employees for speaking out against the introduction of crèche facilities. Other female employees questioned the company's 'rigid sex roles', the maintenance of differentiated uniform rankings 'by a vocal group of senior male cabin crew', the 'degradation' of women through company-sponsored beauty contests and the 'chauvinist editorial policy' of the *BA News*.

Despite some changes (e.g., the lifting of stewardess age restrictions) a 1978 internal account revealed that progress was slow and limited, with women absent from eight of twenty major groupings – including engineering,

Table 7.1   Employee job categories by gender at BA, 1978

Job Category	Percentage of Female Employee
Ramp	0%
Supervisory, engineering and technical	0%
Engineering officers	0%
Pilots	0%
Sn./first officers	0%
Second officers	0%
Medical officers	0%
Senior management	0%
Technical engineering	0.09%
Engineering and maintenance industrial	0.81%
Sn staff SSL	3.3%
Ground services (includes ground catering)	17.9%
Sn Medical Officer[1]	33.33%
Administrative	27.3%
Chief/Sn steward/ess	35.2%
Miscellaneous	61.3%
Clerical	68.45%
Steward/ess (under training)	70.14%
Steward/ess 1	71.74%
Steward/ess 2	75.15%
Total (all employees)	27.5%

Note: This category has only 3 people.

Source: Constructed from *British Airways Manpower Report*, August 1978.

piloting and senior management – and virtually absent from two others (see Table 7.1). In only five groupings were women in the majority, including three different levels of flight attending, and one ('miscellaneous') with just over one hundred employees. More than three-quarters of all BA's female employees were in clerical and cabin crew staffs (see Table 7.1).

Many female employees were unhappy by the lack of progress. A group of women at BA's West London Terminal wrote to complain that, 'despite the Equal Pay Act and the Sex Discrimination Act there is still blatant discrimination against women in British Airways', particularly in regard to employment, pay and promotion (British Airways, 1978b). They noted that 'there are many jobs in British Airways where no women are employed, such as engineering apprentices/graduates, ramp workers, HGV drivers, cargo agents, pilots'; that 'there are jobs which only women are employed to do, such as upholstery seamstresses and secretaries' (ibid.) which are low paid; and that women are concentrated in the lower echelons of the organization (see Table 7.2). In response, Howard Phelps, BA's Personnel Director, argued:

The analysis reveals an imbalance between men and women which British Airways does not find acceptable and policies have to be adopted

Table 7.2 Promotion and the ghettoization of female employees in BA, 1978

	No. of men employed	No. of women employed	% of women
Clerical (C1–C5)	2877	5440	65.41
Admin. (D6–D11)	5000	1509	23.18
Senior Staff (5 SLV, VI, V)	807	17	2.06
Senior Management Levels	240	0	0

Source: Table reproduced from letter in *BA News*, no. 225, 2 June 1978.

to redress the balance, by special alteration to recruitment policy, among other things. The present situation is a reflection of many years and will take many years to change.

(ibid.)

Thus, two years after the Sex Discrimination Act became law BA was still *talking* about changing its recruitment policy. This prompted a female employee to write, 'No more platitudes Mr. Phelps. Let's begin to improve prospects for women now with the opening of a nursery' (British Airways, 1978a). Nonetheless, there were signs that the company was beginning to respond, particularly in the area of piloting, but it would take a company-wide culture change to substantially challenge existing discriminatory practices.

Culture change and the gender gestalt

At BA at the end of the 1970s the gender gestalt was composed in large part of dominant images of white, heterosexual masculinities.[60] But things were beginning to change. At the beginning of February 1979 Wendy Crick became the first woman instructor at the airline's College of Air Training,[61] and later that month Lynn Barton became BA's first female recruit to undergo pilot training.[62] Other breakthroughs included the appointment of Jennifer Clay as Manager Western USA – the first woman to be appointed to an overseas managerial position.

Things took a new turn in 1979 when the new Conservative Government of Margaret Thatcher announced plans to privatize the airline and appointed Sir John King to oversee the process. Meanwhile the airline was 'facing the worst crisis in its history [–] heading for a loss of at least £100 million in' 1980, with the prospect of losses of close to £250 million in two years' (Roy Watts, BA Chair, quoted in Hampden-Turner, 1990: 83). In August of 1980 it was announced that staff numbers – already cut from 60,000 to 52,000 in the previous year – would be reduced by 20,000 over a two-year period (Campbell-Smith, 1986: 93).

There were also changes of a different kind on the horizon with the appointment in 1983 of Colin Marshall as Chief Executive Officer. To deal with the serious financial position and the 'appallingly low morale' of the staff (Campbell-Smith, 1986: 85), Marshall sought a solution in culture change.[63]

The organizational changes

The culture change program – 'Putting People First' (PPF) – was introduced soon after Marshall arrived, and had far reaching outcomes. The aim was to become a more service-oriented business and the key was seen as restructuring, managing emotion labour, tearing down of the old military-bureaucratic culture, and creating a customer-focussed image.[64]

Restructuring involved severe cuts to management, which not only reduced several layers of the management hierarchy and reliance of bureaucratic roles and rules but also downgraded the role of air force experience. King began the process by cutting a number of senior staff, including almost 'all the old, top management hands' (Campbell-Smith, 1986: 49), and hiring his new CEO – Colin Marshall – from the car-rental firm of Avis.[65] Marshall continued the process by reducing the number of senior managers by 70, including 'the last of the pre-King senior management' (Campbell-Smith, 1986: 104). Marshall preferred employees to make decisions and let it be known that in the new culture making mistakes was more forgivable than not deciding in the first place (Hampden-Turner, 1990).

The main thrust of the culture change was an emotional labour 'revolution', with employees as 'emotional labourers whose prime responsibility is to make those they serve feel good and emotionally satisfied' (Georgiades, quoted in Hampden-Turner, 1990: 88–89).[66] Through confidence-building exercises and behaviour-modification techniques, all employees were put through a two-day course aimed at improving the 'whole person' to 'build up their confidence that they could make decisions and could use flexible and ingenious means to fulfill the superordinate goal of satisfying customers' (Mike Bruce, quoted in Hampden-Turner, 1990: 90).[67] This was followed by the development of 'Customer First Teams', based on the notion of quality circles, and then a one-week 'Managing People First' program of residential training for all managers and supervisors, concerned with encouraging 'caring, achievement, creativity, innovation, and profit' (Poulet and Moult, 1987: 62). Managers were not only shown how to coach, train and support their staff but were to be judged on how well they achieved this in practice. In future the progress of a BA manager would depend on how well he or she had achieved 'against goals set in part by themselves, but also on how they had achieved it' (Hampden-Turner, 1990: 92). The aim was to create a very different management style from what had previously existed, 'an organization dedicated to the pursuit of excellence, [where] the best person must get the job' (Georgiades, quoted in British Airways, 1985a).

Gone were the old military titles and uniform rank,[68] as military and bureaucratic management archetypes[69] gave way to the 'good service manager', who was composed of 'an unusual store of personal energy', empathy, ambition, computer literacy, confidence, risk-taking, sound commonsense, emotional commitment, and 'being a good teacher as well as a good team builder' (Bickerstaffe and Hill, 1988: 49). Far from being devoid of masculine reference points, the characteristics of the new archetypal manager were nonetheless ambiguous compared to previous air force and bureaucratic archetypes. The ambiguity was exacerbated by the introduction of a widespread culture change program that emphasized emotionality and service.

Changing images and practices

Despite the passage of anti-discrimination laws BA's culture change program had little to say about employment equity. Nonetheless, the changing practices focussed on emotionality and customer care introduced a radically different discourse into the organization, destabilizing some of the long held associations between management and masculinity.

New gendered imagery and practices appeared, including an advertising campaign built around the notion of the female flight attendant as 'super girl', ready to fly to the aid of passengers in a number of ways.[70] Once again youth, beauty and femininity were stressed but the image was more complex in it's gendering.[71]

The airline continued to be dominated by males but, despite severe cuts in staffing, the number of female employees continued to grow, from 15,300 (26.5% of all employees) in 1978, to 17,000 (33.5%) by 1991 (see Figure 3.1). Change at the top, as exemplified in the airline's organizational charts,[72] was much slower (see Table 7.3). Yet even here there is some movement from 1983 when the BA hierarchy consisted of five layers of management, consisting of 80 senior management positions, with only woman – Fiona Gehring – appearing on the chart.[73] By 1990 BA's 'guide to who's who at the top of British Airways' listed 119 persons, of whom 9 were women,[74] and there were a few women appearing on the organizational charts of sales (17 of 143 managers),[75] ground operations (6 of 45 managers)[76] and marketing (2 of 20 senior managers).[77]

However, for much of the 1980s there were no women on the Board or the Executive (see Table 7.4) and men were in charge of each of the airline's major divisions.[78] Signs of employment equity were uneven. Restructuring and 'streamlining' had led, as in the case of Marketing and Operations, to fewer and then no women among the top management groups but, on the other hand, three women – Gail Redwood, Val Gooding and Valerie Scoulam – joined the Executive and Baroness O'Cathain became a non-executive director of the Board.[79]

Elsewhere in the airline much of the imagery was changing. Perhaps in some small part due to the fact that the 1990s saw the first female editors of

Table 7.3   Percentage of female managers shown on selected organization charts

Division	Period	Percentage of women
British Airways	July 1983	0.8%
Operations department	January 1984	0.0%
Marketing	September 1986	10.0%
Ground operations	October 1986	13.0%
World sales	November 1986	12.0%
Ground Operations, Gatwick	August 1988	8.0%
Marketing services	December 1988	45.0%
Human resources	January 1989	30.0%
Cabin services	March 1989	25.0%
British Airways	January 1990	7.5%
Marketing and operations	February 1990	9.5%
Marketing and operations	November 1990	0.0%

the airline's internal newsletter.[80] Although much of the corporate coverage continued to focus on male leadership and pilots there was increasing coverage of female managers and pilots and their role in the airline.[81]

Heterosexuality

BA's corporate imaging played predominantly to heterosexual sensibilities. Women were now imaged as permanent and long-term employees as well as wives and mothers; occupying a range of professional and managerial as well as the more traditional secretarial and clerical roles. The old archetype of the attractive young maiden had not been replaced but rather added to with one or two new archetypes, including the career woman and the professional. In both these latter cases, reference was often made to the tensions between developing a long-term career and developing a 'family life', and advertising campaigns still featured traditional nuclear families, with the father as the 'breadwinner'.

Even a rare mention of homosexuality assumed an exclusively heterosexual readership. In 1985 the first ever mention of homosexuality was in response to a *Sun* newspaper report that the airline was 'racked with fear' because one of its stewardess' was dying of AIDS in an American hospital. *British Airways News* called this 'highly misleading, inaccurate and sensational' but, nonetheless, referred concerned readers to 'British Airways Medical Memorandum No. 41', which defined AIDS as 'charcterised by suppression of the body's natural defence mechanism'. Reproduced in full, the Memorandum advised that 'with one or two exceptions [AIDS] it is only transmitted by sexual contact' and warned against homosexuals – 'promiscuity among this group should be avoided, also normal sexual activity with them'.[82]

It was around this time that William Davis joined BA as a sales reservations agent. A gay man, Davis found a culture that was, at best, ambivalent

Table 7.4   Women on the board and executive of British Airways and its successors, 1919–91

Name	Airline	Period on Board	Comments
Pauline Gower	BOAC	1943–46	First woman to sit on the Board
Alison Munro	BEA	1966	First woman to sit on the BEA Board
Jennifer Tanburn	British Airways	1973–77	Third woman to serve on the airline's board. BA's first female board member
Dorothy Barrett	British Airways	1977–83	Fourth woman to serve on the airline's board
Gail Redwood	British Airways	1991	Although not a member of the Board, Redwood, as Company Secretary, was the first female member of the Executive
Valerie Gooding	British Airways	1992	Joined the Executive as Director of Business
Valerie Scoulam	British Airways	1992	Joined the Executive as Director of Human Resources
Baroness O'Cathain	British Airways	1993–2004	Fifth woman to serve on the airline's board

towards homosexuality. In a number of ways he 'never felt very comfortable as being a gay man in BA, especially at reservations level', where there was a sense of 'homophobia [...] especially from male supervisors'.[83]

There were 'very few gay male supervisors'. Employees had 'to bend over backwards to fit the macho image' (ibid.). The 'male management tended to be very wary, very heterosexually oriented' and had 'sympathy rather than empathy for gay people'. If, for example, Davis's 'performance wasn't up to date, that [he wasn't] taking an average of about sixty calls a day' the supervisor was 'always very patronizing', saying things like 'Oh well, you're gay and we understand. [How's] your love life and have you got anybody in your life at the moment? So, does this unhappiness have anything to do with your call rate?' Davis also felt that a 'heterosexist' attitude was evident 'when anything gay happened [such as] gay pride day [and] you could not get' time off. The supervisor would say, 'well, I'm sorry if you haven't booked your holiday "x" number of days in advance [but] you've got to do it'. In general 'the horrible shifts always seemed to be the ones that the gay people got or would end up getting [...] like Christmas [and] nights ... because there is no family unit'. He was also angry that his female supervisor – a 'brilliant woman, very well read' and able to speak 'umpteen languages' – had not risen above the rank of supervisor after 20 years at BA because she was a lesbian. For Davis, 'the whole idea of homophobia or lesbaphobia in BA [was] personified through this one particular woman because she had gone through the mill with it all and she'd come out on top but it was very hard going'.

Yet, it seemed to Davis that, with the exception of cabin crew where 'there was a little more leniency', things were worse in other departments where management 'were very much the old BOAC [...] crew who tended to be more patriotic towards the airline than anyone [he'd] ever met'. They seemed to 'humour lesbians and gays or [...] tolerate them but [didn't] want them in [their] positions'. Similarly, the 'maintenance and ground handling side of things [...] was very much a macho world whereby you had to actually carry an airline on your back before you got the job'.

Despite these concerns, Davis reflected, BA was one of the better places that he had worked at. He was drawn to the airline, in part, because of the stereotyping of gays in the airline industry:

> It's very stereotyping but gays do tend to go into all the services [...] and the airline business seems to be full of them [...] Just within Reservations [...] at that time there were [...] probably two hundred [males], and of those, a good sixty to seventy percent were gay or known to be gay.

The fact that there were a large number of gay and lesbian women already working for BA contributed to a culture whereby Davis could feel 'quite relaxed about [his] sexuality'. Indeed, at times it seemed that

> most people enjoyed the BA culture especially if they were lesbian or gay purely because they were allowed to be a little bit more free. It was not [...] as though it became a political issue that you were lesbian or gay [...] but being gay was not unproper. And that made a lot of people feel more secure in their working environment.

Thus, the culture was made tolerable 'by the number of gay people there. There was like a unity in strength through numbers and that you were generally accepted. [You] were tolerated more as a human being because there was so many of you around that they had to tolerate it and they didn't like it'. Although he was 'never openly out' there came a point when he told his supervisor that he was gay and he found her to be 'very, very sympathetic and very understanding'.

Race and ethnicity

In 1978, following the passage of the Race Relations Act, 1977, BA adopted a 'Policy on Racial Discrimination', designed to 'ensure equal opportunity in employment for all staff regardless of race, colour, nationality, or ethnic or national origin' (British Airways, 1978c). Yet, like its policy on sex discrimination, little progress occurred until well into the 1980s, and in 1987 the airline experienced outside pressure to move more speedily. Following 'recommendations forwarded by the Commission for Racial Equality', senior management conducted a company-wide survey to 'safeguard equal opportunities' through the gathering of 'Ethnic Origin Data' under four broad categories – 'white', 'Afro/Caribbean', 'Asian' or 'other'. The survey, completed in 1991, indicated that 'ethnic staff' members (i.e., non-white) constituted 11.4 per cent of BA's employees and 2.4 per cent of its managers; figures that BA felt compared 'favourably with the British norm' but admitted that there was 'still much to be done to ensure current and future employees have true equal opportunity in their careers' (British Airways, 1991). What it had failed to do to this point was reflect the growing employment of people of colour in its corporate materials. For example, in a review of selected newsletters (see Table 7.5[84]) less than four per cent of all employees photographed are perceptually 'non-white' and of these only one in seven, or half a per cent of all employees depicted, are based in the United Kingdom. In only four cases are 'foreign-based' people of colour shown as occupying positions of authority and in all three cases they are men.

One photograph, of Keith Kerr, Senior Manager in internal audit and one of Britain's '50 most influential black people' (British Airways, 1991), was a rare image. For the most part British-based people of colour were shown in relatively low positions within the airline.

Masculinity

Racial imagery was changing but slowly. As late as the mid-1970s BA was still running cartoons that depicted black Africans as ignorant and British-based people of colour were simply ignored. Remarkably, it was not until the very end of the 1960s that the airline newsletters carried reference to men of colour among their UK-based employees, but they had to die to achieve that distinction. Sultan Beg Mirza was one of the first 'non-white' men to receive a mention in *BOAC News*. When he died in 1969, the newsletter noted that Mirza, a catering labourer, had joined BOAC only four months earlier. The following year, death also occasioned an obituary notice for Mehar Singh Judge, 'a head cook, who had been with the company since 1965' (British Overseas Airways Corporation, 1970a). Between 1971 and 1982 less than a handful of the company's UK-based men of colour received any mention in the newsletter – a maintenance worker, a loader-driver, a uniform supplies employee and an apprentice. The only item of any length drew heavily on black stereotypes of the time in its referencing of size, sexuality and aggression, in a story of a man who 'packs a real punch. [The] gentle giant of Heathrow and the man who might lay claim to the title of Mr. Speedbird [...] is Phillip Dubisson, 6ft 4 in tall and no mean fighter. Phillip has worked for

Table 7.5 Content analysis of photographic images of women and visible minorities in selected British Airways newsletters[1]

Period [issues]	Newsletter	Total number of individual employee images[2]	People of colour (%)	UK-based people of colour (%)	Women (%)
1949 (May)	BOAC News Letter	106	0 [0%]	0 [0%]	4 [3.7%]
1965 (Apr. May)	BOAC Review	157	2 [1.3%]	0 [0%]	23 [14.6%]
1966 (All issues)	BOAC News	495	11 [2.2%]	4 [0.8%]	137 [27.7%]
1971 (June; July)	BEA Magazine	119	0 [0%]	0 [0%]	83 [69.7%]
1973	BEA Magazine	21	0 [0%]	0 [0%]	2 [9.5%]
1973 (First Dec. 1973)	British Airways News Issue	82	1 [1.2%]	0 [0%]	14 [17%]
1975 (Apr.; May; Aug.)	Topline	340	5 [1.5%]	5 [1.5%]	74 [21.8%]
1976 (23 Jan; 23 Jan. supplement; 28 Mar.)	British Airways News	94	2 [2.1%]	0 [0%]	27 [28.7%]
1977 (All first quarter issues)	British Airways News	532	35 [6.5%]	1 [0.2%]	174 [33%]
1982 (June special bulletin)	British Airways News	30	0 [0%]	0 [0%]	3 [10%]
1985 (31 May; 31 May supplement; 14 June supplement;10 Aug.)	British Airways News	136	3 [2.2%]	0 [0%]	55 [40.5%]
1987 (3 July)	British Airways News	86	6 [7%]	0 [0%]	15 [17.5%]
1990 (19 Oct.)	British Airways News	34	1 [2.9%]	1 [2.9%]	8 [23.5%]
1992 (24 Apr; 14, 21 and 28 Aug; 23 and 30 Oct.; 6 Nov.)	British Airways New	574	110 [19.1%]	18 [3.1%]	254 [44.3%]
1993 (26 Feb.; 5 and 26 Mar.; 2 Apr.)	British Airways News	556	108 [19.5%]	37 [6.6%]	258 [46.5%]

Notes:
[1] 'Visible minorities' is a term used by the Canadian Royal Commission on Equality in Employment (Abella, 1984: 46) and is defined as 'people who [are] visible non-white'. The newsletters were randomly selected in so far as they were among the few in the possession of the author.
[2] This involves a simple counting of the number of faces that appear in a single photograph.

BOAC for 5 years and is at present a loader-driver' (British Overseas Airways Corporation, 1972).

Femininity

From 1967 to 1982 the newsletters carried items on a very small number of women of colour, including one station clerk, two 'cargo flight documentation' employees, five catering workers, two clerk/typists, a punch operator and a passenger receptionist.

A breakthrough of sorts occurred in 1980 when a black woman – Hazel George – was featured among the leading contestants of the 'Miss British Airways competition'. Until now company-run beauty contestants were more often than not blonde, white, and blue-eyed – features that in this case characterized the eventual winner. Nonetheless, Hazel George was 'a runner-up'. The mould had been broken. Two years later Hazel George was chosen to promote the company's Personality Girl contest and in 1988 another woman of Afro-Caribbean origin – Jacqui Scally – represented BA in the 'Miss Heathrow Airport competition' – she came third.

Finally, by the mid-1990s BA was making conscious efforts not only to recruit and promote people of colour but also to image them as 'normal' employees. Much of its corporate materials presented a 'family' image consisting of a multitude of ethic faces.

The gendering of British Airways

In the 1980s BA went through many of its most profound changes since the onset of Second World War. Ongoing sensemaking experienced a series of shocks in the form of massive lay-offs, new leadership, and culture change that altered the gender gestalt. Some aspects of masculinity proved remarkably resilient, particularly the image of the while-coveralled engineer. Piloting and management, on the other hand, lost some of their deep-rooted links to male activities that made them inexorably masculine. The introduction of a culture change focused on caring and emotionally challenged traditional notions of manhood and opened the door for the employment of more female managers. New, yet conflictual, images of femininity were developing – positing tension between notions of woman as professional and as wife and mother. Beneath the surface of these changes were unresolved issues of sexual orientation and race/ethnicity. BA's heterosexual imagery of the 1990s had implications for all employees, favouring those who appeared to fit the archetypes while in someway excluding or doubting those who did not. The central focus on whiteness also had its implications for the social construction of ideal typical employees and the valuing not only of racial and ethnic types but also of certain forms of masculinity and femininity.

In this era change owed much to internal upheaval as to the broad formative context in which BA was located. If leadership had an impact on the way that people reacted to issues of gender and race it was due more to the introduction of culture change which broke up the ongoing sense of the organization than any direct influence of the leaders themselves. The formative context intruded into the company in the form of legislative changes, the changing demographic and expectations of the UK workforce, and increasing levels of resistance. The company responded to legislative changes but in a largely formalistic way. The disruptions caused by mass layoffs and then company-wide culture change did not simply alter the organizational rules but disrupted the existing understandings of what the rules meant. In the process a new sense of the organization was created as management grappled with new corporate imagery and practices that were far more gender ambiguous than they had been in the past. Finally, they could not have failed to be influenced by events in North American airlines.

Equity struggles in North American airlines

Throughout the 1960s the United States witnessed a number of widespread challenges to structural inequities, including campaigns against racism and sexism in politics and business. This often had a dramatic impact on the public consciousness in North America and other parts of the world, with freedom marches, the March on Washington, race riots and numerous marches for 'women's liberation'.

Flight attendants were among the very first women involved in the new women's movement, and were to the fore in legal challenges to discriminatory practices.[85] Interestingly, one of the first of such challenges to Pan Am was from someone charging sex discrimination because he was turned down for a job as a flight attendant because he was a man. In the subsequent *Diaz v. Pan American World Airways, Inc.* case, in the early 1970s, the airline drew on gendered notions of womanhood to defend their position, arguing that women, 'because of their psychological relationships to persons of both sexes, are better able' than men to deal with typical passenger emotional states of 'apprehension, boredom, and excitement' (quoted in Nielsen, 1982: 96–97). The airline also argued that it had difficulty in finding male flight attendants who possessed traits of 'femininity' (ibid.). Pan Am eventually lost the case[86] and, along with other airlines, began to hire male flight attendants. Pan Am also lost a class action suit from a group of 116 women, former flight attendants, claiming sex discrimination because they 'were disciplined, denied promotion, forced to resign, or fired for being "overweight"' (NAAFA Online, 2005). They were awarded \$.2.3 million.

Shortly after the Diaz case, William Sewell, the 'chairman' of Pan Am, announced that one of the airline's 'targets in 1973 is to increase job opportunities for women – to make the phrase 'Equal Opportunity Employee' even more meaningful within our company' (Pan American Airways, 1973). Referencing Ann Archibald, Sewell – somewhat ingeniously, given the relative absence of women in senior positions – went on to praise Pan Am as 'one of the first, even the first, airline to advance a woman to the status of corporate officer' (ibid). There were no women on the board, no women pilots, and the newest appointment to a senior position was a woman – Wilma Rogalin – placed in charge of the new 'Office of Women's Opportunities' (ibid). At this point, 7500 (or 30%) of Pan Am's employees were women, including just 306 that constituted 7.5 per cent of the airline's managers (Pan American Airways, 1974a).[87]

Over the next years employment equity was debated in the pages of the company newsletter alongside reported commitments to women's opportunities and affirmative action policies. Rhetorical questions were raised about whether a woman would ever be president of the airline, and women readers were pointedly asked if they wanted '*all* the jobs in the company' (Pan American Airways, 1973). The official answer to the latter question was 'of course, "no", but women *do* want the opportunity to compete on an equal basis with men for any job in Pan Am' (ibid.). Nonetheless, it was 1974 when Pan Am caught up with BA in hiring its first female station manager, it was not until 1976 that it appointed a woman – Marietta Tree – to its Pan Am board, and it was a month behind BA (but several years behind comparable US carriers) when it hired is first female pilot – Colleen Burgess – in April 1987.[88] For a variety of reasons the airline went bankrupt in 1991[89] and a number of other US carriers have since followed suit.

In Canada during the 1960s and much of the 1970s the country was preoccupied with issues of nationhood, biculturalism and bilingualism,[90] which led to the Official Languages Act in 1969 – providing federal services in both French and English, where population size warranted it – and the Multiculturalism Policy of 1971 – providing 'official recognition and support to those ethnic groups who sought to preserve their distinctive cultural heritages and ethnic identities within a pluralist society' (Mills, Simmons, and Helms Mills, 2005: 197).

Responding to the new sensibilities, TCA changed its name in 1965 to the more bilingually friendly Air Canada, and in 1968, on the retirement of Gordon McGregor, appointed its first ever Francophone CEO, Yves Pratte, a Quebec City lawyer.[91]

Nonetheless, gender equity was also very much a concern within the airline, which in 1967 employed 5000 women, or 31.25 per cent of Air Canada employees (Fournier, 1967). It was in 1969 when Air Canada heralded its first female – an Executive Assistant to the Senior Vice President of Sales (Air Canada, 1969) – and at the onset of the 1970s senior management announced new personnel policies to 'ensure equality of treatment and opportunities for all employees regardless of race, national origin, colour, religion, age, sex or marital status' (Air Canada, 1973b). In particular, the new policies were seen as 'paving the way for greater participation and advancement of women' but warned that 'policy changes do not provide the full answer', that 'anyone eyeing the corporate ladder must be qualified' (ibid.).

A sign of the discussion around employment equity and women's libera-tion, reminiscent of debates inside BA, was a report on a woman's promotion to management that stated, 'She's in a position that might be considered a victory for some ardent women's liberationists. And quite frankly, Air Canada's first female passenger service duty manager [...] doesn't really care about women's lib anyway' (Air Canada, 1973a).

By 1974 the percentage of female employees had, at 30 per cent, dropped below the national average of 34.4 per cent of women in the labour force as a whole, but the actual *number* of female employees had risen to 6506 com-pared with 1967 (Air Canada, 1975b). There were however some advances, particularly in the field of management. From 1970 to 1974 the number of female managers increased from 130 (4%) to 293 (7.9%); although very low this figure was much higher than the national average of the 2.9 per cent of managerial and administrative positions held by women (ibid). In an other-wise balanced report, Claude Taylor (see Exhibit 7.1) – who was to succeed Yves Pratte in 1975 – argued, that is terms of management qualities 'women appear to excel in the creative and [...] "soft" sciences versus the "hard"

Exhibit 7.1   The president and the agent: Claude Taylor (center) poses with Passenger Agent Jean Helms, 1976

sciences [and are] more sensitive, more creative and probably more willing to work that men' (Air Canada, 1975a).

By the end of the 1980s Air Canada was a long way from fulfilling its equity mandate. It had hired its first female pilot,[91] board member and mechanic but, as the Royal Commission of Equality in Employment found in 1984, its percentage of female employees was falling (to below 30%) (Abella, 1984: 104), and only three per cent of its upper-level managers, and under eight per cent of middle managers were women. There was one woman on the board of directors (Abella, 1984: 112), and women constituted around three-quarters of all the airline's clerical and service workers but less than one per cent of its professional employees (Abella, 1984: 107). And women were less paid than men at all levels (Abella, 1984: 117–21). By the time Air Canada was privatized in 1989 the rhetoric of equity was far from having been translated into reality.

8
From Here to Eternity: Making Sense of the Gendering of Organizational Culture

> The idea of multiple overlapping discourses ... problematizes sharp distinctions between self and other ... undermining oppositional rhetorical strategies.
>
> Steven R. Corman (2000: 10)

> Recognizing our differences and using those differences to push our own and others' understanding does not mean that we must reject the notion of a common ground for organizational theorizing; instead, it suggests that any common ground we do develop will be provisional, partial, and subject to continual critique [...] A politics of affinity recognizes that there is 'nothing about being ''female' that naturally binds women'; rather identities are conceived as the result of 'contradictory social realities of patriarchy, colonialism, racism, and capitalism'... Feminist interested in creating knowledge for social change are left with the responsibility of building unities rather than naturalizing them.
>
> Angela Trethewey (2000: 201–02)

Introduction

As was made clear at the beginning, this book is and is not about British Airways (nor for that matter about Air Canada and Pan American Airways). Clearly, the book is about these airlines in that it attempts to analyse the companies over time, but as case studies designed to shed light on the gendering of organizational culture per se. Certainly there is no intent to single out BA, Pan Am or Air Canada as exemplars of bad organizational practice; there is no evidence to suggest that any of these airlines has a worse than average track record on sex discrimination. BA, for example, appears to have been less willing to hire female clerical staff than other major companies in the 1920s, more advanced than many in the late 1940s with its equity imaging of female flight attendants, more willing to exploit eroticism in the

1960s, and yet among the 1990s leaders in adopting employment equity strategies. Rather, BA's value as a case study depends on methodological issues, including the length of time that it has been in business; the fact that it is still in operation; its prominence as a major, internationally known company; the existence of a corporate archive; and the fact that it has been the subject of several written histories (see Chapter 1). On the other hand, the notion of organizational culture is only useful as a heuristic where it is able not only to identify processes common across organizations but also to make sense of localized realities. In that regard BA, Air Canada and Pan Am are not simply stand-ins for organizational culture but an important study of localized practices in an organization. As they are prominent organizations in the world of organizational realities, study of these airlines is also important in their own right for the light it can shed on the gendered influences of the major corporation.

So, what can we learn from the study of an airline over time? The study has pointed to three key areas for discussion and reflection – the character of sex discrimination and change, methodological issues and concerns, and strategies of change. How we answer this question and deal with the areas of discussion will depend in large part on the perspective we take to (or against) feminism.

This book has, from the beginning, taken an 'aspirational feminist' approach, studying the gendering of organizational culture to identify ways of addressing workplace discrimination. But, as a number of feminists have suggested, there are many feminisms, with roots in different philosophical traditions. Calás and Smircich (1996), for example, outline six major feminism perspectives that provide a useful framework for a review of airlines over time: liberal, radical-cultural, psychoanalytic, socialist, poststructuralist, and (post) colonial feminism. Rather than revisit the particular strengths and limitations of each approach, this chapter takes a multi-lens approach, examining each in turn, for what insights they can collectively generate. To that end the chapter focuses on selected features of each perspective. To avoid the creation of several straw women, it should be pointed out that the simplification of each approach masks the complexity of concerns that characterize each approach. For example, a focus on radical-cultural feminism's concern with the social construction of women does not imply that liberal feminists do not share similar, albeit differently framed, concerns.

Liberal feminism

In its characterization of discrimination and equity, liberal feminism focuses on numbers. This perspective quite literally *counts* inequity as the comparative differences between men and women in terms of positions held and incomes received. From this approach, it is relatively easy to measure social change through statistical analysis. Thus, for example, if we examine the changes in BA over time it is not difficult to conclude that there have been a number of positive changes in the last eighty years, but that the company still has quite a way to go before it achieves full employment equity.

In terms of the positive changes, BA has gone from less than a handful of female employees in 1919 to approximately seventeen thousand female staff in the 1990s; from a situation where they could only find employment in a few, narrowly defined, clerical and secretarial jobs, to one where women were employed in almost all levels and categories of work; from formal rules prohibiting women from airline work to employment equity initiatives designed to encourage women to join the company; and, from a 'chosen instrument' of Britain's imperialist policy to a company anxious to present itself as sensitive to workplace diversity, even replacing the Union Jack on the tail fins of its planes with the work of artists of various nationalities and ethnic backgrounds. On the other hand, this viewpoint needs to be tempered by the fact that changes were a long time coming and that women are still virtually absent from the board and constitute less than one-third of all employees and one-fifth of all managers.

This raises at least two main questions: what brought about 'improvements' (i.e., more women in better positions) in the airline and why did some of these changes take so long? Here liberal feminism guides us to a focus on the impact of perceived differences between men and women on organizational arrangements. We do not have to embrace the essentialism of liberal feminism to accept that large numbers of people live their lives as if there were essential differences between men and women. The question is, 'how do these perceptions influence workplace relationships?' A reading of BA, Pan Am and Air Canada over time confirms that the men in charge did see women as being fundamentally different from women and that influenced the extent to which they were prepared to recruit female labour. This is as true of the male leadership of AT&T in the early 1920s, Pan Am in the late 1920s, TCA in the late 1930s, as is it of most of the male leaders of all three airlines in the 1980s and early 1990s. What changed was the view of women's capabilities, not their essential difference.

Thus, one interesting line of enquiry is what is it that changes the views of powerful men towards the capabilities of women. We have seen that in the United Kingdom prior to 1924, such things as warfare and male dominance of aviation reinforced male views of women and helped to exclude them from commercial airlines. We have also seen that social attitudes – influenced by technical change, economic demands and social activism – can also change perceptions about women's capabilities. Between 1924 and 1939 the recruitment of women to the airlines reflected and contributed to the feminization of clerical work, but was mediated by wider socio-political concerns. In Britain and Canada IAL and TCA respectively were behind the national trend, while in the United States Pan Am went with the flow; and the difference appears to be linked to differences in the initial influences on the composition of each airline – its masculine bases and leadership. The biggest changes in attitude appear to be linked to major 'shocks' to the system (Weick, 1995). Warfare in 1939–45, cultural revolution in the 1960s, and corporate-wide culture change strategies in the 1980s. This is not to suggest that employment equity change is inevitably slow or that it depends on serious social upheaval. It might, however, suggest that successful equity programmes need to be rooted in 'shocks' to ongoing sensemaking. For example, in the 1980s BA spent millions of pounds on culture change to improve its 'bottom line'. A major restructuring that affected the tasks, relationships, communications and thinking of the whole staff accompanied the culture change program. It may take that level of organization-wide upheaval to create a sense of equity.

One important external pressure on companies has been the introduction of anti-discrimination and employment equity laws. If we look at events in all three airlines following the introduction of legislation, it is clear that such laws need to incorporate tougher requirements for compliance, and be accompanied by senior management commitment if they are to have an impact (Abella, 1984). There was, for example, very little change in Pan Am in the 1960s and 1970s following the introduction of the Equal Pay Act and the Civil Rights Act. Similarly, there was very little change in BA following the introduction of the Equal Pay Act, the Sex Discrimination Act and the establishment of an Equal Opportunities Commission. There was a far more visible change in Air Canada following the Abella Commission report, and the same was true for BA in the early 1990s following the commitment of senior management to Opportunity 2000.

Another type of intervention is the use of policies and organizational rules to bring about or inhibit equity. The following examples give clues to the value of such interventions: IAL's ban on female pilots in the 1920s; BOAC/BEA's 'desexualization' policy of the 1940s; BA's anti-discrimination policy of the 1970s and its Opportunity 2000 campaign of the 1990s. In two cases (1920s and 1970s) management did little more than endorse the policy, while in two cases (1940s and 1990s) management took an active role.

In the 1920s IAL's support for the ICAN and ICAO rules against female flight crews was an expression of the strong informal rules throughout the industry, and as such unnecessary. When the official bans were lifted after a legal challenge IAL continued to exclude women from flight crews. Informal practices were clearly stronger than formal rules.

In the mid-1970s, as a legal requirement, BA's introduction of an anti-sex discrimination policy did little to address the various practices and processes that continued to reproduce discrimination. A decade later a Canadian Royal Commission into equity in the workplace found a similar approach in Air Canada and other major Canadian companies. The Abella Commission, as it became known, argued that the problem did not rely on changes to individual attitudes (although that was an important element) but in dealing with 'systemic discrimination' rooted in a multitude of mundane practices and processes (Abella, 1984).

In many ways it was the mundane practices and processes of discrimination that derailed BOAC and BEA managements' desexualization policy of the 1940s. Although both airlines made a point of addressing some of the immediate practices (i.e., imagery, equal pay) the changes were small enough to be overwhelmed in companies whose gender gestalts were increasingly informed by eroticized images of women. Indeed, it can be argued that the gendered concerns of senior management imposed too narrow a sense of womanhood on company employees and encouraged more traditional notions to find its way through informal channels. The changes were less dramatic at Air Canada and Pan Am but that is essentially because those airlines tended to reflect (and reproduce) dominant images of women focussed on bodily beauty at both official and informal levels.

If BA's Opportunity 2000 can be said to have had any success, and that is an open question, it was due, in large part, to the fact that (1) there was already a growing discourse of employment equity within the company, (2) senior management were on one side and (3) equity was perceived as an important contribution to the 'bottom line'.

Arguably, the success of any policy intervention will depend on the extent to which senior management is prepared to deal with the numerous informal (as well as formal) rules, practices and procedures that constitute the culture of an organization. Thus, for example, while all three airlines – BA, Pan Am and Air Canada – were publicly committed to employment equity in the 1970s, none of them addressed the vexing issue of how to present people in text and imagery. Stories of female success and promotion were often accompanied by reference to the woman's looks or domestic responsibilities. And of course none of these airlines opened up dialogue around issues of gender that would have encouraged employees to define their own sense of gendered realities.

As part of the strategy of change, liberal feminists emphasise the role of individual women in changing attitudes by striving for different jobs and higher levels in organizational hierarchies, and by showing what they are capable of. This has been criticized as individualistic, and accepting of the status quo (Calás and Smircich, 1996), but it does speak to experiences of gender gestalts that can have a powerful influence on perception. Kanter (1977), for example, argues that too few women at the top of a hierarchy presents organizational actors with an 'opportunity structure' that influences not only advancement but also the image of organizational worth. Those opportunity structures were reproduced with regularity from the 1950s onwards as the airlines sought to clarify the various chains of command through organizational charts. It may be, as socialist feminists argue, that the long-term solution to inequities is to restructure organizational society, but in the meantime we have to live with gender gestalts composed of inequities based on hierarchical position. The notion of 'the glass ceiling' (Morrison, White and Van Elsor, 1987), for example, captures the feelings of women whose sense of identity is linked with a 'common sense' view of reality in which hierarchies are 'normal' and acceptable. Thus, we might ask, how has the existence and performance of women influenced equity development in the airlines over time?

First, the existence of a large and growing number of women in IAL, for example, did not of itself have much impact beyond the clerical sector to which they were recruited. If anything, it had the effect of feminising clerical work but little else. On the positive side it could be argued that at the very least this opened up areas of 'women's work' where none had existed before; influencing the gendered workplace gestalt to include women, however marginal. It also created spaces where there was a perceived need for female supervisors and a senior administrator to manage female employees. The existence of a large number of female employees may also have made it easier for those in charge to absorb large numbers of women workers during the war years. Certainly, senior managers noted the range of abilities displayed by female employees during the war, making it more difficult to keep females out of a number of post-war jobs. Nonetheless, it is clear that despite the extent, character and positive perception of female labour during the war women were still excluded from management, piloting and engineering for most of the post-war era. Arguably, strategies of change based on the presence and performance of female employees and managers is useful in undermining sexist characterizations of women's abilities and in providing a more positive gender gestalt to new generations of women. But it is effective only to the extent that other factors, such as socio-legal or commercial pressures, are also present. Both the 1974 and 1991 male leaderships of the airlines could point to the competencies of female managers but only the latter made a commitment to hire more women to management.

Radical-cultural feminism

This perspective views workplace inequity as the outcome of male dominance rooted in patriarchal familial arrangements. Here the task is not so much to 'improve' conditions for women within existing hierarchies but to encourage women to break with existing organizational and family arrangements, establishing alternative ways of being. The overt essentialism of this approach, in its celebration of femininity, has found its way into mainstream management practice, as seen in attempts to include 'feminine qualities' in valued management styles (Fondas, 1997; Harriman, 1985). There are examples of this in all three airlines in more recent times, with editorials in praise of 'the feminine touch' in management. Nonetheless, this perspective raises interesting questions about study of the gendering of organizational culture. It encourages examination not simply of discrimination against women but of the relationship between organizational dominance and the social construction of womanhood. It also suggests that organizational cultures should be understood as reflections of broader gendered realities, particularly the family.

Drawing on this perspective, it can be argued that the sources of discriminatory notions of women can be found not only in male dominance of organizations but in corporate practices (i.e., recruitment and promotion) and processes (e.g., the production of advertisements, in-house journals, annual reports, memoranda, etc.) that reproduce and mirror that dominance. Here BA, Pan Am and Air Canada offer conflicted cases. Clearly, corporate practices and imagery contributed to narrow, often negative notions of womanhood over time. Yet, corporate imagery differed over time.

For much of the early years women were simply ignored. Prior to 1939 women were non-persons in BA's culture, a small and marginal part of Pan Am's culture and literally not employed by TCA. In the war years women moved centre stage in the corporate gender gestalt as defenders of the home front. For a brief time in the 1940s BOAC and BEA female flight attendants were characterized as the equal of their male counterparts, but not so in Air Canada and Pan Am. In the 1960s and 1970s the predominant corporate image of women in all three airlines revolved around eroticized images of the body. Yet in the early 1990s images of the female corporate manager vied for attention alongside those of the 'sexy young thing'. Radical-cultural feminists may well contend that this simply illustrates the point that male dominant organizations construct images of womanhood that reflect their own needs.

Notwithstanding the argument that all male-dominant images of womanhood are sexist, there is still the possibility that, in terms of lived experiences, some gender gestalts are preferable to others. For example, Stewardesses for Women's Rights (see Chapter 7) argue that in some senses earlier airline practices were preferable to the situation they experienced in the 1970s: for example, 'stewardesses on the major airlines had much more conservative and professional looking uniforms until Braniff International came along with the couture outfits and strip shows in 1965, and other airlines followed suit in the 1960's' (quoted in Kane, 1974: 88). The earlier days were viewed nostalgically as 'more of a Doris Day kind of thing. We were a sweetheart then, not a sex object' (ibid.). For some, the stewardess profession had lost a lot in the transition: the 'very classic, perhaps even paramilitary uniform [was preferable to] the hot pants kind of thing' (ibid.). In the 'more dignified uniform' the stewardess could look in the mirror and 'see a professional, competent person [with] the authority need[ed] to do the job' (ibid.).

This raises the question of how and why do certain practices develop and change and what can we learn from this? To begin with, it is clear that it is harder to ignore women the more they are part of the organizational landscape: prior to 1939 the corporate neglect of female employees contributed to an image of women as marginal to the workplace. It is also clear that the existence of a large number of female employees does not guarantee the development of positive female images. From 1945 to 1960, with the notable exception of female flight attendants, only narrowly defined, relatively marginalized images of women ever appeared in the corporate gestalt of BOAC, BEA, Air Canada and Pan Am. Ironically, both the desexualization policy of the 1940s and eroticized marketing in the 1960s were the result of commercial pressures. The somewhat more inclusive images of the 1990s seem to be the outcome of resistance, an evolving discourse of equity, and commercial interests ('equity sells'!).

Radical-cultural feminists contend that in the long run women will only find liberated spaces outside existing male-dominant organizations. From this perspective an important strategy for change involves 'consciousness raising', making women aware of their oppression and the processes through which this is normalized. If we look at the history of BA there are only two clear pockets of resistance – an early attempt at stewardess unionization in the early 1960s and the war of words in the mid-to-late 1970s. In the earlier period resistance was aimed at inequitable work and pay, what might be termed a liberal feminist strategy. The latter resistance was aimed at the relationships between work processes and understandings of women, what might be seen as a radical-cultural feminist strategy. This raises some interesting questions for further research.

To begin, there is the simple issue of numbers. On the one hand, we might ask, does it matter whether a few or a large number of women resist? There may have been women in the pre-Second World War era who 'recognised' the male dominant nature of the airline business but unless they engaged in any dramatic form of resistance, either individually (e.g., legal action) or collectively (e.g., attempts to unionize), it may not come to our attention. If we focus on more dramatic evidence of consciousness, then the question is, does there have to be sufficient numbers of women in the workplace for effective consciousness raising to occur? Kanter (1977) and Gutek (1985) have both argued that, along with other conditions, a critical mass of women (i.e., around one-third of employees in a given workplace) is essential to effect far-reaching changes in the workplace. When we look at BA there is no evidence of resistance in the pre-1940 era when the number of females represented less than ten per cent of the airline employees. Also there is no evidence of resistance when women constituted a third of the workforce during the war years. The least we can say is that there were signs of resistance during periods when women constituted at least 25 per cent of the airline's workforce.

Certainly numbers alone is not the issue. Armstrong and Armstrong (1986: 178) contend that 'work has a profound effect on women's view of themselves and on their personalities, and that it should be the starting point for an explanation of women's consciousness'. They argue that there are two processes at work. On the one hand, the boring, dull and routine nature of much of women's work inhibits the potential for individual women to rise above a lowly sense of self let alone a consciousness of the impact of male dominant work on images of womanhood. On the other hand, paid work can provide a welcome outlet from stifling patriarchal home life situations, thus blurring some of the harsher effects. Indeed, Kanter (1977) also suggests that low-paid female work ghettos can encourage conservatism whereby women discourage other women from seeking better employment. If we look at female employment and imagery in BA, Air Canada and Pan Am we find that until the 1960s women were mostly employed in routine jobs and were expected to leave when they married. Prior to Second World War there seems to have been a strong sense among women as well as men in the airlines that female employment was only a phase between school and marriage. In a similar vein, women – including a large number of married women – took on a range of new jobs during the war years but expected this to be temporary. The experience of new and interesting work, coupled with post-war labour shortages, did, however, change women's views of what was 'fit work for women'. By the 1960s the female employee was a 'normal' part of the airlines' gender gestalts, and expectations were changing of women's abilities and workplace careers. It was a period of economic boom and the advent of the birth-control pill, but as of yet, the workplace had not responded to women's changing expectations. The time was ripe for anger and resistance as women not only balked at restricted opportunities but also at the deep-rooted images of womanhood associated with such attitudes.

Pugh (1992) and others (Lewis, 1992; Rowbotham, 1999; Weeks, 1990) suggest that women's consciousness and feminism has gone through different phases that reflect the changing political gains and defeats of the women's movement. In many ways this is mirrored in the history of BA. In the period ending in 1940 IAL hired a growing number of young, middle-class women who fully expected to leave work once they married but who may have shared with their sisters in other jobs the enjoyment of being able to work. Pugh (1992) refers to this as an 'anti-feminist' era where young women were able to combine a new found freedom of being able to work while still preparing for marriage and home life. If anything, according to Pugh (1992) and Rowbotham (1999), the era of new clerical job opportunities encouraged a kind of individualism in young women that they had not previously been able to experience. Warfare, once again, put general feminist concerns on the back burner as everyone rallied together to defeat fascism. This was more than evident in BOAC during those years. The first two decades of the post-war era saw a renewed emphasis on childhood and motherhood and the rise of consumerism. Within Pan Am, Air Canada and the British airlines the normalization of the female employee managed to combine concerns regarding marriagability with the themes of childrearing and motherhood. When the new women's movement developed in the 1960s it is interesting to note that female flight attendants were in the forefront of various struggles. Whatever may have held back female resistance it is certain that corporate imagery and symbolism served to reinforce narrow notions of women and womanhood and may have contributed to an acceptance of the status quo.

Psychoanalytic feminism

This perspective focuses on psychosexual development in the formation of patriarchal organizational structures. Male and female experiences in organizations are seen as being rooted in historically and personally cited childhood practices and sex-role socialization. This has profound implications for women who are seen as being socialized to be passive and ambivalent towards career. This ill prepares women for the world of work where more often than not they 'fall short in the corporate culture, because the rules, norms, ethos of modern business reflect the male developmental experience' (Calás and Smircich, 1996: 230). One strategy of social and organizational change centres on changes in child-rearing practices and another centres on changing the cultural values of organizations to incorporate 'feminine' values.

This perspective directs us to the analysis of such things as personalities, values, organizational rules and business ethos. It is clear from much of the history of the airlines that the values and rules developed from personalities (e.g., Brancker, Trippe, Johnson), events (e.g., warfare), business ethos (e.g., 'chosen instrument' of government policy), and symbolism (e.g., wartime uniforms, ranks and planes) were strongly linked to male-associated activities. The questions I have tried to pose throughout the book are: how much influence did these things have on the gendered character of an organization, are there discernible changes over time, and what are the lessons for feminism?

Over the years all airlines had a series of male leaders. At BA this ranged from Sir Sefton Brancker through to Sir Colin Marshall. Each was associated with a different form of masculinity and employment practices. Brancker, as we have seen, was a Victorian paternalist who favoured the employment of women under certain circumstances. Sir Eric Geddes, also paternalist in his approach to women and men, was less favourable to the employment of women in all but a few clerical positions. Yet under Brancker few, if any, women worked for the airline and he presided over official bans on female flight crews. The Geddes era, on the other hand, is associated with the first consistent hiring of female employees. The main difference between the two men was their influence on the business ethos of commercial aviation at the time. Brancker was associated with a military esprit de corps, which excluded women by dint of its masculinist values of warfare and danger. Geddes imposed a 'hard nosed' commercialism and authoritarian leadership style on the airline, which excluded women from all but clerical work by dint of its masculinist values of aggression and toughness. The employment of women to various secretarial and clerical positions, while significant in itself, was more a reflection of the rapid feminization of clerical work.

The first man to make any real difference at BOAC was Gerard d'Erlanger who, as head of the ATA, was persuaded to recruit female pilots and then, after some reluctance, to allow them to fly the full range of aircraft. Arguably, d'Erlanger's reactions were informed by the perceived necessities of war. Certainly, there is no evidence that he played a role in opening up work to women during his time at BAL, BEA and BOAC. Nonetheless, he could have brought his influence to bear by excluding women from ATA piloting, but he didn't. At the very least, this gives up some clues about the possibilities of change under certain types of male leaders.

Sir Harold Harley presided over the next real 'advance' for women with the introduction of a 'desexualization' policy for the hiring of female flight attendants. This is a case where the action appears to have been influenced by concerns of impropriety rather than equity. The effect was the same but, as a result, was less stable and not enduring because it was not rooted in a concern with equity. Again, the strength of this personality trait probably influenced events because it was in tune with the political ethos of austerity that was prevalent at the time.

As business picked up and Britain moved into a new era Sir Miles Thomas contributed to a normalization of the female employee by a shift in ethos towards performance measurement. Although the various technological reference points of this discourse favoured men over women it did create some element of ambivalence in that 'women's work' was, for the first time, being judged as subject to efficiency standards.

Thomas was something of an enigma. Like Sefton Brancker, Miles Thomas felt that there were certain jobs that women can and should be employed to do and, like Brancker, he held on to a notion of women as girls – essentially wives and mothers. In terms of feminist psychoanalysis, Thomas's biography provides a number of clues to his later behaviour. He was born in 1897, the closing years of the Victorian era, and his father died before he was one year old. Commenting that all the events of his early days 'were dominated by women', Thomas (1964: 11) felt that the whole of his early life 'was predominantly affected by the female sex' because he never knew his father and had 'absolutely no memory of him' (ibid.). He returns to this theme elsewhere when he discusses his religious beliefs: '[In] the atmosphere of inhibited pride and almost prudish domination by women in which I was brought up, one belief [in a greater power] grew strong in my mind, a belief that years of increased acquaintance with science has strengthened' (Thomas, 1964: 18). In the early 1920s Thomas went to work for the Morris car company in Cowley, Oxford and again refers to the issue of female 'domination':

> I do not claim it as a bond of affinity with Bill Morris that both our lives at an early age were dominated by our mothers[... But] it was, I feel sure, the fact that Morris recognised that he had to be the main source of support for his mother that spurred him on to such dynamic physical and commercial efforts.
>
> (Thomas, 1964: 130)

This ambivalence towards women as dominant but important people in his life is also reflected in his personal relationships. As was noted in Chapter 6, Thomas followed a traditional approach in requiring his wife to resign her job following marriage.

Elsewhere we gain glimpses of Thomas's sense of masculinity. On one occasion during the First World War a prostitute approached Thomas in a London street. Somewhat shyly he rebuffed her but went away feeling a 'suspicion of disappointment that [he] had been very unmanly' (Thomas, 1964: 44). On homosexuality, Thomas (1964: 48) had some forthright and chilling comments:

> In [earlier] days, not only among the upper and upper middle classes but at all social levels, homosexuality simply wasn't recognised. Let me be frank and say that until this very day I do not know the mechanics of the practice. Either my dimensions are odd or there is some behaviour that has escaped me entirely. I count myself lucky in these regards; on the other hand, I think that any nasty practice of this kind is like a weed – it flourishes with the light. Once this or any other form of vice became reported tantalisingly in some sections of the Press, revelling in its Freedom like a snake relishes a warm, moist, incest-strewn midden, it became fashionable among queer-minded fellows who, had they been kept in ignorance, would not have had the enterprise to ferret things out for themselves.

That these attitudes and deeply held beliefs had an influence on Thomas's running of the airline is evidenced in certain attitudes and policies but will, for the most part, have depended on the structural constraints and social climate in which he was able to express them.

It was not until the 1990s that any male leader made an attempt to address the issue of employment equity, when Sir Colin Marshall introduced *Opportunity 2000*. It is fair to say Marshall took a lead among business leaders but that whatever his personality his actions were strongly influenced by a growing discourse of equity both within the company and the country as a whole. But it was very much a Thatcherite image of equity, the strong woman who competes successfully in the male world on male terms.

Similar analyses could be done on Juan Trippe and Phil Johnson. Trippe has been described as having 'little interest in women [avoiding] even conversing with them' (Daley, 1980) yet was the first to promote a woman to a senior position in the airlines. Johnson played a role at both UAL and Air Canada in pioneering the hiring of female flight attendants.

If we can say anything about the relationship between personality, structure and gender it is that where structure is decided by a strong personality it will play a key role in the development of practices and processes (Kets de Vries, 1991). Juan Trippe, for example, dominated the structure at Pan Am, only allowing decisions to be made that he approved of. This almost certainly had a bearing on the employment of women in Pan Am. On the other hand, where an established sense of organization is in place then personality may play an important role through reactions to ongoing sensemaking (Whyte, 1956). Wartime leaders of British airlines, for example, reacted to the perceived needs of the day, in many ways facilitating the employment of women but in other ways ensuring that they are not hired to existing structures (e.g., stewardesses).

Socialist feminism

This perspective views the existing (capitalist) structures of organizations (along with patriarchal familial arrangements) as the root of the problem. From this perspective, 'improvements' in the numbers of women in workplace hierarchies are less important than signs that women are challenging the patriarchal character of existing organizational structures. This perspective differs from radical-cultural feminism in its rejection of essentialist notions of women and men. Instead it focuses on the social construction of womanhood through intersections of power located in familial and organizational sites.

Here our attention is directed towards an understanding of how the structuring of capitalist relationships contributes to notions of masculinity and femininity. This often involves analysis of the historical roots of materialist practices and their potential for change over time. Mary Ryan's (1979) study of womanhood in America, for example, traces the development of capitalism in the United States and its impact on how womanhood was understood at various points in time.

In the pre-Second World War era women were hardly noticed in IAL and Pan Am. In the post-war era change was slow, intermittent, sometimes regressive and, at times, confusing. A limited equity policy was introduced in the post-war, state-owned BOAC and BEA. But it was also in the state-owned airlines that the process of eroticization occurred. It was in the era of Thatcherism, when BA had become privatized, that a more concerted effort at equity was introduced. In order to understand the role of power in the social construction of womanhood and manhood we need to understand not only its organizational (and familial) locations but also its exercise.

Examining the history of airlines over time we find different notions of womanhood at different points. None are ultimately positive but, taking into account lived experiences, some are more positive than others. Clearly power relations between men and women are central in the process. When we examine power in the airline over time we find that until recently men dominated all 'circuits of power' (Kanter, 1979) .

In the period 1919–24 the structures, practices and processes of the early British airlines were decided by an elite group of men who had, for the most part, served the war effort in some capacity or other. It was their worldview that dominated the airline, and it was a worldview associated with a specific form of warfare masculinity. The limited notion of womanhood that was produced (or, rather, implied) was due not simply to the fact that males held every power position but that masculine reference points, experienced through a sense of camaraderie and esprit de corps, reinforced associations between aviation and manliness. Those masculine associations were strongly mediated by cut-throat competitive business practices in the United States and bush piloting in Canada.

Men were dominant in IAL but there were at least two dominant forms of masculinity. Under Geddes's leadership a new style of 'hard-nosed' commercialism informed the expected management style. This supplanted the air force camaraderie style of managing. Now the stress was on hierarchical structure, central control and a 'business-like' approach to the day-to-day running of the airline. This contributed to two major archetypes of masculinity that became more-or-less associated with different tasks. The military model continued to dominate the image of the engineer and the pilot. Management, for the most part, became associated with the new business ethos. There were of course tensions between the new masculinity and the old as established air force men felt edged out by newcomers who were recruited for their business sense rather than aviation experience. At other levels the new business ethos was giving rise to the career pilot whose points of reference were 'the corporation' rather than the flying fraternity. The reference points for engineering were also changing. As the new business ethos took hold and the military camaraderie between pilots and engineers gave way to corporate links, aviation engineering turned more to its links with engineering in general and stressed professional training and skill; a new masculinity in the making. A fourth type of masculinity began to develop with the establishment of flight stewards. With no military reference points, this new role drew on characteristics extant in other areas of the travel business.

There were no such apparent sharp divisions in Pan Am, which from the position was dominated by big business concerns and sharp business practices, while TCA came to be dominated by different forms of masculinity at different levels of the company – railwaymen at the board level, competitive business men at the operations level and bush piloting at the service level.

Between them these various forms of masculinity created a gender gestalt in which all positions of power and authority, core tasks, and allied work were inexorably linked to male-associated characteristics. This not only excluded women from the industry but also contributed to notions of womanhood. A role for women was barely visible in the interstices between masculinities. To compound matters the establishment of in-house newsletters served to reflect the lack of imaginative spaces for women in the airline industry. This added a new layer of male power – the editor, who constructed selected images of the predominant masculine worldview. At one end of the organization's discursive practices were the hiring processes and organizational rules enacted by the managers and supervisors. At the other end was the reflection and naturalization of those processes in the airline's in-house newsletters, annual reports, advertisements and other corporate documentation.

The onset of Second World War drastically changed the ethos of the airlines and led to some changes in the imaging of womanhood. In the United Kingdom the era saw a return to the dominance of military masculinity but this was tempered by the need to recruit a large number of women to replace male employees who were required for national service. Those at the top saw themselves as part of the greater war effort in which women were involved at a number of levels. The presence of women across a range of jobs weakened their masculine associations and may have opened spaces for future generations but did not lead to immediate results. In part this may have been due to the fact that very few women attained positions of authority and that the discourse of warfare helped to cast other concerns (e.g., pay equity) as marginal. For the most part, a number of women who went to work for BOAC during the war seem to have accepted their role as 'backroom girls'. That is not to say that women were 'cultural dopes', blithely accepting whatever roles came their way. Women's voices helped to shape the discourse of war and a number of prominent female activists contributed to the notion that women should be recruited to stand alongside their 'menfolk' in uniform and in the workplace. This helped to broaden rather than 'liberate' notions of womanhood. This was particularly the case in the British airlines where male and female employees could in some sense see themselves sharing an important front line, or home front. Things were somewhat different in Canada and the United States. Air Canada was militarized in a more direct sense, seeing themselves as contributing to combat in a number of ways. Pan Am, on the other hand, saw their wartime duties as an extension of existing business practices, where they occupied a special role as the chosen instrument of foreign policy. They were more like diplomats, spies and businessmen than military men. Tripp even turned down a key military commission, preferring to continue in the role of business entrepreneur. In both airlines there was a divide between the men who enlisted and went 'off to war' and the women who stayed behind in places far removed from the so-called theatre of war.

Male associations with power, piloting and professionalism helped to constrain notions of womanhood in the post-war era. In large part this was still due to the continued control of power positions by men. But it was also due to the associations of masculine characteristics with those roles. With the growing presence of female employees some notions of womanhood and femininity were contested. In particular the British airlines' desexualization policies, which imposed a male image of equity on female flight attendants, was eroded by the resistance of women to 'unfashionable', masculine-looking clothes. It was the mediated concerns of male managers and female flight attendants and other uniformed female staff that informed the developing emphasis on 'glamour'. Yet, it we look at the construction of the role of the flight attendant itself we can see other layers of the exercise of power, whereby a form of co-option is embedded in the 'attraction' of the job. For example, in later years, even when militant feminists were protesting the eroticization of the flight attendant image, the various airlines continued to be inundated with applications for the job.

From the 1970s onwards it was the potential for women to occupy established positions – positions associated with power, status and glamour – that drew a number of them into the struggle for employment equity and informed such decisions as the introduction of Opportunity 2000. On the one hand, discriminatory images of women were challenged as women struggled for greater equity. On the other hand, the exercise of male power is still evident in definitions of equity and their link to business efficiency. Nonetheless, it seems that levels of change depend on a combination of factors. First, a critical mass of women may be needed in a given workplace in order for a women's voice to be heard. This can build solidarity and resistance (Pollert, 1981) or conservatism (Kanter, 1977); but, second, the more women are to be found in a range of jobs and job-levels the less likely they are to accept constraints. At some level this can discourage women from action as the world of work affords freedom and status not strictly attainable in domestic situations (Armstrong and Armstrong, 1986; Hochschild, 1990). On the other hand, it can generate resistance where the workplace simultaneously stresses women's abilities while clearly laying out glass walls and ceilings (Morrison *et al.*, 1987). Third, feminist strategies are needed that engage women in short-term struggles over workplace equity and concurrently work with those women to develop long-term alternatives to existing power arrangements.

Poststructuralist feminism

This perspective turns our focus on the discursive nature of 'social reality' and 'subjectivity'. Through an emphasis on language as a system of difference, poststructuralist feminism encourages us to question the creation of, and the limits imposed upon, 'knowledge' by certain privileged discourses.

Drawing on this perspective we can trace how certain 'truths' become embedded in the culture of an organization, what the consequences of those 'truths' are for the development of subjectivities, and how they change over time. Here, we can identify two key strategies of change: (1) weakening the hold of discursive practices on sense of self (or selves) by exposing the relationship between discourse and identity; and (2) taking some control over the development of subjectivities by understanding something of how it develops, is maintained and changes (Thomas, Mills and Helms Mills, 2004).

For poststructuralist feminism, organizational culture is a heuristic for making sense of change. It is a way of framing events to make sense of the present. As such we need to remind ourselves that this is a temporary tool for communication and not a representation of a form of reality. That is, focus on the culture of an organization is a way to communicate ideas about the social construction of gendered identities, but should not be taken to imply a reality in itself. With that caveat, analysis of the culture of an organization over time might usefully highlight the central discourses at play and the traces of subjectivities, exploring the potential relationships between the two.

The exploration of BA, Pan Am and Air Canada reveal several dominant masculinities and femininities over time. Glimpses of subjectivities in the pre-IAL days, for example, suggest that air force thinking, symbolism and camaraderie dominated the early airlines. This appears to have had the effect of reinforcing certain notions of warfare masculinity and recreating it in a commercial setting. Warfare, notions of danger, and national survival heavily informed the emerging organizational discourse of safety and survival. These 'truths' influenced how aviation employees viewed the nature of their jobs and their sense of self. Such discourses contributed to aspects of key subjectivities that associated danger and survival with masculinity, excluding women from flight crews and management. With each changing set of discourses came new or modified masculinities and femininities.

What can we say about the outcomes for gendered selves of organizational discourses over time? First, for the most part, masculinity is privileged over femininity. Powerful discourses have contributed to the exclusion of women from a range of jobs based on their association with feminine traits. There have been two exceptions to this that we need to consider later: (1) masculinity became viewed as inappropriate for flight stewarding in the two decades following Second World War; (2) in the 1990s certain female-associated characteristics (e.g., consideration for others, an ability to listen) were seen as valued aspects of management.

Second, the (re)creation of certain forms of masculinity as privileged characteristics has consequences for women and men: women are (further) marginalized, some men find themselves in a privileged position, and some men find themselves struggling for organizational authenticity. Again, we might note the two exceptions referred to above, where types of femininity are privileged over masculinity.

Third, notions of men and women are relatively unstable and subject to change. But there do appear to be limits. The men and women of IAL almost certainly viewed manhood and womanhood in a different light from their BA counterparts in the 1990s. Nonetheless, the change appears to be around issues of the types and range of characteristics one associates with being a man and a woman rather than any fundamental questioning of the notion of 'man' and 'woman' itself. That is, in the 1990s people still acted as if there were essential differences between men and women.

Fourth, it is difficult, if not too much of a truth claim in its own right, to argue that all notions of femininity have been equally bad. For example, in the pre-war era women were seen as incapable of serving as flight crew. The post-war 'desexualised' female flight attendant was profoundly gendered and problematic but it did open up an important avenue of employment for a number of women. The comments of a number of British, US and Canadian women, who were flight attendants during this era, suggest that many, if not all, valued their time and position and fought to retain rather than change the work. This is not to suggest that women should accept their lot in life or be grateful for certain 'opportunities'; far from it. It is clear that much of the discourses around the notion of flight attending were premised on male notions of what service was being provided (e.g., hostess work) and to whom (i.e., 'the businessman'). Nonetheless, in terms of short-term strategies (and lived experiences), we take account of differences in perceived outcomes and how they contribute to future resistance. Indeed, from this perspective, change is a process not an end. If we cannot escape the power of discursive practice we can understand it. Understanding means to identify the constraining elements of existing discourses, to challenge/resist those elements and then to reflect on the outcome as a new problematic.

Fifth, change is not progressive but contextual. To take flight attending as an example, in simple (modernist) terms it would be difficult to argue that the move from exclusion (1928–46) to desexualization (1946–60), eroticization (1960–75), speed-up and burn-out (1970–85), and formal equity policy (e.g., Opportunity 2000) represented a clean line of progress; with women gaining at every step. Indeed, in some ways it appears to be a roller coaster with some 'gains', some 'losses' and some mixture of the two. This is both optimistic and pessimistic. Pessimism lies in the understanding that change can never deal a final blow to discrimination, just alter the ground – sometimes for the better, sometimes for the worst. But this is also ground for optimism because it tells us that the masculine need not always, and irrevocably, be privileged over the feminine. It tells us that the way that characteristics are valued depends on its relationship to other characteristics and evaluations. For example, when men were hired to become the first of a generation of air stewards they were required to be small and light weight. Their size and weight were related to a number of economic (e.g., fuel costs) and safety (e.g., issues of weight and balance) concerns. They were not gendered concerns. When females were hired as flight attendants the size and weight considerations were still in place but were reconceptualized to take on gendered notions of physical attractiveness. In a similar vein, but with different consequences, 'attentiveness' long devalued in the workplace as a 'feminine' trait has recently been applauded as an essential quality of management (Fondas, 1997). In other words, the possibility exists whereby characteristics long associated as feminine (or as masculine) can take on different meanings and values. There is also the possibility that characteristics associated with femininity (or with masculinity) can become unstable, ambiguous and gender confused (i.e., become associated with individual men or women rather than as categories of men and women). This is of course fanciful and will depend on constant struggles, resistance and deconstruction.

Postcolonial feminism

Finally, the lens of postcolonial feminism encourages us to review our understanding of gender as a 'western project'. This perspective reminds us that gender understandings are refined and acted out in localized contexts, and that those contexts are informed by deep-rooted cultures mediated by the influence of global capitalism and reactions to it.

Using this perspective explorations of airlines over time need to take into account multiple layers of cultural experience and perception, including the culture of the organization, the society in which it is located, and the specific country's relationships with other peoples. These, of course, are all abstract terms. There is, for example, no such thing as an organizational culture, British society and a Britain outside of specific sets of relationships. Thus, we are interested in those relationships that inform people within a particular activity system (Blackler, 1992).

Taking the period 1919–39 as an example, we can see that in the United Kingdom a specific set of relationships was mediated by wartime military experience. If we examine discourse and traces of subjectivity within IAL we can explore the impact of this military thinking on notions of masculinity and femininity. The fact that Britain was an important colonial power at this time may not seem, at first sight, to be of direct importance to our understanding of gender, yet postcolonial feminists would argue that it is of central importance. IAL was not just subject to various ideological influences but was directly engaged in imperial practice in its development, policies and hirings, with its UK bases of operations almost exclusively staffed by 'whites'. Men of colour were employed in menial tasks in the airline's 'outposts'. Women of colour were not employed by IAL. This speaks to issues of race but also of gender in the development of ideas and practices embedded with notions of different forms of manhood and womanhood; different valuations of manhood and womanhood.

This raises questions about the salience of race/ethnicity, mediated relationships, and strategic alliances. Thus, how far should/can struggles against sex discrimination (or women's liberation) be linked to broader struggles for social change? Within BA struggles against desexualization, eroticization, speed-up and so on were largely pursued without reference to broader (anti-colonial) struggles. That may account for their limited successes and also for the limits of those successes. Perhaps one of the biggest changes in attitudes to the employment of women in the airline came during Second World War when on-going struggles were linked to broader issues of anti-fascism and democracy; struggles that stopped far short of embracing anti-colonialist struggle. But it contributed to the normalization of (white) women's work in British airlines.

This raises another issue. How should we value localized change? To what extent can we applaud 'improvements' in opportunity for 'white' British women at a time when women of colour were rarely employed in any capacity by the airline? The answer may not be black or white (pun intended). It may be that overall change depends on a series of challenges at numerous (but not necessarily connected) sites. Whether' victory' at one site weakens or strengthens the struggle at another will depend on the ability of those involved to make conceptual links between the struggles. By reflecting on the various facets of our subjectivities we may be better placed to resist the power of discourse on how we see others and ourselves.

Summary

Discriminatory practices are deep-rooted in society and are not confined to a single organization or even a group of organizations. On the other hand, the survival of gendered practices relies on a multitude of mundane practices and their reproduction on a regular basis. To occur such practices must reside in the actions and regularized relationships of people, whether it is in family relationships or in organizational arrangements. Thus, to confront the deep-rooted nature of discrimination we need to address it where it lives – in specific places, in a multitude of embedded practices, behaviours, symbols and language. This study has focussed on three such 'places' – but on British Airways in particular – its established practices, processes, rules and on-going sensemaking, which we have called its 'culture'. Using a multiparadigmatic approach, where each feminist paradigm directs us to a different aspect of the influence of culture on a sense of gendered identity, various insights and change strategies were suggested. Further studies of the gendering of organizational culture may help to identify (and redress) all the various questions, problems and insights that this study has not managed to generate.

Appendix 1

Table A1.1   British Airways' in–house newsletters, 1926–93

Name	Period of Publication	Size	Style
Imperial Airways Monthly bulletin	1926–31	1 page/1 sided; news sheet monthly	Designed to inform staff about timetables, fares and route developments. It also included items on 'passengers of note' and other comments concerned with building pride in the airline.
Imperial Airways Staff News	1931–39	4 pages; news sheet weekly	Items of company information, plus a number of items on personnel, including company-related issues of recruitment, posting, promotion, organizational achievements and retirements, and more personnel issues of engagements, marriages, births and deaths.
Imperial Airways Weekly News Bulletin	1936–39	2 pages; typed bulletin weekly	Reporting specific company and industry news (leaving items on personnel to the *Staff News*)
BOAC Newsletter	1940–46	4–8 pages; news sheet monthly	Recombined company and personnel news previously divided between the *Bulletin* and the *Staff News*
Speedbird	1946 (Apr.–Aug.)	8 pages; magazine style monthly	Company, industry and personnel news. (This was to remain the format over the years ahead)
BOAC News Letter	1946–50	12 pages; magazine style monthly	—
BEA Magazine	1946–72	16 pages; magazine style quarterly/monthly	—
BOAC Review & Newsletter	1950–51	12 pages; magazine style monthly	—
BOAC Review	1951–67	—	—
BOAC News	1959–73	newspaper broad sheet style weekly	—
BA (European Division) Magazine	1972–73	16 pages; magazine	—
British Airways News	1973–current	12 pages; newspaper weekly	—
Topline	1974–76	24 pages; magazine monthly	—
Touchdown	1979–	news paper format	Items of interest focused on and for retired staff

Appendix 2

Table A2.1 Airline history on film: The British Airways archive collection

Film title (original production date)	Featured airline	(Producers) Subject matter	BA video reference
The Imperial Airway and the work of British Airways (1922)	HPT	('Air Ministry Official Film') Focusses on the safety, speed and comfort of flying.	Vol. 4, 1993
Watch & Ward in the Air (1937)	Imperial Airways	[Imperial Airways] Illustrates the basics of air navigation for land based aircraft and flying boats.	Vol. 2, 1992
Air Outpost (1937)	Imperial Airways	['Made in cooperation with Imperial Airways'] A look at '24 hours at Shajah airport on the Persian Gulf ... all the fascinating preparations for the arrival and the overnight stop of an HP42 airliner en route to Basra'.	Vol. 1, 1992
Aerial Milestones (1939)	Imperial Airways (and BA Ltd)	[Strand Film Company] Traces 'the foundation of the airlines that led to the creation of the great Imperial Airways'. Also deals with BA Ltd.	Vol. 1, 1992
Take It Easy (late 1940s)	BEA	Shows the processes involved in getting passengers to their plane.	Vol. 5, 1993
Michael And The Flying Boats (1949)	BOAC	['Made with the assistance of BOAC'] Through the eyes of a 9 year old boy, explains the operation of flying boats.	Vol. 4, 1993
Vickers Viscount: BEA	BEA	[Vickers Armstrong] focuses on the inaugural flight of the (1953) Viscount.	Vol. 4, 1993
Britain's Comet (1953)	BOAC	Focuses on some of the planning and construction of the Comet 1.	Vol. 7, 1994
Tomorrow Is Theirs	BOAC	A look behind the scenes at BOAC operations. (mid-1950s)	Vol. 3, 1992
Skyport (late 1950s)	BEA	[BEA] Behind the scenes at London airport.	Vol. 2, 1992
Trident For BEA (early 1960s)	BEA	Highlights the first two Trident aircraft.	Vol. 9, 1995
Flight Plan (early 1960s)	BEA	[BEA] Features the role of different personnel within the Airline.	Vol. 7, 1994
Top Flight (1963)	BOAC	[BOAC] Behind the scenes operations, featuring the Boeing 707.	Vol. 6, 1993
The VC10 (?)	BOAC	[BOAC] Introduces attractions of the new plane.	Vol. 3, 1992
Super VC10 (?)	BOAC	[BOAC] Introduces attractions of the new plane.	Vol. 3, 1992
Trident Turnaround (1964)	BEA	Focuses on what is involved in 'turning around' a Trident.	Vol. 5, 1993
Clear To Land (1968)	BEA	[BEA] Explains the advantages and disadvantages of the Automatic Landing System.	Vol. 6, 1993

continued

Table A2.1   Continued

Film title (original production date)	Featured airline	(Producers) Subject matter	BA video reference
Number One In Europe (late1960s)	BEA	Features the training of Cabin Crew.	Vol. 5, 1993
Airline Pilot (1969)	BOAC	[BOAC] Focuses on the training of pilots.	Vol. 8, 1994
The Great British Airline (1970)	BEA	Promotes the image of BEA as a top airline.	Vol. 9, 1995
The Tristar (1975)	BA	[BA] Features the advantages of the new plane.	Vol. 8, 1994
Rotor Flight Into The Eighties (1981)	BA	Focuses on the work of BA Helicopter services.	Vol. 9, 1995

Notes

1: Gender, Culture and Commercial Airways

1. It is more accurately 'aspirational feminist' (Mills, 1994) in that it recognizes the limitations of male embodiedment in trying to represent female experience and attempts to avoid notions of (political) correctness and closure of debate, suggesting that a (male) feminist position is something to be constantly striven for.

2. Family groupings are also important sites for the production and reproduction of gendered understandings (Mackie, 1987). Indeed, a number of feminists would argue that they are the single-most important sites. Reflecting this argument, Savage and Witz (1992) contend that organizational realities are a reflection and reproduction of patriarchal influences that reside outside of organizations. I have contested this viewpoint elsewhere, arguing that gendered understandings should be understood as an ongoing process that relies as much on context as social history (Mills, 1997).

3. Acker argues that there are five gendering processes, including the *idea* of the organization which precedes organizational activity (Acker, 1990); see also Mills and Chiaramonte (1991).

4. Bourdieu (1977) contends that strategies (in the broadest sense) are interest laden but not necessarily consciously so, and may themselves be influenced by cultural legacies.

5. This approach stands in contrast to those who view organizational culture as a real entity, something that an organization has (see Martin, 2002; Smircich, 1983).

6. For example, the pilot and the white-coveralled engineer.

7. For example, the stewardess.

8. Its origins can be traced back to 1919.

9. The most recent World Airline Report placed BA seventh in the world in terms of total operating revenue, and twelfth in terms of passengers carried (Air Transport World, 2004).

10. I am indebted to the feminist historian Barbara Roberts for these criteria. The fact that a company has been in operation for a considerable period of time (e.g., fifty years or more) allows the researcher to follow the development, maintenance and change of key employment practices. The availability of an established and accessible company archive facilitates in-depth study of several aspects of the culture, especially where many of the earlier members of the organization had long since died. The existence of published histories of the company is helpful in gaining a sense of key events, persons, activities and practices as well as in providing valuable clues to gendered understandings of the organization.

11. The study of British Airways was undertaken between 1991 and 1994, Air Canada between 1999 and 2003, and Pan American Airways, begun in 2004, is still in progress. The latter two studies were undertaken with Jean Helms Mills. The Social Sciences and Humanities Research Council (SSHRC) of Canada funded all three studies.

12. United Air Lines (UAL), while of great interest because of its influence on the development of Air Canada's cabin service, refuses pubic access to its corporate archives.

13. Feminists organizational scholars agree that organizational arrangements contribute to notions of femininity and masculinity but disagree on the extent to which organizations *reflect* broad gendered constructions (Witz and Savage, 1992), rather then generate (Ferguson, 1984) or structure (Kanter, 1977) practices that go on to influence social values.

14. For example, laws governing commerce, labour, occupational health and safety, and employment equity.

15. For instance, machinery, tools, skills, work methods.

16. For example, scientific management, re-engineering, TQM.

17. For example, the establishment of unequal pay rates or differentiated recruitment practices based on gender (or race/ethnicity).

18. For example, workplace social clubs, sports teams, dinner-dance events.

19. For example, processes of differentiation or divisionalization as a company moves into new markets or areas. Feminist studies of the various aspects include MacKinnon (1979), Razack (1991) and Wolf (1991) on the law; Hacker (1989) and Cockburn (1985; 1991a) on technology; Schein (1973; 1989; 1994) on management practice; Wolff (1977), Wilson (2002), and Prasad and Prasad (2002) on extra-organizational rules; Crompton and Jones (1984) on social practices; Morgan (1988) and Rogers (1988) on exclusionary practices; Townley (1994) on human relations practices; Kanter (1977), and Witz and Savage (1992) on structure; and Morgan and Knights (1991) on strategy.

20. On occasion an 'unbalanced' personality can have a disproportionate influence on a culture (Kets de Vries, 1989). This was arguably the case of Howard Hughes and his influence on Trans World Airways (TWA) – (Rummel, 1991; Serling, 1983).

21. Indeed, the Canadian government *Report of the Commission on Equality in Employment* argues that, rather than approaching discrimination from the perspective of the single perpetrator and the single victim, the systemic approach acknowledges that by and large the systems and practices we customarily and often unwittingly adopt may have an unjustifiably negative effect on certain groups in society (Abella, 1984: 9–10).

22. For example, internal memoranda, annual reports, advertisements, press statements, in-flight magazines, in-house journals and newsletters.

23. Such as physical structures, stories, language, and so on.

24. Gleaned from interviews, observations, letters, biographies, and other such documented data.

25. Arguably, corporate materials 'are not passive describers of an 'objective reality'; but play a part in forming the world view or social ideology that fashions and legitimizes women's place in society [by promoting] policies, beliefs, attitudes, and practices that perpetuate workplace inequities'(Tinker and Neimark, 1987: 72). That is not to suggest that corporate materials are consciously and deliberately designed to promote discrimination but that, rather, they contribute to a visual mirror of the world in which we live and, regardless of intent, can serve to influence the way people come to view themselves (Burrell, 1987). As several studies have suggested, the hegemonic power of organizational leadership is due to a combination of conscious and unconscious, intended and unintended, deliberate and emergent actions (Gramsci, 1978; Merton, 1940; Mintzberg *et al.*, 1986). This will become clear as we review some of the attitudes and associated images in Imperial Airlines' corporate materials over the years.

26. The notion of 'the juncture' can be seen as a more localized (i.e., organizationally focussed) version of Foucault's notion of 'the episteme' as 'the largely unconscious assumptions concerning intellectual order that underlie the historical states of particular societies [and …] define the mode of being of the objects in the field' (Butler, 2002: 46).

2: The Gendering of Civil Aviation, 1919–24

1. Koninklijke Luchtvaart Maatschappij.
2. The Compagnie Messageries Aériennes (CMA) and Cie. des Grands Express Aériens (CGEA). These two airlines merged in 1923 to form Air Union, the forerunner of Air France.
3. BMAN was established by the Supermarine Aviation Works Ltd and the London and Southwestern Railway. It offered a flying boat operation that flew between Southampton and Le Havre, Cherbourg, and the Channel Islands.
4. It is estimated that some 2000 combat flyers returned to Canada following the First World War, many of whom turned to bush flying to earn a living (Milberry, 1979: 20).
5. Gossage (1991: 17) notes that in Canada, with 'the notable exception of the 3,141 nursing sisters serving in Canada and overseas as officers in the Canadian Medical Corps, during the First World War, there was virtually no female presence, in the military sense'. Women did, however, play a role in war industry at home. Similarly, in the United States women were, reluctantly, recruited to the war industries (Holden and Griffith, 1991) but 13,000 of them were enlisted in the US Navy, mostly doing clerical work, thus becoming the first women in US history to be admitted to full military rank and status (Goldstein, 2001). The US Army, on the other hand, hired women as nurses and telephone operators for overseas work. The women wore uniforms but remained civilians (ibid.). Plans for a female auxiliary corps similar to those operating in Britain were outright rejected by the War Department (ibid.).
6. The interwar novel *Gerald Cranston's Lady*, by Gilbert Frankau, captures the masculine feel of one of the airlines (Instone) of the time with its references to the successful businessman passenger being greeted at the airport by 'a young ground-officer in [a] white sea-cap and dark uniform', bowler-hatted customs officials, 'the leather caps of pilot and observer', and a myriad of male employees, from mechanics to doorway men (a long passage from the book is quoted in Instone, 1938).
7. Captain Donald Greig (General Manager), and General Sir Francis Festing (Commercial Director) rounded out the leadership.
8. Festing, and Greig were also on the board.
9. Lieutenant-Colonel Sholto Douglas was the chief pilot.
10. Captain W. R. Hinchcliffe was the chief pilot.
11. Captain Franklyn Barnard was the chief pilot.
12. The next four sections – on gendered work patterns, symbolism, imagery and interactions – follow Acker's (1992) notion of key processes that constitute the gendered substructure.
13. In February of 1919 the Department of Civil Aviation was formed in the Air Ministry under Winston Churchill. Churchill was Secretary of State for Air until 1921 when his cousin Captain Freddy Guest replaced him. Under Churchill were

Major-General Sir Hugh Trenchard as Chief of Air Staff and Major-General Sir Frederick Sykes as the first Director of Civil Aviation. Trenchard was succeeded by Air Chief Marshall Sir John Salmond and by Air Vice-Marshall Sir Sefton Brancker. Churchill and Guest were both former army officers turned career politicians but all the others were from the higher echelons of the Royal Air Force (RAF).

14. Young was employed at ATT between March and September of 1920 (Young, 1987). It is not clear when or for how long Wyton worked at ATT.

15. CMA employed at least four other women, two at its London operations and two at its Paris offices. Yvonne Didier worked at the company's Croydon airport office for a short time in 1920 and a 'Mademoiselle Liotard', along with 'Miss Wyton' worked at the new London office in 1922 (Bamford, 1986: 29). In the Paris office one woman was employed as the secretary to the office manager, while at the head office Madame Marie Lukinova was the secretary to the airline's Director General (Bamford, 1986: 29).

16. At the end of 1922 the total number of staff employed by Daimler, Instone and HPT combined was 135, including 18 pilots (Jackson, 1995; Penrose, 1980b). Things improved after the introduction of government subsidies and by the time of the staff dinner on 31 March 1924 Instone hosted close to 100 employees – all men (Instone, 1938: plate xxviii).

17. The role has variously been termed 'cabin boys' (Pudney, 1959; Wright, 1985), 'aerial stewards' (Penrose, 1980b) and 'page boys' (Learmonth *et al.*, 1983). They were dressed like hotel pageboys, 'in buttons and tight trousers [and] a stiff wing collar with bow tie and monkey jacket' (Jackson, 1995: 15). Boys were selected because of their weight, and were fined if they exceeded 98 pounds (Learmonth *et al.*, 1983; Wright, 1985). It has been contended that they did not serve food or drinks but 'travelled more for decoration than for any real service' (Pudney, 1959: 276), helped the passengers to stay calm (Wright, 1985: 1) and/or performed similar duties to bellboys (Allen, 1986). There is also some controversy about their recruitment. Wright (1985) argues that they were originally bellhops at luxury hotels. Pudney (1959: 276), on the other hand, states that they were recruited from the families of the Daimler hire drivers, and trained at the Savoy Hotel.

18. Finding a commissionaire drunk at the end of his shift, Instone fired the employee and decided to discontinue the position (Penrose, 1973: 99). The company discontinued the short-lived employment of a steward because the small number of seats on planes at that time did not make the service cost-effective (Instone, 1938). The experiment with cabin boys was ended when one of the boys was killed in a mid-air collision.

19. DiMaggio and Powell (1991) refer to this as 'mimetic isomorphism' whereby an organization adapts to uncertainty by, in effect, mimicking successful aspects of similar, established businesses.

20. Many commercial pilots ended up flying in and out of their old wartime aerodromes, including F. L. Barnard (Instone), W.R. Hinchcliffe (Daimler), Gordon Olley (HPT) who flew from Wadden (renamed Croydon) Aerodrome; R.H. McIntosh (HPT), from Cricklewood; and Major Patteson and Lieutenant Jerry Shaw of ATT, from Hendon.

21. This influenced the French airline Air Union, which tried to capture an 'air of masculine difference' with uniforms that mimicked those worn by Royal Navy officers (Bamford, 1986: 44).

22. By the end of the First World War advertising had become a prominent part of newsprint publications (Ohmann, 1996). Brancker of ATT encouraged

'propaganda' to encourage 'air sense' among the public, while Alfred Instone encouraged 'stunts' (Instone, 1938: 21), by which he meant the 'planting' of stories in the press, to enhance the airline's reputation and achievements. Many of Instone's stunts were designed to link the airline with modernity, advancement, and middle class life styles, through stories such as grouse shooting expeditions and reports of film stars travelling on Instone. Air Union also used advertisements to emphasize the congruence between air travel, social class and celebrity (Hudson and Pettifer, 1979).

23. Similarly, the Lawson Airline Company, a US aircraft construction business, advertized that 'There Has Never Been A Person Hurt In A Lawson Airplane' (Allen, 1986: 55).

24. During the war, opposing air forces made use of publicity to develop heroic images of their pilots (Burrows, 1972; McCaffery, 1988).

25. Some pilots enjoyed the limelight but others, such as Armstrong and McIntosh, were more ambivalent. According to Armstrong (1952: 77), pilots frequently saw their names in the papers but 'these reports and vapourings had a rather unfortunate effect upon us – and on the future of aviation as well. We saw and sensed the admiration of our passengers; some would make it plain to us that they thought we were dashing young adventurers. We almost came to believe that we were a brand of hero'. Similarly, McIntosh (1963: 40) – who was dubbed 'all-weather Mac' for his ability to land in foggy weather – felt that pilots 'soon built up a reputation in the national Press, [which] was not perhaps the best thing that could have happened'.

26. See for example Pudney's (1959: 45–46) account of ATT's Jerry Shaw. Pudney highlights a particular flight by Shaw to exemplify the bravery, technical skills, courage and professionalism of pilots. Shaw is seen as brave and professional in his preparedness to fly in all weathers, and skilful and calm in the face of danger as he lands in 110 mph winds that have clearly blown down trees and damaged buildings. Similar stories are told by Harper (1930), Olley (1934) and Armstrong (1952).

27. In 1914 there were only 7000 women (or a little over 0.5% of the workforce) in the mines and quarries industry, By 1918 the numbers had risen to 13,000 or one per cent. In the transport industry there were only 18, 200 women (1.5%) in 1914. This rose to 117, 200 (10%) by 1918 but almost certainly the great majority of these women was employed on buses, trams and trains.

28. During the First World War Brancker dealt with strikes at Airco and Vickers, accusing the union leaders of being 'pro-German agitators'. Despite his success in getting the strikes called off, Lord Weir of Vickers was unhappy with Brancker's apparent 'breezy manner', and flippant approach to the personnel (Beauman, 1971: 19; King, 1989: 191). On the other hand, when it came to the recruitment of air force mechanics he offered 'the alluring rate of ten shillings a day and [enlisted] more than a thousand of the best craftsmen in the country' (Collier, 1959: 38).

29. Brancker was to state that he had 'been deeply interested in the question of employing women [in the armed forces] since 1915, and was a strong supporter of the movement' (quoted in Beauman, 1971: 19).

30. Brancker's suggestion, although quite radical, should be seen in the context of the time. With the onset of the First World War Emmeline Pankhurst announced a suspension of the activities of her Women's Social and Political Union (WSPU). By October 1915 the WSPU journal – the *Suffragette* – had been replaced by *Britannia*,

which was devoted to the war effort, including advocacy of military conscription, the war of attrition, the internment of 'enemy aliens', and encouragement of women to engage in war work. Pankhurst became a virulent supporter of the war effort, abandoning women's suffrage for the patriotic cause (Pugh, 1992). Thus, by 1918 Pankhurst was a pillar of the war effort and not such a surprising choice for the leadership of a women's organization devoted to contributing to military victory.

31. Brancker argued that the success of the WRAF was due to the wide powers and independence of action that he gave to Gwynne-Vaughan (Escott, 1989: 83).

32. During his time as Master-General of the RAF, he allowed WRAF members to fly as passengers in planes while on duty but they were not allowed to pilot or undertake other combat-related tasks. In 1925 he presided over a meeting of the International Civil Aviation Organization (ICAO) that voted to exclude women from employment as aircraft crews engaged on public transport (Cadogan, 1992; Penrose, 1980b). However, by the onset of the 1930s he was talking openly about the possibility of female combat pilots in a new war, was helping Amy Johnson with her flying career and had engaged a female pilot – Winifred Spooner – to fly him on official duties.

33. This was facilitated by the establishment of relatively small operational units – the squadron – and the fact that the great majority of pilots were themselves officers (James, 1990).

34. Captain McIntosh and Major Brackley of HPT, for example, previously served together during the war, and there were many other former air force pilots who ended up working together in the post-war airlines (Penrose, 1969: 544).

35. Barnard was seen as 'a pilot with every resource – brave, brainy, and exceedingly likeable – everybody's hero' (Instone, 1938: 5).

36. Brancker hired ten pilots from the Communication Squadron (Collier, 1959: 134), including Major Cyril Patteson (who commanded the No.1 wing), Lieutenant Armstrong and Jerry Shaw. Ninety per cent of the flights made by the Hendon Communication Squadrons before they were disbanded were on a route from London to Paris (Pudney, 1959: 43), the same route by HPT.

37. This includes L. C. Pace who went on to become a BOAC staff flown supervisor for the recruitment and training of flight attendants.

38. In those early years McIntosh still flew the same Handley Page bomber 'up and down [the same] peaceful and pleasant piece of coast' (McIntosh, 1963: 61). Similarly, Captain Jerry Shaw drew on memories of 'the anti-aircraft stuff [he] flew through in the War' to deal with concerns about bad flying weather (quoted in Harper, 1936: 133). Captain Bill Lawford, on the other hand, sometimes hankered after his war days. When asked for his passport at Le Bourget (Paris) airport, following his pioneering flight in August 1919, it occurred to him that he'd been 'flying for years in the Royal Flying Corps and the Royal Air Force without a passport' and that this was 'a comedown', he was 'just a mere civilian now' (quoted in Pudney, 1959: 39).

39. McIntosh (1963: 40) felt that 'there was a grand spirit among the early pilots and it was our pride to press on and get our passengers through if humanly possible'.

40. Robert Michel recalls a similar atmosphere among ATT staff at Le Bourget airport in Paris (see Pudney, 1959: 56).

41. Brancker and Brackley left the airlines to take up prominent positions within government – Brancker as Director of Civil Aviation and Brackley as a member of a government Mission to the Imperial Japanese. Woods Humphery helped to form Daimler Airway, and Sholto Douglas rejoined the RAF.

42. In point of fact, airlines were not particularly safe. For example, in 1919 a crash severely injured one of ATT's pilots. In 1920 an ATT plane flew into a tree on take-off, killing the Chief Pilot and two passengers; in 1921 a forced landing destroyed one of Instone's planes; and in 1922 the passengers and crews of two airlines were killed in the first ever mid-air collision.

43. Passenger seating ranged from 4 to 14 seats.

44. According to Anderson and Zinsser (1988: 143), the increasing wealth of the period enabled Europeans to exaggerate the traditional opposition of the sexes. Women were emotional and passive, their virtues were chastity and obedience, and their place was in the home. In contrast, men were meant for public life; rational and aggressive, with virtues of courage and honour (see also Pugh, 1992; Weeks, 1990).

45. The middle class man 'required the legitimacy of all his children not only to protect his possessions from being enjoyed by the offspring of other men but to ensure the loyalty of his sons who might be business partners, and of his daughters who might be essential in marriage alliances' (Weeks, 1990: 29–30).

46. In their battles against 'the evils of industrial life' middle-class social reformers turned much of their attention on the working class family and the role of the mother. Dr. Barnardo, for example, argued that: 'The East End of London is a hive of factory life and factory means that which is inimical to home [...] There is bred in (factory women) a spirit of precocious independence which weakens family ties and is highly unfavourable to the growth of domestic virtues (quoted in Weeks, 1990: 57–58).

47. Rowbotham (1999: 26) agrees that 'attitudes to women's work were bound up with deep-rooted assumptions about women's place' but points out that 'these attitudes were not uniform'. There were regional differences within the working class. In the Staffordshire Potteries, for example, 'it was assumed that women continued to work when they had families. A women who did not contribute to the family income was seen as lazy, and it was customary for men to help with cleaning and child-care'.

48. The average number of children per family in 1925 was 2.2 compared to 5.5 to 6 in the mid-Victorian era (Rowbotham, 1999: 32; see also Weeks, 1990: 45).

49. Far from contesting notions of marriage, many in the Suffragette movement argued for greater rights for women within marriage, including issues of property rights, the legal power of the husband over his wife and children, custody and taxation (Weeks, 1990).

50. This was due in part to the efforts of sympathetic post-master generals. Women first entered government service in large numbers as postal clerks and telegraph operators (Cohn, 1985; Lowe, 1987).

51. Teaching provided the greatest number of new jobs for women prior to the First World War. By 1911 there were 183,298 women employed in teaching, that is almost 73 per cent of the total number of teachers. This compares with 77,000 women in nursing at that time. In the clerical field 'Englishwomen' constituted 51 per cent of the country's post office clerks and 35.9 per cent of the telegraph and telephone operators (Anderson and Zinsser, 1988: 195).

52. Lowe (1987: 17–18) points out that, 'By the turn of the century the new office jobs of "typewriter", "short-hand writer" and short-hand typist had become sex-labelled as female. Victorian social morality only tolerated this new role for women on the understanding that it was merely something temporary until marriage.' By 1911 women constituted 21 per cent of clerical and related work.

53. In the Edwardian era as many of 55 per cent of single women but only 14 per cent of married women were in paid employment, the latter fell to 9.6 per cent by 1911 (Pugh, 1992: 92).
54. Indeed, most organizations insisted on it (Cohn, 1985; Rowbotham, 1999).
55. The era saw the establishment of the National Birthrate Commission, the National Baby Week Council, and the Babies of the British Empire association.
56. The WAAC was the first ever uniformed women's military service. At the suggestion of the Director of Recruitment at the War Office, Brigadier-General Auckland Geddes, his sister, Mary Chalmers Watson, was appointed the Chief Controller (Home) of the WAAC: Watson was the first woman to earn a medical degree from Edinburgh University (Beauman, 1971: 1). Geddes' brother, Eric, became the first 'Chairman' of Imperial Airways in 1924.
57. In the Salvage Workshops women gained some insights into aircraft production through the dismantling of wrecked aircraft. Some of the women who excelled at this level were moved to the Aircraft Repair Shops where crashed planes were rebuilt. Although few in number this work 'prepared the ground for the highly responsible technical work entrusted to RAF women of the future' (Escott, 1989: 41).
58. Eventually the Commandant won permission for WRAF members to travel in aircraft while on duty (Escott, 1989: 69). Commenting on the overall situation, The Daily Express argued that, 'flying is not a woman's job [...] they always lose their head in a sudden emergency' (quoted in Pugh, 1992: 31).
59. The WRAF was placed under the direct control of the Air Council's 'Department of the Master-General of Personnel' (MGP) and delegated to the Director of Manning, where, as section 'M3', it was one of several under his command. The WRAF was 'run, with no doubt the best of intentions, by men, who dealt with matters effecting the WRAF externally'(Escott, 1989: 24).
60. Recommending Crawford's dismissal, Godfrey Paine, the officer in charge, told the Air Council that she 'did not possess the qualities necessary for the organisation of a large body of women' (Beauman, 1971: 9). Crawford, a skilled 'craftswoman' and member of a City Guild, had been in charge of women munitions workers at a Northern England factory when she was appointed as WRAF Commandant (Beauman, 1971; Escott, 1989).
61. Prior to this she had been Commissioner for Wales in the National Health Insurance Commission, and held important positions in a number of organizations, including the London County Council Education Committee, Girl's Youth Clubs and Hospital Units.
62. The House of Lords subsequently deemed the dismissal illegal and unconstitutional (Beauman, 1971; Escott, 1989).
63. Female officers came from the same ranks of the middle and upper classes as their male counterparts. Violet Douglas-Pennant, for instance, was the daughter of Lord Penrhyn, and Dame Helen Gwynne-Vaughan came from an 'impoverished Scottish aristocratic army family' (Escott, 1989: 80). Other officers, were 'chosen as far as possible from the old officer class' (Dame Helen Gwynne-Vaughan, quoted in Beauman, 1971: 36).
64. In civilian life Gwynne-Vaughan had been a campaigner for women's rights, in particular, equal pay for women. But she 'recognised' that some differences should be made for the military where women were not in combatant roles; that pay allowances for women should, as a result, be less than those for men. Sickness and disestablishment provisions, however, should be the same for men and women (Beauman, 1971: 33).

65. This work was not attained without some resistance and hostility from male officer and other ranks. Escott (1989: 27), for example, reports on a female carpenter who felt that she was 'tolerated by the men as another military nuisance'. Similarly, Rowbotham (1999: 75) notes that, 'women in the services could encounter hostility if they invaded a man's terrain. Mrs Stephens, for example, who was one of the first aircraft motorcyclists, found that the men initially refused to speak to her. Nonetheless, a remarkable transformation in women's lives had occurred'.

66. The Conservative Party was unwilling to select her for a winnable seat due to her 'intelligence, feminism, and a reputation for being overbearing in her dealings with men' (Pugh, 1992: 154–55).

67. In 1911 35.32 per cent of women were in the labour force The percentage of the labour force that were women also fell slightly from 29.6 per cent to 29.5 per cent over the same period (Pugh, 1992: 91).

68. These laws include the 1918 Maternity and Child Welfare Act; the 1919 Restoration of Pre-War Practices Act; and the 1920 Employment of Women, Young Persons and Children Act. The latter prohibited night work and, as a result, excluded women from certain industries, including printing. Other legislative acts, such as the 1924 Factory Bill, aimed at protecting women from physical dangers by excluding them from certain jobs.

69. Women outnumbered men 1.176 to 1 among 20 to 24 year olds, and 1.209 to 1 among those aged 25 to 29 (Pugh, 1992: 77).

70. Like a number of terms, 'flapper' was embraced in some quarters and took on a more neutral tone in others (Pugh, 1992: 78).

71. Dr. Cecil Webb-Johnson, writing in *Good Housekeeping*, warned that these women's 'constant craving for change, for amusement, for excitement at any cost' would lead to lined and weary faces, constant headaches, uncertainty and irritability of temper (quoted in Rowbotham, 1999: 120) [...] Barbara Cartland, the romantic novelist, noted that the 'new slimline girl would have weak babies, if she had them at all' (quoted in Pugh, 1992: 78).

72. In the area of dress, clothing increasingly came to stress opposites. While in the eighteenth century men and women of the upper classes had 'dressed far more like each other' in the nineteenth century/early twentieth century women and men were expected to look very different. As a result men who continued to dress in a 'flamboyant or unusual way were criticized for being unmanly and effeminate' (Anderson and Zinsser, 1988: 145).

73. According to Weeks (1990: 101) as late as 1871 'concepts of homosexuality were extremely underdeveloped both in the Metropolitan Police and in high medical and legal circles'.

74. In Britain as late as 1861 the death penalty was still on the statute books for the act of buggery (Weeks, 1990: 99).

75. Interestingly the Criminal Law Amendment Act 1912 did not extend to female homosexuality, perhaps because it was too dire to conceive of by moralists of the time (Weeks, 1990).

76. Young, whose maiden name is not recorded, started work at the age of 16 as a clerk in the Aeronautical Inspection Department of the Air Ministry during the war.

77. Her husband was killed in 1916 at the Battle of the Somme (British Overseas Airways Corporation, 1946g).

78. At the 1919 Peace Conference she served as secretary to Sir Robert Bordern, the Canadian Prime Minister.

79. Mishkind, Rodin, Silberstein and Striegel-Moore (1987) argue that over time several forms of masculine archetypes became traditional, including the soldier, the expert, the breadwinner, the Lord and the frontiersman. We could also add the masculine image of 'the worker' (Collinson, 1988; Willis, 1977).

80. Other inventors include Montague Napier, the aircraft engine designer, who was the son of a car manufacturer. The father of Henry Royce, of Rolls-Royce engines fame, ran a milling business. The Short brothers, the aircraft manufacturers, were sons of the owner of an iron-works. Noel Pemberton Billing, the manufacturer of the Supermarine flying boats, was the son of a Birmingham iron-founder. Aircraft designers Robert Blackburn, Richard Fairey and Roy Fedden were, respectively, the sons of a prominent Leeds manufacturer, a timber merchant and a leading figure in the sugar trade (King, 1989). The Instone brothers were wealthy coal merchants when they moved into the aviation business. Frederick Handley Page, educated at Cheltenham Grammar School, was from a more lowly position than his counterparts as his father was the proprietor of a small furniture and upholstery business.

81. According to the 1911 census there were no women to be found employed as engineers, riveters, or fitters and turners (See Roberts, 1988: 26–27). The engineering union (ASE) continued to exclude women members through the First World War (Pugh, 1992: 27). During the First World War the engineering unions, in a voluntary deal known as the Treasury Agreement, agreed to the entry of unskilled workers, including women, into jobs traditionally held by skilled men. The work was modified or divided in such a way that several women undertook the job previously done by a skilled man. In this way the women undertook 'deskilled' work and could not be classified (or paid) as skilled workers (Pugh, 1992: 27–28).

82. The wife of Alexander Graham Bell, for example, first suggested the idea an aviation association and 'offered to meet the entire cost of the undertaking' to prove that she was serious (Ellis, 1980: 4) […] Yet he is credited as 'the father of Canadian aviation' (Ellis, 1980: 2) for his establishment of the Aerial Experiment Association (in Nova Scotia, Canada) in 1908. Similarly, Katherine Wright, the sister of Orville and Wilbur, contributed to her brothers' aviation ventures, including bankrolling the building of the Kitty Hawk. Several female flyers played important roles in developing flying schools, including Katherine, Marjorie and Emma Stinson in the United States, Hilda Hewlett in the United Kingdom and Melli Beese in Germany. Hewlett purchased her own plane in 1910 and went on to establish a training school some time later; Melli Beese established the Berlin flying school in 1912; and the Stinsons established the Stinson Aviation Company in 1913. All played a role in training the wartime pilots for their respective national air forces, yet their efforts received far less attention than those of male trainers and entrepreneurs. For discussion of the role of women in the development of aviation see Cadogan (1992), Corn (1983), Harper (1936), Holden and Griffith (1991), Lauwick (1960), Moolman (1981), Rich (1993) and Spring (1994).

Female flyers fared little better, their efforts often scoffed at. Thus, for example, when Harriet Quimby became, in 1912, the first women to fly the English Channel C.G. Grey, the editor of the influential 'The Aeroplane', referred to her as 'a woman of *unusual* initiative, determination and ability' but disparaged her technical abilities as 'reckless', claiming that 'she used habitually fly up to 2000 feet without knowing how to glide, and it never occurred to her that she might have difficulty if her engine stopped' (quoted in Cadogan, 1992: emphasis added). Grey never characterized male fliers in the same way. Women flyers were viewed as a departure from the (male) norm. As one female (barnstorming) flyer put it in 1916, 'In aviation there seems no place for the woman engineer, mechanic or flyer. Too often people paid money to see me risk my neck more as a freak – woman freak pilot – than as a skilled flyer'(Blanche Stuart Scott, quoted in Cadogan, 1992: 33).

83. Cranwell, the RFC's officer training school, was a fee-paying institution and would-be officers could only get a permanent commission by paying a sizeable sum of money for entry and tuition (James, 1982).

84. This was also true for the RNAS (James, 1990).

85. By the 1930s as many as three-quarters of all Air Force pilots were officers and that percentage steadily increased up to the 1990s (James, 1990: 133).

86. The School Certificate in those days was attainable by the children of those with money enough to invest in their child's education.

87. See note 74.

88. Indeed, it was women who piloted the last of the balloons (Lauwick, 1960) and female parachutists had proven more popular with audiences than their male counterparts. Part of the attraction may have been in the unconventional combination of danger and femininity. Lauwick (1960: 23), for example, argues, 'Most people are always excited by the sight of a pretty woman in danger.'

89. In 1908 Thérèse Peltier, of France, became the first woman to make a solo flight (Cadogan, 1992: 38; Harper, 1936: 232), but the credit of being the first woman to 'pilot an aeroplane in fully-controlled flights of any duration' went to the Baroness de la Roche in 1909 (Harper, 1936). Edith Maude Cook became the first British woman and Blanche Stuart Scott the first American woman to fly an aeroplane solo (Cadogan, 1992: 38–39). Baroness de la Roche was the first female to receive a pilot's certificate. Mrs Hilda Hewlett, and Harriet Quimby were, respectively, the first British and American women to receive a pilot's certificate (Cadogan, 1992: 57; Harper, 1936: 233).

90. For example, in 1910 Hélène Dutrieu of Belgium flew non-stop from Ostend to Bruges and in 1911 beat a field of male flyers to win the Italian King's Cup air race. That same year Matilde Moisant won the Rodman-Wassamaker altitude trophy. In 1912 Harriet Quimby became the first women to fly the Channel.

91. Only the French and Russian armies allowed women to become pilots but not in combatant roles (Cadogan, 1992: 58).

92. In fact, the idea of female air force flyers was a cause for scandal and disbelief (McCaffery, 1988: 53–54). Nonetheless, some female flyers ended up training men to become air force pilots (Cadogan, 1992; Lovell, 1989), see note 74.

93. The RFC and RAF allowed pilots to wear a moustache and eventually it became the mark of a *corp d'elite* (James, 1990: 183).

94. Imperial Airways, for example, used the term extensively.

95. At the start of the First World War there were only 18,200 women employed in the entire transportation industry of 1,179,200 employees, around 1.5 per cent of the total. The number of women employed in transport rose to 99,000 (or approximately 8.5% of the industry total) by the war's end but it quickly fell back as women were laid off to make way for the return of male employees (Pugh, 1992: 20). With the exception of clerical and office jobs, the great majority of women worked in industries that, by the standards of the time, were unrelated to aviation work. In order of numbers employed, female employees were concentrated in domestic work (3 million), clerical and office work (750,000) textiles (600,000), shop-keeping and shop work (500,000), outwork, homework

and the sweated trades (400,000), dressmaking, millinery and tailoring (350,000), various catering enterprises (120,000), and agriculture (100,000). The categories are adapted from Roberts (1988: 29–43). Figures are compiled from Pugh (1992: 20) and Roberts (1988: 29–43) but should only be taken as very rough estimates due to differences in comparison points (i.e., Pugh compared 1914 with 1918; Roberts compared 1911 with 1931) and databases (i.e., Pugh and Roberts vary in the way that they classify some jobs and under which broad category they place them). Both agree on the relative strengths and trends of female employment.

96. One of the few non-traditional jobs that remained open to women was clerical work but the airlines had few of those jobs and preferred to give them to men. Here the airlines chose to mimic (DiMaggio and Powell, 1991) companies within the transport industry, such as the Great Western Railway, which only hired male clerical workers, rather than the civil service which hired large numbers of female clerical staff: as early as 1872 the Post Office took the lead in breaking down barriers to female clerical work by recruiting large numbers of women (Cohn, 1985).

97. By the end of the war the Wood and Aircraft Trades industry employed 79,000 women in wood-milling, sawing, planing, assembly, painting, polishing, varnishing, doping and metalwork (Griffiths, 1991: 75). Some of these women were employed on the production of flying boats at the Hythe factory of George Holt Thomas (King, 1989: 163). Many worked in what became the post-war aerodromes of Hendon, Cricklewood, Hythe and, Waddon. The National Aircraft Factory No. 1, for example, was based at wartime Waddon and employed upwards of 1000 women, including lathe operators and dope painters. Claude Grahame-White operated a factory at Hendon prior to 1914 and by the middle of the war was employing '1000 men and women'(King, 1989: 172). At the end of the First World War an evaluation by the National Employers' Federation of the performance of women in the aircraft woodwork industry concluded that women's production 'was equal to men's output' and was 'equal to men in most areas of quality' (Griffiths, 1991: 56–57).

98. The enterprises were made possible by the availability of cheap ex-war planes, often selling for as little as CDN$50 (Pigott, 1997).

99. For example, in 1918 Ellwood Wilson, the chief forester of the Laurentide Pulp and Paper Company in Quebec, started an aerial fire spotting service – Laurentide Air Services, as it became known, was eventually sold to Roy Maxwell, a former RAF instructor, with financial backing from Thomas Hall, a Montreal ship builder. In 1921 Imperial Oil started a service from Edmonton (Alberta) to service the company's wells in the North West Territories; and in 1924 the Ontario Provincial government established a forestry patrol service (Ellis, 1980; Pigott, 1997).

100. On the rare occasion a woman was hired it was usually as a stenographer or a basic clerical job. WCA, for instance, in the late 1920s hired a female stenographer (Western Canada Airways, 1929).

101. In 1921 there were 88 airline operators (only 17 of whom were in operation two years later); in 1922 there were 125 operators (less than half of whom were still operating the following year); the number of operators rose to 129 in 1923 but was down to 44 by 1928; in 1929 saw a number of mergers and dominance by four major airlines – UAL, TWA, American Airways (American) and Eastern (Smith, 1944; Williams, 1970).

102. TWA was later renamed Trans World Airways, and Eastern was renamed Eastern Airlines.

103. Connell's (1995) notion of hegemonic masculinity refers to 'an idealized image of masculinity in relation to which images of femininity and other masculinities are marginalized and subordinated' (Barrett, 1996: 130).

3: Thoroughly Modern Milieu – The Feminine Presence in the Airways

1. See Chapter 2, footnote 93.
2. A sixth women – Mrs J. Benkain – was employed as secretary to the manager of the Brussels office. Several of these women remained with the airline for many years. Benkain, for example, remained in her position for 29 years, retiring from BOAC in 1953. Margery Masters worked for the airline for several decades. She died in January 1969. Peggy Russell, by then Mrs Peggy Dovey, stayed with the airline until her retirement in January 1953. In 1926 Mrs 'Mac' left IAL to give birth to a daughter but shortly after found herself a young widow. She soon returned to the airline as a relief telephone operator at Croydon and later became a full-time operator in London at the Airways Terminus. Eventually she became joint supervisor of the switchboard. She died in 1949. (British Overseas Airways Corporation, 1949d).
3. They were joined later by Dennis Handover (Traffic Manager).
4. 'In 1931 she became secretary to the Deputy Air Superintendent of the European Division'; in 1933 worked for several weeks with Major Brackley, the Air Superintendent, typing up the results of his survey of the Australian land plane route, and in 1937 she secretly took part in the founding of the British Air Line Pilot's Association (BALPA), acting as unpaid secretary to the fledgling trade union, taking shorthand notes and typing up reports (British Overseas Airways Corporation, 1965d).
5. Other women joining the company in this period included Lucy Stevens (office staff, 1925), 'Mick' Vivien Smithers ('temp', 1926) and Micky Pace (1930).
6. Between 1931 and 1937 the company's internal newsletter – *Imperial Airways Staff News* – referenced few women among the hundreds of new hires that were announced.
7. IAL's staff numbers doubled from 1800 to 3600 between 1935 and 1938.
8. Referred to as a 'powers operator'.
9. The British aviatrix Lady Heath successfully challenged this ruling in 1926 but informally the practice was continued well into the 1980s in the United Kingdom.
10. IAL was a founding member of ICAO.
11. The forerunner of UAL.
12. Opposition came not only from BAT's executives but other industry leaders. For example, the wartime ace, Eddie Rickenbacker, then in charge of Eastern, pressed BAT not to make aviation 'a laughing stock' by hiring female flight attendants (Nielsen, 1982).
13. KLM soon discontinued the practice as the turnover in stewardesses was very high, with large numbers leaving to get married (Hudson and Pettifer, 1979: 96).
14. Delta adopted the practice in 1940, followed by Continental the following year.
15. Johns, nonetheless, went on to express sympathy with the idea, arguing that 'a young and attractive girl casually serving coffee in an airliner, possibly in rough weather, is certain to create a feeling of confidence among the passengers' (Cadogan, 1992: 213).

16. Mildred Bruce, the owner, hired a 21 year old former typist on its Croydon–Paris service. The woman wore 'a dark, polka-dot dress with a very large, ruched, white collar' (Cadogan, 1992: 213).

17. The letter, 'from a young lady at Versailles,' was printed under the heading, 'Victualling Her Way to Matrimony'. It read:

> Could you not take me on board one of your Company's aircraft as stewardess? This is why. My fiancée is a Captain in the Colonial Infantry and in charge of Biltire. The nearest airport is Geneina. I would like to join him so that we could be married. The air trip to Geneina via Cairo and Khartoum is too dear for me. As a stewardess, however, I could work my passage out there. I am over 21. Quite apart from the sentimental side of the question, I would supply journalistic material to a very large French daily paper. My suggestion will probably surprise you. It is useless to tell you how happy I should be if you would care to consider it.
>
> Imperial Airways (1939h)

18. Ironically, the agreement refers to 'accompanying' wives as 'stewardesses' when engaged in temporary work in transit.

19. In 1939 women were paid between £2.0.0–£2.15.0 compared with a male rate of £3/5/0 – £4/0/0 per week (Imperial Airways, 1939e). Note that the currency was divided into pounds (£), shillings (s) and pence (d.), with twelve pence to a shilling, and twenty shillings to a pound. Thus, for example, '£2.12.6' refers to two pounds, twelve shillings and six pence. In modern terms a shilling translates to 5 pence.

20. In 1938 single men of the general engineering staff earned £3.15.0 per week in their first year (married men were paid more); this was higher than any female employee including the prestigious secretary rank (Imperial Airways, 1938h). In their third year these men earned £4.0.0. per week, comparable to female secretaries in their fourth year. By the seventh year the men were earning £4.10.0 per week which was only bettered by a female secretary in her eleventh year. Among the air crews, stewards' rates of pay varied from £3.5.0 per week in the first year to £3.19.0 by the seventh year (Imperial Airways, 1938m); grade 'B' flight clerks on the 'Empire Services' were paid a starting salary of £3.10.0 per week, rising by annual increments of five shillings to a maximum of £4.10.0 while those in grade 'A' were paid between £4.10.0 and £5.10.0 (Imperial Airways, 1938f);; radio officers received £4.10.0 in their first year, £5.0.0 in their third year and £6.5.0. in their eighth year (Imperial Airways, 1938k); first officers and acting captains were paid £300 per annum (approximately £5.15.0 per week), and captains were paid between £400 and £750 per annum (or approximately £7.14.0 to £14.8.0 per week) (Imperial Airways, 1938c).

21. Within Imperial Airways the title 'secretary' was specifically reserved for that level of work only: the 'appointment of secretaries, other than those for Managers and Heads of Departments, [required] the sanction of the Staff Manager' (Imperial Airways, 1938d).

22. In January 1938 Mrs Spence was appointed supervisor.

23. Sheila Tracy, Miss H. M. Cowan and Miss M. Watson were all promoted in May 1939, to the respective positions of Supervisor, Deputy Supervisor and Senior Section Leader.

24. The 1932 Annual Report indicates that there were 17 women among the 80 'holders of 1000 shares and over' (Imperial Airways, 1933), and the 1933 Report lists

300 proxies from female shareholders out a total of 872 proxies (Imperial Airways, 1934).

25. Male jobs included receptionist, booking clerk, coach driver and baggage handler The visibility of male employees grew over the years as the company added new service positions, including stewards (introduced in 1927), page-boys (1937) and reception officers. Stewards attended to passenger needs during the flight and over time came to serve them meals and beverages. Page-boys attended to the passengers aboard the coach from London to the airport at Croydon where other uniformed page-boys met them and helped them to board (Imperial Airways, 1937a). The job of the reception officer was 'to solve any such incidental travel problems as may arise, and to deal promptly with questions concerning any specific flight' (Imperial Airways, 1937b).

26. The *Imperial Airways Monthly Bulletin* was the first in-house bulletin to be produced, in 1925 (see Appendix 1),

27. The *Imperial Airways Gazette* was introduced in 1930 (see Appendix 1). The first corporate film was produced in 1937 (see Appendix 2).

28. The only mention of a woman was to a Miss D. Miller of the European Division who was listed in the 1934 Annual Report under 'Staff Debtors'. The only visual reference to any woman was a photograph of a female passenger, alongside two male passengers, emphasizing the largeness of the modern airliner in the 1932 Annual Report. Thus, it was hardly surprising that the opening remarks of IAL's 'Chairman' to the Annual General Meeting was addressed to 'gentlemen'.

29. For example: 'Miss Day of Accounts Department, Croydon, has left the Company's services' (Imperial Airways, 1932b).

30. The woman was Frankie Probert.

31. In the 1930s Clause 12 of the Terms and Conditions of First Officers stated:

> You should not marry during the period of this engagement without the consent of the Company previously obtained, which may be withheld without any reason being assigned. Breach of this provision shall entitle the Company to terminate your engagement forthwith without notice or any salary in lieu of notice.

32. Few if any black women worked for IAL at this time.

33. This image, which appeared on an IAL advertising poster, was the only one of a black woman to appear in IAL's corporate materials.

34. For example, on 'the occasion of her wedding the staff presented Miss Bridges with a clock as a mark of their esteem' (Imperial Airways, 1932a).

35. A man headed up the Swimming Club, for example, and two women – Sheila Tracy and Minnie Mann – formed part of the five-person organizing committee. Similarly, the Sports and Social Club had a male Secretary and the ten-member Executive Committee included only two women (Minnie Mann and Doris Moore). In the organization of the dinner and dance, (with the exception of Minnie Mann and Doris Moore) male employees occupied five of the seven committee positions and all four officer posts.

36. Speaking to the issue, at the January 1939 Southampton and Hythe Staff Dinner, Captain Walker, the secretary of the male hockey club, dismissed the women's concerns and their attempt to establish their own team, arguing that 'they haven't met with much success, but at any rate they appeared to be enjoying themselves, and were still plodding along' (Imperial Airways, 1939d). Interestingly, the *Imperial Airways Gazette* characterized Walker's speech as 'masculine condescension' and wondered if that tone would 'have the effect of spurring [the women] on to future hockey glory' (ibid.)

37. Prior to the First World War he was deputy general manager of the North Eastern Railway. During the war his flare for efficiency saw him, in turn, appointed Deputy Director General of the Ministry of Munitions, Brigadier-General on the staff of the Commander in Chief of the British Army in France, Director-General of Military Railways, Inspector-General of Transportation in all theatres of war with the rank of Major-General, and First Lord of the Admiralty. Following the war Geddes was elected to Parliament as a Unionist MP, becoming Minister without Portfolio, Minister of Transport, and then Chairman of the Committee of National Expenditure, charged with making recommendations to the Chancellor of the Exchequer on reductions in the national expenditure on supply services (Penrose, 1973: 140). By now Geddes had attracted the attention of Hungarian financier Frederick Szarvasy who was attempting to put the ailing Dunlop Rubber Company back on its feet. He hired Geddes as Chairman with a mandate to reorganize the business. Interestingly, Szarvasy was also at this time working with George Holt Thomas on a proposal for an 'Imperial Air Transport', a proposal that eventually formed the basis of the establishment of IAL.

38. He retained his 'chairmanship' of Dunlop, and ran the airline almost as an adjunct of the rubber company. The board met in the Dunlop office and employed the same solicitors, auditors and architects. Sir George Beharrell and Sir Hardman Lever, Geddes' closest associates at Dunlop, both sat on the IAL board and, like Geddes, ran the airline from Dunlop's offices.

39. Prior to joining the airline business he had been Director of London's buses, running the system as a private enterprise. When he took over as Managing Director of Daimler Airway in 1920 he found a business that was very inefficient in its operation. Aeroplanes, for instance, were only making one cross-channel journey per day; being stored in a hangar at the end of each journey so that minor repairs and checks could be made. Searle soon changed things, bringing his 'hard business mind to bear on the subject' (Pudney, 1959: 58). As a result, Searle became known for his concentration on safety and high efficiency. At IAL he moved quickly to replace many of the older planes and to standardize the fleet.

40. Even in the mid-1930s 'the most satisfactory way of becoming a pilot on the commercial airways [was] by undertaking a first period of service in the Royal Air Force' (Olley, 1934: 230). Indeed, 'right up to the second world war [IAL's] pilots were mostly the remnants of [the] older men [who] were the survivors of the sketchily-trained pilots turned out by the R.A.F. or the R.F.C. in the [First World] war' (Armstrong, 1952: 112–13).

41. Sidney Albert Dismore was a former pilot with the RFC.

42. These included Air Vice-Marshall Sir Vyell Vyvyan (1925–33) and Air Chief Marshall Sir John Salmond (1933–38).

43. On small exception was Anne Brooks, who joined Imperial Airways in 1934, and was promoted to supervisor of flight administration records by the time she retired in 1966.

44. Through memoranda and in-house newsletters, senior management encouraged employees to 'act and think imperially [to lift] the nation, indeed the whole Empire', out of economic crisis (Imperial Airways, 1931c). From 1931 onwards 'Let Us Act and Think Imperially' became the banner slogan on subsequent issues of the *Imperial Airways Staff News*.

45. For example, a 1934 edition of the *Imperial Airways Staff News* reported on 'an interesting analysis of the nationalities of passengers carried between Karachi and Rangoon [which indicated that] 76% [...] were British, 18% were of Indian nationality, 5% were Burmese, and 1% Chinese'.

46. For example, in 1936 a Mr Shivram was hired as a driver by the Delhi station (a post he retained until 1969); in 1937 Kefas Dubje became 'one of the first Africans taken on to the Durban staff', but in a menial position (British Overseas Airways Corporation, 1947e).

47. As Pett expresses it: 'As you can imagine, there were no women employees down the line' (Letter to the author).

48. Miss Mackay, for example, was hired as a secretary in the Germinston (South Africa) office in 1936, and with the expansion of the company in 1938 a number of typists were hired at the Alexandria (Miss Bell, Miss Epstein, Miss Antoun and Miss Trafralian), Lourenco-Marques (Miss Fragoso), Durban (Miss Marshall), Cairo (Miss Allcourt) and Karachi (Miss Holloway) offices.

49. As Said (1993: ix) contends,

> What are striking in these discourses are the rhetorical figures one keep encountering in their descriptions of 'the mysterious East', as well as the stereotypes about 'the African [or Indian or Irish or Jamaican or Chinese] mind', the notions about bringing civilization to primitive or barbaric peoples, the disturbingly familiar ideas about flogging or death or extended punishment being required when 'they' misbehaved or became rebellious, because 'they' mainly understood force or violence best; 'they' were not like 'us', and for that reason deserved to be ruled.

50. This was not restricted to IAL but was part of a broader discourse of race and empire. The British Board of Film Censors, for example, enacted prohibitions not only of 'white men is a state of degradation amidst native surroundings' but also of 'equivocal situations between white girls and men of other races' (Mackenzie, 1984: 77).

51. Sinha (1987: 217) argues that there is 'a connection between imperialism and the ideal of manliness [with] foreign domination mediated through gender relations and gender identities' (see also Prasad, 1997; Said, 1993). For example, study of British colonial policy in late nineteenth century Bengal suggests that British rule was aided and abetted by the development of a series of racial and culture stereotypes, in particular the notion of 'the effeminate Bengali'. Here the stress is on inadequacy, the need to be led and effeminate behaviour: 'The British questioned the masculinity of the Bengali male and these doubts were often used to justify their unwillingness to share political power and administrative control with the new Bengali middle class' (Sinha, 1987: 218). On the other hand, analysis of the imagery associated with the myth of Lawrence of Arabia stresses different characteristics in the construction of male Arab masculinity. In stories about Lawrence of Arabia 'the desired qualities of Arab masculinity are also the very qualities that mark Arab inferiority, and ultimately subordination to Lawrence's Englishness', that is, 'a constant insistence of the Arab's boyish enthusiasm, innocence and indiscipline [...], 'playfulness' and 'carelessness'. [A] combination of qualities [that is] both epic and childish' (Dawson, 1991: 133).

52. A 1936 newsletter report on 'Air Facilities For Business Men' typifies this approach by focusing on 'the value of air transport to business men' (Imperial Airways, 1936b).

53. Other names include Hadrian ('a Roman Emperor'), Hengist ('the foremost of the [fifth century Saxon] chieftains'), Achilles ('the principle hero of the Iliad, the handsomest and bravest of the Greeks') and Apollo ('god of the sun').

54. In 1919 Lady Astor became the first woman to sit as an MP in the British Parliament, and Mrs Wintringham joined her in 1920. By 1931 there were 15

women MPs, a small percentage of the House but they had, nonetheless, dented the 'masculine world of parliamentary practice and politics, shifting the discourse' (Rowbotham, 1999: 122).

55. In Greater London 17 per cent of all female employees were clerical workers (Halsey, 1978: 26).

56. Even in 1933, when clerical work had become feminized, less than one in six of the GWR's clerks were women.

57. Roberts (1988: 67) argues that this is one of several factors that explain the feminization of clerical work. Other trends include: (1) the ascendancy of corporate capitalism, (2) the growth of large-scale public and private sector bureaucracies, and (3) the rise of the professional class of managers.

58. See note 34.

59. Indeed IAL had strong links with the GWR and began its own railway company in 1929.

60. Lady Astor and Mrs Wintringham managed to ward off the cuts (Horn, 1994). Interestingly, it was Geddes' brother Sir Auckland Geddes, who was responsible for ordering the dismissal of Violet Douglas-Pennant from her post as Woman Commandant of the WRAF (Collier, 1959).

61. Her father was 'a comfortably-off fish merchant' (Cadogan, 1992: 111). Her maternal great-grandfather had been the Mayor of Hull in 1860, and her maternal grandfather had inherited the family linseed-crushing mill. Her mother, a typical middle-class woman of the time, stayed home and tended to the needs of Amy and her two sisters. In 1922 she began studying for a degree in Economics, Latin and French at Sheffield University. Degree in hand, she did what many middle-class daughters of the day were doing and that was to take courses at a commercial college in order to prepare for a career in secretarial work (Horn, 1994; Smith, 1988).

62. She worked for a time as a short-hand typist for a corporate accountant, and then for an advertising agency, and later became a Department Store sales girl before joining the typing staff of a firm of city solicitors.

63. Johnson he became the first woman to earn an aircraft ground engineer's licence in Britain. Lady Heath, in fact, was the first British woman to qualify as a ground engineer but she had obtained her licence in the United States (Cadogan, 1992: 112).

64. The newspapers that were normally a good source of funds for aviation ventures rebuffed her, as did a number of potential backers. An Australian trade minister, for example, told her: 'Better go to Australia by steamer, my girl. You would be foolish to try to fly there' (Moolman, 1981: 77). Undaunted she managed to gain support from her father and from oil magnate Lord Wakefield. Interestingly enough it was Sir Sefton Brancker who helped her to obtain the connection to Wakefield. Johnson had written to Brancker for support and he had effected an introduction to Lord Wakefield. Johnson was later to say that Brancker 'took a certain pride in me, as he doubtless felt – which was perfectly true – that it was his faith in me which led to the achievement of my ambitions' (quoted in Macmillan, 1935: 403).

65. France's Bollard made aviation history when she flew from Argentina to Chile over the Andes. In 1928 Bailey became the first woman to fly solo from England to South Africa, and Heath made the first solo flight from the Cape of Good Hope to Cairo. That same year the Honourable Elsie Mackay, along with IAL Captain W. G. R. Hinchliffe, perished in an attempted East to West Atlantic crossing, but three months later Earhart become famous as the first woman to cross the Atlantic by air.

What these and other women flyers had in common was the ability to access the funding that made flying possible. The typical male flyer had military flight training, flying jobs and 'access to the kind of financial backing that made long-distance flying feasible' (Moolman, 1981: 43–44). Women had none of those opportunities and, at a time when the average family did not own a car, let alone an aeroplane, it is hardly surprising that women flyers came from the upper classes. Many of these women also shared an unconventional childhood interest in activities, as then associated exclusively with males, and had fathers or husbands who helped rather than hindered their flying careers (Cadogan, 1992; Heycock, 1991; Peake, 1993; Smith, 1988).

66. When the first all women's flying meeting was held in Britain in 1931 the press commented that the meeting was 'very appositely of a more emotional nature than usual', and that never have there been 'so high a proportion of good looking and well-dressed young women at any aeronautical function' (quoted in Moolman, 1981: 103).

67. In 1934 the owner, John Sword, was forced out of business. Sword's routes were taken over by Northern and Scottish Airways and there is no indication of what happened to Winifred Drinkwater.

68. The pilot, Grace Brown, was hired in 1938.

69. Major Hap Arnold, Major Carl Spaatz, Major Jack Jouett and Air Corps officer Captain John Montgomery, spurred by nationalist concerns that German airlines could dominate South America, suggested the idea of a US international airline that would operate throughout the region. The US government shared these fears and were willing to support the establishment of an American airline that would compete throughout South America.

70. This was very similar to the relationship between IAL and the British government. IAL was also referred to as the 'chosen instrument' of government policy.

71. Amaury Sanchez, a 19-year-old from Puerto Rico, was hired from a New York fraternity club (Lester, 2000).

72. Like IAL, Pan Am hired a number of non-white 'native' employees on various menial tasks in its imperial backyard. In Bolivia, for example, Pan Am developed an airport at Uyuni by bribing a local official to drive 'across the pampas in a truck, lassoing male Indians, whom he herded into an area enclosed by barbed wire – the site for the airport' (Bender and Altschul, 1982: 164–65). The Indians were then forced to dig up rocks and load them on to trucks. Only once the task was complete were they released. In the United States and the Caribbean the company did employ male and female blacks and Hispanics on jobs other than stewarding. The latter case involved routine clerical tasks but the blacks were only hired for menial jobs. Sibert C. Brown, for example, was hired in 1931 as a Porter in Kingston Jamaica, but was promoted to clerk in 1938 (Pan American Airways, 1956a), and Cecil ('Sharky') Fabien, joined the airline in 1932, in Port of Spain, Trinidad, as a 'boatman and lineservice man at Cocorite Seabase, where he was in charge of the docks'. Roy Young joined the airline in 1931 as a groundsman (sic) (Pan American Airways, 1958).

73. As the April 1936 edition of *Fortune Magazine* commented, Pan Am's 'proper competitors are not the US domestic lines but lines set up to seize the trade routes as the official representatives of their governments, [i.e.,] France's Air France, Germany's Lufthansa, Britain's Imperial Airways, and Holland's K.L.M' (p. 79). IAL/BOAC did not hire stewardesses until after the Second World War. It was Pan Am's closest European ally. Starting in 1928 Juan Trippe established a 'special' working

relationship with George Woods Humphery (Bender and Altschul, 1982: 198) and from 1930 onwards Pan Am and IAL entered into a number of agreements, including a joint development corporation to offer services from Bermuda to New York in 1930, and to cooperate on transatlantic flights in 1939.

74. Prior to working for Pan Am, Archibald spent time in Latin America when her husband, a US army officer, was stationed in Nicaragua. When her husband was killed in a car crash in 1928 Archibald went to work for Pan Am.

75. She was in this role as early as 1933 (Bender and Altschul, 1982: 218).

76. Perhaps he was drawn to the fact that Archibald was 'direct, disarming and, in her thinking, very masculine. She cinches a deal not by weeping on your shoulder but by knowing the facts better than everyone else' (Daley, 1980: 351).

77. The women – Eliane Schlachter and Margaret Fane – were hired by Grant McConachie who, even by bush standards, was seen as something of a maverick (Milberry, 1979; Render, 1992).

78. There was also a link between IAL, Pan Am and the establishment of TCA. In 1935 British, Irish, Newfoundland and Canadian delegates, meeting in Ottawa, agreed to establish a Joint Operating Company as part of a plan to circumvent the globe by air. Part of the plan involved a commitment by Ottawa to establish a national airline, to grant landing rights to IAL and Pan Am in Shediac (New Brunswick), and to cooperate in the establishment of meteorological base in Botwood (Newfoundland) (Pigott, 2001).

79. TCA copied the requirement of other airlines that recruits had to be registered nurses.

4: Their Finest Hour – Mrs Miniver and the World at War

1. See Figure 3.2.

2. Sir John Reith left the company in March 1940 to become Minister of Information. The new BOAC board included Irvine C. Geddes (Deputy Chairman; he was the son of the late Sir Eric Geddes), W. Leslie Runciman (Director General), Harold G. Brown and Gerard d'Erlanger. Pearson and d'Erlanger were outgoing members of the IAL board, Brown was a relative newcomer to commercial aviation and Runciman had, with Constance Leathart, been co-owner of Cramlington Aircraft Ltd.

3. Geddes, Runciman and Brown.

4. In the interim Sir Harold Howitt, a financial expert, was named chairman. He remained on the Knowles Board, along with Air Commodore Alfred Critchley (Director General), Sir Simon Marks, of Marks and Spencer's, (Deputy Chairman), d'Erlanger, Gower, and John Marchbank, a former General Secretary of the National Union of Railwaymen (NUR).

5. BOAC's general 'Employment Agreement' stated that

> The employee shall not marry during his engagement hereunder without the consent of the Corporation. The business of the Corporation requires that a proportion of its staff shall be unmarried and free to travel if required from station to station at short notice and for to live at stations when the Corporation considers it inexpedient for employees to be accompanied by their wives [...].
> (undated BOAC document)

6. For example, married men, 'with one or more children under sixteen', received a bonus of 10 shillings compared to 4 shillings for single men and 7 shillings and

     6 pence for married women, 'with one or more dependent children' (British Overseas Airways Corporation, 1940c).

7. Adams' recollections were shared with the author in letters, dated 12 July and 14 October 1993.

8. Baynham and Battson were responsible for the delivery of air freight, and Chivers' job was to train and test all newcomers and to visit the various bases where women transport drivers worked (British Overseas Airways Corporation, 1942g).

9. Reade studied history and law at Cambridge University and came first in the Bar exams. She gave the address at Call Night at the Inner Temple(British Overseas Airways Corporation, 1942a). She joined the airline in February 1941 as personal assistant to the Assistant Director.

10. As a 'computor' her job was to 'work out the times of darkness between the evening twilight and the morning twilight, to help the pilots when flying at night'. She also had to compute 'the best height and speed to travel over certain routes according to the wind analysis' (British Overseas Airways Corporation, 1942a).

11. She came to BOAC with A, B, C, D and X Ground Engineers' licences, and experience on 30 types of aircraft. She also spoke English, French, Greek, Arabic and Italian (British Overseas Airways Corporation, 1942d).

12. Others included Miss B. P. Wooten, the Assistant Cables Superintendent and Miss B. K. Bennett, the Filing Supervisor in the Accounts and Services Branch.

13. For Grey, women were imbued 'with a certain amount of ability, too much self-confidence, an overload of conceit, a dislike of taking orders and not enough experience to balance one against the other', a characteristic which 'is one of the commonest causes of crashes, in aeroplanes and other ways' (quoted in Curtis, 1985: 11–12).

14. One writer described the situation as an 'encroachment of men's jobs', and that 'such work should be confined to pilots unfit for combat service in the RAF and others above military age' (quoted in Curtis, 1985: 19–20). Another complained that it was 'disgusting' to employ female pilots with 'so many men fully qualified to do the work' (quoted in Curtis, 1985: 20). The women, it was argued, 'are only doing it more or less as a hobby and should be ashamed of themselves!'(ibid.).

15. Memorandum from the Director General of Civil Aviation to the Director of Civil Aviation Finance (quoted in Curtis, 1985: 14).

16. Including Margie Fairweather, the niece of Leslie Runciman. They were soon joined by four new pilots – Lois Butler, Lady Bailey, Grace Brown and Amy Johnson.

17. Among the new recruits was Constance Leathart.

18. In 1945 women constituted 12.6 per cent of all ATA pilots.

19. Pauline Gower and Amy Johnson, for example, had, respectively, 2000 and 2285 flying hours' experience, which was well over the minimum ATA requirement of 250 hours.

20. Johnson joined the ATA on 20 May 1940 and her sister Betty followed her two months later, taking up an ATA secretarial post.

21. In June 1940, for example, the Director-General of BOAC, Leslie Runciman, reported that the ATA had around 111 pilots on call of whom 'one fifth were BOAC pilots doing spells of duty with the ATA between jobs for the Corporation' (Curtis, 1985: 31). Yet for the female pilots of the ATA, whose number included Runciman's niece (Margie Fairweather) and a former aviation partner (Connie Leathart), the reverse was never the case.

22. Rosamond Gilmour, one of the six female stewards, (quoted in British Overseas Airways Corporation, 1964c). Gilmore became a steward on 10 May 1943, and the

following day worked on the airline's DC3 service between the United Kingdom and Portugal.

23. These female-associated reference points were offset, in part, by reference to the boys' 'great aptitude for specialized duties,' and the fact that they are taught 'the most modern catering methods', training for periods of three to six months in the Corporation's restaurants and buffets, and finally in some London clubs, where they learn the quiet, dignified courtesy which is the hallmark of the ideal steward' (British Overseas Airways Corporation, 1946b).

24. At the company's Marine Base, for example, there was a 'ladies cricket team', which included Peggy Russell (now Mrs Peggy Dovey), one of the first women to join Imperial Airways in 1924. The women's rifle shooting section, founded in October 1941, had 50 members by July of the following year, with Miss Masters as the secretary.

25. Including the company-wide Sports and Social Club, the Grand Spa Club (Mrs M. Maclung and Helen Stott) for head office staff, the Marine Base Sports and Social Club, the Scottish Station Welfare Committee, the War Savings Group (Frances Probert), the Friendly Society (Miss Howden) and the Airways Club (Mrs Holdstock). Several women served as Association or Club Secretary. At least one woman – Mrs Pace (Grand Spa Club) – served as Club Vice President, and several women served as Club Treasurer, including Miss Rogers (Grand Spa Club), Helen Stott (Grand Spa Club), Mrs G. C. Courvoisier (Scottish Station Welfare Committee) and Miss Williams (Friendly Society). Numerous other women served on club committees – Mrs E. Walker, Mrs E. Walton, Mrs J. Latty, Mrs I. N. S. Middleton, Miss de Boissiére, Mrs M. R. Roberts (all, Grand Spa Club), Miss Cheesman (Sports and Social Club) and Miss T. L. Julian (Table Tennis).

26. A title, according to the newsletter that the women 'have earned [...] It describes them well, and they deserve it' (British Overseas Airways Corporation, 1942h).

27. For example, a female supervisor with a law degree is described as dividing her time between [work] and her two children.

28. *Imperial Airways Staff News* introduced photographs in the fall of 1938 but made limited use of them; most pictured senior managers, different aeroplane types and occasionally the activities of male employees.

29. Under wartime conditions, women were not required to leave the company's employ if they got married. In fact there is a notable increase in the number of married women employed at various levels of the company during this time. Some were married before they joined the airline, including a few former IAL employees who had previously been forced to resign on marriage, such as Mrs N.C. Jarvis who, as Miss Hall, had joined IAL 1929 and became secretary to the Press Manager, where she served as the typist on the *Imperial Airways Staff News*. She left IAL in 1937 but joined BOAC in January 1943. Others married after they were employed by the airline. In this latter case marriage announcements also served the purpose of informing staff of the employee's new name. Thus, for example, it was noted that Miss M. E. Smith, the Head Office Librarian, was now Mrs I. E. Perry.

30. During the First World War she had been became head driver in the Women's Legion. During the Second World War she went on to become a Company Commander with the ATS.

31. Weick (1979; 1995) refers to organizational changes as 'shocks' to explain how ongoing sensemaking becomes disturbed and forces a rethink of the ways activities, people and events are understood.

32. Before Reith left IAL in 1940 he made his mark not only on the reorganization but on the new leadership, appointing the first Board, and creating the post of

Director General and two Assistant Directors General. He came up with the name – British Overseas Airways Corporation.

33. Other BAL promotions include Major J. R. McCrindle (Assistant Director General for the western hemisphere), Alan Campbell-Orde (Operations Manager) and Captain C. N. Pelly. McCrindle and d'Erlanger had both been involved with *Hillman's Airways Ltd*, a forerunner of BAL. Gerard d'Erlanger got into the airline business when the Hillman family sold their shares in the airline in December 1934. The banking house of Erlanger, of which Gerard d'Erlanger was a director, purchased the shares and d'Erlanger became a director of Hillman's. When Hillman's merged with other companies in 1936 to become British Airways Ltd, d'Erlanger remained on the Board as a director of the new airline. Major Ron McCrindle was the 'chairman' of Hillman's in 1934 and, for a brief period, took over as 'Chairman' of BAL in 1936 before handing over the reigns to Clive Pearson. Between 1936 and 1939 McCrindle served as the Managing Director of BAL.

    Campbell-Orde joined BAL as Operations Manager in 1936 and transferred to the emergent BOAC in April 1939. Pelly had been the Chief Pilot for BAL and had piloted the famous flight of Neville Chamberlain to meet with Hitler in Munich in September 1938. McCrindle, d'Erlanger and Campbell-Orde were all to have an important influence on the airline for years to come – Campbell-Orde as the Development Director, McCrindle as advisor on international affairs, and d'Erlanger as Managing Director (1946–47) and 'Chairman' (1947–49) of BEA and then 'Chairman' of BOAC (1956–60).

34. The post of Air Superintendent was abolished and Brackley was placed under Campbell-Orde.

35. Rising up the ranks of the administrative staff was Keith Granville, who started as a Head Office trainee with IAL in 1929. In 1971 he became the 'Chairman' of BOAC.

36. Although in Runciman and d'Erlanger were two men with experience and some sympathies for women in aviation. Runciman had previously operated an airline in partnership with Constace Leathart, had flown in air races that included male and female flyers and had a niece who was a prominent flyer and ATA pilot. d'Erlanger, as Commander of the ATA, had overseen the recruitment of female flyers though 'it would seem probable that the decision arose from a sheer necessity to make the maximum use of every available pilot, at a time when there was still a shortage of operational pilots' (Curtis, 1985: 96).

37. In 1944, for example, the company's 'capacity ton miles' for the year was, at 31.3 million, up 29.2 per cent on the previous year (at 24.2 million) and up 110.1 per cent on 1941 when it recorded 14.9 million ton miles: 'capacity ton mile' is a measure of output based on 'the number of aircraft operated and the number of hours flown by each aircraft' (British Overseas Airways Corporation, 1941b).

38. Previously Knollys was a courtier and former Governor of Bermuda.

39. Including Brigadier-General Critchley, who was said to be better known for his involvement with greyhound racing and golfing than with aviation (Penrose, 1980b: 135; Sampson, 1984: 59).

40. An editorial by Charles Grey, for example, concluded 'the recent appointments to the Board of the Corporation [suggests] that the Air Ministry discounts experience of air route operation and believes air transport will thrive on business management' (quoted in Pudney, 1959: 208). He characterized the Board as consisting of 'banker, accountant, multiple shop proprietor, trade union organizer, an 'A' licence pilot and a woman 'B' licence pilot [...], whose policy will be carried into doubtless vigorous

effect by an officer who in civil life was a leader in popular sport' (ibid.). As far as Grey was concerned, 'to choose such a Board and arm it with a chief officer who is said 'never to have lost a friend or an enemy' is either an extremely subtle method of obtaining startling results without appearing to plan them, or a naive attempt to mix oil with water' (ibid.).

41. Reflecting on the changed name the editor of the *BOAC Newsletter* expressed regret at the loss of the 'Imperial' name and 'the great achievements' associated with it 'throughout the Empire' (British Overseas Airways Corporation, 1940e). He did, however, recognise that 'in those days 'Imperial' had an almost Nazi significance in certain ears, despite the great good Imperial Airways had done to break down such a tendency throughout the world'. He concluded that, perhaps after the war "British' will be more appropriate than 'Imperial'. And in the British Commonwealth of Nations itself British is the word that counts' (British Overseas Airways Corporation, 1940e).

42. For example, a story from Nairobi reports that 'the native staff includes a boy whom everyone knows as 'Dopey' (British Overseas Airways Corporation, 1940h). Another story refers to a passenger as 'a coolie type [who] did not appear very presentable' (British Overseas Airways Corporation, 1941a).

43. A story from El Geneina typifies Eurocentric superiority by reporting,

> a man turned up asking for a job as a carpenter [and when ...] asked his name and origin, he said he came from Sierra Leone [...] and rejoiced under the good old English name of Thomas Terry – a change from the usual Mohameds, Abduls and Ahmeds to which one becomes so used out here.
> (British Overseas Airways Corporation, 1941c)

And sometimes readers were 'reminded' of the 'strange, exotic' ways of the African, who considers flying ants such a great luxury that 'our boys [become] so intent on filing paper bags with them that they [forget] all about the passengers' luggage' (British Overseas Airways Corporation, 1941d).

44. Approximately 63,000 women were injured over the course of the Second World War and of these 25,000 died. Female deaths constituted just under 42 per cent of all civilians who were killed in the bombings (Braybon and Summerfield, 1987).

45. The Women's Legion was founded in 1934 by Lady Londonderry to prepare women for a number of auxiliary tasks in the event of war: Dame Helen Gwynne-Vaughan – the former Director of the WRAF and President of the OCA – became the Chair. One of the first actions of the Women's Legion was to establish an Officer Training Section, recruiting several women to be trained as female officers. In the fall of 1936 the Women's Legion folded but the Officer Training Section became the basis of a new organization called the Emergency Service, with Dame Helen Gwynne-Vaughan as the 'Chairman' and Lady Trenchard as 'Vice-Chairman'. Initially the Emergency Service, and similar women's organizations, did not receive approval from the Imperial Defence Committee but as the threat of war loomed large it changed its stance. In January 1938 HRH the Duchess of Gloucester became the President of the Emergency Service, signalling royal ascent and the following month it received official recognition from the Imperial Defence Committee.

46. At least 5 Canadian (including Helen Harrison, Francis Horsburgh, Gloria Large, Marion Orr and Margaret Russell), and 26 American women joined the ATA: the Americans included Helen Richey and Jacqueline Cochran (Curtis, 1985).

47. There were exceptions. Curtis (1985: 187) claims that on one occasion her flight engineer reported that she had difficulty flying a particular type of plane. Normally opinions of this type was enough to prevent female flyers from progressing to different types of plane but independent witnesses verified that Curtis had not 'bounced' the plane on landing as her engineer had reported. The flight engineer – Freddie Laker – became famous in the 1960s for the establishment of Laker Air, which offered cheap flights across the North Atlantic.
48. 4.9 per cent of female flyers and 8.1 per cent of male flyers were killed in action.
49. In the case of dental clerk orderlies male dental offices were so impressed that they tried, unsuccessfully, to achieve 100 per cent substitution.
50. This 'cinema of Empire'(Richards, 1986) included such films such as *The Green Goddess* (1930), *Clive of India* (1934), *Sanders of the River* (1935), *Wee Willie Winkie* (1937), *The Drum* (1938), *The Four Feathers* (1939) and *Gunga Din* (1939). Images of colonial people in these films were so invidious to the people that they depicted that in several cases there were sharp responses in the relevant countries. *Lives of a Bengal Lancer* and *Gunga Din*, for example, were said to have 'aroused violent and deeply subversive feelings in Indian viewers [and a] great deal of criticism from Indian leaders' (Glancy, 1999: 190–91).
51. The debate reveals something of the continued discriminatory thinking of those at the highest levels. In 1942 US Army officials were complaining that British troops and civilians were overly fraternizing with their Black troops and, as a consequence, were giving offence to their White troops. Major General Dowler, in charge of administration for the British Southern Command under which the Black American troops were stationed, issued a directive to British troops to avoid friendly relations with the Black troops. He advised his own troops to 'try to find out from American troops how they treat Blacks and to avoid such action as would tend to antagonize the white American soldier' (Bousquet and Douglas, 1991: 72–73). Dowler argued that blacks

    work hard when they have no money and when they have money they prefer to do nothing until it is gone. In short they have not the white man's ability to think and act to a plan [...].... Too much freedom, too wide associations with white men tend to make them lose their heads and have on occasions led to civil strife.

    quoted in Bousquet and Douglas (1991: 73)

    There were some serious complains about Dowler's comments but in general his approach was supported by James Grigg, the Secretary of State for War and upheld by a meeting of Cabinet on 13 October 1942, which concluded that 'it was desirable that the people of this country should avoid becoming friendly with coloured American troops' (Bousquet and Douglas, 1991: 75).
52. The RAF, for example, resisted the recruitment of black women from the colonies, going so far as to state that in the Caribbean it would only accept 'local applications for WAAF [...] from white women of excellent type' (quoted in Bousquet and Douglas, 1991: 92).
53. This invisibility is all the more interesting given the argument that one thing that contributed to women's work in the interwar years was the fact that 'women were suddenly publicly visible in the First War' (Braybon and Summerfield, 1987: 281).
54. Indeed, Colyer and Larsen were Johnson's handpicked officers, recruited from UAL when Johnson took over TCA.

55. By 1942 women constituted 30 per cent of TCA's employees, rising to a peak of 1943 of 34 per cent in 1943 (Trans-Canada Air Lines, 1943e). In some areas women exceeded these percentages, including the traffic department (60%) (Trans-Canada Air Lines, 1943d) and Central Reservation Control (95%) (Trans-Canada Air Lines, 1943c).

56. Although they also began employing female employees in 1870 the Canadian government were far more circumspect in their hiring (Strong-Boag, 1979), restricting women to work as typists, secretaries, stenographers, and 'girl Fridays' while that of clerk remained a 'man's job' (Morgan, 1988: 6–8).

57. The Japanese invasion of China in 1937, seen by many historians as the beginning of the Second World War, seriously affected Pan AM's associate airline China National Aviation Corp (CNAC). In 1939 Pan Am, under direction of the US War Department, began a process of ridding Columbo-German Aerial Transport Company (SCADTA), its Colombian airline, off its German staff. The airline was also involved in a secret War Department contract to build and equip airfields along the Atlantic coasts of Central and South America; Accra (West Africa); and Khartoum in North Africa (Burns, 2005).

58. It grew from 5300 employees in 1940 to 25,000 by the end of 1941.

59. The Japanese attack on Pearl Harbor had a direct effect on Pam Am, as it had a key base at Honolulu. Fortunately, all its planes were in service during the attack and the company was able to redirect them to land elsewhere. The airline's employees in Hong Kong and Wake Island fared less well. Almost all those on Wake Island were killed and the Hong Kong staff was imprisoned for the duration of the war. A post-war report indicated that 49 Pan Am personnel were interned, 9 killed and 33 were missing, and the airline suffered 1M $ in lost or destroyed equipment'.

60. The airline also lost a number of female employees to the armed forces but the real challenge was to replace the much larger exodus of male employees from a much-depleted pool of manpower (sic).

61. There is, however, something of the Mrs Miniver imagery in the following account:

> To PAA in May, 1942 came blonde, soft-spoken Nettie Harp. No career woman she, but determined to do all she could to speed the return of her navy husband ... Transition from knitting doilies to splicing cables in the control shop has been quite agreeable to Mrs. Harp. Today, like many another American housewife, she finds pleasure, satisfaction in performing what was formerly considered a man's work. Interesting as the work has been, Mrs. Harp plans to give up her jog at war's end. Says she: 'When the boys come back they'll be needing jobs. And they should have them. I wouldn't feel right in keeping this one'.
>
> (Pan American Airways, 1945a)

62. For example, in a report on the return of former employees 'who took military leaves of absence' it was noted that other 'recently hired war veterans include; Doris F. Duval, staff sergeant in the Marine Corps, hired as a Link trainer operator [...], Irma E. Davis, Sp T 3/c in the Navy, hired as secretary in Industrial Relations [...] and Marie F. Guidone, Y 2/c in the Navy, hired as Traffic clerk' (Pan American Airways, 1943c). After the war returning veterans included 'Evelyn Sanches, [who] was with the WACS, [and] spent 14 months in the Southwest Pacific [... where she] received two battle stars as part of her war record. She worked for PAA seven

months before joining the service, [and] now is back in the metal shop'(Pan American Airways, 1946a).

63. According to Pan Am, 'increased wartime services and man-power problems necessitated a departure from [the] custom' of only hiring male stewards (Pan American Airways, 1944).

64. Established in 1942, almost 2000 women pilots belonged to the WASPS. When the organization was disbanded at the end of December 1944 the female pilots 'went home to spend the rest of their young lives on the ground', no commercial airline would hire them (Keil, 1979: 306).

65. Priester, the chief engineer with vast responsibility over much of the airline's operations, was described as 'the prototype of the tough, unreasonable operations boss of airline literature and film' (Bender and Altschul, 1982: 157).

5: Angels With Dirty Faces – Strategies of 'Normalization' and 'Equity' in the Immediate Post-War Era

1. In fact, the government initially divided the routes between three new state-run airlines – British South America Airways (BSAA), responsible for South American routes; BOAC, responsible for all other transcontinental routes; and BEA, responsible for European destinations. In 1949, after a number of operational difficulties, BSAA was merged with BOAC.

2. Legally the ground had been prepared by the introduction of the *Restoration of Pre-War Practices Act 1942*, which was similar in design to the 1919 Act of the same name.

3. Following the war the company did continue to employ one female engineer, but hired a number of young men as the new generation of stewards. Despite their wartime flying experience, not a single female ATA pilot – or any other female pilot – was hired as commercial airline pilots by BOAC and BEA.

4. In 1944 Gower married Wing Commander Fahie and retired from the Board at the end of Second World War. In 1947 she was preparing to give birth to twin boys when she died in childbirth.

5. BSAA also recruited stewardesses at the same time.

6. From a peak of 35 per cent in 1943, female employment constituted 29 per cent of TCA employees in 1944 and 23 per cent at the end of 1945 (Pigott, 2001: 216). The figures for Pan Am are unavailable but there are various indications that large numbers of women were replaced at the war's end.

7. This was at least the case at TCA where the number of women fell from a peak of 820 in 1943 to 752 by the end of 1945, a drop of eight per cent. Although comparable numbers for Pan Am are unavailable it is clear that the total number of employees fell by over 68,000 between 1943 and 1946.

8. During the war a number of women had worked in TCA's sheet metal shops but by 1946 the only woman left in the Winnipeg Sheet Metal Shop was a female 'Steno Clerk' (Trans-Canada Air Lines, 1946b). Pan Am had recruited a number of female mechanics during the war but they were almost all displaced by 1946: a 1952 newsletter report refers to the fact that a Mrs Carrie Suthard, based in Miami, 'was one of the few, if not the only, female electrical mechanic employed in the aviation industry' (Pan American Airways, 1952).

9. The percentage of women fell across all staffs but the actual number of female employees remained fairly stable. The United Kingdom remained the dominant location, accounting for 78 per cent of all BOAC's female employees – up by 5 per

cent from the previous year. At the same time the percentage of BOAC's UK female staff fell to 45 per cent of all Head Office staff and 18 per cent of other UK staff. A corresponding drop in the percentage of female employees was experienced in the Middle East (5%), South Africa (8%) and Western Atlantic (22%) regions.

10. Kanter (1977) and Gutek (1985) suggest that a critical mass of female employees (i.e., where a 'female presence' can have some influence on work practices) is around one-third of all the employees.

11. Betty Paige's story was told to the author in a letter and in a follow-up interview in the summer of 1994.

12. She originally was with FANY but joined the WAAF because she thought this 'a jolly good idea because the Battle of Britain was starting then and I thought of all those handsome men in their flying machines'. In the WAAF she moved on to 'odd jobs in the medical section' before being assigned to a RAF station on the Sussex coast where she was involved in ground control interception.

13. This convinced her that 'the qualifications for a job in BOAC was to know nothing'.

14. Her BOAC job involved 'sitting in an office, pushing a pen on a piece of paper. [It was a] terrible, terrible flop as you can imagine. I am going to sit here just taking telephone calls all my life and writing names on pieces of paper and putting them in a book'. In contrast, her wartime job involved working through the nighttime hours as part of a small team 'in front of radar sets weaving the height and the numbers if possible at the sound of the incoming bombers ... vectoring [British] fighters onto [German] bombers'. The job involved providing 'very accurate information as to the height and the incoming aircraft direction'.

15. She was told, 'we have to be careful with our Middle East clientele as Arabs won't speak to women'.

16. This is a reference to the No. 45 Group of RAF Transport Command.

17. As BOAC's senior management noted in 1947, the company 'had now to face the problems of becoming a commercial airline and holding its own against rapidly growing international competition' (British Overseas Airways Corporation, 1947c). Competition was fierce. In the second half of 1947, while BOAC made 418 North Atlantic crossings, US airlines (American Overseas Airways, Pan American Airways and Trans-World Airways) made 3104 crossings, and European airlines (including Air France, KLM, Scandinavian Airlines System and Sabena) flew a total of 1012 crossings (British Overseas Airways Corporation, 1948c).

18. In 1946 the tiny UK airline Airwork hired two female 'air hostesses' – Zoë Jenner and Jo Woodward – for their European flights. Jenner and Woodward flew with the old Imperial pilot R. H. McIntosh, who was now the chief pilot of Airwork. They were soon joined by Dorothy Coton, Ann Ellis, Helen Goff, Sheila Hodgson, Cynthia Turner and several other female flight attendants (McIntosh, 1963: 247–49)

19. The company emphasized the 'stewardess' title to eschew the glamour and frivolity thought to be associated with the title of 'air hostess' (Edwards and Edwards, 1990).

20. In this regard a precedent had already been established on the wartime UK – Portugal route (see Chapter 4). The company's post-war uniforms evolved from the armed forces wartime uniforms. BOAC purchased its uniforms from a naval training company.

21. Yet the company was not prepared to face the consequences of a marriage bar that continually required them 'to recruit new stewardesses to replace those who leave the corporation's services, particularly to marry, [making] their average period of

employment as stewardesses [...] comparatively short' (British Overseas Airways Corporation, 1954c).

22. That year BOAC employed 264 stewards (48%) and 283 stewardesses (52%) (British Overseas Airways Corporation, 1960b).

23. RAS's first stewardess was Robina Christie (Stroud, 1987).

24. From 26 female stewards in 1946, the number grew to 324 by August 1961.

25. Interview with Betty Chapel, now Betty Lindsey-Wood, in July 1994.

26. Eventually, suffering from hearing loss, Betty Chapel was grounded and given a job taking bookings at BOAC's Victoria terminal. For Chapel, this 'was doing all the hum drum things while the girls flew in the sky'. Bored, she left the company in 1951 and went on a nursing career.

27. In 1944 Henderson was made Head Office Staff Superintendent with responsibility for 3000 staff, of whom 52 per cent were men (British Overseas Airways Corporation, 1947f).

28. Within 2 years of the ending of Second World War the number of female managers was reduced from four (3.5% of all managers), to one (0.8%), to none.

29. The Croydon Sports and Social Club, for example, saw the formation of several male-associated activities, including cricket, football, and fencing and shooting. A club badge was designed specifically for men and consisted of gold wings across a white circle, with a 'Corporation blue center'.

30. Similarly the BOAC Speedbird Club was established in 1947 with only one woman on the 16-member committee. The '25 Club' for employees with 25 years of more service consisted of 18 men, no women, and of the 11 social club sections, women chaired only 3 – the Debating, Dramatics and Social sections. The Cricket, Squash, Tennis, Swimming, Table Tennis, Football, Rugby and Hockey sections were all under male leadership, and the Aircrew Club 'was specifically designed to meet the needs of the large number of Corporation flying men' (British Overseas Airways Corporation, 1946g).

31. A number of these women, including Howden, Stott, Cheesman and Attwood, had all been active social club members during the war years (see Chapter 4).

32. Including Major R. H. Thornton (board member, 1946–55); Major Ron McCrindle (the Deputy Director General; Managing Director, External Affairs; and Advisor on International Affairs 1940–58); Air Commodore Alfred Critchley (Director General, 1943–46); and Whitney Straight (Managing Director; Deputy Chairman, 1947–55).

33. As a state-owned enterprise the airline also included several men on the Board with experience of government service, including Knollys (former governor of Bermuda), Hartley (chairman of the government sponsored Associated Airways Joint Committee), Thomas (Board of Colonial Development), Sir Harold Howitt (Finance Member of the Air Council), Lord Burghley (wartime controller of aircraft repairs, Ministry of Aircraft Production), Lord Trefgarne (former Labour MP and chair of a television advisory committee) and Major Thornton (served on the Brabazon Committee on commercial airline production).

34. Trade unionists John Marchbank and Hugh Newlands, along with Labour Peers, Douglas, Trefgarne and Rothschild, reflected the new reality of state ownership under Labour Government.

35. They included Sir Simon Marks (Marks & Spencer), Major Thornton (director of the Alfred Holt shipping company), Sir Clement Jones (director of Alfred Booth and Co. Ltd), Lord Knollys (Managing Director of Employers Liability Assurance Company), John Booth (Shipping owner; founder of British Latin-American Airlines), Sir Miles Thomas (Managing Director of Wolseleys) and Sir Harold Howitt (financial expert and past-president of the Institute of Chartered

Accountants). Apart from Booth, three other men had business experience in commercial aviation – d'Erlanger (BAL), McCrindle (BAL) and Hartley (RAS).

36. Hartley had a long association with the airline dating back to 1934 when he became chair of the newly formed Railway Air Services (RAS). RAS was part-owned by IAL and operated out of offices in IAL's Terminus in London. In 1940 Hartley became chairman of the Associated Airways Joint Committee (AAJC), which was established by the government to oversee a number of the smaller domestic airlines during wartime (see Figure 1.1). He came onto the board of BOAC in January 1946 but resigned on 1 August to become chair of BEA. Before returning a year later as head of BOAC.

37. When Sir Miles Thomas succeeded Hartley he was disturbed by 'the poor quality of BOAC's Press Relations' (Thomas, 1964: 273), which he felt was due to the personality of Hartley who was 'extremely irritated' by any criticism of the airline and particularly of his leadership in the press. At the head of the Public Relations department Thomas found 'a tall, good-looking ex-RAF Group Captain who seemed to think that it was his duty to prevent anything from getting into the papers that gave any information at all about the Corporation' (Thomas, 1964: 273).

38. Sir Miles Thomas was appointed to BOAC in 1948 as 'deputy chairman' by the Minister of Aviation, Lord Nathan, who saw in Thomas a 'businessman who would be responsible for reorganising the nationalised Airways Corporation so that it did not lose money' (Thomas, 1964: 256).

39. For Thomas this was particularly pressing given that BSAA was merged with BOAC and created a serious 'overlap in staffing needs' (Smallpiece, 1980: 29).

40. Thomas was of the opinion that leadership had to be shown at the top so took a personal approach to informing the executives that they were to be fired (Thomas, 1964: 276).

41. This contributed to an atmosphere of cooperation in which Thomas managed to drastically reduce staff numbers without a major strike.

42. For instance, accounts, engineering and development, operations, traffic, route licensing, sales promotion and so on.

43. Whitney Straight and John Booth led the team. Sir Victor Tait became the operations manager. John Brancker, the son of Sir Sefton Brancker, was made general manager of commercial activities and Keith Granville was made responsible for worldwide sales.

44. As Thomas expressed it, the image of the Chief Executive 'should be built up by personal appearances whenever possible, by his walking through the shops, at events like sports meetings, by appropriate gatherings at suitable times; he should be recognisable and known' (Thomas, 1964: 300).

45. See Morgan (1988) and Ferguson (1984) for discussions of gender and bureaucracy.

46. See Cockburn (1985; 1991a) on gender and engineering work.

47. Some of this approach can be seen in Thomas's attitude towards secretarial staff. In the late 1940s it was still the practice of 'a number of businessmen in high places to have young men as personal assistants' but in Thomas' view 'an efficient female secretary' was preferable (Thomas, 1964: 275).

48. Interestingly, Thomas states that BOAC's training school for stewardesses is 'appropriately enough an ex-convent' (Thomas, 1964: 284). One can only wonder why he thought it appropriate.

49. d'Erlanger was the wartime Commander of the ATA (see Chapter 4) and Douglas was Marshall of the RAF.

50. When Nick Georgiades first visited BEA in the early years he was invited to the office of BEA's head of engineering and taken to the window to view the airline's entire operational fleet lined up on the tarmac at 6.30 p.m. For the engineering head the view was comforting. When Georgiades asked a hypothetical question about how a businessman, say, in Zurich, could return to Britain that evening when all the planes were on the tarmac, the engineering head's annoyed response was, 'You fly Swissair'. This reminded Georgiades of wartime flying attitudes: 'One of our aircraft is not missing. We'd counted our boys back home'. The wartime air force culture 'was so strong because it had worked. They remembered the Second World War and they wouldn't let it go' (quoted in Hampden-Turner, 1990: 84–85).

51. These only constituted 38 per cent or 625 of BEA's 1641 staff in August 1946.

52. In a number of cases senior staff of the smaller airlines were either not employed by the new airline or were offered much lower positions within it. In addition, there was some bitterness at what appeared to be a high-handed approach to the overall problems of merger on the part of some senior BEA management (Bao, 1989).

53. By 31 March 1947 BEA's staff numbered 5731, which included only 1607 employees of the original collection of airlines that constituted BEA.

54. The percentage of female staff at BOAC grew from 13 per cent to 26.5 per cent over the same period, from 1946 to 1966.

55. For one thing, Gerard d'Erlanger, who had played a role in bringing women into the ATA during the war, led BEA for two of its formative years.

56. Including 32.9 per cent from the RAF, 13.9 per cent from the army, 5.1 per cent from the navy and 2.3 per cent from the ATA.

57. For example, one picture shows a man and a younger woman under the caption: 'Mr. Colin McPhail [...] and his assistant, Miss Mary Munn' (British European Airways, 1948d).

58. The *BOAC Newsletter*, for example, established a regular 'Congratulations' column, devoted to births and marriages that included a report that widowed employee, Mrs Reede had 'relinquished her post to get married to Mr. Beale' (British Overseas Airways Corporation, 1946e).

59. Feldberg and Glenn (1979) refer to this as the 'gender' as opposed to the 'job model' of indexing male and female activities, whereby work or 'the job' is viewed as central to a man's workplace activities whereas home and family are viewed as central explanations of women's activities both inside and outside of the workplace.

60. Sheila Darragh left Glasgow High School in 1935, and although 'her mother was somewhat taken aback' she set out to become an aircraft mechanic. Despite hostility from men in the industry, Darragh went on to obtain the 'C' licence and then went to the de Havilland School (Hatfield), where being 'the only woman among 200 men from all parts of the world, she took her 'B' licence in 1939'. With the onset of the war she transferred to the Air Inspection Department of the Air Ministry and then on to Short's land plane factory at Stroud, Kent, 'where she trained women recruits to inspect spare parts for Stirling bombers'. She went on to join the ATA as an engineering instructor at its White Waltham Engineering School until it was disbanded and taken over by BOAC. The airline retained Darragh – the only female aircraft engineer in Britain holding 'A' and 'B' licences – and her 40 male colleagues.

61. Around this time a similar story was told of Nora Bevis, the company's *last* remaining female coxswain. Bevis joined BOAC in 1943 and was originally one of

eighteen women to be employed as coxswains but the only one left when she retired in 1947. In spite of the fact that she had been 'sailing boats almost ever since she could walk, owned her own 14-footer, and was a yacht racer', the newsletter felt moved to comment that she was able to handle a launch as well as any of the men and is fully accepted by her male colleagues (British Overseas Airways Corporation, 1947a).

62. In April 1947 she became the first female member of the 25 Club, joining its 26 male members.

63. The blue pilot uniforms came complete with gold stripes that signified rank, with three-and-a-half stripes for a senior captain, and one-and-a-quarter to two-and-a-half stripes for junior captains. First Officers and Navigation Officers (First Class) wore two-and-a-half stripes while Second Officers and Navigation Officers (Second Class) wore one-and-a-half stripes. Operations staff, including Marine Inspectors 1st Class, Coxswains 1st Class, Seamen, Van Boys and Raft Hands, were dressed in light blue. Traffic staff (including Catering Officers [I], Pursers 1st Class, Station Stewards and Stewards 1st Class) wore white uniforms, while those in catering wore rose, and reception clerks were dressed in green. Symbols and titles of rank was almost exclusively the preserve of male staff.

64. Prasad (2005: 271) refers to this as a discourse of 'primitivism'.

65. Peoples of the Middle East and Asia are imaged somewhat differently but the contrasts serve the same general racial hierarchy. Arabs are often portrayed as warrior-like, backward, exotic, and 'colourful' and Chinese are referred to as 'coolies' or 'boys'. Indian and Pakistani peoples are virtually absent. Examples of the former include a photograph from Aden, which contrasts the ancient and the modern through the juxtaposition of a camel and an aeroplane, with a uniformed pilot talking to a 'passing camel driver'. Another picture shows an Arab man who, the accompanying text informs us, is 'a colourful tribesman of the Hadhramaut. Arms are carried by most tribesmen when flying and one of the captain's pre-flight checks is to see that no bullets are in the breech' (British Overseas Airways Corporation, 1952). These images correspond to Said's (1979) notion of orientalism.

66. The reference was to 'Miss Markarian, from the Sales Manager's Department in Egypt' (British Overseas Airways Corporation, 1946a).

67. For example, a report on the recruitment of Hong Kong women shows a photograph of 'Miss Winthrop' training five Chinese women (British Overseas Airways Corporation, 1949a).

68. Three of the five women featured were Eurasian, four were Convent-school educated, and all were from wealthy backgrounds.

69. Between 1948 and 1963 serious labour shortages in the United Kingdom encouraged the British government to make efforts to attract people from the Commonwealth to work in Britain. Initially large numbers of people came to Britain from Jamaica and Guyana, then from India and Pakistan, and eventually, in smaller but sizeable numbers, from former African colonies, Malaysia and Hong Kong. Between 1951 and 1961 people of West Indian origin in the United Kingdom rose from 15,300 to 171,800, those of Indian origin from 30,800 to 81,400; Pakistani origin from 5,000 to 24,900; and of Far Eastern origin from 12,000 to 19, 600 (Rees, 1984).

70. Nonetheless, these shortages did not lead to improved wages for women. Most of the new work was in low-paid jobs and in 1948 when the demand for female labour was at its peak, women's wages actually fell from 53 per cent to 45 per cent of men's wages (Rowbotham, 1999: 244)

71. Transport was one of the targeted job areas of government recruitment.
72. Begun in June 1947, the government utilized posters, newspaper and film advertisements, mobile recruitment vans and ministerial appeals to women.
73. While in 1930 6 per cent of employees worked in agriculture, 46 per cent in industry, and 48 per cent in the growing services and administrative sector, by 1950 the respective figures were 6 per cent, 37 per cent and 57 per cent. Although women's percentage share of the labour force only grew from 30 per cent to 31 per cent over this period, there was a tremendous shift in the type of work available to women. From 1930 to 1950 the percentage of female employees engaged in agriculture dropped from 2 per cent to 1 per cent and in industry from 38 per cent to 24 per cent, but grew from 61 per cent to 74 per cent in the services and administrative sector (Pott-Buter, 1993: 100). Between 1931 and 1951 the number of female clerks more than doubled to the point where, at 59.6 per cent of all clerks, women constituted a majority (Simonton, 1998: 240). While in 1931 10.3 per cent of all female workers were employed as clerical workers that percentage had almost doubled to 20.3 per cent by 1951. Over the same time period the percentage of male workers employed in clerical work rose from only 5.1 per cent to 6 per cent (Halsey, 1978: 26). The growth of government employment, especially with the proliferation of welfare policies, speeded up the growth of clerical work. By 1951 the number of female clerks and typists stood at 1,408,000 (Pugh, 1992: 287). Within Imperial Airways/BOAC over the same period, female employment, which was concentrated in the clerical and administrative grades, grew from around 500 to more than 3000.

    The growth of female clerical and administrative workers is also evidenced in unionization. In 1946 the Clerical and Administrative Workers Union (CAWU) consisted of 15,907 (59%) female members and 10,863 (41%) male members; and the Civil Service Clerical Association (CSCA) had 73, 857 (60%) female members and 49,240 (40%) male members. The Transport and General Workers Union (TGWU), which along with the CAWU, was the main organizer of BOAC and BEA clerical workers, had 815,675 (84%) male members and 159,090 (16%) female members across a range of transport companies (Trades Union Congress, 1946)
74. The number of women employed in those three areas of work rose from 45,000 in 1939 to 110,000 by April of 1946 (Trades Union Congress, 1946: 167).
75. This compares with 1931 when half of all female employees were under 25 years and only 10 per cent of married women worked outside of the home. Economic necessity and government campaigns aimed at married women helped to ensure that pre-war marriage bars were not reintroduced across a number of areas of work.
76. The Labour Government introduced the measure despite the fact that the Royal Commission on Equal Pay – established in 1944 – concluded that women were of an inferior value to employers because of lower efficiency and expressed concern that equal pay might further weaken the traditional role of women as stay-at-home wives and mothers.
77. The family metaphor appeared on numerous occasions including the Christmas address by the respective chairmen of BOAC and BEA, referring to staff as 'a big family' (British Overseas Airways Corporation, 1948d) and 'the family of BEA' (British European Airways, 1947b).
78. There were challenges to this powerful discourse, with some critically acclaimed films – such as *A Letter to Three Wives* and *Adam's Rib* – portraying women as successful outside of the home.

79. At the New York Office Gertrude Maume was supervisor of Purchasing Files, and her sister Catherine was Supervisor of Engineering Files (Pan American Airways, 1947d).
80. The story of Jerry Galindo, who became a Pan Am steward in 1934, is referred to as 'full of a boy's passion for flying' (Lester, 2000: 6).
81. Developed from the word steward.
82. According to one former stewardess, 'the male pursers didn't like having women on board. They did half the work for twice our pay of $160 a month' (quoted in McLaughlin, 1994: 87).
83. Female flight attendants were not appointed to the rank of purser until well into the 1970s.

6: The Invasion of the Body Snatchers – The Jet Age and the Eroticization of the Female Employee

1. The same issue carried a picture of a BOAC employee who had won the 'Miss Jamaica 1961' title. In a similar vein, the front cover of a BEA newsletter carried a picture of an ex-stewardess in a bathing suit (British European Airways, 1960a).
2. By the end of the 1950s approximately 35 per cent of all BOAC's employees, the vast majority of whom were men, were in the Engineering and Maintenance Department (British Overseas Airways Corporation, 1961e). In that same time frame more than ten per cent of the Corporation's female employees were one of 269 secretaries, 205 stenographers or 66 copy typists (British Overseas Airways Corporation, 1959e).
3. For example, in 1956 women constituted less than 21 per cent of BEA's flight crews, with men occupying all captain, first and second officer, and radio officer positions and 40 per cent of all flight attending positions. (British European Airways, 1956b).
4. Similarly, a BEA report on the job of a 'sister-in-charge', for example, states that the job holder 'personifies the nurse ... [being] quiet, reassuring, sympathetic and – above all – kind' (British European Airways, 1952b).

   Hochschild (1983) notes that airlines make use of women's emotional labour to smooth relations between the company and the customers. See also Tancred-Sheriff (1989) who discusses the auxiliary role of female labour.
5. Numerous articles, including book reviews also reinforced the idea that piloting was for men and flight attending for women. In a book review of *Careers in Civil Aviation* the reader is told that 'every small boy aspires to become an airline captain, and his sister wants to earn her wings, too, and is fascinated by the idea of becoming an air stewardess' (British Overseas Airways Corporation, 1963c).

   Toy companies also reinforced the differences through 'replicas of a B.O.A.C. captain's and stewardesses' uniform for youngsters' that was produced by British Artwear Ltd during the spring of 1957. Even in the late 1990s the Dutch airline, KLM, in co-operation with the Disney Corporation, was producing a Micky Mouse doll in an airline captain's uniform and a Minnie Mouse doll in a stewardess uniform.
6. Kimmel (1987: 14) argues that 'masculinity and femininity are socially constructed within a historical context of gender relations'.
7. As one aviation expert justifies it, women's exclusion from piloting is 'not merely an expression of male prejudice [but because] companies are fearful that the large costs which they incur in converting newly engaged pilots to a commercial

airliner will be wasted when a young woman marries and takes on family responsibilities' (Jackson, 1975: 78–79).

8. In-house newsletters constantly pointed to the long service of individual pilots and the difficulties in retaining stewardesses for more than two years, due to marriage.

9. Some commentators argue that the early post-war era was a period of masculine angst as men struggled to regain a new sense of masculinity. Quart and Auster (1984) and O'Connor and Jackson (1980) suggest that this sense of masculine angst is reflected in the imagery of the Hollywood movie of the time.

10. In 1942, and again in 1947, articles appeared on BOAC's 'only female engineer'. The first article had featured 'Miss' Halliwell and the second article, Sheila Darragh. In 1966 it was 'Miss' D. L. M. Smith's turn. After almost two decades BOAC had not gotten beyond the fact of hiring solitary female engineers and, once again, the article said more about the male dominance of the work than the skills of Smith. Smith, it turns out, had originally joined BOAC as a clerk in the service-engineering department in July 1941. Through training and support she managed to become appointed as a development engineer in April of 1961 (British Overseas Airways Corporation, 1966c).

11. The cartoon was based on a story in an earlier newsletter where, referring to windy conditions at BEA's Kirkwall station in Scotland, it was said that 'There was a whisper among the male element on the staff, of a certain stenographer who was scared to walk across the tarmac in case her new-look skirt ballooned her into the air over Kirkwall Bay' (British European Airways, 1948d).

12. The marriages of male employees were rarely mentioned except where they involved a female colleague. This is because when men married it did not affect their working situation, while women usually ended up leaving the airline's employ.

13. Reports on unmarried women who had been with the airline for a considerable period of time are few and far between, usually reserved for retirement notices. Such reports usually involved a bald listing of the woman's career-path with the airline and were devoid of any domestic referencing. This was a rare example of where the activities of male and female employees were reported in a similar way, although female employees received far less coverage.

14. In the same issue a profile of 'Miss' Daphne Comfort, the staff travel office chief, refers to 'her vivid personality' and 'tall slim figure' (British European Airways, 1949d).

15. Letter to the author, 15 August 1993. A decade later, by then a cabin crew instructress, Lardner still felt that 'the good stewardess candidate has a genuine interest in people and experience in working with the general public, a charming personality, patience and a sense of humour' (British Overseas Airways Corporation, 1964b).

16. For example, a *BOAC Newsletter* item on the role of stewardesses detailed how the job provided the ability to see and buy all manner of goods and services that were unattainable and in short supply in Britain (British Overseas Airways Corporation, 1947d).

17. Indeed, both airlines turned down thousands of aspiring stewardesses. BEA and BOAC accepted less than two per cent of the respective 9000 and 1500 applications they received each year (British Overseas Airways Corporation, 1952; 1959e).

18. Letter to the author, 5 February 1994.

19. Interview with the author, summer, 1994.

20. Interview with Jeannie Lardner, now Jeannie Sutherland, in the summer of 1994.

21. Interview with Francine Carville, summer, 1994.
22. According to Francine Carville stewardesses 'didn't even see the stewards [once they] were on the aircraft. You were kept totally separate'.
23. Lardner interview, 1994.
24. Lardner was given 'a couple of days sessions with the lady from the London School of Deportment' before taking over (ibid.).
25. In a circular argument, the company blamed segregation in light services for the introduction of segregated training, stating that in 'the past stewardesses were expected to have the same technical knowledge as stewards [but] this knowledge was very rarely put to full use as, by the very nature of the division of duties on board an aircraft, any work relative to this was done by stewards' (British European Airways, 1969).
26. Nonetheless, it was not until September 1960 that BOAC stewardesses became eligible for the 'long service' payments enjoyed by male stewards and not until June 1961 that a stewardess – Terry Barzilay – was appointed to the rank of senior steward.
27. By the late 1950s BOAC was 'losing' some 50 to 60 stewardesses each year due to marriage (British Overseas Airways Corporation, 1959a).
28. Lardner interview, 1994.
29. According to Lardner, a 'cabin crew instructoress' in 1964, this was 'fair enough'.
30. The ten-year rule was well established when Francine Carville joined BOAC. 'We were under contract for ten years and then we had to leave, there were no promotions available to Stewardesses!' In fact she managed to make a longer career out of it – retiring from BOAC in the early 1980s (letter to the author, 10 July 1993).
31. In the early days the weight and balance of the plane was critical to the aircraft's takeoff. Passengers were allowed a maximum weight limit that included their own weight as well as their baggage. Passengers were weighed along with their luggage and, based on averaged weights, women received a lower weight limit than men. Today airlines still use averages for passenger weights but the calculations are made in advance. Thus, for example, for a Boeing 737–400 the average male is assumed to be around 78 kg, females 65 kg, and children 42 kg (Simons, 1993: 110).
32. BOAC recruiter and Staff Supervisor L. C. Pace found 'interviewing such charming girls [...] a pleasant task' (British Overseas Airways Corporation, 1953).
33. A version of this was in practice in American Airlines and United Airlines. American cultivated the 'all American girl' image, while United went for the 'girl next door' look (Kane, 1974).
34. Lardner interview, 1994.
35. Carville felt that many stewards – recruited from the merchant navy and the railways – 'didn't have to have A-levels or languages'(Carville interview, 1994).
36. BOAC had trained its 1000th stewardess – Jayne Lapworth – seven years earlier, in 1954 (British Overseas Airways Corporation, 1954a).
37. Competitions developed at local (e.g., Miss London Airport), job (e.g., Miss Travel Agent), company (e.g., Miss Airways), industry (e.g., Holiday Girl Competition) and international (e.g., Miss International Air Hostess) levels.
38. In some cases attempts were made to link personality with beauty, but personality was clearly secondary, as in the 1955 Queen of the Air competition, where competitors were 'judged not only for beauty but for personality, charm, and deportment' (British Overseas Airways Corporation, 1955a).

39. Sir Miles Thomas has a very traditional view of womanhood. He described his upbringing as being 'dominated by women' and the 'whole of his early life' as being 'predominantly affect by the female sex, [creating] an atmosphere of inhibit pride and prudish domination by women'. As far as Thomas was concerned females were very fundamentally different from males. As a young schoolboy Thomas saw a nine-year-old girl without her clothes on. Commenting on the memory he states, 'that was the first time I saw a female form in the nude and realised that it was much more tidy and smooth in shape than the male equivalent'. Thomas's married life also followed a traditional route. His bride-to-be, Hylda, had a busy work life that ended with marriage. As Thomas explains it, 'Our early married life naturally demanded adjustments. Hylda had been used to arriving at the office promptly at nine o'clock in the morning and being kept busy until the early evening. Suddenly she found herself with nothing to do except look after a cottage that was already run [by housekeepers]'. That is not to say that Thomas had problems with women working. It was he that stressed that stewardesses were hard working members of the flight crews. His attitude to women and to women at work seems to reflect an 'old fashioned gentlemanly' approach whereby women were to be respected *as women* and afforded some measure of opportunity to work in a range of traditionally female roles (see Thomas, 1964).

40. *BOAC News* was the first to use this kind of imagery. *BEA Magazine* took up the animal theme much later, beginning with the front cover of its March 1957 issue with a stewardess shown with chicks. The newsletters suggested that work with animals was a normal part of the job done by the featured women, but this was far from the case. Interviews with former staff suggest that many of the women photographed with animals were chosen for their looks and had little to do with animal care. For example, a former BEA receptionist, based at London airport in the 1950s, says that she appeared in several publicity shots with an elephant, a tiger cub and several other animals even though it was no part of her job to deal with animals: 'I suppose it was about looks really. Whenever they wanted a certain kind of publicity shot they would call me up. I was happy to do it' (interview, July 1994).

41. Announcing the series, *BEA Magazine* urged readers to 'pick a pretty face' by sending in photographs for the back-cover (British Overseas Airways Corporation, 1966f).

42. This may have had something to do with the fact that

> American soldiers fighting in the jungles of Vietnam were captured by a BOAC advertisement. It was the elegant pair of legs in that mini-skirt advertisement that caught their eyes[...] It has become the op pin-up with men of the 214th combat aviation battalion.
>
> British Overseas Airways Corporation (1967a)

43. A number of British colonies had gained independence after long periods of struggle, including India, the newly created Pakistan and Ceylon (1947); Sudan (1956); Ghana and Malaysia (1957); Singapore (1958); and Nigeria (1960) (See Smith, 1975).

44. A photograph of members of the 'Karachi 25 Club' in a 1961 newsletter shows 'long-service certificates [being] presented to 25 Club members' but we do not find out who the recipients are, let alone what they do. This is all the more remarkable given that Karachi had one of the greatest number of long-serving employees of any of BOAC's overseas stations (British Overseas Airways Corporation, 1961b). By 1968 they had 34 staff members with a combined total of 910 years of service (British Overseas Airways Corporation, 1968d).

45. Najeeb Halaby, a former President of Pan Am, argued that American stewardesses should be more like the kimono-clad geishas of Japan, prepared to flatter and entertain the male passenger (Kane, 1974: 52).

46. Perhaps the earliest evidence of Afro-Caribbean employees is a photograph, in a 1957 newsletter, of 27 British West Indian Airways' (BWIA) stewardesses including two visibly black women (British Overseas Airways Corporation, 1957b). Two years later the *BOAC News* carried a photograph of a group of women, including Ghanaians, who had flown into London for training as BOAC stewardesses.

47. Miss G. O Dean, employed in the airline's UK Signals Centre in the late 1950s, was a rare example.

48. Ironically, Shen had already worked for BOAC as a secretary for five years in the airline's Flight Operations department in Hong Kong.

49. As Thomas, expresses it, the airline

> even put Japanese hostesses on our Japanese routes, with considerable expenditures on kimonos. We served the best foods, the best wines; but unless we were in a position to offer, above all, speed plus punctuality, we should see a drop in load factors, and unless an airline on average fills two out of three seats offered it is not going to remain in business long.
>
> (ibid.)

50. The film was made in 1937 in co-operation with TWA.

51. This 1940 movie, made in co-operation with American Airlines, focussed on romance between pilots and stewardesses.

52. *Coffee, Tea, or Me?* was very much a book of its time. It reflected the fact that the image of the stewardess 'was shifting from that of an attractive wife-to-be (with all the inherent limitation that that implied) to a much more sexually explicit Playboy Bunny or torch singer' (Kane, 1974: 103–04). Purported to be written by airline stewardesses Trudy Baker and Rachel Jones, the book was in fact written by a former public relations man for American Airlines (Kane, 1974: 104). Subtitled the 'uninhibited memoirs of two airline stewardesses, the book set out to reveal the sexual situations and encounters of the stewardess's job, by referencing the supposedly natural feminine qualities of the women involved:

> A stewardess is a girl. She wears a uniform and works at thirty-thousand feet. But above all she is a girl, female and subject to all the whims and desires of all females.
>
> One of our desires is that you know more about us, our lives, our loves and laughter. That's why we put together our similar minds and wrote this book. Smoking is permitted, and seatbelts are at your discretion. Welcome!
>
> Baker and Jones (1967: 13)

The book is lavishly illustrated by Bill Wenzell of *Esquire Magazine*, and shows large breasted, scantily dressed and sexually provocative stewardesses. The publishers managed to get a local female chairperson of the Air Line Stewards and Stewardesses Association (ALSSA) to praise the book as 'wacky, naughty and authentic' (Baker and Jones, 1967: 13).

53. Murray was the Director of Stewardess Training at the Aviation School in Boston. Unlike Britain, where the airlines trained their own flight attendants, in the United States would-be stewardesses had to train, at their own expense, at a certified training school like the one run by Murray.

54. The Executive Editor of *Air Travel* magazine.

55. A Foreword by aviation writer Robert Serling suggests a comparison between women and racehorses:

> I share with [the author] that respect and even affection [for stewardesses]. They are a wonderful breed, these girl-women who are a strange mixture of soft femininity and brisk efficiency. They have humor, endurance, warmth and – when the chips are down – guts. They make treasured friends. They also make excellent wives, with the lowest divorce rate of any female group in the United States.
>
> Saunders (1968: 13)

56. The central elements of the book deal with the supposed glamorous aspects of the process, in an entertaining but facile way, including chapters on 'High Style for High Flyers', 'Highball? Martini? Bloody Mary?', 'Galloping Galley Girls', 'Airborne Florence Nightingales', 'Like Caesar's Wife', 'Extra-Curricular Duties', 'Spare Time Galore', 'Cupid Usually Wins', 'It isn't All Seriousness' and 'Shades of Nellie Forbush'.
57. Lardner letter, dated 5 February 1994.
58. Carville interview, 1994.
59. Similarly, the following poem speaks to the glamour associated with being a stewardess:

> Saga of a Stewardess
> 'Twas many, many moons ago
> When I first felt ambition's glow.
> A glamour queen of air I'd be
> And everyone would envy me.
> British European Airways (1955b)

60. Lardner interview, 1994.
61. On the other hand, nothing was made of the stewards' looks, age and opportunities for marriage. Here experience rather than youth was stressed in the recruitment of stewards. Marriage was not a barrier to the recruitment or retention of stewards. Thus, little or no attention was paid to marriages by stewards because it did not affect the company. They had no need to find replacements.
62. In 1944 Ada Brown, a former UAL stewardess organized 300 women into the first stewardesses union (Omelia and Waldock, 2003: 38). Pan Am flight attendants joined the Transport Workers Union (TWU) in 1946 (Nielsen, 1982: 3), and TCA stewardesses formed the Canadian Air Line Stewardesses Association (CALSA) in 1947 (Newby, 1986: 12).
63. A typical example is the following report: 'Dan cupid this week lured the first airline stewardesses to fly the Pacific away from their jobs with Pan American World Airways. After flying for more than two years ... Mary Lyman and Beverly Morgensen are leaving to make plans for November weddings' (Pan American Airways, 1947c: 1–2).
64. In most cases adding a touch of glamour to the newsletter is the only obvious purpose of the images. The January 1947 front cover, for example, shows two stewardesses holding a salmon. The accompanying story is about 'lucky ticket holders at the National Air Show' (Trans-Canada Air Lines, 1947).
65. Variations on the theme include two voluptuous women with badges on their chests clearing security, and one comments on the male guard that 'you'd think it was war-time – how close he checks our badges' (Pan American Airways, 1953b).

66. In an issue of Pan Am's Clipper there is a photograph of a stewardess in a bathing suit who is said to be involved in a 'feature story on the glorious life led by PAA stewardesses' (Pan American Airways, 1957a: 7).

67. Other competitions included – at Pan Am: 'Queen of the Bond Drive', 'Miss Tequesta Queen' and 'Miss Soft Shoulder of 1948;' at TCA: 'Miss TCARA', 'Miss Apple Queen' and 'Miss Yachting'.

68. Pan Am, for example, ran a 'Pretty Girl Picture' competition, advising readers that if they 'have an idea for a pretty girl picture' send it to the Clipper (Pan American Airways, 1945c: 3).

69. Such descriptors were applied to all women, regardless of rank or professional standing. Thus, for example, one issue of Pan Am's Clipper refers to 'blonde Kay Keener, on of Seattle's solicitors' (p. 1), pictures a female employee in a bathing suit (p. 4), discusses 'a bevy of Pan American's loveliest' women in the traffic department (p. 7), and welcomes 'the new brunette lovely at LAX switchboard' (p. 7) (Pan American Airways, 1947b).

70. Pan Am explains the activities of the man as making 'sure the nylons fit'.

71. In 1968 TCA officially changed its name to the more bilingual friendly Air Canada.

72. The story was in fact about the international character of the airline and the varied nationalities that constituted its female workforce. In an earlier newsletter cartoon a bank loan officer is saying to an attractive woman: 'Offering yourself as collateral, Miss LaRoo, is somewhat irregular, but ...' (Pan American Airways, 1955: 7).

73. This questions the voracity of Collinson and Hearn's (1994) concept of multiple masculinities.

74. Mishkind, Rodin, Silberstein and Striegel-Moore (1987: 46–47) argue that there are five traditional archetypes of masculinity – soldier, frontiersman, expert, breadwinner and lord – that are 'archaic artifacts, although the images remain'. They go on to argue that the frontiersman and the lord are no longer viable roles for anyone and that the breadwinner and expert 'are no longer exclusively male'. They conclude that contemporary men may be left 'grasping for the soldier arche-type (which) conveys the image of the strong, muscle-armored body ... in an exaggerated attempt to incorporate what possible options remain of the male images they have held since youth'. This seems to describe the situation at BOAC and BEA in the post-war era leading up to 1970.

7: Close Encounters of the Third Kind – Towards an Employment Equity Discourse

1. In 1973 Frontier Airlines began the first airline in this era to hire a woman – Emily Howell Warner – as one of its pilots. A number of airlines followed suit, including Delta (in 1973), Eastern (1973), Braniff (1974) and Republic. TWA (1978), UAL (1978) and US Air (1979) were a little slower to respond. Pan Am (1987) was one of the last.

2. It was reported that some of Redwood's female colleagues 'felt encouraged by the appointment' (British Airways, 1991).

3. Ground Operations at Gatwick, for instance, included Barbara Giel, Passenger Services Manager responsible for all the activities of the passenger services staff and the development of the airline's customer service standards. A level below her was Sonia Barter, Special Services Manager. In Human Relations women held two

of the six General Manager posts. Jane Gunn, formerly Personnel Director for Coca Cola, UK, joined BA in the late 1980s as Head of HR Marketing before her promotion to HR General Manager responsible for cargo, sales, central marketing and external recruitment. Eva Lauermann, previously a research chemist then personnel officer with the chemical firm of ICI, joined BA in 1988 as HR Manager Engineering Services. Quickly promoted to HR General Manager, Lauermann was responsible for flight crew, engineering, Gatwick airport and HR Strategy and Planning (British Airways, 1988b). Of the 29 management positions below Gunn and Luermann women held 8 – including Jan Shaw (Head of Recruitment), Sheila Thompson (Head of HR North America), Jill Espley (HR Manager Property), Shirley Rae (HR Manager Logistics and Ops Control), Pam Sloan (HR Manager Catering), Ruth Matthews (Head of HR Finance), Jenny Sharp (General Manager Corporate Training) and Ruth Gillespie (Manager Management Development).

Women were also in the higher levels of Marketing Services where, again, they occupied two of six departmental headships. Mary Bartram, as Market Research Manager, was charged with providing top management 'with continuous feedback on what the airline's passengers think of its products and services' (British Airways, 1988a). Two of her four managers were women – Krystyna Monks and Michele Heyworth – both in charge of different aspects of Research Planning. Jill Parker, Controller Distribution Development, was responsible for the Customer Database Marketing System that enabled the airline to 'better understand its core customers' in order to keep ahead of the competition (ibid.). Three of her four project managers were women, including Beverley Burnham-Stevens, Sally Bouch and Carol Mickleburgh.

Other high profile female managers included Patricia Stanley (Chief of Cabin Services), Val Gooding (Head of Cabin Services), Judy Robson (Senior Cabin Services and Operations Training Manager), Barbara Johnson (Sales and Customer Service Training Manager) and Julie Morosco (HR Manager International). Each of these managers headed up BA teams designed to improve the airline's operation. Gooding was Chief of Cabin Services for Gatwick and UK Stations before being promoted to run the whole of cabin services in the February of 1990. Stanley, former Group Brands Manager, headed up Cabin Services for wide-bodied aircraft. Robson, a former stewardess and cabin crew instructor, joined Cabin Services in 1988 and was made Cabin Crew Training Manager in 1989 before being promoted to Senior Manager in 1990. In the two years prior she had seen the department grow from 90 to 220 instructors (British Airways, 1990a). Johnson came from BA's Super Shuttle Department in 1989 to head up a newly structured sales and customer service training department consisting of 11 teams of consultants. Morosco headed up four teams in the Selection Division of the Selection and Assessment Unit.

4. She was followed into the airline by two other experienced commercial airline pilots, Wendy Barnes and Jill Devlin. Barnes began as a co-pilot on BAC I-11s, and Devlin as a co-pilot on BAe 748s. By the following summer the number of BA's female pilots had increased to 14 and in 1989 the airline's first course at its new BAe Flying College graduated 2 women and 14 men. One woman, who graduated from BA's Training College at Kidlington, Oxford in 1989, was Sally Griffiths, a former stewardess who financed herself through the training because she was 'two years over the required age limit' when applying to BA for sponsorship. When she graduated she was assigned to BA's Highlands and Islands Division as a First Officer. Another female graduate of the time – Anna Riis – made history of a different kind when she and her husband Morten joined BA at the same time and became the airline's first ever married piloting couple.

5. This represents less than two per cent of the 14,826 commercial airline pilots in the United Kingdom at that time (see Cadogan, 1992: 262).
6. Sue Miller, HR Adviser Cabin Crew, for example, was an early DBA graduate, and Melanie Bower (Senior Project Executive), Susanne Gray (General Manager Marketing), Delia Hickson (Project Manager BSOR), Sheila Smith (Assistant Human Resources Manager) and Jane Whittle (Pricing Executive) were among the 12 women in BA's first class of 50 MBA participants.
7. The other women included Alison Stanley (from Legal and Government Affairs), Ros Hawley (Telephone Sales, and Central Marketing), Kwai Lin Lim (Information Management) and Linda Moir (Cabin Services). Kwai Lin Lim was the only person from any 'visible minority' group to be represented on the ESG (British Airways, 1991).
8. In 1991 BA estimated that its 'ethnic staff' members constituted 11.4 per cent of its employees and 2.4 per cent of its managers (British Airways, 1991).
9. There were those who were even less charitable, complaining that the equity policy was 'only good news for women's lib and equal opportunities groups' (British Airways, 1990c).
10. BEA introduced the rank of 'first class stewardesses' in the 1950s.
11. Henderson, educated at New Hall and Chelmsford, had been a qualified nurse prior to becoming a BOAC stewardess in 1950.
12. The ten women who passed the Chief Steward exam that year had between 12 and 26 years of service with the airline.
13. Female passengers were seen as largely consisting of 'secretaries going on holiday, or wives accompanying their husbands' but it was conceded that some were also 'executives travelling on business'(British Overseas Airways Corporation, 1961d).
14. The new sales opportunity was open to women 'in the seventeen to eighteen age group who have a good general knowledge of one foreign language' (British Overseas Airways Corporation, 1961d). The first three trainees were employed on 17 March 1961.
15. Wright had worked at the airline's City office for a few years and had always entertained the idea of becoming a sales representative, but job ads were always directed at male applicants. In 1970 she noticed that the 'important word 'male'' had been dropped from advertisements, so she applied and was accepted (quoted in British European Airways, 1972).
16. Both BOAC and BEA were slower than most companies to hire female sales staff due to deep-rooted resistance. In the United Kingdom women constituted a sizeable minority (37%) of those working in sales in the inter-war period (1931). By 1951 they constituted 51.5 per cent of the sales force and by 1961 they were 55 per cent. Many of these women served as counter staff in shops but some worked in other aspects of sales (Halsey, 1978).
17. In 1951, with only 15 hours flying to her credit, she won the Club's solo 'forced landing' competition.
Other women members included Yvonne Sintes, a stewardess on BOAC's South American routes (who joined in the early 1950s); Joyce Lane, a clerk in BOAC's invoice clearing section (1953); 'Miss' Stansfield, from BEA's Air Terminal (1954); Betty Dillon-Trenchard, a BEA stewardess (1955); and Sue Firmin, a stewardess on BOAC's New York route (late 1960s).
18. Adnams served as the Association's Treasurer in 1961 and Tucker became the Secretary-Treasurer in 1971.
19. Van den Hoek was originally turned down for a stewardess position because she was told she was overweight, and had to lose around 35 pounds to meet the maximum weight requirement.

20. Hook, in fact, served as a unit commander of the WJAC.
21. Hughes began flying in 1935 and was part of the very first group of female pilots to join the ATA. In July 1941 when female ATA pilots were 'cleared' to fly operational aircraft Hughes was one of four women chosen to test fly the planes. She served with the ATA – at the rank of Flight Captain – for a period of six years, ending on December 1945. From there she went on in 1946 to work as a flying instructor at the newly established London Aero Club until 1961, when she joined the BOAC/BEA flying club. When Sheila Scott was planning to break Amy Johnson's 1936 record flight to Cape Town she turned to Joan Hughes for advice (Scott, 1968: 191–92).
22. The airline pilot of the late 1960s was still strongly imaged as a man of authority and power:

> What is a captain? For centuries a ship's captain has been acknowledged as a man with virtually ... unlimited authority. He had the power of life and death ... and could marry, or bury, or clap in irons, any of his passengers or crew. An airship captain, with slightly less powers, has the same kind of responsibilities.
>
> British Overseas Airways Corporation (1968a)

Ironically neither BOAC nor BEA had any trouble in supporting Sheila Scott's bid to fly solo around the world. BOAC in particular provided constant support and advice as did Peter Masefield, the former CEO of BEA, and by then the Managing Director of the Beagle Aircraft company. BEA also sent messages of support. It appears that BOAC and BEA had little trouble with the idea of a female pilot so long as she wasn't flying for them!
23. Agazarian, a Third Officer with the ATA, served from October 1943 to September 1945.
24. One of the Autair/Court pilots was Elizabeth Overbury, described by Sheila Scott as 'the most successful and efficient woman pilot I know' (Scott, 1968). She was encouraged to fly in the late 1940s by a 'very forward-thinking' female careers teacher and, working at three jobs to pay for flying lessons, obtained a Private Pilots Licence by the time she was 17. In the late 1960s she obtained a job flying jets as a co-pilot for the Autair/Court Line, becoming one of at least six women pilots flying for commercial airlines in the United Kingdom; one of the leading British independent airlines had engaged three women pilots and three other British independent airlines each employed one woman pilot, all first officers – one flying 'a BAC 111 twin-jet, another a Carvair on the car ferry to the continent and the third a Canadair CL44 ... four-engined turbo-prop freighter' (Jackson, 1975: 79). When Autair/Court collapsed in the mid-1970s Overbury moved to Dan Air.

BALPA and the Guild of Air Pilots and Air Navigators both 'accepted women members and they were entitled to hold office' (Jackson, 1975: 79) and Sheila Scott became the first women pilot to be awarded the Guild's Silver Medal of Merit for a 'single feat'.

When, in 1965, Sheila Scott established the British Section of the Ninety Nines – a US organization of women flyers founded in 1929 with Amelia Earhart as its President – Beryl Sanders, Elizabeth Overbury and other female commercial airline pilots joined. When Scott resigned as the organization's first governor Overbury took over.

25. Once she gained her Private Pilots Licence she joined the RAF Volunteer Reserve and worked towards an Assistant Instructor's Rating in 1953. When her husband died in 1957 she was left with two young sons to look after so took up a job as a flying instructor with a newly formed commercial training flying school. After a while she moved out of instructing and joined air traffic control, becoming – in 1961 – the first woman Air Traffic Controller to work for the Ministry of Aviation.

26. In 1965 Sintes was the only female among BALPA's 2826 members. The only previous time there had been a female member of BALPA was in 1953. Although most of the male pilots at Morton Air Services were in support of the union none would take on the job of running local branch and it fell to Sintes who became the 'Pilots Local Council Chairman'. In the end all but Sintes gave in to the Company's demands and she was fired.

27. When Captain Arthur Larkman was examining pilots for an Instrument Rating Examiners' course at Stansted he was taken with the skills of pilot Beryl Sanders, 'who was remarkably good'. Indeed Sanders had established a reputation as a competitive flyer – winning air races with her co-pilot Sheila Scott. Larkman 'persuaded' Dan Air to employ Beryl Sanders as a First Officer (Simons, 1993: 113) and she became that airline's first female pilot. Gillian Cazalet and Claire Roberts soon joined her. Both friends of Sheila Scott, Roberts and Cazalet had written their commercial pilots licence exams at the same time as Scott.

    Ironically, Dan Air was slower to employ male fight attendants: it was not until 6 March 1978 that the airline graduated its first four male stewards (Simons, 1993: 143)

28. This was 12 years before BA hired Wendy Barnes and Lynn Barton.

29. In the 1970s both memberships were low, with only six women among BALPA's nearly 4500 members.

30. Numerous feminist studies have drawn attention to the role of science and mathematics in the gendering of the engineering profession (Cockburn, 1985; Cockburn, 1991a; Hacker, 1989; Keller, 1989) and the use of humour on the engineering shop floor to reinforce forms of masculinity (Collinson, 1988, 1992; Pollert, 1981).

31. A typical example is a story of 'Stewardesses Jill Mathieson and Wynifred Behenna [being] shown something of the work done in the engineering side of an airline [by watching] fitter Patrick Parks working on a "Check II" (British Overseas Airways Corporation, 1957a).

32. In the 1950s only about six per cent of engineers as a whole and fewer than four per cent of TUC-affiliated union members in the Group 5 Division of 'Engineering, Founding, and Vehicle Building' were women (Trades Union Congress, 1950; 1951). The relatively low number of female members of engineering unions may, in good part, be explained by the resistance of employers and unions alike to females entering engineering (Collinson, Knights and Collinson, 1990; Marty, Appleby and American Academy of Arts and Sciences, 1994; Pollert, 1981). Male resistance to female unionization in general is discussed elsewhere(Beynon and Blackburn, 1984; Hunt, 1984; Purcell, 1984; Walby, 1986).

33. A rare exception was a 1966 newsletter feature on female operatives, which reveals a depth of service and experience that was not usually attributed to women in engineering. It was reported,

    BOAC has 37 women operatives in the Engine Overhaul factory at Treforest of whom no fewer than four are in their 25th year of service while three more are little more than a year behind. [...] They and their 30 colleagues are engaged on the initial inspection of fuel burners, turbine and compression blades, flame tubes, anti-friction bearings, and fuel and oil pipes.

British Overseas Airways Corporation (1966d)

34. Typical of the sensemaking accounts of the (male) manager during this period is the 'portrait' of Ernest Edward Rodley, Officer in charge of training, BOAC Comet Fleet:

To be described as anything so dramatic as a 'war hero' would appall him, but you didn't get a DSO, two DFC's and an AFC for services to the camp blind. His hard-won wartime reputation for flying, leading and instructing ability, achieved during his civil flying in the early post-war years, paved the way for the achievements that crowd the recent examples of the Rodley success story ... . [One] of the first two BOAC men to learn to fly the Comet, [...] and the] world's first pilot to have his licence endorsed for a pure-jet airliner. Despite his casual, free and easy way of telling a story, the qualities that make Rodley a good instructor, [include] his pride in accuracy and thoroughness and skill.

British Overseas Airways Corporation (1954d)

35. In fact, on her retirement that year, the airline noted that Portch had risen to 'the highest office yet attained by a woman in BOAC' (British Overseas Airways Corporation, 1964a), failing to note that two other women – Lady Henderson and Pauline Gower – had held higher rank at an earlier point and Doris Clayton, Portch's predecessor, was appointed to the same position during Second World War.

The novelty of a female manager was such that it made an impression on those who joined the airline over the years. Geoffrey Pett, for example, remembers that when he joined IAL as a Commercial Trainee in 1933 'the women folk [...] were mostly secretaries or junior clerks', including Sheila Portch who was the Traffic Manager's secretary. 'Subsequently, Sheila rose to a very senior position in BOAC' (Letter to the author, November 1993). Things had not changed much when Betty Paige joined BOAC in 1946. There were some female duty officers in the lower ranks but 'the Customer Relations Manager was considered the most senior' (Paige interview, 1994).

36. Paige interview, 1994.
37. Letter to the author, from Major Michael Vaughan, 11 July 1993. Vaughan was, at one time, BEA's Personnel Manager Scotland during the time of Catherine Macpherson's term of office.
38. Vaughan letter, 1993.
39. Conditions had changed little in the airline's 'remotest places on [its] network'. Macpherson was operating out of a 'wooden hut which serves as "airport" office' (British European Airways, 1969).
40. The High Mistress of St. Paul's School, Munro joined the Board as a part-time member.
41. Lardner interview, 1994.
42. Carville interview, 1994.
43. Carville interview, 1994.
44. Hochschild (1983) has noted the use of similar strategies of handling emotional labour among US flight attendants.
44. Former American Airlines stewardess, Pauline Kane describes the process of disillusionment she experienced. She joined the airline because of the glamour and her initial expectations were more than filled, 'staying in the best hotel in the city [...], treated almost like movie stars [...], wined and dined in a frantic night life'

(Kane, 1974: 48–49). But eventually conflict between the attractions and the penalties of airline glamour confronted her in a profoundly personal way, and on one particular day she 'didn't want to put [her] uniform on, and when [she] finally forced [herself] to, [she] felt worthless, an object, a robot that wasn't supposed to have a brain. [She] looked at [her]self in the mirror again and [she] saw just a body detached from my mind' (Kane, 1974: 65). For Kane and a number of other female flight attendants the experience of emotional labour premised on sexuality took its toll. She felt like she had reached a state of rootlessness and loss of identity: 'There is a saying among stewardesses that a pilot gains his identity by putting on his uniform and a stewardess loses hers' (Kane, 1974: 73).

46. At the end of 1971 two former Eastern Airlines stewardesses – Sandra Jarrell and Jan Fulsom – organized *Stewardesses for Women's Rights* (SFWR) which played an active role over the next few years. In 1973, a group of 12 experienced stewardesses formed a group – Mary Poppins – to agitate against the airlines' age rules.

47. Carville interview, 1994. Like Lardner before her, Carville noted 'stewardesses loathed unions because they were such a privileged group'.

48. A 'closed shop' refers to a requirement that, as a condition of their contract, new employees join a designated union.

49. The earliest newsletter, the *Imperial Airways Monthly Bulletin*, was introduced in 1926 and was designed to inform staff about timetable, fares and route developments. It was soon expanded in scope to include items on 'passengers of note' and other commentary concerned with building pride in the airline (see Appendix 1). In the early 1930s the, now weekly, newsletter included reports on personnel that dealt with not only company-related issues of recruitment, postings, promotions and achievements but also items on engagements, marriages, births, and deaths. In the post-war era the newsletter's role in building company morale was made more explicit. *BEA Magazine*, for instance, was redesigned in 'accordance with the desire of the General Manager (Staff and Services)' to 'tell' staff 'what B.E.A. is doing and what are its aims; it will tell you of our successes and mistakes. It will be something to which you can all contribute ideas; it will help us to know one another even if we are far apart, and you must help to make it something of which we can all be proud' (British European Airways, 1947c). At BOAC senior management believed that the newsletter was a useful way to pass 'information and plans, decisions, research and thinking up and down the line of authority'(British Overseas Airways Corporation, 1959b), with the aim of promoting 'a better sense of common purpose and a better team spirit throughout the corporation' (British Overseas Airways Corporation, 1959c).

50. Following Second World War the newly established BEA consulted the editors of 'various old-established journals' including the editor of *Shell Magazine* who provided a number of useful insights (Mills, 1996: 195). The company hired Eric Cecil ('Cheese') Cheesman as founding editor of the new *BEA Magazine*. Cheesman edited the magazine over the next 15 years, until 1961. Like many of those in positions of authority, Cheesman's wartime record figured largely in his recruitment to BEA. He served as a Probationary Flight Officer with the RNAS during First World War and was driver for the ATA during the Second World War (British Airways, 1975a). With his retirement the editorship fell to a series of other male editors. Similarly the BOAC in-house newsletters were edited and staffed by male employees. Raymond Bassett, for example, edited the *BOAC Review* in the mid-1960s. Bill Stevens was the Assistant Editor (1970–72) and then the Editor (1972–74) of *BOAC News*. Stevens had previously been a journalist with the *Daily Mirror* and the *Sunday*

Express before joining the airline. Even in the mid-1960s the editor, staff writers, printers and supervisory staff of *BEA Magazine* were all men. The women working on the magazine included a secretary, a handful of packers and a newly appointed staff writer – Gillian Edwards (British European Airways, 1965c).

51. In response, John Tilsley, the manager of Selection Services, agreed that 'BOAC experience can outweigh academic qualifications' but only for certain jobs: '[The] number of jobs requiring specialist qualifications tends to increase as the airline business becomes more and more advanced and it has to be admitted that it is not as easy for women over 40 to obtain specialist qualifications as it is for the younger ones' (ibid.).

52. In December 1973, for example, Beverly Taylor became the first woman 'in the South-West Pacific' to be promoted to Chief Reservations Officer.

53. In fact, there was at least one other female engineer – Doris Smith – who joined BOAC in 1941 and became the airline's 'first woman development engineer' in 1961 (British Airways, 1975b). Smith retired in August 1975 and was replaced by Patricia Smith.

54. Pilots were also feeling the pinch from a greatly increased tempo of work (Hudson and Pettifer, 1979).

55. In her opinion the stewardess 'still had to have languages' but not 'the same educational qualifications [as] earlier on. Once there were the 747s [jumbo jets] you were recruiting about one thousand more people in a very short space of time. So there were big changes in demand. [The airline] wanted to choose girls who would more emphasize with' the new types of passenger being flown (Carville interview, 1994).

56. Tancred-Sheriff (1989) refers to this as auxiliary emotion work.

57. One of the women, who was retiring from the company after 33 years, is credited with the development of promotional ideas – such as fashions for travelling and beauty kits – 'that treated the women passenger as a traveller in her own right'. The other woman – Marion Porter – is heralded as 'the mother who is going back to school'. Here the focus is on how a female manager copes with issues of childcare, as she becomes the first women in the company to 'attend a specific management training course'. Porter is quoted as saying: 'The big handicap was that when women got married and had children, they gave up their jobs. If they had a senior job, they couldn't come back to it. I had a marvellous boss in Betty Cook and we agreed that, if women were allowed to do this in countries like Japan and America, why weren't they allowed to do this in Britain?' (British Airways, 1976a).

58. One writer pointed out that large numbers of female employees were between the ages of 15 and 45, and reminded readers that surveys of exiting female staff indicated that pregnancy accounted for 28 per cent (British Airways, 1977c). In response a self-described 'mere married male chauvinist pig with three children' contended that women have children 'with a view to staying at home, enjoying them and encouraging their development' (British Airways, 1977d). Other contributors to the debate agreed that the man was indeed a 'male chauvinist pig'.

59. The men's uniforms included a set of gold rings on the sleeve which indicated 'the wearer's status in the company hierarchy', while the women's uniform was adorned with 'cute little stars' that could be 'taken as decoration' (British Airways, 1977d). Other readers wrote in to argue against the use of rank markings on any uniform in a 'modern, jet-propelled, egalitarian society' (British Airways, 1977e).

60. Using the analogy of gestalt psychology (Kohler, 1961), it can be argued that an organization takes on a particular gendered form or shape for individuals, whose perceptions are influenced by a configuration of rules and associated behaviours.

The sense of gender of a female airline clerical worker, for example, may be influenced by a context in which various masculinities (e.g., piloting, managing, engineering) are valued over femininities, and in which some femininities, such as stewarding, are highlighted over others.

61. Crick expressed the hope that she would 'be treated just like any other instructor' (British Airways, 1979a).

62. *BA News* hailed this as a defeat for 'the anti-feminist lobby' and quoted her male colleagues as having 'no objections' to her presence even though it stops them 'from behaving childishly' (British Airways, 1979b). Barton is quoted as hoping to marry one day but accepting the impossibility of 'integrating marriage, children, and a career as a full-time pilot' (British Airways, 1979b).

63. He was influenced in his decision by Jan Carlzon's apparent success at SAS (Carlzon, 1987) and commissioned the same consultants to help BA through the process.

64. When Marshall joined BA in February 1983 it was 'obvious' that 'the organization was extremely introverted [and] had really no grasp of what the market place wanted, what the customer wanted' (quoted in Hampden-Turner, 1990: 86). Subsequent surveys indicated that customers found BA staff to 'be professional and competent but 'cold, aloof, uncaring and bureaucratic' in their responses to customers' (Hampden-Turner, 1990: 87).

65. Marshall had spent a lifetime in the service industry, beginning as a purser with the Orient Steam Navigation Company, before working his way up the corporate ladder of Hertz and then on to Avis where he ended up as Chief Executive Officer.

66. Dr. Nick Georgiades, a former university lecturer in occupational psychology, was appointed as BA's Human Relations Director in 1984, and was strongly committed to the management of emotional labour. Curiously, although he clearly borrowed the term from Hochschild's (1983) study of the damaging effects of emotional labour on flight attendants (and debt collectors), Georgiades cautioned that 'we have not realized what this sort of labour costs those who do it for a living' (quoted in Hampden-Turner, 1990: 88–89).

67. Employees were told: 'If you feel OK about yourself you are more likely to feel OK about dealing with other people' (Young, 1989). Staff were taught to 'express feelings about their jobs, set personal goals and re-examine all their relationships so that they would be seen as whole people, not just roles' (Mike Bruce, quoted in Hampden-Turner, 1990: 90). Yet customer satisfaction remained paramount. Colin Marshall told staff that, 'We have always to treat the passenger with that extra touch of warmth, and with a smile' (British Airways, 1983). For Georgiades, caring for employees was linked to concern with customer satisfaction and organizational success: 'We have to take care of one another because it is only by doing that that we ensure that, in turn, we care for the customer. It is only by caring for the customer that we continue to exist' (ibid.). Asked what he meant by 'caring', Georgiades explained:

> It is not a sloppy, sentimental caring. It is more a sense of support. We have to ensure our people are managed in a sensitive and intelligent way which takes account of their needs as helpers, providers of service, whether they serve our customers directly or serve the staff that do. Everyone must have opportunities for personal growth in terms of training, and a chance to think and rethink what it is they are trying to achieve at work. Also, we have to ensure that people work in teams, generating a feeling of team spirit in understanding one another's work; so we can spot when one of us needs help, and give assistance.
>
> (ibid.)

68. Soon after his appointment someone addressed Colin Marshall by the military term 'CX' (for chief executive) and he responded sharply, saying 'My name is Colin Marshall. I'd like you all to remember that' (Hampden-Turner, 1990: 86). There were also changes to the uniforms. The pilots' uniform retained an air force look but the rings denoting rank were dropped. All other uniforms were designed around a corporate identity of customer service, losing much of its air force reference points in the process (Labich, 1988; Reed, 1990).

69. According to Mike Bruce (1987: 25–26) of the HR Department:

> The company was aware that the attitudes and management style it was seeking were very different from the prevailing ethos. Many managers had joined British Airways from the RAF soon after the war and brought a military approach to management with them. Subsequent managers tended to be recruited on the basis of analytical skills or intellectual capacity rather than experience of managing a service industry [...] British Airways was a classical transport bureaucracy, somewhat analogous to the railways, whose primary agenda was to keep the aircraft flying safely [...] As with all such cultures performance was organised by roles and procedures. The underlying values were order, rationality, dependability, and system. The belief was that performance could be monitored by information systems rather than by face-to-face contact with people who do the work. Essentially the relationships were paternalistic but impersonal and depersonalised.

70. From flying through the air with a tray of food and drinks ready to serve passengers, to rescuing a lost briefcase for a harried male passenger.

71. The old practice of using female sexuality to stress the power of the male office holder was still very much alive and well. In photographs of senior male managers it seemed almost compulsory to picture each individual flanked by attractive young females. For example, at the launch of new uniforms for *all* uniformed staff in 1985 Colin Marshall is pictured with four 'stewardesses' in their 'new outfits' (British Airways, 1985b).

72. These charts are one means of depicting what Kanter (1977) calls the 'opportunity structure' of an organization.

73. Gehring, in charge of Training (Customer), is one of fifty General Managers at the fifth and lowest level of the hierarchy.

74. Val Gooding, the highest placed female manager, is at the fourth layer of the hierarchy – two layers below the directorship level; Gail Redwood and Eva Lauermann are at the fifth level; with Rosanne Beal, Dr. Sandra Mooney, Caroline Boone, Claire Lane and Helen Cahill at the sixth level. Jean Cowan is found at the eighth and lowest level of the Health Services Division.

75. Towards the top, answering only to the Head and Deputy Head, was Gillian Parker the 'World Sales Support Manager'.

76. The Division's chart for October 1986 includes Ann Doggert, the Operations Training Manager, who is only below the General Manager and his Deputy. At the next level below is Valerie Scoulam as Passenger Services Manager. In 1992 Scoulam became only the third woman to join the Executive of BA (see Figure 7.1). Three levels below Scoulam is Jane Lloyd and Siobhan Simpson and, below them, Jennie Anderson and Barbara Gayford.

77. The September 1986 organizational chart shows Ruth Gillespie ('Head of HR') on the third layer, with Marilyn Cox ('General Manager and Department Head of Product Brands') at the fourth layer.

78. Those areas where women constituted a significant minority included Cabin Services, Human Resources and Marketing Services. The respective charts indicate that of senior managers women constituted 3 of 12 in Cabin Services, 10 of 33 in Human Resources, and 17 of 38 in Marketing Services in the period December 1988 to March 1989 (see Table 7.3). Despite the fact that Cabin Services had been dominated by female employees for much of that post-Second World War era men had occupied almost all the senior management positions until now. As it moved into the 1990s Patricia Stanley and Val Gooding were the respective Cabin Services Chiefs for Wide Bodied Aircraft (WBA) at Gatwick and UK Stations. Judy Robson was Cabin Crew Training Manager. Three years later Gooding became the third women ever to serve on the Executive. In the new Human Resources Division Janet Gunn and Eva Lauermann served as two of the six General Managers below the Director, Robert Ayling.

79. Interestingly, the Baroness – Detta O'Cathain – was one of the very few people outside of the airline to join the board with commercial airline experience. She had started her working career in the mid-1950s as an accounts clerk with Aer Lingus, before serving as an assistant economist with the airline from 1959 to 1966. She resigned from the Board of BA in July 2004 amidst charges of homophobia.

80. Jane Johnston became the first female editor of *British Airways News* in the early 1990s and her deputy, Yolanda Foster, succeeded her in the mid-1990s.

81. For example, Barbara Harmer, 'the world's only commercial female supersonic pilot and a British Airways Concorde Senior First Officer'(British Airways, 1997), was often featured in *BA News* and corporate press releases as were other female pilots.

82. Fourteen years later, although still silent on the issue of homosexuality, BA contributed to a series of events designed to raise awareness of AIDS. Symbolic red ribbons were tied on BA's giant Concorde model at London's Heathrow Airport as support for World Aids Awareness.

83. Interview with the author, summer 1995. The name William Davis is a pseudonym.

84. 'Visible minorities' is a term used by the Canadian Royal Commission on Equality in Employment (Abella, 1984: 46) and is defined as 'people who [are] visibly non-white'. The newsletters were randomly selected in so far as they were among the few in the possession of the author.

85. See for example, Cooper v. Delta Airlines (filed in 1967), Neal v. American Airlines, Inc (1968) and Colvin v. Piedmont Aviation, Inc. (1968), which all challenged airline 'no marriage' rules (Nielsen, 1982).

86. Ironically, the lower court deemed that the plaintiff was not eligible to be a flight attendant because, at age 30, he was too old (Nielsen, 1982: 98).

87. According to the airline, the number of employees was around the national average of the 'total female work force (ranging from 27% to 31%)' but argued that its percentage of female managers compared badly with American Airlines, Eastern Air Lines, TWA and UAL that 'report a slightly larger proportion of women in management (ranging from 8.2 percent to 10.4 percent)' (Pan American Airways, 1974a). The following year the number of female managers rose to 8.1 percent (Pan American Airways, 1974b).

88. In fact Pan Am inherited a female pilot – Susan Horstman – when it merged with National Airlines in 1980. Pan Am retained Horstman, who became a pilot for National in 1979, but they failed to hire any female pilots for seven more years.

89. See for example Gandt (1995).

90. The 'October Crisis' in Quebec exacerbated the situation in 1970, when the *Liberation Front of Quebec* (FLQ) was involved in bombings and the kidnapping and murder of a government minister in 1970. In response the federal government of Pierre Trudeau invoked the War Measures Act, putting the province under a form of martial law.

91. Pratte felt that he was resented by a number of people throughout the airline because of his French–Canadian background and the political nature of his appointment. Others contend that if he was resented it was more likely because of his position as CEO and the decisions he took (Smith, 1986: 292).

92. Judy Cameron – in April 1978; but this was exactly five years after rival Canadian International Airways (CIA) introduced its first female pilot – Rosella Bjornson.

Bibliography

Abella, R. S. (1984) *Equity in Employment. A Royal Commission Report.* Ottawa, Canada: Ministry of Supply and Services.

Acker, J. (1990) 'Hierarchies, jobs, bodies: A theory of gendered organizations', *Gender & Society*, 4, 139–58.

—— (1992) 'Gendering Organizational Theory'. In A. J. Mills and P. Tancred (Eds), *Gendering Organizational Analysis*: 248–60. Newbury Park, CA: Sage.

Air Canada. (1969) 'First woman exec. named', *Between Ourselves*, October (334), 1.

—— (1973a) 'Female duty manager. Barbara's job a victory'? *Horizons*, December 3 (401), 6.

—— (1973b) 'Personnel policies spell out equality', *Horizons*, August 30 (395), 6.

—— (1975a) 'Air Canada's world of women', *Horizons*, December 15 (449), 4–5, 7.

—— (1975b) 'The world of women', *Horizons*, June 16 (437), 6–7.

Air Transport World. (2004) 'World Airline Financial Results 2003', Air Transport World ATWOnline, http://www.atwonline.com/channels/dataAirlineEconomics/index. html (accessed 15 August 2005).

Allen, O. E. (1986) *The Airline Builders* (Third edn). Alexandria, VA: Time-Life Books.

Allen, R. (1978) *Pictorial History of KLM.* London: Ian Allan.

Anderson, B. S. and Zinsser, J. P. (1988) *A History of Their Own. Women in Europe.* New York: Harper & Row.

Armstrong, P. and Armstrong, H. (1986) *The Double Ghetto. Canadian Women and their Segregated Work* (Revised edn). Toronto: McClelland and Stewart.

Armstrong, W. (1952) *Pioneer Pilot.* London: Blandford Press.

Association of Flight Attendants – CWA. (2005) 'Milestones', Washignton, DC Association of Flight Attendants – CWA, http://www.afanet.org/default.asp? nc56336&id537 (24 October).

Baker, T. and Jones, R. (1967) *Coffee, Tea or Me? The uninhibited Memoirs of Two Airline Stewardesses*: Bartholomew House.

Bamford, J. (1986) *Croissant at Croydon.* London: London Borough of Sutton Libraries & Arts Services.

Bao, P. L. (1989) *An Illustrated History of British European Airways.* Feltham, Middlesex: Browcom Group Plc.

Barrett, F. J. (1996) 'The Organizational Construction of Hegemonic Masculinity: The Case of the US Navy', *Gender, Work & Organization*, 3 (3), 129–42.

Beauman, K. B. (1971) *Partners in Blue. The story of women's service with the Royal Air Force.* London: Hutchinson.

Ben-Tovim, G. and Gabriel, J. (1984) 'The politics of race in Britain, 1962–1979: a review of the major trends and of recent debates'. In C. Husband (Ed.), *'Race' in Britain. Continuity and Change*: 145–74. London: Hutchinson.

Bender, M. and Altschul, S. (1982) *The Chosen Instrument. Juan Trippe. Pan Am. The rise and fall of an American entrepreneur.* New York: Simon & Schuster.

Benschop, Y. and Meihuizen, H. E. (2002) 'Reporting gender. Representations of gender in financial and annual reports'. In I. Aaltio and A. J. Mills (Eds), *Gender, Identity and the Culture of Organizations*: 160–84. London: Routledge.

Benson, S. P. (1978) ' "The Clerking Sisterhood." Rationalization and the Work Culture of Saleswomen in American Department Stores, 1890–1960', *Radical America*, 12, 41–55.

—— (1981) 'The Cinderella of Occupations: Managing the Work of Department Store Saleswomen, 1900–1940', *Business History Review*, LV (1), 1–25.

—— (1986) *Counter cultures: Saleswomen, managers, and customers in American department stores, 1890–1940*. Urbana.: University of Illinois Press.

Best, S. and Kellner, D. (1991) *Postmodern Theory. Critical Interrogations*. New York: The Guildford Press.

Beynon, H. and Blackburn, R. (1984) 'Unions: the men's affair'? In J. Siltanen and M. Stanworth (Eds), *Women and the Public Sphere*: 75–88. London: Hutchinson.

Bickerstaffe, G. and Hill, R. (1988) 'Profile: Sir Colin Marshall. A career in service', *Director* (June), 46–49.

Blackler, F. (1992) 'Formative Contexts and Activity Systems: Postmodern Approaches to the Management of Change'. In M. Reed and M. Hughes (Eds), *Rethinking Organization*: 273–94. London: Sage.

Bourdieu, P. (1977) *Outline of a theory of practice*. Cambridge; New York: Cambridge University Press.

Bousquet, B. and Douglas, C. (1991) *West Indian Women At War. British Racism in World War II*. London: Lawrence & Wishart.

Bowen, E. (1980) *Knights of the Air*. Alexandria, Virginia: Time-Life Books.

Braverman, H. (1974) *Labor and Monopoly Capital*. New York: Monthly Review Press.

Bray, W. (1975) *The History of B.O.A.C., 1939–1974*. Camberly, Surrey: Wessex Press.

Braybon, G. and Summerfield, P. (1987) *Out of the cage: women's experiences in two world wars*. New York: Pandora Press.

British Airways. (1967) 'Pricilla Joins Heathrow', *British Airways News* (25), 15 September.

—— (1973) 'Editorial', *British Airways News*, 1 (December).

—— (1974a) *British Airways News* (24 May).

—— (1974b) *British Airways News* (15), 22 March.

—— (1975a) *Topline*, 2 (4), April.

—— (1975b) *British Airways News* (88), 11 August.

—— (1976a) *British Airways News* (105), 9 January.

—— (1976b) *British Airways News* (146), 29 October.

—— (1976c) 'British Airways News', *British Airways News* (28 May).

—— (1976d) 'Group Instruction No. 53', *Memorandum from the Managing Director to group managers*, 12 March.

—— (1977a) *British Airways News* (183), 29 July.

—— (1977b) *British Airways News* (181), 15 July.

—— (1977c) *British Airways News* (160), 11 February.

—— (1977d) *British Airways News* (161), 8 February.

—— (1977e) *British Airways News* (165), 18 March.

—— (1978a) *British Airways News* (234), 4 August.

—— (1978b) *British Airways News* (225), 2 June.

—— (1978c) 'Policy on Racial Discrimination', *BA Internal Memorandum* (27 June).

—— (1979a) *British Airways News* (259), 2 February.

—— (1979b) *British Airways News* (262), 23 February.

—— (1983) *British Airways News* (466), 1 July.

—— (1985a) *British Airways News* (May 3).

—— (1985b) *British Airways News*, June 14.

—— (1988a) *British Airways News* (December 16), December16.

—— (1988b) *British Airways News* (December 2).

—— (1990a) *British Airways News* (787), February 9.

—— (1990b) *British Airways News* (April 6).

—— (1990c) *British Airways News* (March 2).

—— (1991) *British Airways News* (877), November 1

—— (1994) 'Special Anniversary Issue (insert)', *British Airways News* (August).

—— (1997) 'BA on-line press release', http://press.britishairways.com (October 3).

British European Airways. (1947a) *Annual Report, 1946–1947*. London: HMSO.

—— (1947b) 'A Christmas Letter from Mr. Gerard d'Erlanger', *B.E.A. Magazine* (5), Christmas.

—— (1947c) 'Editorial', *B.E.A. Magazine* (5), Christmas.

—— (1947d) 'We Had To Kill The Stewardess', *BEA Magazine*, September.

—— (1948a) *B.E.A. Magazine*, November (10).

—— (1948b) *B.E.A. Magazine*, June (5).

—— (1948c) *B.E.A. Magazine*, March.

—— (1948d) 'B.E.A. Areas No.6. The Scottish Division', *B.E.A. Magazine* (10), Christmas, 5–12.

—— (1948e) 'Orchids for Terminella', *B.E.A. Magazine*, June.

—— (1949a) *B.E.A. Magazine*, September (16).

—— (1949b) 'Chairman's Message', *B.E.A. Magazine* (18), November.

—— (1949c) 'Message from Chairman', *B.E.A. Magazine* (12), April.

—— (1949d) 'Profile No. 7', *B.E.A. Magazine* (16), September.

—— (1950a) *B.E.A. Magazine* (25), June.

—— (1950b) *B.E.A. Magazine*, 23 (April).

—— (1952a) *B.E.A. Magazine*, February.

—— (1952b) *B.E.A. Magazine* (45), April.

—— (1954) *B.E.A. Magazine* (66), March.

—— (1955a) *B.E.A. Magazine* (78), April.

—— (1955b) 'Saga of a Stewardess', *B.E.A. Magazine*, January (75).

—— (1956a) *B.E.A. Magazine* (86), January.

—— (1956b) *Annual Report, 1955–1956*. London: H.M.S.O.

—— (1960a) *B.E.A. Magazine*, January.

—— (1960b) *B.E.A. Magazine* (135), July.

—— (1961) '1,000 Bar One', *B.E.A. Magazine* (147), August.

—— (1962) *B.E.A. Magazine* (156), May.

—— (1965a) *B.E.A. Magazine* (189), February.

—— (1965b) *B.E.A. Magazine* (196), September.

—— (1965c) *B.E.A. Magazine* (January).

—— (1967) 'Matcha Pretty Face', *B.E.A. Magazine*, May.

—— (1968) *B.E.A. Magazine* (227), May.

—— (1969) *B.E.A. Magazine* (237), March.

—— (1972) *B.E.A. Magazine* (281), November.

British Overseas Airways Corporation. (1940a) *B.O.A.C. Newsletter*, 7 (August).

—— (1940b) *B.O.A.C. Newsletter*, 8 (September).

—— (1940c) 'Cost of Living Bonus. Notice To UK Staff. No. 26', (11 October).

—— (1940d) 'Draft Notice to be posted up in each office of Grand Spa Hotel', (11 October).

—— (1940e) 'Editorial: What's in a Name', *B.O.A.C. Newsletter*, 11 (December).

—— (1940f) 'Goodbye to Marguerite Mundy', *B.O.A.C. Newsletter*, 11 (December).

British Overseas Airways Corporation. (1940g) 'Memorandum from the Administrative Director to Heads of Department', (17 July). British Overseas Airways Corporation (1940h) 'Nairobi', *B.O.A.C. Newsletter*, 10 (November).

—— (1940i) 'Staff vacancy Notice No. 14', (27 December).

—— (1941a) *BOAC Newsletter*, 21 (October).

—— (1941b) *Annual Report*. London: HMSO.

—— (1941c) 'El Geneina', *B.O.A.C. Newsletter*, 18 (July).

—— (1941d) 'Kisumu', *B.O.A.C. Newsletter*, 16 (May).

—— (1941e) 'Memorandum from G.E.O. to C.A'., (1 May).

—— (1941f) 'Sudan Outpost', *BOAC Newsletter*, 14 (March).

—— (1942a) *B.O.A.C. Newsletter*, 29 (June).

—— (1942b) *B.O.A.C. Newsletter*, 28 (May).

—— (1942c) *B.O.A.C. Newsletter*, 24 (January).

—— (1942d) *B.O.A.C. Newsletter*, 31 (August).

—— (1942e) *B.O.A.C. Newsletter*, 32 (September).

—— (1942f) *B.O.A.C. Newsletter*, 25 (February).

—— (1942g) 'Femininity in Baltimore', *B.O.A.C. Newsletter*, 31 (August).

—— (1942h) 'Our Women at War', *B.O.A.C. Newsletter*, 29 (June).

—— (1942i) 'Stewards-To-Be', *B.O.A.C. Newsletter*, 34 (November).

—— (1944a) *BOAC Newsletter*, 57 (October).

—— (1944b) '25 Years Ago – Our First Air Service', *BOAC Newsletter*, 55 (August).

—— (1945a) *BOAC Handbook*. London: HMSO.

—— (1945b) 'The A.T.A'., *B.O.A.C. Newsletter* (August).

—— (1946a) *BOAC News Letter*, 6 (September).

—— (1946b) *BOAC News Letter*, 72 (January).

—— (1946c) *Speedbird*, 3 (June).

—— (1946d) *Annual Report*. London: HMSO.

—— (1946e) 'Congratulations', *BOAC News Letter*, 9 (December).

—— (1946f) 'The Men Who Came Back', *B.O.A.C. News Letter* (October).

—— (1946g) 'Mrs. D. Clayton. Chairman's Tribute at Farewell Party', *Speedbird*, 5 (August).

—— (1947a) *BOAC News Letter*, 13 (April).

—— (1947b) 'Art of the Steward', *B.O.A.C. News Letter*, 20 (November).

—— (1947c) *B.O.A.C. Annual Report, 1947*. London: HMSO.

—— (1947d) 'By air to 'Aladdin's Cave', *BOAC News Letter* (10), January.

—— (1947e) 'Chairman's African Tour', *BOAC News Letter*, 10 (January).

—— (1947f) 'White Waltham's Only Woman Engineer', *BOAC News Letter*, 12 (March).

—— (1948a) *BOAC News Letter* (February).

—— (1948b) *BOAC News Letter* (April).

—— (1948c) *B.O.A.C. Annual Report, 1948*. London: HMSO.

—— (1948d) 'Chairman's New Year Message', *B.O.A.C. News Letter* (22), January.

—— (1948e) 'The Two 'Babies', *B.O.A.C. News*, October.

—— (1949a) *BOAC News Letter*, 37 (April).

—— (1949b) *B.O.A.C. Annual Report, 1949*. London: H.M.S.O.

—— (1949c) 'Beauty and the Beast', *B.O.A.C. News*, October.

—— (1949d) 'Obituary: Mrs.Mac', *B.O.A.C. Review*, 41 (August).

—— (1950a) *B.O.A.C. Review* (51), June.

—— (1950b) *BOAC Review* (August).

—— (1950c) *B.O.A.C. Review* (46), January.

—— (1950d) 'Pygmy Land', *BOAC News Letter*, October.

—— (1951) 'Cover Girl', *B.O.A.C Review*, March.

—— (1952) 'Advertisement. More Pilots Needed', *B.O.A.C. Review* (January).

—— (1953) *B.O.A.C. Review* (January).

—— (1954a) *B.O.A.C. Review* (March).

—— (1954b) *BOAC News Letter* (May).

—— (1954c) *B.O.A.C. Annual Report 1953–1954*. London: HMSO.

—— (1954d) 'Portrait of a Pioneer', *B.O.A.C. Review*, August.

—— (1955a) *B.O.A.C. Review* (April).

—— (1955b) *B.O.A.C. Review* (June).

—— (1957a) *B.O.A.C. Review* (December).

—— (1957b) *B.O.A.C. Review* (February).

—— (1957c) *B.O.A.C. Review*, June.

—— (1957d) 'Advertisement. *Your* Chance To Fly – Engineering Officers Needed', *B.O.A.C. Review* (November).

—— (1958a) *B.O.A.C Review*, January.

—— (1958b) *B.O.A.C. Review* (June).

—— (1958c) 'Picture of the Month', *B.O.A.C Review*, January.

—— (1959a) *B.O.A.C. Review* (November).

—— (1959b) *B.O.A.C. News*, 1 (40), October 16.

—— (1959c) *B.O.A.C. News*, 1 (1), January 9.

—— (1959d) *B.O.A.C. News*, 1 (18), May 15.

—— (1959e) 'It's A Woman's World – They've Even Invaded Judo', *B.O.A.C. Review* (December).

—— (1959f) 'Job of the Month', *B.O.A.C Review*, January.

—— (1959g) 'Wanted 500 Stewards and Stewardesses', *B.O.A.C. Review* (November).

—— (1960a) *B.O.A.C. News* (63), April 1.

—— (1960b) *B.O.A.C. Annual Report 1960*. London: HMSO.

—— (1960c) 'Shirley – First Asian Girl in Flight Ops'? *B.O.A.C. News* (82), 19 August.

—— (1961a) *B.O.A.C. Review*, October.

—— (1961b) *B.O.A.C Review*, August.

—— (1961c) *B.O.A.C. Review* (November).

—— (1961d) 'Advertisement. Wanted – Saleswomen', *B.O.A.C. News* (110), March 10.

—— (1961e) *B.O.A.C. Annual Report, 1960–1961*. London: H.M.S.O.

—— (1961f) 'East Goes Further West', *B.O.A.C. News* (149), 15 December.

—— (1961g) 'East Meets West', *B.O.A.C Review*, January.

—— (1962a) *B.O.A.C. Review* (196), November 20.

—— (1962b) *B.O.A.C. Review* (November).

—— (1962c) *B.O.A.C. Review* (March).

—— (1962d) *B.O.A.C. Review*, December.

—— (1962e) *B.O.A.C. News* (192), November 2.

—— (1962f) 'Women in a 'Man's World', *B.O.A.C. Review* (April).

—— (1963a) *B.O.A.C. News* (249), December 20.

—— (1963b) *B.O.A.C. Review*, June.

—— (1963c) *B.O.A.C. Review* (October).

—— (1964a) *B.O.A.C. Review* (January).

—— (1964b) *B.O.A.C. Review* (April).

—— (1964c) *B.O.A.C. Review*, July.

—— (1964d) *B.O.A.C. Review* (October).

—— (1965a) *B.O.A.C. News* (308), 19 February.

—— (1965b) *B.O.A.C. News* (309), 26 February.

British Airways Overseas Corporation (1965c) 'Sunshine Smiles', *B.O.A.C News*.

—— (1965d) 'Women's World. Miss Eileen R. 'Minnie' Mann', *BOAC Review* (April).

—— (1966a) *B.O.A.C. Review* (375), 24 June.

—— (1966b) *B.O.A.C. Review* (July).

—— (1966c) *B.O.A.C. News* (386), 9 September.

—— (1966d) *B.O.A.C. News* (372), 3 June.

—— (1966e) 'Battle of the Stiff Collar Won Our Girls Freedom to be Feminine', *B.O.A.C. Review* (April).

—— (1966f) 'Pick a Pretty Face', *B.O.A.C. Review*, November.

—— (1967a) *B.O.A.C. News* (157), July.

—— (1967b) *B.O.A.C. News* (25), 15 September.

—— (1967c) 'In a Woman's World, Ron Is the Odd Man Out', *B.O.A.C. News* (19), August 4.

—— (1968a) *B.O.A.C. News* (52), March 29.

—— (1968b) *B.O.A.C. News* (80), October 4.

—— (1968c) *B.O.A.C. Review* (February).

—— (1968d) 'Take Note! Here's How To Treat A Boss', *B.O.A.C. News* (81), 11 October.

—— (1969) *B.O.A.C. News* (118), 11 July.

—— (1970a) *B.O.A.C. News* (183), 23 October.

—— (1970b) *B.O.A.C. News* (181), October 9.

—— (1970c) *B.O.A.C. News* (180), October 2.

—— (1971a) *B.O.A.C. News* (213), June 4.

—— (1971b) *B.O.A.C. News* (223), 13 August.

—— (1972) *B.O.A.C. News* (276), 1 September.

—— (1973) *B.O.A.C. News* (338), November 23.

—— (undated) 'Compensation for War Injuries for Civilians. Notice to UK Staff No. 25', (British Airways Archive Collection, London).

Bruce, M. (1987) 'Managing People First – Bringing the Service Concept to British Airways', *ICT* (March/April), 21–26.

Bryman, A. (1986) *Leadership and Organizations*. London: Routledge & Kegan Paul.

Burns, G. E. (2005) 'The War Years', *Pan American World Airways*, 11 (4), http://www.panam.org/cgi-bin/_textdisplay_0.asp?display=WARYEARS&refer=696964263&call=D.

Burrell, G. (1984) 'Sex and Organizational Analysis', *Organization Studies*, 5 (2), 97–118.

—— (1987) 'No accounting for sexuality'. *Accounting, Organizations, and Society*, 12, 89–101.

—— (1992) 'Sex and Organizational Analysis'. In A. J. Mills and P. Tancred (Eds), *Gendering Organizational Analysis*: 71–92. Newbury Park, CA.: Sage.

Burrows, W. E. (1972) *Richthofen*. London: Granada Publishing.

Butler, C. (2002) *Postmodernism: A Very Short Introduction*. Oxford: Oxford University Press.

Cadogan, M. (1992) *Women with Wings*. London: MacMillan.

Calder, A. (1969) *The People's War 1939–1945*. London: Cape.

Calás, M. B. and Smircich, L. (1992) 'Using the "F" word: Feminist theories and the social consequences of organizational research'. In A. J. Mills and P. Tancred (Eds), *Gendering Organizational Analysis*: 222–234. Newbury Park, CA: Sage.

—— (1996) 'From "The Woman's" Point of View: Feminist Approaches to Organization Studies'. In S. R. Clegg, C. Hardy and W. R. Nord (Eds), *Handbook of Organization Studies*: 218–257. London: Sage.

Campbell-Smith, D. (1986) *Struggle for Take-Off. The British Airways Story*. London: Coronet/Hodder & Stoughton.

Carlzon, J. (1987) *Moments of Truth*. Cambridge, MA: Ballinger Publishing Co.

City of Yellowknife. (1984) *Yellowknife Homecoming*. Yellowknife: City of Yellowknife.

Clegg, S. (1981) 'Organization and Control', *Administrative Sciences Quarterly*, 26, 532–545.

Cluett, D., Nash, J. and Learmonth, B. (1980) *Croydon Airport 1928–1939. The Great Days*. Sutton, Surrey: London Borough of Sutton Libraries & Arts Services.

Cockburn, C. (1985) *Machinery of Dominance*. London: Pluto Press.

—— (1991a) *Brothers. Male Dominance and Technological Change*. London: Pluto Press.

—— (1991b) *In The Way of Women: Men's Resistance to Sex Equality in Organizations*. Ithaca, New York: ILR Press.

Cohn, S. (1985) *The Process of Occupational Sex-Typing. The Feminization of Clerical Labour in Great Britain*. Philadelphia: Temple University.

Collier, B. (1959) *Heavenly Adventurer. Sefton Brancker and the Dawn of British Aviation*. London: Secker & Warburg.

Collins, D. H. (1978) *Wings Across Time. The story of Air Canada*. Toronto: Griffin House.

Collinson, D. L. (1988) 'Engineering humour: Masculinity, Joking and Conflict in Shopfloor Relations', *Organization Studies*, 9 (2), 181–99.

—— (1992) *Managing the Shopfloor: Subjectivity, Masculinity and Workplace Culture*. Berlin: de Gruyter & Co.

Collinson, D. L. and Hearn, J. (1994) 'Naming Men as Men: Implications for Work, Organization and Management', *Gender, Work and Organization*, 1 (1), 2–22.

—— (Eds). (1996) *Men as Managers, Managers as Men*. London: Sage.

Collinson, D. L., Knights, D. and Collinson, M. (1990) *Managing to Discriminate*. London: Routledge.

Connell, R. W. (1987) *Gender and Power*. Stanford: Stanford University Press.

—— (1995) *Masculinities*. Berkeley, CA: University of California Press.

Corke, A. (1986) *British Airways. The Path to Profitability*. London: Frances Pinter.

Corman, S. R. (2000) 'The Need for Common Ground'. In S. R. Corman and M. S. Poole (Eds), *Perspectives on Organizational Communication*: 3–13. New York: The Guilford Press.

Corn, J. J. (1983) *The Winged Gospel. America's Romance With Aviation, 1900–1950*. New York: Oxford University Press.

Crompton, R. and Jones, G. (1984) *White-Collar Proletariat: Deskilling and Gender in Clerical Work*. London: The Macmillan Press Ltd.

Curtis, L. (1985) *The Forgotten Pilots*. London: The Eastern Press.

Czarniawska, B. and Calás, M. B. (1997) 'Another Country: Explaining Gender Discrimination with 'Culture'', *Hallinnon [Finnish Journal of Administrative Studies]*, 4, 326–41.

Daley, R. (1980) *An American Saga. Juan Trippe and His Pan Am Empire*. New York: Random House.

Davis, N. Z. (1994) 'What is women's history'? In J. Gardiner (Ed.), *What is history today?* 85–87. London: Macmillan.

Dawson, G. (1991) 'The Blond Bedouin. Lawrence of Arabia, imperial adventure and the imagining of English-British masculinity'. In M. Roper and J. Tosh (Eds), *Manful Assertions. Masculinities in Britain since 1800*: 113–44. London: Routledge.

Deal, T. E. and Kennedy, A. A. (1982) *Corporate Cultures*. Reading, MA: Addison-Wesley.

Dellheim, C. (1986) 'Business in time: the historian and corporate culture', *The Public Historian.*, 8 (2), 9–22.

Denhardt, R. (1981) *In the Shadow of Organization*. Lawrence, KS: Regents Press of Kansas.

DiMaggio, P. and Powell, W. (1983) 'The Iron cage revisited: Institutional Isomorphism and Collective Rationality in Organizational Fields', *American Sociological Review*, 48, April, 147–60.

DiMaggio, P. J. and Powell, W. W. (1991) 'The Iron Cage Revisited: Institutional Isomorphism and Collective Rationality in Organizational Fields'. In W. W. Powell and P. J. DiMaggio (Eds), *The New Institutionalism in Organizational Analysis*: 63–82. Chicago: University of Chicago Press.

Douglas, M. (1986) *How Organizations Think*. Syracuse, NY: Syracuse University Press.

Due Billing, Y. and Alvesson, M. (1994) *Gender, Managers, and Organizations*. Berlin: de Gruyter.

Edwards, M. and Edwards, E. (1990) *The Aircraft Cabin*. Aldershot: Gower Technical.

Ehrenreich, B. and English, D. (1974) *Witches, Midwives, and Nurses: A History of Women Healers*. New York: The Feminist Press.

Eldridge, J. E. T. and Crombie, A. D. (1974) *The Sociology of Organisations*. London: George Allen & Unwin Ltd.

Ellis, F. H. (1980) *Canada's Flying Heritage*. Toronto: University of Toronto Press.

Escott, B. E. (1989) *Women in Air Force Blue*. Northamptonshire: Patrick Stevens.

Feldberg, R. L. and Glenn, E. N. (1979) 'Male and Female: Job Versus Gender Models in the Sociology of Work', *Social Problems*, 26 (5), 524–38.

Ferguson, K. E. (1984) *The Feminist Case Against Bureaucracy*. Philadelphia, Penn: Temple University Press.

Fondas, N. (1997) 'Feminization Unveiled: Management Qualities in Contemporary Writings', *The Academy of Management Review*, 22 (1), 257–82.

Foster, J. A. (1990) *The Bush Pilots*. Toronto: McClelland & Stewart.

Fournier, M. (1967) 'Those Daring Young Women in Their Flying Machines', *Speech to the Women's Ad and Sales Club of Hamilton*, 13 November.

Gandt, R. (1995) *Skygods. The Fall of Pan Am*. New York: William Morrow and Comany, Inc.

Gherardi, S. (1995) *Gender, Symbolism, and Organizational Culture*. London: Sage.

Gibbons, D. (1950) 'Selecting Stewards', *B.E.A. Magazine* (23), April.

Gil, A. (1990) 'Air transport deregulation and its implications for flight attendants', *International Labour Review*, 129 (3), 317–31.

Ginsburg, F. and Lowenhaupt Tsing, A. (Eds). (1990) *Uncertain Terms: Negotiating Gender in American Culture*. Boston: Beacon Press.

Glancy, H. M. (1999) *When Hollywood loved Britain: the Hollywood 'British' film 1939–1945*. Manchester: Manchester University Press.

Goldstein, J. S. (2001) *War and Gender: How Gender Shapes the War System and Vice Versa*. Cambridge: Cambridge University Press.

Gossage, C. (1991) *Greatcoats and Glamour Boots*. Toronto: Dundurn Press.

Gramsci, A. (1978) *The Modern Prince and Other Writings*. New York: International Publishers.

Griffiths, G. (1991) *Women's Factory Work in World War I*. Bath, Avon: Alan Sutton.

Gutek, B. A. (1985) *Sex and the Workplace*. San Francisco: Jossey-Bass.

Gutting, G. (1996) 'Introduction: Michel Foucault: A user's manual'. In G. Gutting (Ed.), *The Cambridge Companion to Foucault*: 1–27. Cambridge: Cambridge University Press.

Hacker, B. C. (1988) 'From Military Revolution to Industrial Revolution: Armies, Women and Political Economy in Early Modern Europe'. In E. Isaksson (Ed.), *Women and the Military System*: 11–29. New York: St. Martin's Press.

Hacker, S. (1989) *Pleasure, Power & Technology*. Boston, MA: Unwin.

Halsey, A. H. (1978) *Change in British Society*. Oxford: Oxford University Press.

Hampden-Turner, C. (1990) *Corporate Culture. From Vicious to Virtuous Circles*. London: Hutchinson.

Harper, H. (1930) *The Romance of a Modern Airway*. London: Marston & Co.

—— (1936) *Riders of the Sky*. London: Hodder and Stoughton Ltd.

Harriman, A. (1985) *Women/Men, Management*. New York: Praeger.

Hatch, M. J. (1997) *Organization Theory: Modern Symbolic and Postmodern Perspectives*. Oxford: Oxford University Press.

Hearn, J. and Parkin, P. W. (1987) *'Sex' at 'Work' – The Power and Paradox of Organizational Sexuality*. Brighton: Wheatsheaf.

Helms Mills, J. and Mills, A. J. (2000) 'Rules, Sensemaking, Formative Contexts and Discourse in the Gendering of Organizational Culture'. In N. M. Ashkanasy, C. P. M. Wilderom and M. F. Peterson (Eds), *Handbook of Organizational Culture and Climate*: 55–70. Thousand Oaks, CA.: Sage.

Henry, W. (Ed.). (1983) *Unchartered Skies. Canadian Bush Pilot Stories*. Edmonton, Alta: Reidmore.

Herald Telephone. 1930, January 11 ed. Miami.

Heycock, B. (1991) *Put It Down To Experience*. Titchmarsh: Marlow Durndell.

Higham, R. (1960) *Britain's Imperial Air Routes 1918 to 1939*. London: G.T.Foulis & Co.

Higonnet, M. R. and Higonnet, P. L. R. (1987) 'The Double Helix'. In M. R. Higonnet, J. Jenson, S. Michel and M. C. Weitz (Eds), *Behind the Lines. Gender and the Two World Wars*: 31–47. London: Yale University Press.

Higonnet, M. R., Jenson, J., Michel, S. and Weitz, M. C. (Eds). (1987) *Behind the Lines. Gender and the Two World Wars*. London: Yale University Press.

Hobsbawm, E. (1994) *Age of Extremes*. London: Michael Joseph.

Hochschild, A. R. (1983) *The Managed Heart*. Berkeley, CA: University of California Press.

—— (1990) *The Second Shift*. New York: Avon.

Holden, H. M. and Griffith, C. L. (1991) *Ladybirds. The untold story of women pilots in America*. Mt.Freedom, NJ.: Black Hawk Publishing Co.

Horn, P. (1994) *Women in the 1920s*. Frome, Somerset: Alan Sutton Publishing Ltd.

Hudson, K. (1972) *Air Travel. A social history*. Somerset: Adams &Dart.

Hudson, K. and Pettifer, J. (1979) *Diamonds in the Sky. A social history of air travel*. London: Bodley Head/BBC Publications.

Hufton, O. (1974) *The Poor of Eighteenth-Century France, 1750–1789*. Oxford: Oxford University Press.

—— (1994) 'What is Women's History'? In J. Gardiner (Ed.), *What is History Today?* London: MacMillan.

Humphreys, S. (1994) 'What is women's history'? In J. Gardiner (Ed.), *What is history today?* 87–89. London: Macmillan.

Hunt, P. (1984) 'Workers side by side: women and the trade union movement'. In J. Siltanen and M. Stanworth (Eds), *Women and the Public Sphere*: 47–53. London: Hutchinson.

Imperial Airways. (1926) *Annual Report, 1925*. London: Imperial Airways Ltd.

—— (1927) 'Ladies Only', *Imperial Airways Monthly Bulletin* (July).

—— (1929) *Annual Report, 1928*. London: Imperial Airways Ltd.

Imperial Airways. (1931a) *Imperial Airways Staff News*, 38 (28 August).

—— (1931b) *Imperial Airways Staff News*, 42 (2 October).

—— (1931c) 'Editorial: Let Us Act and Think Imperially', *Imperial Airways Staff News*, 40 (11 September).

—— (1931d) 'Hanno', *Imperial Airways Staff News*, 49 (20 November).

—— (1932a) *Imperial Airways Staff News*, 55 (1 January).

—— (1932b) 'Appolo', *Imperial Airways Staff News*, 63 (26 February).

—— (1932c) 'A broadcast by the High Commissioner in London of the Union of South Africa on the opening of a through service to the Cape', *Imperial Airways Staff News*, 60 (5 February).

—— (1932d) 'Story From the South Africa Division', *Imperial Airways Staff News*, 71 (26 April).

—— (1933) *Annual Report, 1932*. London: Imperial Airways Ltd.

—— (1934) *Annual Report, 1933*. London: Imperial Airways Ltd.

—— (1935) 'An amusing letter from a former hangar boy at Bulawayo to the station-manager at Germiston station', *Imperial Airways Staff News*, 232, 15 June.

—— (1936a) *Imperial Airways Weekly News Bulletin*, 23, 25 August.

—— (1936b) 'Air Facilities For Business Men', *Imperial Airways Weekly News Bulletin*, 14 (23 June).

—— (1936c) 'The Air-Liner Stewards of Imperial Airways. Men On A New Calling. Serving Meals in Aircraft While In Flight', *Imperial Airways Weekly News Bulletin*, 25 (8 September).

—— (1936d) *Annual Report, 1935*. London: Imperial Airways Ltd.

—— (1936e) 'In the Control-Cabin of an Airliner the Work of the Captain and First Officer. Modern Wonders of Science and Mechanics', *Imperial Airways Weekly News Bulletin*, 24 (1 Septtember).

—— (1936f) 'Pilots' Room', *Imperial Airways Weekly News Bulletin*, 21 (11 August).

—— (1936g) 'A Romance of the Air', *Imperial Airways Weekly News Bulletin*, 1 (24 March).

—— (1937a) *Imperial Airways Weekly News Bulletin*, 82 (12 October).

—— (1937b) *Imperial Airways Weekly News Bulletin*, 63 (1 June).

—— (1937c) *Imperial Airways Weekly News Bulletin*, 64 (8 June).

—— (1937d) *Annual Report, 1936*. London: Imperial Airways Ltd.

—— (1937e) 'Veteran Civil Airman's 1,100,000 miles of flying', *Imperial Airways Weekly News Bulletin*, 59 (4 May).

—— (1937f) 'Work of a Modern Air Captain: An Imperial Airways Pilot Talks to Rotary Club Members', *Imperial Airways Weekly News Bulletin*, 44 (19 January).

—— (1938a) *Imperial Airways Staff News*, 8 (3), 18 January.

—— (1938b) *Imperial Airways Gazette*, 10 (4).

—— (1938c) *Captains, Acting Captains, First Officers. Pay and Allowances*. London: Imperial Airways Ltd.

—— (1938d) *Female Office Staff Salaries. 1938*. London: Imperial Airways Ltd.

—— (1938e) *Flight Clerks Pay & Allowances*. London: Imperial Airways Ltd.

—— (1938f) *Flight Crews (Empire Services Only) Pay and Allowances*. London: Imperial Airways Ltd.

—— (1938g) 'Hints for Uniformed Staff', *Imperial Airways Staff News*, 8 (4), 25 January.

—— (1938h) *Memorandum, Imperial Airways General Engineering Staff (including Coxswains) on overseas contract. Pay and Allowances 1938*. London: Imperial Airways Ltd.

—— (1938i) 'Men Lead The Way', *Imperial Airways Staff News*, 8 (1), 1 April.

—— (1938j) 'Overheard on a Bus', *Imperial Airways Staff News*, 8 (43), October.
—— (1938k) *Radio Officer. Pay and Allowances*. London: Imperial Airways Ltd.
—— (1938l) 'Staff Vacancies', *Imperial Airways Staff News*, 8 (45), 11 November.
—— (1938m) *Stewards Pay & Allowance (Regulations) 1938*. London: Imperial Airways Ltd.
—— (1939a) *Imperial Airways Staff News*, 9 (23), 9 June.
—— (1939b) *Imperial Airways Staff News*, 9 (9), 3 March.
—— (1939c) *Annual Report, 1938*. London: Imperial Airways Ltd.
—— (1939d) 'Southampton and Hythe Staff Dinner', *Imperial Airways Staff News*, 9 (2), 13 January.
—— (1939e) 'Staff Vacancies', *Imperial Airways Staff News*, 9 (32), 11 August.
—— (1939f) 'Staff Vacancies', *Imperial Airways Staff News*, 9 (30), 28 July.
—— (1939g) 'Staff Vacancies', *Imperial Airways Staff News*, 9 (3), 20 January.
—— (1939h) 'Victualling Her Way to Matrimony', *Imperial Airways Staff News*, 9 (9), 3 March.
—— (1939i) 'Women Staff Supervisor', *Imperial Airways Staff News*, 7 (9), 17 February.
Instone, A. (1938) *Early Birds*. London: Western Mail & Echo Ltd.
Isaksson, E. (Ed.). (1988) *Women and the Military System*. New York: St.Martin's Press.
Jackson, A. S. (1975) *Civil Aviation. Flight Crews*. London: David and Charles.
—— (1995) *Imperial Airways and the First British Airlines 1919–1940*. Lavenham: Terence Dalton.
James, G. W. (Ed.). (1982) *Airline Economics*. Lexington, MA.: D.C. Heath.
James, J. (1990) *The Paladins*. London: Macdonald & Co.
Jenkins, K. (1994) *Re-Thinking History*. London: Routledge.
John, A. V. (1994) 'What is Women's History'. In J. Gardiner (Ed.), *What is History Today?* 89–91. London: Macmillan.
Josephson, M. (1944) *Empire of the Air*. New York: Harcourt, Brace and Company.
Kane, P. (1974) *Sex objects in the sky*. Chicago, Ill.: Follett.
Kanter, R. M. (1977) *Men and Women of the Corporation*. New York: Basic Books.
—— (1979) 'Power failure in management circuits'., *Harvard Business Review*, 57 (4), 65–75.
Keil, S. V. W. (1979) *Those Wonderful Women in their Flying Machines*. New York: Rawson, Wade Publishers Inc.
Keller, E. F. (1989) 'Women, Science, and Popular Mythology'. In J. Rothschild (Ed.), *Machina Ex Dea. Feminist Perspectives on Technology*. New York: Pergamon Press.
Kets de Vries, M. F. R. (1989) 'The Leader as Mirror: Clinical Reflections', *Human Relations*, 42 (7), 607–23.
—— (1991) *Organizations on the couch: clinical perspectives on organizational behavior and change* (First edn). San Francisco: Jossey-Bass.
Kieser, A. (1989) 'Organizational, Institutional, and Societal Evolution: Medieval Craft Guilds and the Genesis of Formal Organizations', *Administrative Science Quarterly*, 34, 540–64.
—— (1994) 'Why Organization Theory Needs Historical Analyses – And How This Should Be Performed', *Organization Science*, 5 (4).
Kimmel, M. S. (Ed.). (1987) *Changing Men. New Directions in Research on Men and Masculinity*. Newbury Park, CA.: Sage.
King, P. (1989) *Knights of the Air*. Iowa City: University of Iowa Press.
Kohler, W. (1961) *Gestalt Psychology*. New York: Mentor Books.
Labich, K. 1988. The Big Comeback at British Airways, *Fortune International*: 104.
Lansbury, R. D. (1978) *Professionals and management: a study of behaviour in organizations*. Hemel Hempstead: University of Queensland Press.

Lauwick, H. (1960) *Heroines of the Sky*. London: Frederick Muller.

Learmonth, B., Nash, J. and Cluett, D. (1983) *The First Croydon Airport 1915–1928*. London: Sutton Libraries and Arts Services.

Lester, V. (2000) *Fasten Your Seat Belts! History and Heroism in the Pan Am Cabin*. McLean, Virginia: Paladwr Press.

Lewis, J. (1992) *Women in Britain since 1945*. Oxford: Blackwell.

Lovegrove, K. (2000) *Airline. Identity, Design and Culture*. New York: teNeues Publishing Co.

Lovell, M. S. (1989) *The Sound of Wings. The Biography of Amelia Earhart*. London: Hutchinson.

Lowe, G. S. (1987) *Women in the Administrative Revolution*. Toronto: University of Toronto Press.

Mackenzie, J. (1984) 'The Cinema, Radio and The Empire'. In J. Mackenzie (Ed.), *Propaganda and Empire: The manipulation of British public opinion 1880–1960*.: 67–95. Manchester: Manchester University Press.

Mackie, M. (1987) *Constructing Women & Men*. Toronto: Holt, Rinehart and Winston of Canada Ltd.

MacKinnon, C. (1979) *Sexual Harassment of Working Women*. New Haven, Conn: Yale University Press.

Macmillan, N. (1935) *Sir Sefton Brancker*. London: William Heinemann Ltd.

Maddock, S. (1999) *Challenging Women. Gender, Culture and Organization*. London: Sage.

Maier, M. (1997) ''We Have to Make a Management Decision': Challenger and the Dysfunctions of Corporate Masculinity'. In P. Prasad, A. J. Mills, M. Elmes and A. Prasad (Eds), *Managing the Organizational Melting Pot: Dilemmas of Workplace Diversity*: 226–54. Newbury Park, CA: Sage.

Marshall, J. (1984) *Women Managers: Travellers in a male world*. Chichester: John Wiley & Sons.

Martin, J. (2002) *Organizational Culture. Mapping the Terrain*. Thousand Oaks, CA: Sage.

Marty, M. E., Appleby, R. S. and American Academy of Arts and Sciences. (1994) *Accounting for fundamentalisms: the dynamic character of movements*. Chicago: University of Chicago Press.

May, G. (1971) *The challenge of BEA: the story of a great airline's first 25 years*. London: Wolfe.

McCaffery, D. (1988) *Billy Bishop Canadian Hero*. Toronto: James Lorimer & Co.

McIntosh, R. H. (1963) *All-Weather Mac*. London: Macdonald.

McLaughlin, H. (1994) *Footsteps in the Sky*. Denver, CO: State of the Art, Ltd.

Merton, R. K. (1940) 'Bureaucratic Structure and Personality'., *Social Forces*, XVII, 560–68.

Milberry, L. (1979) *Aviation in Canada*. Toronto: McGraw-Hill Ryerson.

Millett, K. (1971) *Sexual Politics*. New York: Avon Books.

Mills, A. J. (1988a) 'Organization, gender and culture', *Organization Studies*, 9 (3), 351–369.

—— (1988b) 'Organizational Acculturation and Gender Discrimination'. In P. K. Kresl (Ed.), *Canadian Issues, X1 – Women and the Workplace*: 1–22. Montreal: Association of Canadian Studies/International Council for Canadian Studies.

—— (1994) 'No Sex Please, We're British Airways: A model for uncovering the symbols of gender in British Airways' culture, 1919–1991', *Paper presented at the 12th annual conference of the Standing Conference on Organizational Symbolism (SCOS), Calgary, Alberta*.

—— (1996) 'Corporate Image, Gendered Subjects And The Company Newsletter – The Changing Faces of British Airways'. In G. Palmer and S. Clegg (Eds), *Constituting Management: Markets, Meanings And Identities*.: 191–211. Berlin: de Gruyter.

—— (1997) 'Practice Makes Perfect: Corporate Practices, Bureaucratization and the Idealized Gendered Self', *Hallinnon Tutkimus (Finnish Journal of Administrative Studies)* (4), 272–88.

—— (1998) 'Cockpits, Hangars, Boys and Galleys: Corporate Masculinities and the Development of British Airways', *Gender, Work & Organization*, 5 (3), 172–88.

Mills, A. J. and Chiaramonte, P. (1991) 'Organization as Gendered Communication Act', *Canadian Journal of Communications*, 16 (4), 381–98.

Mills, A. J. and Murgatroyd, S. J. (1991) *Organizational Rules: a framework for understanding organizations*. Milton Keynes: Open University Press.

Mills, A. J. and Ryan, C. (2001) 'Contesting the Spiritual Space: Patriarchy, Bureaucracy, and the Gendering of Women's Religious Orders', *Tamara: Journal of Critical Postmodern Organization Science*, 1 (4), 60–79.

Mills, A. J., Simmons, T. and Helms Mills, J. (2005) *Reading Organization Theory: A Critical Approach to the Study of Organizational Behaviour and Structure. Third Edition.* Toronto: Garamond Press.

Mills, A. J. and Tancred, P. (Eds). (1992) *Gendering Organizational Analysis*. Newbury Park, CA.: Sage.

Mintzberg, H., Brunet, J. P. and Waters, J. A. (1986) 'Does Planning Impede Strategic Thinking? Tracking the Strategies of Air Canada From 1937 to 1976'. In R. Lamb and P. Shrivastava (Eds), *Advances in Strategic Management*, Vol. 4: 3–41. Greenwich, CT.: JAI Press.

Mishkind, M. E., Rodin, J., Silberstein, L. R. and Striegel-Moore, R. H. (1987) 'The Embodiment of Masculinity: Cultural, Psychological, and Behavioral Dimensions'. In M. S. Kimmel (Ed.), *Changing Men. New Directions in Research on Men and Masculinity*.: 37–52. Newbury Park, CA.: Sage.

Moolman, V. (1981) *Woman Aloft*. Alexandria, VA: Time-Life Books.

Morgan, G. and Knights, D. (1991) 'Gendering Jobs: Corporate Strategies, Managerial Control and Dynamics of Job Segregation', *Work, Employment & Society*, 5 (2), 181–200.

Morgan, N. (1988) *The Equality Game: Women in the Federal Public Service (1908–1987)*. Ottawa: Canadian Advisory Council on the Status of Women.

Morris, J. (1989) *Riding the Skies. Classic Posters From The Golden Age of Flying*. London: Bloomsbury.

Morrison, A., White, R. and Van Elsor, E. (1987) *Breaking the Glass Ceiling*. Reading, MA: Addison Wesley.

Murray, M. F. (1951) *Skygirl. A Career Handbook for the Airline Stewardess*. New York: Duell, Sloan and Pearce.

NAAFA Online. (2005) 'Recent Lawsuits about Fat Discrimination. Pan American World Airways', Oakland, CA National Association to Advance Fat Acceptance, http://www.naafa.org/info/legal/court.html (24 October).

Newby, N. J. (1986) *The Sky's The Limit*. Vancouver, B.C.: Mitchell Press Ltd.

Nielsen, G. P. (1982) *From sky girl to flight attendant. Women and the making of a union*. New York: ILR Press.

O'Brien, G. (1983) 'Negotiating Order in the Workplace: The case of the air hostess', *Journal of Irish Business and Administrative Research*, 5 (2), 3–13.

O'Connor, J. E. and Jackson, M. A. (Eds). (1980) *American History/American Film*. New York: Frederick Ungar Publishing Co.

Oakley, A. (1972) *Sex, gender and society*. London: Temple Smith.

Ohmann, R. (1996) *Selling Culture. Magazine, Markets, and Class at the Turn of the Century*. London: Verso.

Olley, G. P. (1934) *A Million Miles in the Air*. London: Hodder & Stoughton Ltd.

Omelia, J. and Waldock, M. (2003) *Come Fly With Us! A Global History of the Airline Hostess*. Portland, Oregon: Collectors Press.

Ouchi, W. (1981) *Theory Z*. Reading, MA: Addison-Wesley.

Pan American Airways. 'People Are Talking About', *Pan News Atlantic*, 2 (21), 3.

—— (1932) ''Hush, Baby, Hush' Sings Helpful Steward', *Pan American Air Ways*, July, 15.

—— (1941) *New Horizons*, February, 27.

—— (1943a) *New Horizons*, XIII (12), 23.

—— (1943b) *New Horizons*, XIII (3), 11–12.

—— (1943c) 'The Welcome Mat', *New Horizons*, XIII (12), 2.

—— (1944) 'In the Americas', *New Horizons*, January.

—— (1945a) 'Behind the Wrench', *Clipper, Pacific Alaska Division*, 3 (18), July 1, 4.

—— (1945b) 'L.A.D. Chief Flight Stewardess Visitor in N.Y.O'., *Clipper (New York)*, 1 (10), April, 3.

—— (1945c) 'Somebody Said'., *Clipper (New York)*, 3 (7).

—— (1946a) 'More Ex-GIs On The Job at Pan American', *Clipper, Pacific Alaska Division*, 3 (34), Feb. 15, 7.

—— (1946b) 'Nice Work If You Can Get It', *Clipper. Pacific Alaska Division*, 3 (40).

—— (1946c) 'Pursers and Stewardesses Train for Flight Service in Six Crowded Weeks', *Clipper Atlantic Division*, 5 (1), May 23, 3.

—— (1947a) *Clipper Pacific Alaska Division*, 3 (74), October 1, 8.

—— (1947b) *Clipper. Pacific Alaska Division*, 3 (75).

—— (1947c) *Clipper Pacific Alaska Division*, 3 (74), October, 1.

—— (1947d) 'The Sisters Maume', *Skywriter*, 1 (4), July, 2.

—— (1948) 'PAA Stewardesses Learn Latest Beauty Technique. Madame Raymonde Instructs in Use of Beauty Preparations', *Clipper Pacific Alaska Division*, 4 (8), July 28, 8.

—— (1951) 'Young Women Must Work Hard To Be Stewardesses', *The Clipper. Latin American Division*, 8 (10), October.

—— (1952) 'London Airport News', *Pan American World Airways Clipper. Atlantic Division*, 11 (12), December, 4.

—— (1953a) 'Cartoon', *Pan American World Airways Clipper. Atlantic Division*, 12 (7), 1.

—— (1953b) 'Cartoon', *Clipper. Atlantic Division*, 12 (5), 3.

—— (1954) 'Cartoon', *Clipper. Atlantic Division*, 5 (May).

—— (1955) 'Cartoon', *Clipper. Atlantic Division*, 14 (7).

—— (1956a) 'Clipper Log Book: Kingston Salesman Wins 25 year Pin', *Clipper Latin American Division*, 13 (7), 2.

—— (1956b) 'Glamorous Travel Rewards Miami-Trained Stewardesses', *Clipper Latin American Division*, 13 (9), September, 6.

—— (1957a) *System Sales Clipper*, NY, 15 (7).

—— (1957b) 'Our Girls Can Say 'No' in 20 Different Languages', *Clipper. Atlantic Division*, 16 (5).

—— (1958) 'Veteran Gets 25-Year Pin', *Clipper, Latin American Division*, XV (2), February, 2.

—— (1969) *Management Memo*, 8 (October).

—— (1973) 'Chairman's Corner', *Pan Am 73*, May, 3.

—— (1974a) 'No nonsense about women's opportunity', *Pan Am 74*, August, 24–26.

—— (1974b) ''Steam' escapes as coemps explore job opportunities', *Pan Am 74*, October/November, 21.

Pascale, R. T. and Athos, A. G. (1981) *The Art of Japanese Management: Applications for American Executives*. New York: Simon & Schuster.

Peake, D. F. (1993) *Pure Chance*. Shrewsbury: Airlife.

Penrose, H. (1969) *British Aviation: The Great War and Armistice*. New York: Funk & Wagnalls.

—— (1973) *British Aviation. The Adventuring Years*. London: Putnam.

—— (1980a) *British Aviation. Ominous Skies, 1935–1939*. London: H.M.S.O.

—— (1980b) *Wings across the world. An Illustrated History of British Airways*. London: Cassell, Ltd.

Petit, C. 1991. Suburbs in the Sky. Television programme, '40 Minutes' series. B.B.C. Television: London, 40 Minutes.

Pettigrew, A. (1979) 'On Studying Organizational Cultures', *Administrative Science Quarterly*, 24, 570–81.

—— (1985) *The Awakening Giant*. Oxford: Basil Blackwell.

Pigott, P. (1997) *Flying Colours. A History of Commercial Aviation in Canada*. Vancouver: Douglas & McIntyre.

—— (1998) *Wing Walkers. A History of Canadian Airlines International*. Maderia Park, BC: Harbour Publishing.

—— (2001) *National Treasure. The History of Trans Canada Airlines*. Medeira Park, BC: Harbour Publishing.

Pollert, A. (1981) *Girls, Wives, Factory Lives*. London: The MacMillan Press Ltd.

Pott-Buter, H. (1993) *Facts and fairy tales about female labor, family, and fertility: a seven-country comparison, 1850–1990*. Amsterdam: Amsterdam University Press.

Poulet, R. and Moult, G. (1987) 'Putting Values Into Evaluation', *Training and Development Journal* (July), 62–66.

Prasad, A. (1997) 'The Colonizing Consciousness and Representations of the Other: A Postcolonial Critique of the Discourse of Oil'. In P. Prasad, A. J. Mills, M. Elmes and A. Prasad (Eds), *Managing the Organizational Melting Pot: Dilemmas of Workplace Diversity*: 285–311. Thousand Oaks, CA: Sage.

Prasad, A. and Prasad, P. (2002) 'Otherness at Large: identity and difference in the new globalized organizational landscape'. In I. Aaltio and A. J. Mills (Eds), *Gender, Identity and the Culture of Organizations*: 57–71. London: Routledge.

Prasad, P. (2005) *Crafting Qualitative Research. Working in the Postpositivist Traditions*. Armonk, NY: M. E. Sharpe.

Prasad, P. and Mills, A. J. (1997) 'From Showcase to Shadow. Understanding the Dilemmas of Managing Workplace Diversity'. In P. Prasad, A. J. Mills, M. Elmes and A. Prasad (Eds), *Managing The Organizational Melting Pot: Dilemmas of Workplace Diversity*: 3–27. Thousand Oaks, CA: Sage.

Pudney, J. (1959) *The Seven Skies*. London: Putnam.

Pugh, M. (1992) *Women and the Women's Movement in Britain 1914–19591914–19591959*. London: MacMillan.

Purcell, K. (1984) 'Militancy and Acquiescence among women workers'. In J. Siltanen and M. Stanworth (Eds), *Women and the Public Sphere*: 54–67. London: Hutchinson.

Quart, L. and Auster, A. (1984) *American Film and Society Since 1945*. London: MacMillan.

Rakow, L. F. (1986) 'Rethinking gender research in communication', *Journal of Communication*, 36 (4), 11–24.

Razack, S. (1991) *Canadian Feminism and the Law: The Women's Legal Education and Action Fund and the Pursuit of Equality*. Toronto: Second Story Press.

Reed, A. (1990) *Airline. The Inside Story of British Airways*. London: BBC Books.

Reed, M. (1992) *The Sociology of Organizations:Themes, Perspectives and Prospects*. London: Harvester Wheatsheaf.

Rees, T. (1984) 'Immigration policies in the United Kingdom'. In C. Husband (Ed.), *'Race' in Britain. Continuity and change.*: 75–96. London: Hutchinson.

Render, S. (1992) *No Place for a Lady. The Story of Canadian Women Pilots 1928–1992*. Winnipge: Portage & Main Press.

Rich, D. L. (1993) *Queen Bess*. Washington, D.C.: Smithsonian Institution Press.

Richards, J. (1986) 'Boy's Own Empire. Feature Films and Imperialism in the 1930s'. In J. Mackenzie (Ed.), *Imperialism and Popular Culture*. Manchester: Manchester University Press.

Riley, D. (1987) 'Some Peculiarities of Social Policy concerning Women in Wartime and Postwar Britain'. In M. R. Higgonnet, J. Jenson, S. Michel and M. C. Weitz (Eds), *Between the Lines: Gender and the Two World Wars*: 260–71. New Haven: Yale University Press.

Roberts, E. (1988) *Women's Work 1840–1940*. Macmillan: London.

Rogers, B. (1988) *Men Only: An Investigation Into Men's Organisations*. London: Pandora.

Rose, M. (1978) *Industrial Behaviour*. Harmondsworth: Penguin.

Rowbotham, S. (1973) *Women's Consciousness, Man's World*. Harmondsworth: Pengiun.

—— (1999) *A Century of Women. A History of Women in Britain and the United States*. London: Penguin.

Rowlinson, M. and Procter, S. (1999) 'Organizational Culture and Business History', *Organization Studies*, 20 (3), 369–96.

Rummel, R. W. (1991) *Howard Hughes and TWA*. Washington, DC.: Smithsonian.

Ryan, M. (1979) *Womanhood in America*. New York: Viewpoints.

Said, E. W. (1979) *Orientalism*. New York: Vintage.

—— (1993) *Culture and Imperialism*. New York: Vintage.

Sampson, A. (1984) *Empires of the Sky. The politics, contests and cartels of world airlines*. New York: Random House.

Saunders, K. (1968) *So you want to be an airline stewardess*. New York: ARCO Publishing.

Savage, M. and Witz, A. (1992) 'The gender of organizations'. In M. Savage and A. Witz (Eds), *Gender and Bureaucracy*. Oxford.: Blackwell.

Sawicki, J. (1996) 'Foucault, feminism and questions of identity'. In G. Gutting (Ed.), *The Cambridge Companion to Foucault*: 286–313. Cambridge: Cambridge University Press.

Schein, E. H. (1992) *Organizational Culture and Leadership* (Second edn). San Francisco: Jossey-Bass.

Schein, V. E. (1973) 'The relationship between sex role stereotypes and requisite management characteristics among female managers', *Journal of Applied Psychology*, 57, 89–105.

—— (1989) 'Sex Role Stereotypes and Requisite

Management Characteristics Past, Present and Future, *National Centre for Management Research and Development, Working Paper* (NC 89–26, November).

—— (1994) 'Managerial Sex Typing: A Persistent and Pervasive Barrier to Women's Opportunities'. In M. J. Davidson and R. J. Burke (Eds), *Women in Management. Current Research Issues.*: 41–52. London: Paul Chapman Publishing Ltd.

Schultz, M. (1995) *On Studying Organizational Cultures. Diagnosis and Understanding*. Berlin: de Gruyter.

Scott, J. W. (1987) 'Rewriting History'. In M. R. Higonnet, J. Jenson, S. Michel and M. C. Weitz (Eds), *Between the Lines. Gender and the two world wars*. London: Yale University Press.

Scott, S. (1968) *I Must Fly*. London: Hodder and Stoughton.

Serling, R. (1983) *Howard Hughes' Airline. An informal history of TWA*. New York: St.Martin's/Marek.

Shaw, M. M. (1964) *Bush Pilots*. Clark, Irwin & Co.: Toronto.

Simons, G. M. (1993) *The Spirit of Dan-Air*. Peterborough: GMS Enterprises.

Simonton, D. (1998) *A History of European Women's Work 1700 to Present*. London: Routledge.

Sinha, M. (1987) 'Gender and Imperialism: Colonial Policy and the Ideology of Moral Imperialism in Late Nineteenth-Century Bengal'. In M. S. Kimmel (Ed.), *Changing Men. New Directions in Research on Men and Masculinity.*: 217–31. Newbury Park, CA.: Sage.

Smallpiece, S. B. (1980) *Of Comets and Queens*. Shrewsbury: Airlife.

Smircich, L. (1983) 'Concepts of Culture and Organizational Analysis', *Administrative Science Quarterly* (28), 339–58.

Smith, C. B. (1988) *Amy Johnson* (Third edn). Bury, St. Edmunds: Patrick Stephens.

Smith, H. L. (1944) *Airways. The History of Commercial Aviation in the United States*. New York: Alfred A. Knopf.

Smith, P. (1986) *It Seems Like Only Yesterday*. Toronto: McClelland & Stewart.

Smith, T. (Ed.). (1975) *The End of the European Empire. Decolonization after World War II*. Lexington, MA: D. C. Heath and Company.

Spring, J. (1994) *Daring Lady Flyers. Canadian Women In The Early Years of Aviation*. Lawrencetown Beach, N.S.: Pottersfield Press.

St.John Turner, P. (1976) *Pictorial History of Pan American Airways*. Shepperton: Ian Allan.

Stevenson, G. (1987) *The Politics of Canada's Airlines*. Toronto: University of Toronto Press.

Strong-Boag, V. (1979) 'The Girl of the New Day: Canadian Working Women in the 1920s', *Labour/Le Travailleur*, 4, 131–64.

Stroud, J. (1987) *Railway Air Services*. Shepperton, Surrey: Ian Allan.

Tancred-Sheriff, P. (1989) 'Gender, Sexuality and the Labour Process'. In J. Hearn, D. L. Sheppard, P. Tancred-Sheriff and G. Burrell (Eds), *The Sexuality of Organization*: 44–55. London: Sage.

The Star. (1946) 'Glamour Not Wanted Here', *The Star newspaper. London*, 23 August.

The Times. (1927) 'Report on the Annual General Meeting of Imperial Airways', *The Times Newpaper*, 30 November.

Thomas, R., Mills, A. J. and Helms Mills, J. C. (Eds). (2004) *Identity Politics at Work: Gendering resistance, resisting gender*. London: Routledge.

Thomas, S. M. (1964) *Out On A Wing*. London: Michael Joseph.

Thompson, E. P. 1977. Happy Families, New Society, Vol. 8 September.

Time-Life. (1983) *The Bush Pilots*. Chicago, Ill.: Time-Life Books.

Tinker, T. and Neimark, M. (1987) 'The role of annual reports in gender and class contradictions at General Motors: 1917–1976', *Accounting, Organizations and Society*, 12 (1), 71–88.

Townley, B. (1994) *Reframing Human Resource Management: Power, Ethics and the Subject at Work*. London: Sage.

Trades Union Congress. (1946) *78th Annual Report, 1946*. London: Trades Union Congress.

Trades Union Congress. (1949) *T.U.C. Report 1949*. London: Trades Union Congress.

—— (1950) *1950 Annual Report*. London: Trades Union Congress.

—— (1951) *1951 Annual report*. London: Trades Union Congress.

Trans-Canada Air Lines. (1938a) *Annual Report*.

—— (1938b) 'Flying Across Canada. Airmail, Passenger and Express Services', *TCA corporate brochure*.

—— (1940) *Trans-Canada Air Lines News*, 4 (March).

—— (1942) 'We Welcome Our Ladies', *Between Ourselves*, 1 (February).

—— (1943a) 'Airline Lodge 714. Are the Girls Holding Their Own', *Between Ourselves*, 6 (June), 14.

—— (1943b) 'Just Graduated', *Between Ourselves*, 23 (August).

—— (1943c) 'The New Central Contol', *Between Ourselves*, 8 (August), 6–8.

—— (1943d) 'Traffic's Third Wartime Year', *Between Ourselves*, 3 (March), 12.

—— (1943e) 'Trans-Canada Air Lines in 1942', *Between Ourselves*, 3 (March), 4–5.

—— (1945) 'Between Ourselves', *Between Ourselves*, October: (32), October.

—— (1946a) 'Those Fabulous Nylons', *Between Ourselves*, March (37), March.

—— (1946b) 'Winnipeg Sheet Metal Shop', *Between Ourselves*, January (35), 21.

—— (1947) *Between Ourselves*, 46 (January).

—— (1949a) *Between Ourselves*, May.

—— (1949b) 'Winnipeg. Crusing Down the River', *Between Ourselves*, September.

—— (1950) 'On Becoming a Stewardess', *Between Ourselves* (June), 4–6.

—— (1959) *Between Ourselves*, April (212).

Trethewey, A. (2000) 'The Shifting Common Ground: Feminism(s), Organizational Communication, and Productive Paradigmatic Tensions'. In S. R. Corman and M. S. Poole (Eds), *Perspectives on Organizational Communication*: 200–07. New York: The Guilford Press.

Trice, H. and Beyer, J. (1984) 'Studying Organizational Cultures Through Rites and Ceremonies', *Academy of Management Review*, 9 (4).

—— (1993) *The cultures of work organizations*. Englewood Cliffs, NJ: Prentice Hall.

Ussher, J. (1991) *Women's madness. Misogyny or Mental Illness?* Hertfordshire: Harvester Wheatsheaf.

Walby, S. (1986) *Patriarchy at work: patriarchal and capitalist relations in employment*. Minneapolis: University of Minnesota Press.

Weeks, J. (1990) *Sex, Politics & Society*. (Second edn). London: Longman.

Weick, K. E. (1979) *The Social Psychology of Organizing* (Second edn). Reading, MA: Addison-Wesley.

—— (1995) *Sensemaking in Organizations*. London: Sage.

Western Canada Airways. (1929) *The Bulletin* (August), August.

Whyte, W. (1956) *The Organization Man*. New York: Simon & Schuster.

Wicks, D. (1998) 'Organizational Structures as Recursively Constructed Systems of Agency and Constraint: Compliance and Resistance in the Context of Structural Conditions', *The Canadian Review of Sociology and Anthropology*, 35 (3), 369–90.

Williams, B. (1970) *The Anatomy of an Airline*. New York: Doubleday.

Willis, P. (1977) *Learning to Labour*. Farnsborough: Saxon House.

Wilson, E. M. (1997) 'Exploring gendered cultures', *Hallinon Tutkimus*, 4, 289–303.

—— (2001) 'Organizational Culture'. In E. M. Wilson (Ed.), *Organizational Behaviour Reassessed*: 168–87. London: Sage.

—— (2002) 'Family Man or Conqueror? – Contested Meanings in an Engineering Company', *Culture and Organization*, 8 (2), 81–100.

Witz, A. and Savage, M. (1992) 'The gender of organizations'. In M. Savage and A. Witz (Eds), *Gender and Bureaucracy*: 3–62. Oxford: Blackwell.

Wolf, N. (1991) *The Beauty Myth*. London: Vintage.

Wolff, J. (1977) 'Women in Organizations'. In S. Clegg and D. Dunkerley (Eds), *Critical Issues in Organizations*: 7–20. London: Routeledge & Kegan Paul.

Wright, C. (1985) *Tables in the Sky. Recipes from British Airways and the Great Chefs*. London: W. H. Allen.

Young, D. (1987) 'A.T. & T. Remembered', *Croydon Airport Society Journal* (11).

—— (1989) *British Airways: Putting the Customer First*. Ashridge Strategic Management Centre.

Author Index

Subject Index